New Advances in Financial Economics

edited by
Dilip K. Ghosh
Suffolk University, Boston

Pergamon

UK   Elsevier Science Ltd, The Boulevard, Langford Lane, Kidlington,
        Oxford OX5 1GB, UK

USA   Elsevier Science Inc., 660 White Plains Road, Tarrytown,
        New York 10591-5153, USA

JAPAN   Elsevier Science (Japan), Tsunashima Building Annex, 3-20-12 Yushima,
        Bunkyo-ku, Tokyo 113, Japan

First edition 1995

Library of Congress Cataloging in Publication Data
New advances in financial economics/edited by Dilip K. Ghosh.
        p.cm.—(Series in international business and economics)
        Includes bibliographical references and index.
        1. Finance.   2. Economics.   3. International finance I. Ghosh,
        Dilip K. (Dilip Kumar), 1942–   .   II. Series.
        HG173.N38   1995   332—dc20   94-46677

British Library Cataloguing in Publication Data
A catalogue record for this title is available from the British Library.

ISBN 0-08-042408-2

1828678X

*Typeset by Gray Publishing, Tunbridge Wells
Printed in Great Britain by Biddles Ltd, Guildford*

Contents

Contributors

Dilip K. Ghosh—Editor, *The International Journal of Finance*, Professor of Finance, Suffolk University, Boston, Massachusetts 02108, and Director of Research, The Institute of Policy Analysis, Princeton, New Jersey 08544, U.S.A.

Enrique Arjona—Professor of Finance, Colegio de Postgraduados-Chapingo, Mexico, D.F.

Somnath Basu—Assistant Professor of Finance, University of Denver, University Park, Denver, Colorado 80208, U.S.A.

Lloyd P. Blenman—Associate Professor of Finance, University of Mississippi, Oxford, Mississippi 38655, U.S.A.

G. Geoffrey Booth—Professor of Finance, Louisiana State University, Baton Rouge, Louisiana 70803, U.S.A.

Mustafa Chowdhury—Assistant Professor of Finance, Louisiana State University, Baton Rouge, Louisiana 70803, U.S.A.

Rafiq Dossari—CEO, Jardine Fleming (India) Ltd, India.

Gilles Duteil—Professor of Finance, CETFI, University of Aix–Marseilles III, & Groupe E.I.A.–ISEFI, France.

Edward A. Dyl—Professor of Finance, University of Arizona, Tucson, Arizona 85721, U.S.A.

Vihang R. Errunza—Director of Research, and Professor of Finance, McGill University, Montreal, PQ, H3A 1G5, Canada.

O. David Gulley—Assistant Professor of Economics, Bentley College, Waltham, Massachusetts 02154, U.S.A.

Shahid Hamid—Assistant Professor of Finance, Florida International University, Miami, Florida 33199, U.S.A.

Ki C. Han—Associate Professor of Finance, Suffolk University, Boston, Massachusetts 02108, U.S.A.

John J. Hatem—Assistant Professor of Finance, Georgia Southern University, Statesboro, Georgia 30460, U.S.A.

Kose John—Professor of Finance, New York University, New York, NY 10003, U.S.A.

Ira G. Kawaller—Vice President–Director of Research, New York Office, Chicago Mercantile Exchange, New York, NY 10005, U.S.A.

Ramakrishnan S. Koundinya—Associate Professor of Finance, University of Massachusetts–Dartmouth, N. Dartmouth, Massachusetts 02747, U.S.A.

K. Thomas Liaw—Associate Professor of Finance, St. John's University, Jamaica, NY 11439, U.S.A.

Otto Loistl—Professor of Finance, Wirtschaftsuniversitat Wien, Austria

Rosewell E. Mathis, III—Doctoral Fellow, Florida International University, Miami, Florida 33199, U.S.A.

Ike Mathur—Editor, *Journal of International Financial Markets, Institutions & Money, Journal of Multinational Financial Management,* and Professor of Finance, Southern Illinois University–Carbondale, Carbondale, Illinois 62901, U.S.A.

Robert N. McCauley—Vice President, Federal Reserve Bank of New York, New York, NY 10005, U.S.A.

Robyn McLaughlin—Associate Professor of Finance, Suffolk University, Boston, Massachusetts 08102, U.S.A.

Arthur F. Moreau—Associate Professor of Finance, McGill University, Montreal, PQ, H3A 1G5, Canada.

Abraham Mulugetta—Associate Professor of Finance and International Business, Ithaca College, Ithaca, NY 14850, U.S.A.

S. Nagarajan—Assistant Professor of Finance, McGill University, Montreal, PQ, H3A 1G5, Canada.

Edgar Ortiz—Professor of Finance, Universidad Nacional Autonoma de Mexico, Mexico, D.F.

Ali M. Parhizgari—Professor of Finance and International Business, Florida International University, Miami, Florida 33199, U.S.A.

George C. Philippatos—Editor, *The Financial Review*, and Professor of Finance, University of Tennessee, Knoxville, Tennessee 37996, U.S.A.

Efi Pilarinu—Vice President, Latin American Research, Bankers Trust, New York, NY 10017, U.S.A.

Arun K. Prakash—Professor of Finance, Florida International University, Miami, Florida 33199, U.S.A.

Dev Prasad—Assistant Professor of Finance, University of Texas–San Antonio, San Antonio, Texas 78249, U.S.A.

John D. Schatzberg—Associate Professor of Finance, University of New Mexico, Albuquerque, New Mexico 87131, U.S.A.

Rama Seth—Economist, Federal Reserve Bank of New York, New York, NY 10005, U.S.A. and International Bank for Settlement, Basel, Switzerland.

Michael W. Smyser—Assistant Professor of Finance, Southern University, Baton Rouge, Louisiana 70813, U.S.A.

Vijaya Subrahmanyam—Assistant Professor of Finance, Clark Atlanta University, Atlanta, Georgia 30314, U.S.A.

Michael A. Sullivan—Assistant Professor of Finance, Florida International University, Miami, Florida 33199, U.S.A.

Robert A. Taggart, Jr—Professor of Finance, Boston College, Chestnut Hill, Massachusetts 02167, U.S.A.

Maurice K. S. Tse—Assistant Professor of Finance, Indiana University, Bloomington, Indiana 47405, U.S.A.

Jamshed Y. Uppal—Assistant Professor of Finance, Catholic University of America, Washington, DC 20064, U.S.A.

Gopala K. Vasudevon—Assistant Professor of Finance, Suffolk University, Boston, Massachusetts 02108, U.S.A.

Preface

For quite a while I have been reflecting on the status of financial economics in general ever since I recognized the lack of mutual respect between economists and finance scholars. After a long, hard look at this unusually strained relationship, I began to talk to several outstanding scholars who are eminent economists and at the same time top members of finance faculty—Franco Modigliani, Merton Miller, Harry Markowitz, William Sharpe, Stephen Ross—to mention only a few names. Very soon I realized that the rift was only at the lower level. After further research I came to the conclusion that the scholars in the upper echelon of finance would like to be recognized as economists rather than being branded as financial pundits. Even though one may think that the honor of the Nobel Prize for economics might be the reason for this position of some of the high-profile researchers in finance, one should not lose sight of the fact that the *Journal of Financial Economics* had been in business long before Professor Franco Modigliani won that unique world-class accolade.

It is evidently clear today that financial economics is a better title or characterization than finance *per se*, and this nomenclature has gained a distinct advantage in both fields of finance and economics even with parochial interest at heart. That is not, however, the reason why I am using this expression as part of the name of this study. I feel that financial economics is a study of economics with issues of financial interest as we witness it today and in the recent past. This year I wrote three books and a number of papers for various academic journals, and have been engaged in editing the *International Journal of Finance*, as well as other editing and reviewing activities. In the midst of this fun-filled work I realized that there were many remaining areas which I could not effectively touch upon. Immediately I decided to edit a book of materials on the cutting edge of financial economics. After hard labor, lots of luncheon meetings, and finally, of course, with lots of luck, I convinced all the authors for this volume to contribute, and here we are with this book.

I have to express my gratitude to a number of people whose support and substantive guidance have helped me to keep my mind in focus. Since the number is very large and I know the Publisher will not allow me to use that much of space in the Print Castle, I shall send my appreciation to all of these friends personally. But I must acknowledge the extensive support from *The Savid Group*, and help from my wife, Shyamasri, and my daughters, Dipasri (Dee) and Debasri (Debbie) for putting up with me while I was doing all this work in Boston, 312 miles away from our home in Cherry Hill, where they were doing their school work and homework most effectively.

DILIP K. GHOSH
Princeton

Introduction

DILIP K. GHOSH

The history of economics as a science is quite old, but history of finance as a subject or recognized discipline is fairly new. The *Journal of Finance* as one of the first vehicles for research publication in finance came into being in 1946, and yet most financial researchers were still finding their outlets through *The American Economic Review*, the *Quarterly Journal of Economics*, and other economic journals. In fact, most researchers felt that finance was a branch of economics. Franco Modigliani and Merton Miller—both trained as economists—published their seminal papers on corporation finance and then on dividend policy in the *American Economic Review* (1958), and in the *Journal of Business* (1961). Most business schools in the United States under the influence of the American Assembly of Collegiate Schools of Business (AACSB) recognized finance as a discipline quite separate from economics, and so economics and finance departments got their distinct identities.

Slowly, but surely, everyone felt that finance was a special branch of economics, and thus financial economics as a nomenclature came into being. In the mid-1970s, in clear recognition of this reality, some of the major scholars in finance decided to launch a journal, and titled it the *Journal of Financial Economics*. It is currently one of the most prestigious periodicals publishing serious research, theoretical as well as empirical, coming from all parts of the globe. New studies and results are constantly being presented through the pages of several finance and economics journals. Although no one can identify the formal debut of financial economics, it will not be much of a matter of debate if one argues that contemporaneous publication of Harry Markowitz and A. D. Roy on portfolio diversification in the *Journal of Finance* (1952) and *Econometrica* (1952), the work on capital structure and cost of capital, and later piece on dividend payout by Franco Modigliani and Merton Miller, already cited, William Sharpe's illuminating research on capital asset pricing model mark the starting points for the literature on financial economics. Following those pieces of fundamental value, one witnesses the significant studies in the area of contingent claims by Fischer Black and Myron Scholes, managerial behavior, agency costs and ownership structure by Michael Jensen and W. Mechling, arbitrage pricing theory on capital asset pricing by Stephen Ross, and then incentive-signalling approach to the determination of financial structure by Stephen Ross again. Various analyses on take-over, restructuring and mergers, initial public offerings (IPOs) mostly on the closed economy environment, and exchange rate structures, forward and futures contracts, other innovations in the currency markets, sovereign and corporate borrowings, and so on have also colored the landscape of financial economics in the past two decades.

In this book, we have brought out new advances in financial economics. The book is divided into two distinct sections: Part I and Part II. Part I presents 14 new and informative studies, dealing with diverse issues that relate directly to domestic economy. This section begins with the codetermination of optimal capital structure and optimal dividend policy within the framework of a unified dynamic model of assets growth and intertemporal utility maximization. Dilip Ghosh—the editor of this study—develops the dynamic analytical structure via Pontryagin's optimum control theory, shows that Modigliani–Miller's two major and disjoint studies on capital structure and on dividend payout policy can be put together in a unified framework, and then asserts that under conditions of growth of capital assets, none of the Modigliani–Miller results hold. In Chapter 2, Edward Dyl, John Schatzberg, and Somnath Basu examine the daily frequency of ex-dividend dates and consider its implications for daily pattern of returns on common stocks. They suggest that the day-of-the-week pattern of ex-dividend dates does not appear to explain the weekend effect, and they conclude that the existence of this pattern since 1968 makes the continued presence of a weekend effect in daily stock returns an even greater puzzle. In Chapter 3, Jamshed Uppal, Ki Han, and Maurice Tse demonstrate, following the partial adjustment model of Lintner, that a reasonable approximation to the dividend growth over time is provided by a quadratic function. Assuming a quadratic function for dividends over an initial period, this work develops an expression for computation of the price of a stock. In Chapter 4, Geoffrey Booth, Mustafa Chowdhury, John Hatem, and Otto Loistl use the Grassberger–Procaccia correlation dimension to provide support for the contention that German stock returns exhibit nonlinear dependence. This dependence is found not to be chaotic, and it appears to be consistent with ARCH process. This conclusion supports the notion that German stock returns follow a martingale, thereby making short-run prediction impossible. The ability to make accurate predictions over long-run intervals, however, is not ruled out. Efi Pilarinu and George Philippatos, in the next chapter, view chaos as an alternative approach to modeling complex and random behavior. They observe that daily individual stock prices exhibit the same static (spatial) but different dynamic (temporal) properties than daily index levels. The chapter by Kose John and G. Vasudevon next takes up the role of banks in debt restructuring. In Chapter 8, 'Stock Prices, Merger Activity and the Macroeconomy', by Ike Mathur and Vijaya Subrahmanyam, examination of resource allocation decisions related to stock prices and merger activity directs attention to a system of interrelationships among stock prices, mergers, business failures, bond yields, and industrial production. By using the multivariate vector autoregressive system of equations within the framework of Granger causality, these authors identify these interrelationships. These results indicate that stock price movements influence merger activity, and industrial production conditions impact business failures. In the next chapter, Dev Prasad examines the extent of underpricing in initial public offerings (IPOs) in stock exchanges. Here the author argues that IPOs should be distinguished on the basis of the type of offering, and on that taxonomic basis there are three basic types: pure primary offerings, pure secondary offerings, and mixed offerings. This study shows that the average level of underpricing is least for pure primary offerings and most for pure secondary offerings, and the extent of underpricing of the mixed offerings lies somewhere in between the extent of the other two. In Chapter 10, 'Assessment of Investment Quality of Securities: A Fuzzy Set Theory Approach', Ramakrishnan Koundinya examines the problem of investment quality assessment of securities, and proposes a model based on the calculus of fuzzy sets for grading securities in terms of quality as perceived by investors. In the next chapter, 'Equity Markets with Frictions: An Examination', Abraham Mulugetta and Gilles Duteil study the microstructure of equity markets in the presence of frictions and distortions captured by ask–bid spread, existence of circuit breakers, taxes, information costs, and so on. The timing of order placement, the price of the order, the number of shares in an order, mechanism of trading process bearing on whether the order will be executed and, if it is, at what transaction costs are all part of this examination. In Chapter 12, Robyn McLaughlin and Robert Taggart present the opportunity cost of excess capacity, using real options analysis of capital budgeting. It is shown here that the true opportunity cost of using the excess capacity a firm has is the change in the value of the firm's options that is caused by diverting capacity to some other purpose. Chapter 13 asks the question: is the real interest rate stable? David Gulley after reexamining the existing literature on the issue finds that the time-series properties of inflation rates vary across sample periods, which then leads him to conclude that inferences concerning the *ex ante* real interest rate are difficult to make. Furthermore, he asserts that *ex post* real interest rate also varies across sample periods. In the final chapter in Part I, Thomas Liaw employs a principal-agent dynamic game to examine the use of an employee stock ownership plan (ESOP) to reduce agency costs. It is established that the adoption of an ESOP improves corporate investment and hence reduces agency costs, which, in turn, make stockholders and employees better off.

Part II deals with issues and questions in the arena of international finance. The first chapter in this section by Ira Kawaller discusses the innovations in currency markets and examines rolling spot contracts. Designed in a manner consistent with spot market pricing conventions, the author argues that these contracts will be easy to assimilate by the interbank trading/dealing community; the automatic daily swap arrangements will save time and money and substantially reduce the prospects of costly errors. In Chapter 16 Lloyd Blenman develops a generalized and yet testable model of the pricing of forward and futures contracts which exist in an environment where there is heterogeneity of information, wealth and trading goals. Here it is shown that even in the absence of stochastic interest rates, forward and futures contracts are generally equivalent, and therefore they need not be priced at par. Both contract prices are shown to be fundamentally dependent on expected futures spot prices at contract maturity, future terms structure of interest rates, marginal utility of terminal wealth, past contract prices and expected net profits. Conditions are derived under which the general model is reduced to that of Richard and Sundaresan. In the next chapter, 'Exchange Rate Determination in the Forward Exchange and Foreign Currency Futures Markets', Ali Parhizgari and Roswell Mathis explore the relationship between forward exchange markets and foreign currency futures markets by using data on the British pound, German mark, Japanese yen, and Swiss franc. Based on the tests for causality in conformity with the Granger method, the results indicate that a strong bidirectional feedback exists between the two markets. In Chapter 18, Michael Sullivan investigates the characteristics of the term structure of currency futures prices, and then demonstrates that in efficient markets prices in a given contract and the difference between contemporaneous prices in distinct contracts will have a unit root in their time series representation. It is further concluded that tests for unit roots and cointegration for the British pound, Canadian dollar, German mark, Japanese yen, and Swiss franc give evidence to support the hypothesis that currency futures markets are efficient. In the next chapter, Vihang Errunza, Arthur Moreau, and S. Nagarajan model the problem faced by the stockholders of a domestic firm targeted for a takeover by two bidders—a domestic bidder and a foreign bidder—as a mechanism design problem under asymmetric information. It is shown that the optimal takeover mechanism for the target shareholders discriminates between the domestic and foreign firms. If the foreign bidder values the target more than the domestic bidder on average, then the takeover mechanism favors the domestic firm at the expense of the foreign firm. Chapter 20 by Robert McCauley and Rama Seth examines the evidence on offshore bank loans to U.S. business and enunciates the implications of offshore loans. The authors study both the rapid growth in the pile-up of offshore credit in the 1980s, and its slow-down since the elimination of the relevant reserve requirements in 1990, and attempt to provide the explanation for these occurrences. Edgar Ortiz and Enrique Arjona conclude this study with their thoughts on sovereign and corporate borrowing and sustainable growth with their prescription on the strategies and design of loan payments.

With all these selected chapter of fundamental research and useful results, many of which sharpen the focus on the existing literature and some of which extend and/or refute the old propositions, we make new advances in financial economics. Since it is a growing subject, it is impossible to exhaustively provide new findings in every sub-field, and it will be simply pretentious even to attempt to make such a claim. I hope this work will give sufficient ideas and new directions for further work and more studies and thus take the field to new heights in the days to come.

References

BLACK, F. and SCHOLES, M. (1973) The pricing of options and corporate liabilities, *Journal of Political Economy*, 81, 637–654.

GHOSH, D. K. (1992) Optimum capital structure redefined, *Financial Review*, August.

GHOSH, D. K. and KHAKSARI, S. (eds.) (1994) *Managerial Finance in the Corporate Economy*, Routledge & Kegan Paul, London.

GHOSH, D. K. and KHAKSARI, S. (eds.) (1994) *New Directions in Finance*, Routledge & Kegan Paul, London.

Ghosh, D. K. and Ortiz E. (eds.) (1994) *The Changing Environment of International Financial Markets: Issues and Analysis*, Macmillan Press, London.

Hirshleifer, J. (1965) Investment decision under uncertainty: Choice theoretic approaches, *Quarterly Journal of Economics*, LXXIX, 4, 509–536.

Jensen, M. C. and Meckling, W. H. (1976) Theory of firm: managerial behavior, agency costs and ownership structure, *Journal of Financial Economics*, 3, 305–360.

Miller, M. H. and Modigliani, F. (1961) Dividend policy, growth, and the valuation of shares, *Journal of Business*, XXXIV, 411–433.

Modigliani, F. and Miller, M. H. (1958) The cost of capital, corporation finance, and the theory of investment, *American Economic Review*, XLVIII, 3, 261–297.

Lintner, J. (1956) Distribution of incomes of corporations among dividends, retained earnings and taxes, *American Economic Review*, XLVI, 97–113.

Lintner, J. (1963) The costs of capital and optimal financing of corporate growth, *Journal of Finance*, 11, 292–310.

Markowitz, H. M. (1952) Portfolio selection, *Journal of Finance*, March.

Markowitz, H. M. (1959) *Portfolio Selection: Efficient Diversification of Investment*, Cowles Foundation Monograph, Yale University Press.

Sharpe, W. F. (1964) Capital asset prices: a theory of market equilibrium under conditions of risk, *Journal of Finance*, September.

Ross, S. A. (1976) The arbitrage theory of capital asset pricing, *Journal of Economic Theory*, December.

Ross, S. A. (1977) The determination of financial structure: the incentive-signalling approach, *Bell Journal of Economics*, 8, 23–40.

Roy, A. D. (1952) Safety first and the holding of assets, *Econometrica*, XX, 431–449.

Walter, J. E. (1956) Dividend policies and common stock prices, *Journal of Finance*, XI, March.

Walter, J. E. (1963) Dividend policy: its influence on the value of the enterprise, *Journal of Finance*, XVIII, 2, May.

Walter, J. E. (1967) *Dividend Policy and Enterprise Valuation*, Wadsworth.

Part I

1

Capital Structure and Dividend Policy in an Intertemporal Optimization Model

DILIP K. GHOSH

Introduction

The classic irrelevance propositions on capital structure and on dividend policy (of Modigliani and Miller (1958, 1959) and Miller and Modigliani (1961)) have undergone extensive scrutiny, and it is well established that within the analytical structures envisaged by these authors, their results remain unscathed.[1] However, in the presence of market distortions or imperfections caused by taxes, financial distress, agency costs or information asymmetry, it has been demonstrated theoretically, as well as empirically, that corporations are not really indifferent to different capital structures or dividend distribution policies. DeAngelo and Masulis (1980), Kim (1978), Ross (1977), Myers (1977, 1984), Rozeff (1982), and Jensen and Meckling (1976), among others, show that there exists an optimal capital structure; and we also find that optimal dividend payout is not definably nonunique. Long and Malitz (1985) and Bradley *et al.* (1989) have examined the relation between leverage and earnings and established that firms with fluctuating income utilize less debt. In a recent study, Hansen *et al.* (1989) reported that firms which face higher costs of raising funds pay less dividend—the result also noted in an earlier work by Rozeff (1982). Crutchley and Hansen (1989) note aptly that earlier studies have examined either dividend policy or capital structure in isolation, and then they make an effort through this work to integrate these issues by studying the same set of firms empirically. Theoretical works

1

dealing with the optimality of capital structure and dividend policy in a unified framework are still conspicuous by their absence in the received literature.

In this chapter an attempt is made to reexamine the optimality of capital structure and dividend policy in one theoretical structure, and it is established that optimal equity debt ratio exists for a firm and that optimal capital structure is uniquely related to the optimum dividend payout policy. Within the framework of intertemporal utility maximization, subject to the dynamics of debt and equity accumulation, in perfectly competitive market conditions, the simultaneous determination of optimum dividend and optimal capital mix is made by employing the control theory proposed by Pontryagin *et al.* (1962). This work is important for a number of reasons. First, in conditions of perfect competition in which Modigliani and Miller establish the nonuniqueness of optimum capital structure and dividend payout policy, the contrary claim is demonstrated, and thus this result is strikingly new since market imperfection or distortion is not needed, as has been the case in the existing literature, to assert the optimality. Second, here not a static one-shot, but a true dynamic structure is utilized to explain the behavior of the firm and investor, and in this sense it is a more general and extensive analytical device. Finally, it provides an insight as to why the Modigliani–Miller results are different from what we derive through our model.

In this work, I plan to demonstrate my claim by using two different analytical structures. The first is directly grounded on the works of Lintner (1956, 1963), Baumol (1962), Sau (1969), and a more recent paper by Jorgensen *et al.* (1989), and another by Lee *et al.* (1990); the second structure is related to the works of Ghosh (1990, 1991). It is shown that the capital structure that maximizes the payout—which in essence signifies the maximization of the value of the firm—is optimal in both counts: dividend maximization and value maximization. In the second section we build the formal structures and derive the results. In the third section, the analysis is concluded by comparing the model developed here with the Lintner–Sau model and then with the Modigliani–Miller models.

The Analytical Structures

Aggregated Capital

Consider a firm that produces its, as Sau (1969) calls it, "income or net earnings" as follows:

$$Y = f(S), \tag{1}$$

where $df(S)/dS \equiv f'(S) > 0$, and $d^2f(S)/dS^2 < 0$, for $0 < S < \infty$, Y is the income of the firm and S is its stock of capital. The restrictions on this income-generating function $f(S)$ mean that income rises with every (positive and finite) increase in capital stock at diminishing rates. Assume that no taxes or market distorting conditions exist. Against the backdrop of this 'production function', as Sau puts it, we postulate that our investor wants to maximize his or her utility level, where utility is the function of dividend he or she receives. This approach is first introduced by Lintner in the static instantaneous framework, which is subsequently visible in the work of Baumol (1962), but this function is extended to the full dynamic framework by Sau (1969), Ghosh (1990, 1991), and Ghosh and Ndubizu (1993). The dynamics are characterized by the rate of change of capital stock, and the consideration of the intertemporal utility function, as given in equations (3) and (2), respectively. The problem for our investor (who is also the ultimate owner of the firm) is as follows:

$$\max U = \int_0^\infty U(D)e^{-\delta t}dt, \tag{2}$$

subject to

$$\dot{S} = b \cdot f(S) - \lambda S, \tag{3}$$

or, alternatively

$$\dot{S} = f(S) - \lambda S - D, \tag{3.1}$$

$$S(0) = S_0, \quad 0 \leqslant b \leqslant 1, \tag{4}$$

where $U(D)$ is the utility function $[U'(D) > 0, U''(D) < 0]$, D (that is dividend) is the argument of the utility function, $\dot{S} \equiv dS/dt$, b is the plowback ratio, and λ is the rate of loss of capital. $S(0) = S_0$ is the initial stock of capital (that is capital stock at time $t = 0$). The constraint given by (3) is the equation of capital accumulation, and it is this fundamental equation that defines the dynamics for the investor who seeks, under the given constraints, the maximum attainable utility level throughout the time horizon.

Since this is a problem in the optimum control theory proposed by Pontryagin *et al.* (1962), consider the following Hamiltonian function as the maximand

$$H = [U(D) + \mu \cdot \{b \cdot f(S) - \lambda S\}] \cdot e^{-\delta t}. \tag{5}$$

The solution to this problem is the optimal time profile for dividend (D^*) and the optimal time profile for capital (S^*) for time (t) from the beginning ($t \geqslant 0$). Here μ is the dynamic Lagrange multiplier (co-state variable). The term in the square brackets is the sum total of investor's utility and the second part, $\mu \cdot \{b \cdot f(S) - \lambda S\}$, is the imputed value of incremental capital, measured in utility terms. Thus, the term in the square brackets is the imputed value of earnings, and this term multiplied by $e^{-\delta t}$ is the imputed value discounted back to the initial (beginning) time. Note here that although we started out with utility maximization, we are now in value maximization through the process of intertemporal optimization.

Let us now ascertain the maximality of the Hamiltonian. According to the maximum principle, the optimal control (optimum dividend) maximizes the Hamiltonian at each instant if the following necessary conditions are satisfied

$$\partial H/\partial D = 0; \tag{6}$$

$$\partial H/\partial S = -(d\mu e^{-\delta t})/dt; \tag{7}$$

and

$$\lim_{t \to \infty} \mu e^{-\delta t}. \tag{8}$$

Equation (6) yields

$$U'(D) = \mu, \tag{6.1}$$

which means that the imputed value (that is the shadow price) of capital accumulation along the optimal path is the marginal utility of dividend. From equation (7) we get (by making use of equation (6))

$$\dot{\mu} = (\delta + \lambda)\mu - U'(D)f'(S), \tag{7.1}$$

which, in view of equation (6.1), can be rewritten as follows:

$$f'(S) + (\dot{\mu}/\mu) = (\delta + \lambda). \tag{7.2}$$

Equation (7.2) states that along the optimal time path the marginal income due to an incremental capital, $f'(S)$, plus the capital appreciation, $(\dot{\mu}/\mu)$, equals the loss owing to interest rate (δ: which is the rate of discount) and the rate of depreciation of capital (λ), which signifies the condition of zero profit. Equation (8), which is called the *transversality condition* in the optimum control literature, means that the discounted value of the shadow price at infinity is zero. Note now the remarkable similarity between the Sau equation (22) and our equation (7.2). If λ is zero, as is the case with Sau, both these equations are identical, even though we have employed the optimum control theory and Sau has made use of the classical calculus of variations.

A slight algebraic manipulation of equation (6.1) yields

$$\dot{\mu}/\mu = \{U''(D)/U'(D)\} \cdot D \equiv - \xi(D) \cdot \dot{D}/D, \tag{9}$$

where $\xi(D) \equiv -\{U''(D)/U'(D)\} \cdot D$ is the elasticity of marginal utility (and the Arrow–Pratt measure of risk aversion). Now, combining equation (9) with equation (7.2), we obtain the following relation

$$\dot{D} = (D/\xi(D)) \cdot \{f'(D) - (\delta + \lambda)\}. \tag{10}$$

It is clear now that for intertemporal optimality to take place the desired values of dividend (D^*) and capital (S^*) must satisfy the following differential equations

$$\dot{D} = (D/\xi(D)) \cdot \{f'(S) - (\delta + \lambda)\}. \tag{11}$$

and

$$\dot{S} = f(S) - \lambda S - D. \tag{3.1}$$

The nontrivial solution to this pair of differential equations is that neither D nor S change over time (that is $\dot{D} = 0$ and $\dot{S} = 0$), in which event, $D = D^*$ and $S = S^*$, and that means

$$f'(S^*) = \delta + \lambda, \tag{12}$$

and

$$D^* = f(S^*) - \lambda S^*. \tag{13}$$

By virtue of the characteristics of $f(S)$ one can easily see that S^* and D^* exist, are unique, and the following is true

$$0 < D^* < f(S^*), \tag{14}$$

and thus S^* and D^* are the optimum capital and dividend. Remember that the solutions to equations (11) and (3.1) have been obtained without paying attention to the boundary condition, given by equation

(4). Therefore, it is instructive that we do that. In order to do so, let us go through the diagrammatic exposition and the phase diagram (Fig. 1.1). The upper panel of Fig. 1.1 (in which horizontal and vertical axes represent capital and income of the firm, respectively) exhibits the income function, $f(S)$, as described by equation (1), and the λS line. The vertical difference between them, that is $f(S) - \lambda S$, measures, as equation (3.1) shows, $\dot{S} + D$ (which is also represented by the vertical axis of the upper panel of Fig. 1.1). Here the horizontal axis of the lower panel, as in the upper panel, measures capital stock, but the vertical axis measures only dividend (D), which means the curve OGHM in this lower panel (that measures the vertical distance between $f(S)$ and λS for each value of K) defines the curve, $\dot{S} = 0$. Note that at $S = S^*$, $f'(S) = \delta + \lambda$. From equation (11) it is now obvious that

$$\dot{D} \lessgtr 0 \quad \text{if} \quad f'(S) \lessgtr \delta + \lambda, \tag{15}$$

or, as seen from Fig. 1.1

$$\dot{D} \lessgtr 0 \quad \text{if} \quad S = S^*. \tag{15.1}$$

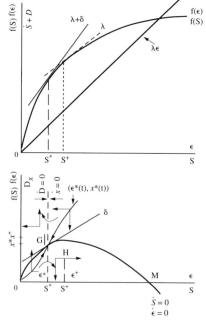

FIGURE 1.1

In the lower panel we thus depict the curve, $D = 0$, which is the vertical line at S^*. As already noted, the humped curve OGHM is the graphic view of $\dot{S} = 0$. Obviously, then one can see, as equation (3.1) demonstrates

$$\dot{S} \lesseqgtr 0 \quad \text{if} \quad D \lesseqgtr f(S) - \lambda S. \tag{16}$$

Now, we see that the intersection of $\dot{S} = 0$ and $\dot{D} = 0$ determines the optimal value of capital (S^*) and the optimal value of dividend (D^*). Taylor expansion around the optimal point (S^*, D^*) gives the appropriate characteristic equation from which the eigenvalues

$$\{\delta \pm (\delta^2 - (4D^*f''(S^*)/\xi(D^*)^{1/2}\}/2,$$

are evidently real and opposite in sign, which implies that the optimum at (S^*, D^*) is a saddle point.[2] What transpires from all of these is the following: if initial capital $S_0 = S^*$, then both D^* and S^* are optimally invariant over time; but if $S_0 < S^*$, then both D^* and S^* will increase over time (and if $S_0 > S^*$, then both D^* and S^* will decrease over time), moving toward the optimum.

We thus note that optimum capital and dividend are ascertained in one framework. However, a moment's reflection should remind us that we have so far taken an aggregated view of capital. Our S is the summation of equity capital (E) and debt capital (D). Let us define S as follows:

$$S = E + P_D \cdot D,$$

where E is measured in terms of the unit in which income (Y) has been expressed, but D is the number of debt instruments and P_D is the price of a debt instrument, measured in units of income. Let the price of an equity capital be unity (that is, $P_E = 1$, a standard normalization), which means that E may be interpreted as the number of equity capital instruments as well. Since Y is a function of S and, now as we find, S is a function of E and D, we can then rewrite equation (1) as follows:

$$Y = f(E, D). \tag{1'}$$

Remember that we already have determined the optimal value, S^*. So, given this optimal S^*, and hence $S^* = E + P_D \cdot D$, the problem of determining the optimum capital structure is simply as follows:

$$\max F(E, D) \tag{17}$$

$$\text{subject to: } S^* = E + P_D \cdot D. \tag{18}$$

The solution to this constrained maximization determines the optimal equity debt ratio of the firm. To demonstrate this point more vividly, consider equation (1′) to be as follows:

$$Y = E^\alpha D^{1-\alpha}. \tag{1″}$$

Now, the Lagrangian optimization

$$\max L = E^\alpha D^{1-\alpha} + \rho \cdot (S^* - E - P_D \cdot D)$$

yields

$$\text{optimal capital structure, } (E/D)^* = (\alpha/(1-\alpha)) \cdot P_D. \tag{19}$$

Disaggregated Capital

Consider, in this section, the disaggregated capital, that is, capital in its component structure. The components of capital, as already noted in the previous section, are equity capital and debt capital. The income generating function is now equation (1′), and assume that it exhibits constant returns to scale. That is, if both the capitals are increased by, say, $h\%$, the income of the firm increases by $h\%$. From this then one can easily derive the modified income function as follows:

$$y = f(E), \quad f'(\varepsilon) > 0, f''(\varepsilon) < 0, \tag{20}$$

where $y \; (\equiv Y/D)$ is income per unit of debt, and $\varepsilon \; (\equiv E/D)$ is the equity debt ratio. The dynamics of component capital assets are then expressed by

$$\dot{E}(t) = bY(t) - \gamma \cdot E(t), \tag{21}$$

and

$$\dot{D}(t) = \beta \cdot D(t), \tag{22}$$

where γ is the rate of loss of capital (if $\gamma > 0$, and vice versa), and β is the rate of growth of debt. Equation (21) states that equity build up equals the retained earnings minus its dilution, and equation (22) shows that growth rate of debt is exogenously given. Together these two equations define the firm's dynamics of income generation. A differentiation of E with respect to time (t) and some algebraic manipulation of equations (20)–(22) then yield

$$f(\varepsilon) = (1 - b) \cdot f(\varepsilon) + (\beta + \gamma) \cdot \dot{\varepsilon} + \varepsilon. \tag{23}$$

Equation (23) shows that the income of the firm per unit of its debt equals the sum of total payout, $[(1 - b) \cdot f(\varepsilon) \equiv x]$, the value required to maintain its equity debt ratio, $(\beta + \gamma) \cdot \varepsilon \equiv \lambda\varepsilon$, and the net growth in its equity debt ratio, ε. Alternatively, it states that the retained earnings of the firm are equal to the value required by the firm to maintain its existing capital structure and the rate of growth of equity debt ratio. In view of the relation (23), one can exhibit equation (23) graphically once again by Fig. 1.1 (upper panel), where the horizontal axis now represents equity debt ratio (ε) and the vertical axis measures y and $\lambda\varepsilon + \dot{\varepsilon}$.

In the lower panel of the diagram, the horizontal axis represents the same as it does in the upper panel, but the vertical axis measures dividend payout, x. It is evident then that if payout maximization is the objective, then ε^+ and the corresponding payout amount, x^+ (that is, $\varepsilon^+ H$ in this diagram) are the optimal values of equity debt ratio and dividend payout. However, we have already set out to determine the optimality on the basis of the maximization of the utility function which, in its modified form, is given by

$$U = U(x). \tag{24}$$

The maximization problem then is defined by

$$\max U = U(x) \tag{25}$$

$$\text{subject to:} \; \dot{\varepsilon} = bf(\varepsilon) - \lambda\varepsilon, \tag{26}$$

$$\text{and } \varepsilon(0) = \varepsilon_0, \quad 0 \leqslant b \leqslant 1. \tag{27}$$

Forming the Hamiltonian function in the following way, as already done in equation (5) in the previous section

$$H = [U(x) + v \cdot \{bf(\varepsilon) - \lambda\varepsilon\}] \cdot e^{-\alpha}, \tag{28}$$

(where v is the dynamic Lagrange multiplier in this maximand), and doing the routine exercises on this Hamiltonian, we get

$$U'(x) = v, \tag{29}$$

and

$$f'(E) + (dv/dt)/v - (\lambda + \delta) = 0. \qquad (30)$$

The interpretations of these equations are exactly the same as those of equations (6) and (7). Next, note that the substitution of (29) into (30) results in the expression

$$dx/dt = \xi^{-1} \cdot \{f'(\varepsilon) - (\delta + \lambda)\} \cdot \varepsilon. \qquad (31)$$

Following the dynamic optimization principle, as outlined by Pontryagin *et al.* (1962), one can now find that equity debt ratio and dividend payout are simultaneously and intertemporally optimum at ε^* and x^*, respectively, when equations (31) and (26) are satisfied. If the time derivatives, $dx/dt = 0$ and $d\varepsilon/dt = 0$, that is, if x and ε remain time-invariant, then we get

$$f'(\varepsilon^*) = \delta + \lambda, \qquad (32)$$

and

$$x^* = f(\varepsilon^*) - \lambda\varepsilon^*. \qquad (33)$$

Figure 1.1 (lower panel) depicts the loci of $dx/dt = 0$ and $d\varepsilon/dt = 0$, and the intersection of these loci defines the optimum, that is, the utility-maximizing capital mix and dividend. The arrows describe the dynamic movements of these variables. It is clear that if initial equity debt ratio is equal to ε^*, then this capital structure remains optimally the same over time. However, if initial capital structure is different from the optimum structure, it will converge toward the optimum structure by moving down the stable branch of the saddle point.

The Lintner–Sau and the Modigliani–Miller Models Revisited

As already stated, building upon the Lintner model "in which the criterion of optimizing shareholders' utility is identified with the maximization of the market value of common stock," Sau has extended the analytical structure to a dynamic framework by using the classical calculus of variations. The Euler–Lagrange condition, defining the optimum in the model, is *his* equation (22), and the more general version of that equation is our equation (7.2) in the subsection on aggregated capital and (30) in the subsection on disaggregated capital. But beyond such identifications, we can note that the Sau model and our model in the subsection on aggregated capital are quite alike except that our analytical vehicle is optimum control theory in place of his calculus of variations. In the subsection on disaggregated capital, where we present the capital components, *optimum* capital structure and dividend payout are uniquely determined without additional gyrations that we have to go through in the subsection on aggregated capital (and which are not spelled out in the Sau model).

Let us now focus on the Modigliani–Miller (MM) model. In their regime, note they start off with *constant* net earnings over time, and the perpetual stream of fixed income discounted by the constant interest rate yields the constant value of the firm. In their demonstration, they state that

$$V_i = E_i + D_i = X_i/\delta,$$

where V_i, E_i, D_i and X_i are the ith firm's value, equity, debt and earnings, all measured in the same units (dollars), and δ is the discount rate, respectively. In view of our analysis in the second section of this chapter, it is now evident that since income function is not examined in the Modigliani–Miller's analytical structure, it is not realized that the constant income is not possible without a unique capital structure sustaining growth and optimizing a chosen objective function. It is instructive now that we bring out the Modigliani–Miller demonstration of their proposition at this point to compare it with our result. Their proof that the value of a firm is independent of its capital structure is as follows: let the first firm be fully levered, and the second firm be incompletely levered (that is, the firm has some debt and some equity). If an investor, in their paradigm, holding μ_2 dollars' worth of equity capital of firm 2, representing a fraction ρ of firm 2's outstanding stock of equity S_2, his return from this asset holding (R_2) is then

$$R_2 = \rho(X - k_D \cdot B_2) \tag{34}$$

where X is the net earnings of firm 2 (and also of firm 1). Now, if this investor liquidates his $\mu_2 = \rho \cdot S_2$ and acquires instead the asset in the amount of $\mu_1 = \rho(S_2 + B_2)$ of the stock of firm 1, by borrowing the amount $\rho \cdot B_2$ by pledging his new holdings in firm 1 (made possible by his realized liquidity of μ_2), then his share of firm 1 now is $\mu_1/S_1 = \rho(S_2 + B_2)/S_1$, and his share of earnings of this firm then must be (R_1)

$$R_1 = \frac{\rho(S_2 + B_2)}{S_1} X - k_D \cdot \rho \cdot B_2 = \rho \frac{V_2}{V_1} \cdot X - k_D \cdot \rho \cdot B_2. \tag{35}$$

Now, if one compares equations (32) and (33), one immediately finds that the equality between R_1 and R_2 (which is the condition of competitive equilibrium) dictates the equality between V_1 and V_2, and that means that the value of the levered firm is equal to the value of the unlevered firm, and hence the proof is complete that the value of a firm is independent of its capital structure. In the MM framework, note that X is same for both firms, and constant over time, and this is crucial to the proof of the MM proposition on value invariance. If $X_1 \neq X_2$, the MM proposition 1 does not remain unscathed. However, it should be pointed out that in our framework both the firms use both types of capital ($0 < E_i/D_i < \infty$), but in the MM regime, one firm, as already noted, is fully unlevered (that is, $E_i/D_i \rightarrow \infty$). Next, one may bring out the point made by Baumol and Malkiel (1967) that if there is cost in the MM arbitrage process, then the leverage irrelevance proposition may not hold good. If perfect competition does not prevail, Modigliani and Miller (1958, 1959) also admit that the value of a firm is not independent of its capital structure. Baumol and Malkiel (1967), Stiglitz (1969, 1972, 1973, 1974), and a few others reaffirm the same point; later a host of works defines the optimality of capital structure in the presence of factors such as taxes, financial distress leading to bankruptcy, and so on.[3] On dividend issue, Lintner's conclusion that "generalized uncertainty" would suffice to insure that shareholders would not be indifferent to whether cash dividends were increased or decreased by substituting new equity issues for retained earnings to finance given capital budgets stems out of the our framework quite nicely. A significant work by Wallingford (1972), who has brought the optimum dividend issue out of the closet of static analytical structure in which Miller and Modigliani have argued in terms of dividend capitalization by recognizing that new investments can be financed externally and proven that the existence or the absence of dividend payments should be a matter of indifference to investors. Following the lead of Gordon, Lintner (1956, 1963) and Ghosh and Ndubizu (1993) have correctly and convincingly pointed out that the MM result on dividend payout hinges entirely on the assumption of invariance of the discount rate to changes in dividend policy. Wallingford's (1972) intertemporal approach to optimization to dividend policy with predetermined investments yields an approximation of the payout ratio

$$\text{payout ratio} \approx [(r-g)/r]\{1 + g/3(g+i)\},$$

where r is the mean rate of return on assets, g is the predetermined growth rate in assets independent of the firm's dividend policy, presumably reflecting the expectations of investors, and i is the risk-free rate of interest. If $g = 0$, one then arrives immediately at the conclusion that optimum payout should be 100 percent, a result long established by Walter (1956). Our result comes close to this, and yet our framework ties up both the works of Modigliani and Miller in a unified analytical structure.

Notes

1. See Ghosh (1991) for details on this point as discussed in the existing literature.
2. Taylor expansion about the equilibrium points (S^*, D^*):

$$\dot{D} \simeq \{D^*f''(S^*) \cdot (S - S^*)\}/\xi(D^*),$$

$$\dot{S} \simeq -(D - D^*) + \delta(S - S^*),$$

   yield the following eigenvalues

$$[d \pm \sqrt{\{d^2 - 4D^*f''(S^*)/\xi(D^*)\}}]/2.$$

   Since these characteristic roots are real and opposite in sign, the equilibrium point is a saddle point, and the stable branch of this equilibrium is $\{S^*(t), D^*(t)\}$, as shown in the lower panel of Fig. 1.1.
3. For more bibliographic references on this result, see Ghosh (1991).

References

BAUMOL, W. J. (1962) On the theory of expansion of the firm, *American Economic Review*.

BAUMOL, W. J. and MALKIEL, B. (1967) The firm's optimal debt–equity combination and the cost of capital, *Quarterly Journal of Economics*, 91, No. 4.

BRADLEY, M., JARRELL, G. A. and KIM, E. H. (1984) On the existence of an optimal capital structure: theory and evidence, *Journal of Finance*, July.

CRUTCHLEY, C. E. and HANSEN, R. H. (1989) A test of the agency theory of managerial ownership, corporate leverage, and corporate dividends, *Financial Management*, 18, No. 4.

DEANGELO, H. and MASULIS, R. (1980) Optimal capital structure under corporate and personal taxation, *Journal of Financial Economics*, March.

GHOSH, D. K. (1990) Optimum dividend: a new analytical approach, *Advances in Quantitative Analysis in Finance and Accounting*, October.

GHOSH, D. K. (1991) Optimum capital structure redefined, *Financial Review*, August.

GHOSH, D. K. and G. A. NDUBIZU (1993) Optimum dividend: a reexamination, *Advances in Quantitative Analysis in Finance and Accounting*, July.

HANSEN, R. S., KUMAR, R. and SHOME, D. (1989) Dividends and agency costs: empirical evidence from the electric utilities case. Working paper, The University of Michigan.

JENSEN, M. C. and MECKLING, W. H. (1976) Theory of the firm: managerial behavior, agency costs and ownership structure, *Journal of Financial Economics*, October.

JORGENSEN, S., KORT, P. H. and van SCHIJNDEL, G.-J. C. T. (1989) Optimal investment, financing, and dividends: a Stackelberg differential game, *Journal of Economic Dynamics Control*, 13, No. 3.

KIM, E. H. (1978) A mean variance theory of optimal capital structure and corporate debt capacity, *Journal of Finance*, March.

LEE, C. F. and GUPTA, M. C. (1977) An inter-temporal approach to the optimization of dividend with pre-determined investment: a further comment, *Journal of Finance*, 32, No. 4, 1358–1361.

LEE, C. F., RAHMAN, S. and LIAW, K. T. (1990) Interaction of investment, financing and dividend policy: a control theory approach. Presented at the TIMS/ORSA Annual Meetings, Las Vegas, Nevada.

LINTNER, J. (1956) The cost of capital and optimal financing of corporate growth, *Journal of Finance*, XI, No.1.

LINTNER, J. (1963) Optimal dividends and corporate growth under uncertainty, *Quarterly Journal of Economics*, November.

LONG, M. S. and MALITZ, I. B. (1985) Investment patterns and financial leverage. In FRIEDMAN, B. S. (ed.) *National Bureau of Economic Research: Corporate Capital Structures in the United States*, The University of Chicago Press, Chicago.

MILLER, M. H. and MODIGLIANI, F. (1961) Dividend policy, growth and the valuation of shares, *Journal of Business*, October.

MODIGLIANI, F. and MILLER, M. H. (1958) The cost of capital, corporation finance and the theory of investment, *American Economic Review*, June.

MODIGLIANI, F. and MILLER, M. H. (1959) The cost of capital, corporation finance, and the theory of investment: reply, *American Economic Review*, September.

MYERS, S. C. (1977) Determinants of corporate borrowing, *Journal of Financial Economics*, November.

MYERS, S. C. (1984) The capital structure puzzle, *Journal of Finance*, July.

PONTRYAGIN, L. S., BOLTYANSKII, V. G., GAMKRELIDZE, R. V. and MISHCHENKO, E. F. (1962) *The Mathematical Theory of Optimal Processes*, (translated by TRIROGOFF, K. N.), John Wiley, New York.

ROSS, S. A. (1977) The determination of financial structure: the incentive signalling approach, *Bell Journal of Economics*, Spring.

ROZEFF, M. S. (1982) Growth, beta and agency costs as determinants of dividend payout ratios, *Journal of Financial Research*, Fall.

SAU, R. K. (1969) The optimal rate of investment in a firm, *Journal of Finance*, XXIV, No. 1.

STIGLITZ, J. (1969) A re-examination of the Modigliani–Miller theorem, *American Economic Review*, December.

STIGLITZ, J. (1972) Some aspects of the pure theory of corporate finance: bankruptcies and takeovers, *The Bell Journal of Economics and Management Science*, Autumn.

STIGLITZ, J. (1973) Taxation, financial policy, and the cost of capital, *Journal of Public Economics*, February.

STIGLITZ, J. (1974) On the irrelevance of corporate financial policy, *American Economic Review*, 64, No. 6.

WALLINGFORD II, B. A. (1972) An inter-temporal approach to the optimization of dividend with pre-determined investment, *Journal of Finance*, 27, No. 3, 627–635.

WALTER, J. E. (1956) Dividend policies and common stock prices, *Journal of Finance*, XI, March.

2

Ex-dividend Days and Daily Stock Returns

EDWARD A. DYL, JOHN D. SCHATZBERG AND SOMNATH BASU

Introduction

Numerous studies have documented the existence of a daily pattern in the returns on common stocks.[1] The most puzzling aspect of this pattern in daily returns is that, on average, returns are actually negative on Mondays—a phenomenon that has come to be known as the weekend effect.[2] Levi (1988) recently pointed out that one problem with the studies that find a weekend effect in stock returns

> . . . is the exclusion of dividends from stock returns. If stocks tend to go ex-dividend on Mondays there is a good reason for expecting an average negative return on Mondays in data that exclude dividends (p. 46).

This study examines the daily frequency of ex-dividend dates and considers its implications for the daily pattern of returns on common stocks.

Companies declare dividends payable to investors who are stockholders as of a certain date (called the date of record). The current convention in the brokerage industry is that investors who purchase the stock five or more business days before the date of record are entitled to the dividend. The stock is said to go ex-dividend on the fourth business day before the date of record. Open limit buy orders on the specialists' books are marked down by the amount of the dividend at this time and normally the price of the stock drops by roughly the amount of the dividend on the exdividend day. Thus, a concentration of ex-dividend days on Mondays may provide a simple institutional explanation for the weekend effect.

This chapter is organized as follows. The first section documents the presence of a day-of-the-week pattern in ex-dividend dates. The second section shows the effect of dividends on daily stock returns, and the final section summarizes our conclusions.

Ex-dividend Dates and the Day of the Week

Several researchers have noted that the frequency of ex-dividend dates may vary according to the day of the week. Eades *et al.* (1984), who studied returns to common stocks on ex-dividend days from 1962 through 1980, noted that a ". . . tabulation of ex-days for common stocks by the day of the week shows the highest percentage of ex-days occurring on Mondays" (p. 24). The purpose of their observation was to demonstrate that the unusually *high* returns they observed for common stocks on ex-dividend dates was not due to the day-of-the-week effect. Lakonishok and Smidt (1988) examined dividends on the stocks comprising the Dow Jones Industrial Average in 1941 and in 1981, and found a high proportion of ex-dividend dates occurring on Mondays during 1981 but not during 1941. They concluded that the high dividend return on Mondays is a recent phenomenon. Phillips-Patrick and Schneeweis (1988) reported high dividend yields on Mondays for the Center for Research in Security Prices (CRSP) value-weighed and equally-weighted indices during the period 1982–1985, and concluded that this pattern ". . . can partially account for the observed negative returns over the weekend" (p. 120). However, none of these studies provide a definitive analysis of the ex-dividend/day-of-the-week phenomenon.

We examine dividends paid for all stocks listed on the CRSP Daily Master File that paid a taxable quarterly dividend during the period from July 2, 1968 through to December 31, 1986. This sample comprises a total of 134,124 individual dividends. Before February 9, 1968, stocks traded ex-dividend beginning on the third business day before the date of record set by the company; since then they have traded ex-dividend beginning on the fourth business day before the date of record. We therefore divided our sample into two subperiods—before and after February 9, 1968. The frequency of ex-dividend dates falling on a particular day of the week during the two subperiods is shown in parts A and B of Table 2.1, respectively.

If ex-dividend dates are uniformly distributed across days of the week, we would expect to find roughly 20 percent of the observations occurring on each day. Instead we find that before February 9, 1968, the largest proportion of ex-dividend dates (39.9 percent) fell on Tuesday and after that date the largest proportion occurred on Monday. Apparently, companies declaring dividends prefer to have the date of record, which is

TABLE 2.1 *Frequency Distribution of Ex-dividend Dates by the Day of the Week*
*The sample comprises common stocks listed on the CRSP Daily Master File that paid a
taxable quarterly dividend during 1962–1986. Before February 9, 1968, stocks traded ex-
dividend on the third business day before the date of record set by the company; since then
they trade ex-dividend on the fourth business day before the date of record*

	Monday	Tuesday	Wednesday	Thursday	Friday	Total
A. July 2, 1962–February 8, 1968						
Number of dividends	4,420	10,987	5,559	3,113	3,437	27,516
Percent	16.1%	39.9%	20.2%	11.3%	12.5%	100%
B. February 9, 1968–December 31, 1986						
Number of dividends	39,771	22,263	12,359	12,715	19,500	106,608
Percent	37.3%	20.9%	11.6%	11.9%	18.3%	100%

when they close their stock transfer books and prepare the list of stock-holders who are to receive the dividend, fall on a Friday. This preference, together with the change in brokerage procedures mentioned in the preceding paragraph, would explain why the largest proportion of ex-dividend dates has been on Monday since 1968, whereas previously it was on Tuesday.

The existence of the weekend effect both *before* and *after* 1968 is well documented.[1] Although we find that ex-dividend days have been concentrated on Mondays since 1968, this pattern did not exist before 1968. It is therefore unlikely that the concentration of ex-dividend dates on Mondays explains the weekend effect.

Dividends and Daily Returns

Daily dividend yields, percentage price changes, and total returns for the CRSP equally-weighted index from February 9, 1968, through to December 31, 1986, are shown in Table 2.2.[3] The *t*-statistics test whether the mean value observed for a given day is different from the mean observed for the other four days of the week. A positive *t*-statistic indicates that the mean is higher than on the other four days, and a negative *t*-statistic indicates that it is lower.

The mean dividend yield is highest on Monday, which is not surprising in view of the concentration of ex-dividend dates on Monday during this period reported in Table 2.1. Daily percentage stock returns

TABLE 2.2. *Mean Daily Returns (percent) for the Equally-weighted CRSP Index from February 9, 1968, through to December 31, 1986*
Daily returns have two components: the daily dividend yield and the daily change in price. The numbers in parentheses are t-statistics testing the null hypothesis that the mean observed for a particular day of the week is equal to the mean for the remaining four days of the week

	Monday	Tuesday	Wednesday	Thursday	Friday
Dividend yield	0.0232	0.0128	0.0073	0.0073	0.0114
	(33.42)	(1.35)	(−14.57)	(−14.57)*	(−2.48)*
Price change	−0.1489	−0.0184	0.1221	0.1021	0.2127
	(−8.57)	(−3.19)	(2.87)*	(2.01)	(6.72)*
Total return	−0.1257	−0.0056	0.1294	0.1094	0.2241
	(−8.12)*	(−3.17)*	(2.66)*	(1.79)	(6.72)*
Number of observations	916	973	954	951	950

*Significant at the 0.01 level.

excluding dividends, shown in the second row of the table, exhibit the familiar weekend effect. Total daily returns are shown in the third row the table. The negative total return on Monday is less negative when the high Monday dividend yield is included, but it is still negative and the *t*-statistics for the mean daily returns with and without dividends are virtually identical. This latter result implies that the failure of earlier studies to consider dividends did not impart an important bias to their findings.

In fact, the weekend effect is now an even greater puzzle. It is well documented that common stocks exhibit abnormally *high* returns on the day they begin to trade ex-dividend. This peculiarity was first noted by Campbell and Beranek (1955) and was studied extensively by Eades *et al.* (1984). Common stock returns are negative on Mondays *despite* the fact that an inordinately large number of stocks go ex-dividend on Monday, therefore presumably earning abnormally high returns on that day! This anomalous implication of the relationship between day-of-the-week patterns in ex-dividend dates and stock returns has not been discussed heretofore.

Conclusions

Since 1968 a large proportion of ex-dividend dates for common stocks has fallen on Monday, although this was not the case before 1968. Corporations declaring dividends apparently choose to have the date of record fall on a Friday. However, this day-of-the-week pattern of ex-dividend dates does not appear to explain the weekend effect. In fact, the existence of this pattern since 1968 makes the continued presence of a weekend effect in daily stock returns an even greater puzzle.

Notes

1. See, for example, French (1980), Gibbons and Hess (1981), Keim and Stambaugh (1984), and Lakonishok and Smidt (1988).
2. In recent years the negative return has occurred during the weekend (i.e. between the close of the market on Friday and the open on Monday) rather than during trading on Monday. See Rogalski (1984), Harris (1986), and Smirlock and Starks (1986).
3. We also examined the CRSP value-weighted index, and found essentially the same results.

References

CAMPBELL, J. A. and BERANEK, W. (1955) Stock price behavior on ex-dividend dates, *Journal of Finance*, 10, 425–429.

EADES, K. M., HESS, P. J. and HAN KIM, E. (1984) On interpreting security returns during the ex-dividend period, *Journal of Financial Economics*, 13, 3–34.

FRENCH, K. R. (1980) Stock returns and the weekend effect, *Journal of Financial Economics*, 8, 55–69.

GIBBONS, M. R. and HESS, P. J. (1981) Day of the week effects and asset returns. *Journal of Business*, 54, 579–596.

HARRIS, L. (1986) A transaction data study of weekly and intradaily patterns in stock returns, *Journal of Financial Economics*, 16, 99–117.

KEIM, D. and STAMBAUGH, R. (1984) A further investigation of the weekend effect in stock returns, *Journal of Finance*, 39, 819–835.

LAKONISHOK, J. and SMIDT, S. (1988) Are seasonal anomalies real? A ninety-year perspective, *Review of Financial Studies*, 1, 403–425.

LEVI, M. (1988) Weekend effects in stock market returns: an overview. In DIMSON E. (ed.), *Stock Market Anomalies*, Cambridge University Press, New York, 43–51.

PHILLIPS-PATRICK, F. J. and SCHNEEWEISM, T. (1988) The 'weekend effect' for stock indexes and stock index futures: dividend and interest rate effects, *Journal of Futures Markets*, 1, 115–121.

ROGALSKI, R. (1984) New findings regarding day of the week returns over trading and non-trading periods, *Journal of Finance*, 39, 309–327.

SMIRLOCK, M. and STARKS L. (1986) Day-of-the-week and intraday effects in stock returns, *Journal of Financial Economics*, 17, 197–210.

3

A Quadratic Growth Approach to the Two-stage Dividend Discount Model

JAMSHED Y. UPPAL, KI C. HAN AND MAURICE K. S. TSE

Introduction

It is well accepted in finance theory that the value of a share of stock is equal to the present value of its expected future dividends stream. In order to operationalize this concept assumptions regarding the time path of future dividends have to be made. The Gordon model (Gordon, 1959) assumes that dividend growth will be constant and will continue into the indefinite future. The constant growth model is based on the assumptions of a stable dividend policy and a stable return on new equity investment over time. These assumptions may be plausible in the long run, but it seems logical to assume that in the short run a firm will experience a growth rate either below or above its long run growth rate. If positive NPV projects are not available at the same rate, return on equity will decline which may also be followed by a reduced retention rate further lowering the growth rate.

A method of dealing with the initial above 'normal' growth rate is the familiar two-stage growth model based on a somewhat unrealistic assumption that the initial growth rate declines in a single shift to a normal rate after a certain number of years. Brigham and Pappas (1966) discuss four alternative time paths allowing for the super-growth rate to decline gradually over a number of years. They suggest that "a decelerated decline might be applicable to an innovative firm whose market position is protected for some time," but faces declining margins and growth "when competitors' new capacity comes on-line." On the other hand "an accelerated decline is typical of many small new companies." The other two time paths, linear decline and S-shaped decline, represent compromise between these two methods. The discussion of different time patterns of growth rates are entirely intuitive and in practice an analyst is likely to be left on his/her own to choose a certain growth pattern. Moreover, having postulated a certain pattern of growth decline, the analyst still has to estimate the duration of the abnormal growth.

In order to deal with non-normal and nonconstant growth rates, and growth rates exceeding the discount rate, researchers have extended the two-stage model to multiple stages, where the growth rate is different over various stages but ultimately equals a long run and constant growth rate. For example, see Brooks and Helms (1990), Bauman (1969), Fuller and Hsia (1979, 1984), and Molodovsky *et al.* (1965). The multistage models allow for some flexibility in conforming the projected growth to some plausible patterns but at the same time increase the difficulties in implementation of the model, since for each stage of growth a growth rate as well as its duration must be estimated. Moreover, an abrupt shift from one growth stage to the next is unlikely, a shortcoming partially addressed by the three-phase model of Fuller and Hsia (1979), but at the cost of increased parametrization and approximation. Brigham and Pappas (1966) suggest using geometric average of different growth rates, which again requires estimating growth rates as well as their durations over the abnormal growth period. The difficulties associated with implementation of the dividend discount models have been one major reason for a lack of clear empirical evidence in support of the model; see, for example, Hickman and Petry (1990) and Sorenson and Williamson (1985).

As opposed to the deductive approach of the dividend discount models an empirical description of the dividend policies is provided by the partial adjustment model of Lintner (1956). Lintner surveyed the dividend payment decisions of the corporate managers and described their policies by his famous four 'stylized facts'. He further developed a model consistent with these stylized facts to explain empirically observed dividend policies. Following Lintner, dividends can be expressed as a weighted average of current and past earnings (see Brealey and Myers (1988)). Fama and Babiak (1968) tested Lintner's hypothesis and confirmed it in an extensive empirical study. The model has found further empirical support in studies by Fama (1974), and Marsh and Merton (1987).

This paper attempts to integrate Lintner's behavioral model with the inductive approach of the dividend discount models. We trace implication of Lintner's model for the pattern of decline in growth rates and show that an implication of Lintner's partial adjustment model is that the growth rate in dividends will follow an accelerated decline path. We further suggest that the accelerated decline in growth can be reasonably approximated by a function which is quadratic in time and, based on such a function, develop an expression for the computation of the price of a stock. The rest of this chapter is organized as follows: in the next section implications of Lintner's partial adjustment models for the growth patterns are discussed. The third section develops the quadratic model which is followed by sections containing an illustration, comparisons with other growth patterns and numerical simulation. The conclusions and summary are presented in the last section.

The Partial Adjustment Model

According to Lintner's model, firms have long-term target dividend payout ratios. For any year (t) the target dividends (D_{it}^{*}) are related to firm i's earnings (E_{it}) such that dividends bear a target payout ratio (k_i) to its earnings, i.e. $D_{it}^{*} = k_i E_{it}$. In a particular year a firm will only partially adjust towards the target dividend level so that the change in dividend payments from year $t - 1$ to year t is modeled as

$$\Delta D_t = D_t - D_{t-1} = j + m(D_t^* - D_{t-1}) + \mu_t. \qquad (1)$$

Here, we have dropped the subscript i for convenience. We can interpret j, a positive constant, as the firm's annual increase in dividends and m, $0 \leqslant m \leqslant 1$, as its dividend adjustment speed. μ_t represents an error term with an expected value of zero; $E[\mu_t]=0$ for all t. Given that m is less than 1, the firm slowly adjusts towards the target dividend. Dividends $D(t)$ will increase in absolute value approaching target dividend level D_t^* at a decreasing rate. Taking limit as $\Delta t \to 0$, equation (1) can be written as

$$dD/dt = j + m[D^*(t) - D(t)]. \qquad (2)$$

The rate of change in dividends is a constant amount plus a fixed ratio of the difference between the target dividend and the actual dividend paid. Empirical studies by Fama and Babiak (1968), Petit (1972), Watts (1973) and Marsh and Merton (1987) have supported Lintner's model.

We can view the firm's target dividends as following a long-term 'normal' rate of growth. In case the target dividends grow at a continuous constant rate of g the differential equation (2) can be solved to obtain a function describing the time path of dividends (see the Appendix). Assuming an initial position where the actual dividends are less than the target dividends the management can be thought to increase dividends until these reach the target level, i.e. $D^*(t) \geq D(t)$ for all t. This implies that the rate of increase in actual dividends has to be higher than the rate of increase in target dividends, $dD/dt \geq dD^*/dt$, in order for the firm to catch up with its target dividend level. Under these assumptions, following the Lintner model, it can be shown that dividends will increase with time at a decreasing rate, i.e. $dD/dt \geq 0$ and $d^2D/dt^2 < 0$. The dividend growth rate implied by Lintner's model declines with time at a decreasing rate, i.e. $dg_L/dt \leq 0$ and $d^2g_L/dt^2 \geq 0$ (see the Appendix for derivations).

It is, however, not practical to use Lintner's model to estimate price of the stock as the *future* target dividends as well, as the parameters j and m will have to be estimated. Instead it is proposed that the stream of future dividends $D(t)$ may be reasonably represented by a quadratic function.

Quadratic Growth Model

Consider a dividend stream with the following time path

$$D(t) = D_0 + at - bt^2 \tag{3}$$

over time $0 \leq t \leq T$, the range of $D(t)$ being $(0, +\infty)$. For a company currently growing at an above normal, but decreasing rate which will converge to its long run 'normal' rate, a and b are positive constants with the further constraint that $a \geq 2bt$. Thus the dividends increase at a decreasing rate $\{D'(t) = a - 2bt \geq 0$ and $D''(t) = -2b < 0\}$. Further, the growth rate of dividends is not constant, but decreases at a decreasing rate, i.e. $g_Q/dt \leq 0$ and $d^2g_Q/dt^2 \geq 0$, thus closely follows the growth pattern implied by the Lintner model.

The time T is defined by one of the following events.

(i) The firm eventually enters a decline phase and dividends approach zero, $D(t) \to 0$. Here, T is given by the positive root of the equation

$$0 = D_0 + at - bt^2. \tag{4}$$

(ii) The firm achieves a constant and known dividend level D_c, which is maintained for the indefinite period beyond T. Here, T is given by the positive root of the equation

$$D_c = D_0 + at - bt^2. \tag{5}$$

(iii) The firm achieves a maximum dividend level (D_m), after which the dividend level is maintained. This will be a condition where

$$D'(t) = a - 2bt = 0, \text{ and } T = a/2b.$$

(iv) The firm achieves a steady-state growth rate (g_n) which is then maintained into the foreseeable future. In this case at time T, the slope of the dividend function in equation (3), dD/dt, would be equal to the slope of the line prescribed by the dividends growing at g_n, following an exponential growth function, $D(t)=D_0e^{gt}$, with $dD/dt = D(t)g_n$. Then

$$a - 2bt = D(t)g_n \tag{6}$$

and

$$D(t)= D_0 + at - bt^2. \tag{7}$$

T is then given by the simultaneous solution to equations (6) and (7) with the condition that T is the minimum positive root of the resulting quadratic equation.

The above four possibilities are akin to various scenarios on which investors may base their expectations of the future course of the dividends. In all cases T is determined. To derive the dividend function the investor requires an estimation of the coefficients a and b. Now coefficient a can be interpreted as the current growth rate, while b may be regarded as the rate of deceleration in the dividends and may be based on investors' expectations. Both coefficients may also be estimated empirically, given *ex post* dividends, or derived algebraically given values of $D(0)$ and forecasts of dividends, $D(t)$ and $D(t + n)$, at two points in time.

Now consider scenario (iv) without loss of generality. The firm achieves a steady state at time T and grows at a constant rate g_n thereafter. The price of the stock P_0 is the present value of future dividends (D_t) discounted at an appropriate rate (r). Assuming continuous compounding we have

$$P_0 = \int_0^T (D_0 + at - bt^2)e^{-rt}dt + \int_T^\infty D_Te^{gt-rt}dt. \tag{8}$$

The solution to which (see the Appendix) is:

$$P_0 = D_0 \frac{1}{r}(1 - e^{-rT}) + \frac{e^{-rT}}{r}\left[bT^2 + \left(T + \frac{1}{r}\right)\left(\frac{2b}{r} - a\right)\right]$$

$$- \frac{1}{r^2}\left(\frac{2b}{r} - a\right) + \frac{D_T(1 + g_n)}{(r - g_n)e^{-rt}} \tag{9}$$

The first term in equation (9) is the present value of an annuity of current dividends (D_0) up to time T. The last term represents the present value of dividends beyond time T growing at a constant rate. The middle term sums up the present value of amounts paid over the current dividends up to time T.

Under scenario (iii), the firm achieves a maximum dividend level which is then maintained. Here $T = a/2b$ and the last expression in equation (9) will be $D_T(1/r)e^{-rT}$.

Illustration

Suppose an analyst forecasts a firm's dividends as $1.00, $1.18, and $1.32 for the years 1990, 1991, and 1992. The analyst assumes a long-term 'normal' growth rate of 4 percent and estimates the discount rate to be 10 percent.

(i)   Taking 1990 dividend as D_0, and using equation (3), we solve for a and b as $a=0.20$ and $b=0.02$.
(ii) Using equations (6) and (7) we solve for time T when the dividend growth rate would equal the long-term growth rate, g_n. Value of T thus calculated is 3.5 years.
(iii) The price of the share at $t = 0$ is then computed using equation (9) to be $21.30.

For more than three forecasted dividend values OLS regression can provide unbiased estimates of the parameters D_0, a, and b. The parameters may also be estimated empirically by using historical data, regressing *ex post* dividends on time (t) and time squared (t^2).

Comparison With Other Dividend Discount Models

As noted earlier, in application of the dividend discount model there has been a pervasive realization that the rate of growth in dividends will decline over time. It is intuitive to think that growth declines from an above normal rate g_a in a linear manner such that $g(t) = g_a - ct$, implying that the dividend function is $D(t) = D_0\exp(g_a t - \frac{1}{2}ct^2)$. Unfortunately, this function is not only inconsistent with the empirically observed dividend behavior over time, but also yields no closed-form solution.

The H-model, developed by Fuller and Hsia (1984), comes close to the linear decline assumption, but is actually an approximation of the three-stage growth model. The three-stage model assumes that dividends would grow at an initial 'abnormal' rate during the first stage. The growth rate will then decline linearly over an intermediate stage, followed by the final stage of constant and 'normal' growth rate. Although the H-model produces a reasonable approximation of the three-stage model, it does not work well with a wider range of parameters especially when the duration of the first stage is close to zero and the growth declines linearly from the very start.

Table 3.1 provides a summary of the rate of change in dividends and growth rates with respect to time for various dividend models (the derivation can be obtained from the authors). The table shows that the rates of change in dividends and growth have the same signs for the Lintner and the quadratic models; for both models the dividends increase with time at a decreasing rate, $dD/dt \geqslant 0$ and $d^2D/dt^2 < 0$, with the implied growth rate which decreases in time at a decreasing rate, $dg/dt \leqslant 0$ and $d^2g/dt^2 \geqslant 0$. The table also shows that the rates of change in dividends and growth for the constant growth model and for the linearly-declining-growth model have different signs than for the Lintner model. This indicates that the quadratic model would be a better approximation of the dividend function implied by the Lintner model.

Figure 3.1 plots the time pattern of growth rate implied by the Lintner model (equation (1)), g_{lint}, the quadratic model (equation (3)), g_{quad}, and under the assumption of a linear decline in growth, g_{lin}. The figure shows that the dividend growth rate under the quadratic model is a better approximation of the growth pattern implied by Lintner's model. Note that for all models the growth rate declines with time, but the growth rate decreases at a decreasing rate for both the quadratic and Lintner's models.

TABLE 3.1 *Comparison of Rates of Change in Dividends and Growth Rates*

	Lintner's model	Quadratic model	Linear decline in growth rate	Constant growth
Dividends				
dD/dt	$\geqslant 0$	$\geqslant 0$	$\geqslant 0$	$\geqslant 0$
d^2D/dt^2	$\leqslant 0$	$\leqslant 0$	$\geqslant 0$	$\geqslant 0$
Growth				
dg/dt	$\leqslant 0$	$\leqslant 0$	$\leqslant 0$	$= 0$
d^2g/dt^2	$\geqslant 0$	$\geqslant 0$	$= 0$	$= 0$

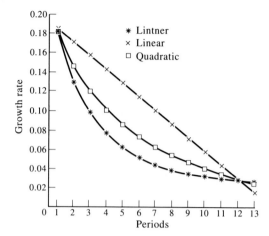

FIGURE 3.1   *Growth Rates Over Time*

Numerical Simulation

In order to test the accuracy of the quadratic model as given in equation (9) it was assumed that the dividends actually follow a time path defined by the Lintner model, equation (1). The target dividends themselves were assumed to grow at a constant rate, g_n. Prices based on the discounted value of future dividends given by Lintner's model and the prices computed using the quadratic model were compared for different parameter values. The results of the tests are reported in Table 3.2 which were obtained using the following procedure:

(i) Dividends over time were generated using Lintner's model, equation (1), assuming different values of dividend at time 0, $D(0)$ = $D\{\$D:0.20, 0.40, 0.60, 0.80\}$, and different speed of adjustment parameter, $m = m\{m:0.2, 0.4, 0.6, 0.8\}$. These are shown in columns 2 and 3 of Table 3.2.

(ii) Price (P_L) was computed by discounting the dividends given by Lintner's model from step (i) above (column 7).

(iii) A quadratic equation of the form $D(t) = D_0 + at - bt^2$ was fitted to the dividends given by step (i) above, using least-square regression.

(iv) Estimated parameters D_0, a, and b from step (iii), (columns 4, 5, and 6) were used in equation (9) to find price (P_Q) of the stock (column 8) according to the quadratic model.

(v) Percentage error was computed as $(P_Q/P_L - 1) \times 100$ for each set of parameters, and is shown in column 9.

In all cases the long-term growth rate, g_n, is assumed to be 4 percent,

TABLE 3.2   *Comparison of the Prices Calculated by Quadratic Model and by Discounting Dividends Given by Lintner's Model (Fixed Parameters: $g_n = 4\%$, $D^*(0) = \$1.00$, $j = 0.10$, $r = 10\%$)*

Case No. (1)	Lintner model Assumed values		D (4)	Quadratic model Estimated values		Stock price		Percent error % (9)
	D(0) (2)	m (3)		a (5)	b (6)	L-model (7)	Q-model (8)	
1	0.2	0.2	0.3150	0.1980	0.0060	18.48	18.43	−0.24
2	0.2	0.4	0.4817	0.2234	0.0110	18.99	19.03	0.25
3	0.2	0.6	0.6160	0.2439	0.0215	19.11	18.86	−1.30
4	0.2	0.8	0.7925	0.2139	0.0215	19.14	18.49	−3.38
5	0.4	0.2	0.4959	0.1698	0.0045	19.09	19.44	1.85
6	0.4	0.4	0.6011	0.2016	0.0104	19.49	19.28	0.12
7	0.4	0.6	0.7277	0.1987	0.0139	19.23	19.11	−0.64
8	0.4	0.8	0.8954	0.1446	0.0109	19.18	19.06	−0.67
9	0.6	0.2	0.6669	0.1465	0.0041	19.67	19.73	0.33
10	0.6	0.4	0.7318	0.1735	0.0093	19.48	19.43	−0.23
11	0.6	0.6	0.8135	0.1777	0.0135	19.36	19.13	−1.12
12	0.6	0.8	0.9337	0.1334	0.0117	19.23	19.02	−1.10
13	0.8	0.2	0.8430	0.1207	0.0032	20.28	20.37	0.48
14	0.8	0.4	0.8877	0.1277	0.0059	19.76	19.84	0.40
15	0.8	0.6	0.9163	0.1440	0.0115	19.45	19.17	−1.43
16	0.8	0.8	1.0042	0.0995	0.0068	19.27	19.27	−0.00

the initial target dividend, $D^*(0)=\$1.00$, the parameter $j=0.10$ and the discount rate $r = 10$ percent.

As can be seen from column 9 of Table 3.2, the percentage error in price computation is quite small. The maximum error is 3.38 percent. The percentage error tends to be higher when the actual dividends approach the target dividends in a relatively short period and relatively fewer observations do not allow us to compute the model parameters a and b with sufficient accuracy. Overall the model shows a fair amount of accuracy in estimating the price of the stock.

Summary

In order to use the dividend discount model, future expected dividends have to be estimated. Assumption of constant growth in dividends has offered simple, but unrealistic pricing models. The realization that the dividend growth rate declines over time has led to the development of multistage growth models. Though more realistic, the multistage models have increased the complexity of the analyst's problem, since for each additional stage two more parameters, growth rate and the duration of the growth period, have to be estimated. This study has shown that following Lintner's description of empirical dividend behavior, the growth in dividends declines at a decreasing rate and can be reasonably approximated by a quadratic function. An expression for the computation of the price of the stock was developed which, it was shown, prices stock with reasonable accuracy given that the dividends actually follow a time path as described by Lintner. The advantage of using the quadratic model is that one needs to estimate fewer parameters compared with multistage models. Moreover, it has been shown that the model conforms closely to the empirically observed dividend policies.

The discussion here has been limited to cases in which short-term growth rate exceeds long-term growth rates. Although this relationship may apply to a large proportion of firms, there will be dividend growth patterns where the quadratic model is not applicable. For some companies the model presented here may be suitably modified. For example, for a company currently experiencing negative growth but expected to revert back to its long-term growth rate, the parameters a and b will both be negative. In other situations the future pattern of expected dividends may be more suitably represented by other models or even by an n-degree polynomial function on the lines developed here.

The quadratic model can be applied in estimation of the cost of capital for public utilities. Although the model does not provide a closed-form solution to the implied required rate of return, the same can be estimated iteratively given the other parameters.

References

BAUMAN, S. W. (1969) Investment return and present values, *Financial Analysts Journal*, 25, 107–120.

BREALEY R. A. and MYERS, S. C. (1988) *Principles of Corporate Finance*, McGraw-Hill, New York.

BRIGHAM, E. F. and PAPPAS, J. L. (1966) Duration of growth, changes in growth rates, and corporate share prices, *Financial Analysts Journal*, 22, 157–162.

BROOKS, R. and HELMS, B. (1990) An *N*-stage, fractional period, quarterly dividend discount model, *Financial Review*, 25, 651–657.

FAMA, E. F. (1974) The empirical relationship between the dividend and investment decisions of firms, *The American Economic Review*, 64, 304–318.

FAMA, E. F. and BABIAK, H. (1968) Dividend policy analysis, *American Statistical Association Journal*, 63, 1132–1161.

FULLER, R. J. and HSIA, C. (1979) Programming the three-phase dividend discount model, *Journal of Portfolio Management*, 5, 28–32.

FULLER, R. J. and HSIA, C. (1984) A simplified common stock valuation model, *Financial Analysts Journal*, 40, 49–56.

GORDON, M. (1959) Dividends, earnings and stock prices, *Review of Economics and Statistics*, 41, 99–105.

HICKMAN, K. and PETRY, G. H. (1990) A comparison of stock price predictions using court accepted formulas, dividend discount, and P/E models, *Financial Management*, 19, 76–87.

LINTNER, J. (1956), Distribution of incomes of corporations among dividends, retained earnings, and taxes, *American Economic Review*, 61, 97–113.

MARSH, T. A. and MERTON, R. C. (1987) Dividend behavior for the aggregate stock market, *Journal of Business*, 60, 1–40.

MOLODOVSKY, N., MAY, C. and CHOTTINER, S. (1965) Common stock valuation-principles, tables and applications, *Financial Analysts Journal*, 20, 104–123.

PETIT, R. R. (1972) Dividend announcements, security performance and capital market efficiency, *Journal of Finance*, 27, 993–1007.

SORENSEN, E. H. and WILLIAMSON, D. A. (1985) Some evidence on the value of dividend discount models, *Financial Analysts Journal*, 41, 60–69.

WATTS, R. (1973) The information content of dividends, *Journal of Business*, 46, 191–211.

Appendix

Derivation of the Quadratic Model, Equation (9)

Following the dividend discount model: $P_0 = \sum_{t=1}^{\infty} D_t/(1 + r)^t$, and assuming that $D_t = D_0 + at - bt^2$, for $0 \leq t \leq T$, we can write the present value of the dividends, employing continuous compounding, from $t = 0$ to $t = T$ as

$$P_0 = \int_0^T (D_0 + at - bt^2)e^{-rt}dt \tag{A1}$$

or

$$P_0 = \int_0^T D_0 + e^{-rt}dt + \int_0^T ate^{-rt}dt - \int_0^T bt^2e^{-rt}dt. \tag{A2}$$

The first expression in equation (A2) equals $D_0/r(1 - e^{-rt})$. Integrating by parts, the second term in equation (A2) equals

$$\frac{a}{r}e^{-rt}\left(-t - \frac{1}{r}\right). \tag{A3}$$

Integrating by parts, the third term in equation (A2) equals

$$\frac{b}{r}e^{-rt}\left(-t^2 - \frac{2}{r}\left(t + \frac{1}{r}\right)\right). \tag{A4}$$

Combining results from equations (A3) and (A4) and simplifying we get

$$\frac{1}{r}e^{-rt}\left(bt^2 + \left(t + \frac{1}{r}\right)\left(\frac{2b}{r} - a\right)\right). \tag{A5}$$

Integrating from 0 to T

$$\frac{1}{r}e^{-rt}\left(bt^2 + \left(T + \frac{1}{r}\right)\left(\frac{2b}{r} - a\right)\right) - \frac{1}{r^2}\left(\frac{2b}{r} - a\right). \tag{A6}$$

Substituting results of integration and noting that the present value of dividends from T to ∞ at time T is $D_T(1 + g)/(r - g_n)$

$$P_0 = D_0(1 - e^{-rT}) + \frac{e^{-rT}}{r}\left(bT^2 + \left(T + \frac{1}{r}\right)\left(\frac{2b}{r} - a\right)\right)$$

$$- \frac{1}{r^2}\left(\frac{2b}{r} - a\right) + \frac{D_T(1 + g_n)}{(r - g_n)e^{-rT}}. \tag{A7}$$

To Derive Dividend Function From Equation (2)

Assuming $D^*(t) = D_0^* e^{gt}$, from equation (2) we have

$$\frac{dD}{dt} = j + mD_0^* e^{gt} - mD \qquad (A8)$$

or

$$\frac{dD}{dt} + mD = j + mD_0^* e^{gt}$$

Multiplying both sides by e^{mt}

$$e^{mt} \frac{dD}{dt} + mDe^{mt} = je^{mt} + mD_0^* e^{(g+m)t}. \qquad (A9)$$

Integrating both sides with respect to t

$$\int_0^t e^{ms} \frac{dD(s)}{ds} ds + \int_0^t mD(s)e^{ms} ds = \int_0^t je^{ms} ds + \int_0^t mD_0^* e^{(g+m)s} ds \qquad (A10)$$

or

$$D(t)e^{mt} - D_0 = \frac{j}{m} e^{mt} - \frac{j}{m} + \frac{m}{(g+m)} D_0^* e^{(g+m)t} - \frac{m}{(g+m)} D_0^* \qquad (A11)$$

or

$$D(t) = \frac{j}{m} + \frac{m}{(g+m)} D_0^* e^{gt} + \left[D_0 - \frac{j}{m} - \frac{m}{(g+m)} D_0^* \right] e^{-mt}. \qquad (A12)$$

To Derive the Partial Derivatives

Lintner's Model. From an initial position where the actual dividends are less than the target dividends, $D_0^* > D_0$, the firm is assumed to increase dividends until these reach the target level, i.e. $D^*(t) \geqslant D(t)$ for all t. This implies that the rate of increase in actual dividends has to be higher than the rate of increase in target dividends, $dD/dt > dD^*/dt$, in order for the firm to catch up with its target dividend level. We also assume that $dD/dt = gD^* \geqslant 0$ and $d^2D^*/dt^2 = g^2D^* > 0$, as, for example, is the case for the constant growth model.

1. Rate of change in dividends:
   (i) From equation (A8) $dD/dt = j + m[D^*(t) - D(t)] \geqslant 0$ since $D^*(t) > D(t)$ for all t.
   (ii) $d^2D/dt^2 = m[dD^*(t)/dt - dD(t)/dt] < 0$ since $dD^*(t)/dt < dD(t)/dt$.

2. Rate of change in growth:
   (i) From equation (A8) we have $g_L = dD/dt(1/D) = 1/D(j + mD*(t) - mD(t))$, then

$$\frac{dg_L}{dt} = \frac{1}{D(t)^2}\left[D(t)\left(m\frac{dD*(t)}{dt} - \frac{dD(t)}{dt}\right) \right.$$

$$\left. -\left(j + m\left(D*(t) - D(t)\right)\right)\frac{dD}{dt}\right].\qquad(A13)$$

From above we have $dD*(t)/dt - dD(t)/dt < 0$ and $j + m[D*(t) - D(t) > 0$. Therefore, $dg_L/dt < 0$.
   (ii) Taking the derivative of dg/dt w.r.t. t, we obtain (dropping the time subscript)

$$\frac{d^2g_L}{dt^2} = \frac{1}{D^4}\left[D^2\left(Dm\left(D*'' - D''\right) - \left(j + m\left(D* - D\right)\right)D''\right)\right.$$

$$\left. - 2\left(\frac{dg_L}{dt}D^2\right)D\cdot\frac{dD}{dt}\right]\qquad(A14)$$

$$\frac{d^2g_L}{dt^2} = \frac{1}{D^4}\left[D^2\left[Dm\left(D*'' - D''\right)\right] - \left(j + m\left(D* - D\right)\right)D''\right.$$

$$\left. - 2D^3\frac{dD}{dt}\frac{dg_L}{dt}\right].\qquad(A15)$$

Given that $dD/dt > 0$, $d^2D/dt^2 < 0$ and $d^2D*/dt^2 \geqslant 0$, we have the first term

$$D^2[D(m(D*'' - D''))] > 0,$$

the second term

$$-(j + m[D* - D])D'' > 0,$$

and, the third term

$$-2D^3\frac{dD}{dt}\frac{dg}{dt} > 0,$$

as $dD/dt > 0$ and $dg/dt < 0$. Therefore, $d^2g_L/dt^2 > 0$.

Quadratic Growth Model. From equation (3) we have $D(t) = D_0 + at - bt^2$. Let $g(s)$ be the implied dividend growth rate as a function of time s, continuously compounded. Then

$$D(t) = D_0 e^{\left(\int g(s)ds\right)} = D_0 + at - bt^2. \qquad (A16)$$

1. Rate of change in dividends:
   (i) By assumption

   $$\frac{dD(t)}{dt} = g(t)D(t) = a - 2b > 0. \qquad (A17)$$

   (ii)

   $$\frac{d^2D}{dt^2} = g(t)\frac{dD}{dt} + D(t)\frac{dg(t)}{dt} = -2bt < 0. \qquad (A18)$$

2. Rate of change in growth:
   (i)

   $$\frac{dg(t)}{dt} = -\left(2b + g(t)\frac{dD}{dt}\right)\frac{1}{D}. \qquad (A19)$$

   Since $D(t) > 0$ for $t \in [0, T]$, and $dD/dt > 0$, $dg(t)/dt < 0$.
   (ii) From the expression for $d^2D(t)/dt^2$, using product rule we obtain

   $$g\frac{d^2D}{dt^2} + \frac{dD}{dt}\frac{dg}{dt} + D\frac{d^2g}{dt^2} + \frac{dD}{dt}\frac{dg}{dt} = 0 \qquad (A20)$$

   $$D\frac{d^2g}{dt^2} = -\frac{dg}{dt}\frac{dD}{dt} - \frac{dD}{dt}\frac{dg}{dt} - g\frac{d^2g}{dt^2} \qquad (A21)$$

   $$\frac{d^2g}{dt^2} = -\frac{1}{D}\left[2\frac{dg}{dt}\frac{dD}{dt} + g\frac{d^2g}{dt^2}\right] > 0. \qquad (A22)$$

Since $dg/dt < 0$, $dD/dt > 0$ and $d^2D/dt^2 < 0$, $d^2g/dt^2 > 0$.

4

The Nature of the Predictability of German Stock Returns

G. GEOFFREY BOOTH, MUSTAFA CHOWDHURY, JOHN J. HATEM AND
OTTO LOISTL

Introduction

The manner in which stock prices evolve is of importance to both
investment management professionals and financial researchers. The
most prevalent view is that stock returns follow a martingale and,
therefore, are not predictable.[1] Noting the restrictions that must be
imposed for this hypothesis to hold in a general equilibrium context,
Sims (1984) and Lehmann (1990) developed the instantaneously
unpredictable hypothesis. This hypothesis suggests that although
stock returns are not predictable in the short-run because they follow
a martingale, they need not follow a martingale in the long-term and
thus may be predictable in this time frame. Fama and French (1988)
and Jegadeesh (1990) provide empirical support for the latter
conjecture. Recently, a sharply contrasting hypothesis, chaos, has
emerged. If chaos is present, stock returns may be able to be
predicted over short time intervals, but they may not be able to be
predicted over long intervals. From a modeling perspective, the
attraction of chaos is that it is capable of explaining large and abrupt
changes that otherwise might be considered outliers. Interestingly,
Scheinkman and LeBaron (1989), Brock and Malliaris (1989), and
Gennotte and Marsh (1986) report evidence of chaos in U.S. stock
returns, while Hseih (1991), Liu et al. (1991), and Ramsey et al. (1990)
provide evidence against this phenomenon.

The purpose of this study is to determine whether nonlinearities
are present in German stock returns and if there are, whether they

39

can be classified as chaotic and whether they can be modeled. Previous investigations into the evolution properties of German returns generally find that returns are linearly independent but ignore the issue of nonlinear dependence. Möller (1984) provides a comprehensive survey of early descriptive work, which typically focuses on whether the unconditional distribution of stock returns conforms to normality. Examples of estimating stochastic models that assume linear and nonlinear independence, such as the stable laws and mixed processes, are provided by Akgiray *et al.* (1989b). Examining the notion of dependence, these same authors (1989a) use autoregressive conditional heteroscedastic (GARCH in particular) techniques to model German stock returns derived from a comprehensive stock index. However, they do not provide evidence as to whether their models fully account for the observed non-linearities, and they report that a GARCH model does not adequately explain the behavior of the index during the months surrounding the October 1987 worldwide stock market crash. The results of this study support the assertion that German stock returns are nonlinearly dependent, but that they are not chaotic. They also support the use of GARCH techniques to model these returns, thereby reinforcing the notion that German returns follow a martingale, at least in the short-run.

The plan of the chapter is as follows. The second section provides a brief discussion of the chaos techniques used. The next section describes the data. The fourth section presents the empirical results, with conclusions being offered in the final section.

Research Method

Recently a number of papers have addressed the potential importance of chaos in economic and financial modeling and the corresponding statistical tests that may be used to detect its presence. Baumol and Benhabib (1989), Brock and Malliaris (1989), and Rosser (1991) provide useful insights into the role of chaos in economics. Key references concerning the various statistical tests include Grassberger and Procaccia (1983), Brock (1986), Brock *et al.* (1991), and Hsieh (1991). Since the exposition of these combined works is quite comprehensive, only a brief discussion of their contents is presented below.

A chaotic process is a nonlinear, deterministic process that has first and second moment properties identical to those of a stochastic series. A special case occurs if these properties also indicate white noise. If this is the case and if the time series is analyzed using conventional time-series techniques, the chaotic series may be mistakenly identified as a stochastic white noise process. Examples of such chaotic series include the tent map, certain logistic functions, the Hénon map, the Mackey–Glass equation, and the quasi-periodic five-torus process.

Key to determining whether a process is chaotic is the correlation dimension, which provides topological information on the underlying system generating the data. For truly random data, the correlation dimension monotonically increases with the dimension of the space within which these data are contained. This spatial dimension is called the embedding dimension. In contrast, for chaotic data, the correlation dimension remains small even when the embedding dimension increases. Thus the correlation dimension may be thought of as indicating the 'nonlinear degrees of freedom' or complexity of the time series.

The concept of correlation dimension is based on the correlation integral. To define the correlation integral, let $\{r_t, t = 1, \ldots, T\}$ be a time series of length T. Define $M(m)$ to be the embedding dimension such that M is a symbol for the Mth embedding dimension and m is the value of M used in mathematical operations. Then create M-dimensional vectors, referred to as M-histories, such that $r = \{r_t, r_{t+1}, \ldots, r_{t+m-1}\}$, thereby converting a single time series to a set of time series with overlapping entries. The correlation integral measures the spatial correlation among the points in the M-histories for a specific embedding dimension and is defined as:

$$C^M(\varepsilon, T) = 2\left[(T - m + 1)(T - m)\right]^{-1} \sum_{1 \leq i < j \leq (T-m+1)} I_\varepsilon\left(r_i^M - r_j^M\right), \qquad (1)$$

where I_ε is an indicator function that equals 1 if $\|r_i^M - r_j^M\| < \varepsilon$ and zero otherwise. $\|\cdot\|$ is a measure of the distance between r_i^M and r_j^M, and the distance measure employed herein is the *sup-norm*. The correlation integral, therefore, measures the fraction of the pairs of all points that are within a distance ε of each other.

For a finite series, the correlation dimension, $D^M(T)$, is specified as

$$\ln C^M(\varepsilon, T) = \gamma + D^M(T) \ln \varepsilon. \qquad (2)$$

An estimate of $D^M(T)$ is obtained by regressing $\ln C^M(\varepsilon, T)$ on $\ln \varepsilon$. To obtain the requisite inputs for this regression, appropriate values of ε and M must be chosen, and this choice is influenced by the length of the series. For a given series length and a given M, it is necessary to find an ε that is neither too large nor too small. If it is too large, $C^M(\varepsilon, T) = 1$ and no information is gained. A similar problem occurs when ε is too small such that $C^M(\varepsilon, T) = 0$. Operationally, the procedure is to select various values of ε so that neither of these two extremes occur.

In practice, $0.5\sigma \le \varepsilon \le 1.5\sigma$, where σ is the original series' standard deviation, often provides appropriate values. Further, since the estimate of the series' true dimensionality is constrained by the size of M, M should be as large as possible for a given ε. Moreover, since r is an observable realization of the true state variable, the larger the M, the more closely the dynamical behavior of the M-histories of r will mimic the law of motion of the true state variable. For a given finite sample size, however, as M increases the regression estimate of $D^M(T)$ becomes progressively biased.

By itself, the correlation dimension may be used in one of two ways. First, it may be compared to the $D^M(T)$ of a Gaussian series or, as Scheinkman and LeBaron (1989) and Frank and Stengos (1989) suggest, the original series after it has been scrambled (scrambling maintains the existing distribution but presumably destroys any existing time-series structure). The object of both comparisons is the same. That is, if nonlinearities exist, the $D^M(T)$ for either of the random series should be noticeably higher than the original series. In fact, the $D^M(T)$ for a truly random series is infinite. Thus the null hypothesis is that the original series is random. Second, the original series' $D^M(T)$ may be compared to the $D^M(T)$ of the residuals of a linear or smooth nonlinear series. Brock (1986) shows that if a series is generated by deterministic chaos, the residuals of such a transformation will have the same $D^M(T)$ as the original series. If the $D^M(T)$ of the transformed series is greater than the $D^M(T)$ of the original series, the original series is not chaotic. The equality of the two $D^M(T)$ indicates that chaos may or may not be present, since there still may be a transformation for which the $D^M(T)$ will be greater than that of the original series.

Data Environment and Empirical Characteristics

The DAX (*Deutscher Aktienindex*) is used to proxy the performance of the German equity market. A detailed description of this index is provided by von Rosen (1988) and Fischer (1990). By way of summary, the DAX is a stock price index containing 30 German blue-chip stocks that are traded on the Frankfurt Stock Exchange, which is the largest of Germany's eight exchanges, accounts for the majority of transactions on these exchanges, and is the fourth largest exchange in the world. DAX stocks represent those that are the most actively traded, provide an early price quote, and have the largest market capitalization. Moreover, DAX stocks as a whole enjoy greater capitalization than all the other Frankfurt exchange stocks combined. Examples of the larger companies in the index in terms of capitalization include Daimler-Benz, Bayer, Hoechst, and Deutsche

Bank. The index is constructed by weighting the share price of the component stocks by listed capital. Listed capital is defined to be the sum of preferred and common capital (including new issues) that are reported to the Frankfurt Stock Exchange. According to Fischer (1990), listed capital has historically been a reliable indicator of volume, and, therefore, the DAX may be thought of as a volume-weighted index as opposed to the more common market-value-weighted or equally-weighted indexes.

The database consists of 2361 daily observations for the period beginning January 2, 1981 and ending June 29, 1990.[2] This period contains several important structural and market oriented events. For instance, in 1985 not only was a market for German stocks instituted in London, but also the Association of German Stock Exchanges was formed in an effort to create an efficient inter-exchange trading network. Further, 1987 and 1989 witnessed worldwide October stock market crashes. Finally, in January 1990, trading on the Frankfurt Stock Exchange opened one hour earlier, resulting in a three-hour trading day beginning at 10:30 a.m. In most analyses, special attention is given to important events such as these. These events, however, may be considered part of a chaotic system, their impact being accounted for in the aggregate analysis.

Since the application of the augmented Dickey–Fuller test results in the inability to reject the null hypothesis that the index contains a unit root, the DAX is transformed into a stationary process by converting it into share price relatives. This is accomplished by taking the first difference of the natural logarithm of the index values, which results in a series of continuous rates of return. Several statistics describing this return series are presented in Table 4.1.[3] Turning to the first column in the table, it is clear that the unconditional distribution is thicker-tailed than a normal distribution and is somewhat negatively skewed. The returns also appear to exhibit some linear dependence.

It may be that some of these empirical characteristics are caused by a day-of-the-week effect. Indeed, the existence of this phenomenon in German stock returns is documented by Frantzmann (1987) and Akgiray *et al.* (1989a). To measure this possible effect and remove linear dependence, returns are regressed on variables signifying the day-of-the-week plus past returns. Specifically

$$r_t = \sum_{j=1}^{5} a_j D_{jt} + \sum_{i=1}^{s} b_i r_{t-i} + e_t, \tag{3}$$

where r_t is the return in time t, D_{jt} are indicator variables denoting the day of the week (Monday, $j = 1; \ldots ;$ Friday, $j = 5$), and e_t is an error term.

TABLE 4.1 Empirical Characteristics of DAX Returns, Mean-filtered Returns, Mean/variance-filtered Returns and GARCH Standardized Residuals

Statistics	DAX returns		Mean-filtered returns		Mean/variance-filtered returns		GARCH standardized residuals	
Number of observations	2360		2353		2353		2353	
Shape and location								
Mean	0.0006	(2.37)	0.0000	(0.00)	0.0000	(0.00)	-0.0186	(-0.90)
Variance	0.0001		0.0001		1.0004		1.0014	
Skewness	-1.13	(-22.38)	-1.13	(-22.45)	-.62	(-12.30)	-.35	(-6.87)
Kurtosis	14.81	(146.92)	14.51	(143.60)	9.29	(91.96)	2.56	(25.41)
$\chi^2_{normal}(35)$	168.21		166.40		134.09		36.54	
Linear dependence								
Q-statistic Lag(6)	2.99		0.06		1.57		13.64	
Lag(24)	45.83		24.69		26.88		40.43	

Notes: At the 1 percent significance level, the critical values for Q(6) and Q(24) are 16.81 and 42.98, respectively. The critical value for the equiprobable $\chi^2_{normal}(35)$ test is 57.40; the number of classifications (degrees of freedom) is determined by a procedure designed to maximize the power of the test and is described in Kendall and Stuart (1977). Where appropriate, *t*-statistics (assuming the null value is zero) are provided in parentheses.

The results of this regression are presented in the first column of Table 4.2. The number of autoregressive terms, s, is determined by noting the lag at which the regression residuals (the mean-filtered returns) become linearly independent as determined by the Q(24) statistic. A review of the parameters indicates that there is a significant day-of-the-week effect on the mean of the series. Frantzmann's (1987) Monday effect is confirmed and there appears to be a Wednesday and Friday effect as well. That the two- and seven-day autoregressive terms are significant and five days apart is also suggestive of some sort of a periodic (weekly) dependence. As is indicated in the second column in Table 4.1, however, the unconditional distribution of the mean-filtered returns is still thick-tailed and negatively skewed. In fact, the values of the statistics signifying these non-normal characteristics are virtually the same as before the removal of linear dependence and the day-of-the-week effect. Thus both the return and mean-filtered return series are examined for chaotic and nonlinear properties.

Empirical Results and Discussion

Various chaos related statistics pertaining to the DAX returns and mean-filtered returns are presented in Table 4.3. For both series, correlation dimensions for embedding dimensions $M = 5$, 10, and 15 are given. In all cases, the estimated values of the $D^M(T)$ from equation (2) are larger than the true values. This overstatement is the result of the small sample bias that has been commented on by Nerenberg and Essex (1990) and Ramsey and Yuan (1989), among others. Solving Nerenberg and Essex's (1990) equation (3.23) using this study's sample size and their recommended scaling factor of 2 yields an estimate of the upward bias of 0.26, 0.75, and 1.22 for $M = 5$, 10, and 15, respectively. Results for greater dimensions are not reported because small sample related bias tends to exert itself dramatically for M beyond 15. For dimensions greater than 15, the plots of $\ln C^M(\varepsilon, T)$ versus $\ln \varepsilon$ tend to flatten as M increases, whereas they should not change in slope if the true dimensionality is reached and the sample size is sufficiently large.

In most instances, the $D^M(T)$ values are estimated by the procedure outlined in the second section using values for ε ranging from 0.5σ to 1.5σ in increments of 0.01σ. For some of the larger dimensions, however, this is not possible since there are no pairs to be found for small ε. Thus the correlation dimension is estimated from the first nonzero correlation integral. For instance, in the case of DAX returns, for $D^{15}(T)$, the lowest nonzero value for ε is 0.51σ. In all cases, however, the lowest ε value for the dimensions reported is less than 0.72σ.

TABLE 4.2 *Filtering Regressions*

Independent variable/ statistic	Dependent variable	
	e_t	$e^2_t (\times 10^2)$
D_1	−0.0016 (−2.97)	0.0193 (7.72)
D_2	0.0001 (0.27)	0.0138 (5.63)
D_3	0.0014 (2.68)	0.0128 (5.14)
D_4	0.0009 (1.64)	0.0113 (4.49)
D_5	0.0019 (3.51)	0.0094 (3.78)
r_{t-1}	0.0367 (1.78)	
r_{t-2}	−0.0550 (−2.67)	
r_{t-3}	0.0083 (0.40)	
r_{t-4}	−0.0164 (−0.08)	
r_{t-5}	0.0015 (0.56)	
r_{t-6}	0.0372 (−1.81)	
r_{t-7}	0.0764 (3.71)	
F-statistic	4.767	30.409

Notes: *t*-statistics contained in parentheses; critical values at the 1 percent level are ± 2.58. The critical values for the *F*-statistic for the e_t and e regressions are 2.18 and 3.02, respectively.

An examination of the $D^M(T)$ for the DAX and mean-filtered returns indicates that their values are about the same. They reach a value of nearly 10 when the embedding dimension equals 15. It is worth observing, even accounting for small sample estimation bias, that this is approximately two-thirds larger than the values reported by Scheinkman and LeBaron (1989), Brock (1986), and Gennotte and Marsh (1986) for U.S. common stock returns. In total, these authors investigated three stock indexes (CRSP value-weighted, NYSE value-weighted, and NYSE equal-weighted) as well as several individual stocks. It is also interesting to note that it is about two-thirds larger than the values for the correlation dimension reported by Frank and Stengos (1989) for London gold and silver prices and it is many times greater, according to Brock and Malliaris (1989), than the correlation dimension for U.S. Treasury bills.[4]

That there is some type of nonlinear dependence in both the German return series is evinced by comparing the $D^M(T)$ for the original series to the $D^M(T)$ of their scrambled counterparts.[5] To accomplish this, following Frank and Stengos (1989) each series is scrambled 100 times and the $D^M(T)$ for each scrambled series calculated.[6] Two benchmarks for comparison purposes are particularly relevant. One is the 1-percentile and 5-percentile $D^M(T)$ values and the other is the t-ratio. The t-ratio denotes the number of standard deviations that the $D^M(T)$ for the original series is away from the mean $D^M(T)$ of the 100 scrambled series. These two benchmarks and the mean $D^M(T)$ values for the DAX and the mean-filtered series are reported in the first two panels of Table 4.3. A review of these panels indicates that, for each M, the 1-percentile $D^M(T)$ values are larger than the $D^M(T)$ for both return series. In addition, relying on the finding that it is not possible to reject the hypothesis that the distributions of the scrambled $D^M(T)$ are normal, in all cases the t-ratio far exceeds the 1 percent level of significance. Specifically, the t-ratios range from -2.69 to -11.31; the critical value is -2.33 for a one-tailed test. Both comparisons suggest that the scrambling of the data destroyed (or at least measurably reduced) the initial nonlinearity. These comparisons and subsequent similar ones are not affected by small sample bias, however, because the bias depends only on M, T, and the scaling factor, all of which are the same for the $D^M(T)$ that are compared.

Given that nonlinear dependence and possibly deterministic chaos exist, it is only natural to ask what is the nature of this relationship. Before exploring this question, it is useful to investigate, as suggested, for example, by Akgiray *et al.* (1989a) and Foster and Viswanathan (1990), whether the conditional variance might partially depend on the day-of-the-week. Thus the following regression is estimated

$$e_t^2 = \sum_{j=1}^{5} c_j D_{jt} + u_t, \tag{4}$$

where e_t^2 is the squared residual from the mean-filtering regression, equation (3), and serves as a proxy for the conditional variance, and u_t is the regression's error term. The results of this regression are presented in the second column of Table 4.2. Again the Monday effect is evident. As revealed by pairwise t-tests, Monday's variance is significantly higher than that of Friday, with the other three days being statistically indistinguishable from Friday.

Therefore, a new series is constructed that removes the day-of-the-week effect on both the mean and the variance as well as linear dependence.[7] In particular

$$R_t = e_t/(e_t^{2} - u_t)^{0.5}, \tag{5}$$

where R_t is defined to be the mean/variance-filtered return, and e_t and u_t are defined by equations (3) and (4), respectively. Descriptive statistics for this new return series are displayed in the third column of Table 4.1. By construction, the series has a zero mean and unit variance. Nevertheless, it is still thick-tailed (although less than the mean-filtered series), slightly skewed, and decidedly non-normal. Similar to the mean-filtered series, the mean/variance-filtered series does not exhibit linear dependence.

That nonlinear dependence still remains, however, is demonstrated by the correlation dimensions presented in the bottom panel of Table 4.3. Similar to the DAX returns and mean-filtered returns, $D^{15}(T)$ for the mean/variance-filtered returns is slightly less than 10. Further, although this value is minutely higher (9.76 versus 9.74) than the 1-percentile value for the scrambled $D^{15}(T)$, it is much lower than the corresponding 5-percentile value. In addition, the t-ratio for the $D^{15}(T)$ is −2.70.

A potential explanation for the observed nonlinearity is that the conditional variance follows an autoregressive conditional heteroscedastic path. This modeling approach was introduced by Engle (1982) and later generalized by Bollerslev (1986). This type of nonlinearity in stock returns has been modeled by Bollerslev (1987), Akgiray (1989), Akgiray *et al.* (1989a), Baillie and DeGennaro (1990) and Booth *et al.* (1991), among others. Bollerslev *et al.* (1992) provide a comprehensive survey of autoregressive conditional heteroscedastic modeling of asset returns.

To investigate the possibility of this type of nonlinearity, the following simple GARCH model is estimated using the method of

TABLE 4.3 *Correlation Dimensions for DAX, Mean-filtered, and Mean/variance-filtered Returns*

	Embedding dimension	Returns	Scrambled returns			
			Mean	Percentile 1	5	*t*-Ratio
DAX	5	3.60	3.91	3.84	3.86	−11.31
returns	10	6.63	7.85	7.54	7.64	−8.45
	15	9.69	11.41	10.11	10.42	−3.11
Mean-	5	3.65	3.92	3.85	3.87	−9.78
filtered	10	6.81	7.86	7.54	7.58	−6.80
returns	15	9.82	11.38	10.01	10.35	−2.69
Mean/variance-	5	3.68	3.94	3.87	3.89	−9.32
filtered	10	6.88	7.92	7.53	7.63	−6.37
returns	15	9.76	11.44	9.74	10.35	−2.70

Notes: The scrambled statistics summarize the results of 100 time series, which are created using computer generated random numbers from a uniform distribution to reorder the returns. For each embedding dimension, the *t*-ratio is the difference between the $D^M(T)$ for the returns and mean $D^M(T)$ for the scrambled returns divided by the standard deviation of the scrambled returns' distribution. Application of the Shapiro–Wilk test indicates that the null hypothesis that the distributions of $D^5(T)$, $D^{10}(T)$, and $D^{15}(T)$ for the scrambled returns are normal cannot be rejected at the 5 percent significance level. This conclusion is supported by Monte Carlo studies reported in Brock and Baek (1991) and Ramsey and Yuan (1990). Thus, assuming normality, the *t*-ratio is equivalent to the calculated *t*-statistic, and critical values for a one-tailed significance test are −1.65 and −2.33 for the 5 and 1 percent levels, respectively.

maximum likelihood as suggested by Berndt *et al.* (1974)

$$R_t | \Omega_t \sim N(\mu, h_t) \tag{6}$$

$$h_t = \alpha_0 + \alpha_1 (R_{t-1} - \mu)^2 + \beta_1 h_{t-1}, \tag{7}$$

where N denotes a normal distribution with mean μ and conditional variance h_t.[8] Although Bollerslev *et al.* (1992) point out that the inclusion of only one period lag in the variance equation is usually sufficient to capture the dynamics of the process, undoubtedly the specification of this model can be improved if institutional changes and true (to this model) outliers are recognized. For examples of such modeling efforts, see Akgiray *et al.* (1989a), Lamoureux and Lastrapes (1990), and Booth *et al.* (1991).

The parameter values for equations (6) and (7) are as follows, with the *t*-statistic provided in parentheses

$$R_{t|}\Omega_t \sim N(0.0156, h_t) \tag{8}$$
$$(0.93)$$

$$h_t = 0.0401 + 0.1784(R_{t-1} - 0.0156)^2 + 0.7894h_{t-1}. \tag{9}$$
$$(5.01)* \quad (17.98)* \qquad\qquad (51.89)*$$

Statistical significance at least at the 1 percent level is denoted by an asterisk, and with the exception of the mean, all of the conditional variance parameters are significantly different from zero at this probability level. Descriptive statistics for the standardized GARCH residuals, $(R_t - \mu)h_t^{-0.5}$, are presented in the last column of Table 4.1. Compared to the three preceding return series, skewness has dropped and tail thickness has dramatically diminished. An overall equiprobable χ^2 test indicates that the hypothesis of normality cannot be rejected, thereby validating the specification of the conditional distribution.

As Hsieh (1989, 1991) points out, nonlinearity can be either multiplicative or additive. Autoregressive conditional heteroscedastic processes are a form of multiplicative nonlinearity, and they retain the martingale property. If, however, the nonlinearity is additive or is a combination of additive and multiplicative, the martingale property is violated.[9] The success of the simple GARCH model in describing the mean/variance-filtered returns suggests that these returns do not exhibit additive nonlinearity. This assertion is further supported by the results of Hsieh's (1989) third-order moment test. Application of this test to the mean/variance-filtered returns fails to reject the null hypothesis of no additive nonlinearity.

The correlation dimensions for the GARCH standardized residuals are presented in Table 4.4. Also presented in this table are the comparison correlation dimensions for 100 random number series (each containing 2500 observations) generated from a standard normal distribution. The $D^M(T)$ for the standardized residual series are similar to the mean of their scrambled standardized residual series and their random number series counterparts. Specifically, $D^{15}(T)$ is in the neighborhood of 12 to 13 instead of slightly less than 10 as before. Thus, the requirement of Brock's residual test is not met, indicating that the series is not generated by deterministic chaos. It is worthwhile to highlight the observation that the standardized

TABLE 4.4 Correlation Dimensions for GARCH Standardized Residual Returns

Embedding dimension	Returns	Scrambled returns				Standardized Normal Random numbers			
		Mean	Percentile 1	Percentile 5	t-Ratio	Mean	Percentile 1	Percentile 5	t-Ratio
5	4.27	4.22	4.17	4.19	2.16	4.30	4.22	4.24	-1.07
10	8.86	8.49	7.96	8.21	1.77	8.60	8.11	8.22	1.13
15	12.26	12.12	10.05	11.00	0.19	12.30	9.39	10.70	-0.04

Notes: See Table 4.3 notes. Similar to the scrambled series statistics, the random number results are derived from 100 random series (2500 observations) generated from a standard normal distribution. In addition, the null hypothesis that the distributions of each of the $D^M(T)$ for the standardized normal random numbers is normal cannot be rejected at the 5 percent significance level.

residual series $D^M(T)$ for every M are larger than the 5-percentile $D^M(T)$ values for both the scrambled and random number series. In fact, in the majority of cases they are higher than the means of the two comparison series. Further, none of the t-ratios are statistically significant at the 5 percent level. These results mean that the nonlinear dependence which is observed in the German returns is not chaotic and appears to be attributed to GARCH effects.[10] Nevertheless, a caveat is necessary. Since all pseudo random number generators are deterministic chaotic processes, both the scrambled and the standardized normal random series are not random in the theoretical sense, although they are random in the financial sense. Nevertheless, it is impossible to rule out completely a difficult to detect chaotic process.

Summary and Conclusions

By way of summary, the returns derived from the DAX exhibit significant linear and nonlinear dependence. Linear dependence can be removed by a simple autoregressive process and by accounting for the day-of-the-week effect. This latter effect also influences the conditional variance. Eliminating its presence, however, does not remove the observed nonlinearity. Nevertheless, a simple GARCH model seems to remove the nonlinearity. This removal, as indicated by the comparison of the $D^M(T)$ to their scrambled and random number counterparts, and the failed Brock's residual test, suggests that the observed nonlinear dependence is not generated by deterministic chaos but that it can be modeled using an autoregressive conditional heteroscedastic framework. That the volatility of the DAX is able to be modeled in this manner is of practical importance to the measurement and management of financial risk. For example, the conditional and not the unconditional variance should be used to calculate optimal hedges with futures, mean/variance trade-offs, and option prices.[11]

These findings contradict the conclusions of Scheinkman and LeBaron (1989), Brock and Malliaris (1989), and Gennotte and Marsh (1986) for U.S. stock returns. Further, they are in sharp contrast with Scheinkman and LeBaron's (1989) observation that GARCH models are not capable of eliminating the nonlinear dependence that they observe in U.S. stock returns. They also provide evidence against Brock and Malliaris' (1989, p. 339) contention that GARCH processes are not capable of accounting for all nonlinear dependence found in asset prices. Nevertheless, the findings complement Hsieh's (1991) contention that U.S. stock returns are not chaotic and that the observed nonlinearities are effectively removed by GARCH processes.[12] They also complement Ramsey *et al.*'s (1990) assertion that the Scheinkman and LeBaron (1989) results are caused by a single, short, anomalous period.

In conclusion, the results of this study suggest that either the martingale or the instantaneously unpredictable hypotheses holds for German stocks. A caveat, however, must be made because of the observed low level of linear dependence in the original DAX return series. Nevertheless, as has been pointed out many times, this amount of dependence cannot be used to generate trading profits after transaction costs have been met. Thus, in this case, a martingale process may be considered a reasonable approximation of reality for short-term German stock returns. This conclusion is consistent with Granger's (1992) assertion that it is unlikely that a stock's price, which is determined by thousands of speculations, can be deterministically modeled.

Notes

1. The short-term dependencies that have been observed are very small, and it is not possible to exploit them to make trading profits, especially after transactions costs have been considered. For an extensive treatment of this issue, see the early classic work of Fama (1965).
2. The Frankfurt Stock Exchange in collaboration with the *Börsen-Zeitung* (a daily newspaper) and the other seven German stock exchanges (via the Association of German Stock Exchanges) initiated the DAX Index at the end of 1987. This index evolved from the *Börsen-Zeitung* Index, which consisted of daily quotes. The DAX Index was created to provide minute by minute quotations throughout the trading day in order to support derivative securities. Because of the similarity in construction of the two indexes and the comprehensive intraday coverage of the DAX Index, the *Börsen-Zeitung* Index was discontinued. The database, therefore, contains DAX quotes from 1988 onward, with its quotations in prior years being created by chain-linking the DAX to the *Börsen-Zeitung* Index.
3. This large sample has implications for the statistical tests that are subsequently applied. In particular, the 1 percent level is used to determine statistical significance. The selection of this value recognizes that statistical tests used on large samples reject the null hypothesis more often than they should. For discussion on this point in the context of financial research, see Connolly (1989).
4. Hsieh (1991) examines the CRSP value-weighted and equal-weighted indexes as well as the S&P 500 index. However, he does not report correlation dimension values. Instead, Hsieh relies on BDS statistics (which are based on the correlation dimension), third-order moment tests, locally weighted regressions, and autoregressive conditional heteroscedastic models to support his claim that U.S. stock returns are nonlinearly dependent but not chaotic.

5. Simulation experiments indicate that random series with thick-tailed (low entropy) distributions (e.g. Student-t and power exponential) are sometimes characterized by relatively lower $D^M(T)$ than the corresponding $D^M(T)$ for a Gaussian series. Examples of this stylized fact may be observed by comparing the mean $D^M(T)$ for all of the thick-tailed scrambled series in Table 4.3 with the mean $D^M(T)$ for the scrambled and standardized normal random number series displayed in Table 4.4. This observation supports one of the major conclusions of Ramsey and Yuan (1989).

6. Frank and Stengos (1989) use 30 replications. Further, Brock in an address to the 1991 Annual Meeting of the Financial Management Association suggested that the number of replications be partly determined by the computer power available. This advice recognizes the enormous amount of computer time needed to calculate the correlation dimension.

7. These mean and variance day-of-the-week effects are different from those discussed in Akgiray *et al.* (1989a) and clarified by Booth and Loistl (1992). It appears that the statistical indication of the presence of these effects may depend on the particular sample of returns. For instance, the strong Monday variance effect in these sample data may be because the series (2360 days) contains the 1987 and 1989 October crashes, both which occurred on Monday. Akgiray *et al.*'s (1989a) crash period (42 days) contains the 1987 crash. In their analysis, Monday's volatility is higher than that of the other four days but it is not significantly so. The statistical difference between the two samples is not the magnitude of the day-of-the-week effects as measured by the regression parameters in equation (7); rather, the parameter variance/covariance values for the 2360-day period are much smaller than the 42-day period.

8. Other autoregressive conditional heteroscedastic models include AARCH (asymmetric ARCH), NARCH (nonlinear ARCH), and SPARCH (semi-parametric ARCH), to name but a few. See Engle (1993) for a readable summary of these and other ARCH models.

9. Most bilinear and threshold autoregressive models are capable of describing additive nonlinear behavior. The GARCH in the mean model is able to handle both additive and multiplicative nonlinear dependence. It should be noted, however, that Baillie and DeGennaro (1990) use daily U.S. stock returns to demonstrate that the additive component in a GARCH in mean model is, at best, weak. See also Nelson (1991). However, the transformation of the German GARCH model to include an 'in mean' term results in no additional explanatory power. Thus, the results of this hybrid model to detect differences in the nonlinearities between the two markets is inconclusive.

10. This assertion is supported by Brock *et al.*'s (1987) BDS test, which examines whether $C^M(\varepsilon, T)$ is significantly greater than $C^1(\varepsilon, T)^m$. For $M = 15$ and $\varepsilon = \sigma$, the BDS statistic for the standardized GARCH residuals is -1.10. According to critical value tables provided by Brock *et al.* (1991), this value is not significantly different from zero, thereby indicating the absence of nonlinearity. A second supplementary test is to see if the evolution of the standardized GARCH residuals is sensitive to the initial conditions. Eckman *et al.* (1986) show that this trait can be measured by the Lyapunov exponent.

This statistic is not considered, however, because, as Scheinkman (1990) points out, its distributional properties are not known.

11. For a treatment of these issues, see, among others, Cecchett *et al.* (1988), Bollerslev *et al.* (1988), and Engle and Mustafa (1992). Also, see Hsieh (1993) for a discussion of the use of conditional variances to determine minimum capital requirements for a margin position.

12. Along these lines, Frank and Stengos (1989) report that GARCH models do not remove the nonlinear dependence contained in gold and silver prices. In contrast, Hsieh (1989) finds that these models describe the nonlinear behavior of the Canadian dollar, Swiss franc, and German mark but perform poorly for the British pound and the Japanese yen. Regardless of the fit, however, Hsieh (1989) maintains that diagnostics show that his GARCH models account for most of the observed nonlinearity. A similar conclusion is drawn by Booth *et al.* (1994) concerning the nonlinear behavior of a broad-based Finnish stock index.

References

AKGIRAY, V. (1989) Conditional heteroscedasticity in time series of stock returns: evidence and forecasts, *Journal of Business*, 62, 55–80.

AKGIRAY, V., BOOTH, G. G. and LOISTL, O. (1989a) German stock markets resiliency to world-wide panics, *Zeitschrift für Betriebswirtschaft*, 59, 968–978.

AKGIRAY, V., BOOTH, G. G. and LOISTL, O. (1989b) Statistical models of German stock returns, *Journal of Economics*, 50, 17–33.

BAILLIE, R. T. and DEGENNARO, R. P. (1990) Stock returns and volatility, *Journal of Financial and Quantitative Analysis*, 25, 203–214.

BAUMOL, W. J. and BENHABIB, J. (1989) Chaos: significance, mechanism, and economic applications, *Journal of Economic Perspectives*, 3, 77–105.

BERNDT, C. K., HALL, B. H., HALL, R. E. and HAUSMAN, J. A. (1974) Estimation and inference in nonlinear structural models, *Annals of Economic and Social Measurement*, 4, 653–665.

BOLLERSLEV, T. (1986) Generalized autoregressive conditional heteroskedasticity, *Journal of Econometrics*, 31, 307–327.

BOLLERSLEV, T. (1987) A conditional heteroskedastic time series model for speculative prices and rates of return, *Review of Economics and Statistics*, 69, 542–547.

BOLLERSLEV, T., CHOU, R. Y. and KRONER, K. F. (1992) ARCH modeling in finance: a review of the theory and empirical evidence, *Journal of Econometrics*, 52, 5–59.

BOLLERSLEV, T., ENGLE, R. F. and WOOLDRIDGE, J. M. (1988) A capital asset pricing model with time varying covariances, *Journal of Political Economy*, 96, 116–131.

BOOTH, G. G., HATEM, J., VIRTANEN, I. and YLI-OLLI, P. (1991) Stochastic modeling of security returns: evidence from the Helsinki exchange, *European Journal of Operational Research*, 56, 111–119.

BOOTH, G. G. and LOISTL, O. (1992) Wie reagiert der Wiener Aktienmarkt auf weltweite Kurseinbrüche?: Kommentar zu den vorstehen den Ausführungen von Dr. Alois Geyer, Wien, *Zeitschrift für Betriebswirtschaft*, 62, 1207–1211.

BOOTH, G. G., MARTIKAINEN, T., SARKAR, S., VIRTANEN, I. and YLI-OLLI, P. (1994) Nonlinear dependence in Finnish stock returns, *European Journal of Operational Research*, 74, 273–283.

BROCK, W. A. (1986) Distinguishing random and deterministic systems: abridged version, *Journal of Economic Theory*, 40, 168–195.

BROCK, W. A. and BAEK, E. G. (1991) Some theory of statistical inference for nonlinear science, *Review of Economics Studies*, 58, 697–716.

BROCK, W. A., DECHERT, W. and SCHEINKMAN, J. (1987) A test for independence based on the correlation dimension. Working paper, University of Wisconsin-Madison, University of Houston, and University of Chicago.

BROCK, W. A., HSEIH, D. A. and LEBARON, B. (1991) *Nonlinear Dynamics, Chaos and Instability: Statistical Theory and Economic Evidence*, MIT Press, Cambridge, MA.

BROCK, W. A., and MALLIARIS, A. G. (1989) *Differential Equations, Stability and Chaos in Dynamic Economics*. North Holland, Amsterdam.

CECCHETTI, S. G., CUMBY, R. E. and FIGLEWSKI, S. (1988) Estimation of the optimal futures hedge, *Review of Economics and Statistics*, 70, 623–630.

CONNOLLY, R. A. (1989) An examination of the robustness of the weekend effect, *Journal of Financial and Quantitative Analysis*, 24, 133–169.

ECKMAN, J. P., KAMPHORST, S. O., RUELLE, D. and CILIBERTO, S. (1986) Lyapunov exponents for time series, *Physical Review A*, 34, 617–656.

ENGLE, R. F. (1982) Autoregressive conditional heteroscedasticity with estimates of the U.K. inflation rate, *Econometrica* 50, 987–1008.

ENGLE, R. F. (1993) Statistical models for financial volatility, *Financial Analysts Journal*, January–February, 72–78.

ENGLE, R. F. and MUSTAFA, C. (1992) Implied ARCH models from options prices, *Journal of Econometrics*, 52, 289–311.

FAMA, E. F. (1965) The behavior of stock market prices, *Journal of Business*, 38, 34–105.

FAMA, E. F. and FRENCH, K. R. (1988) Permanent and temporary components of stock prices, *Journal of Political Economy*, 98, 247–273.

FISCHER, A. (1990) *DAX Information*. Frankfurter Wertpapierbörse, Frankfurt.

FOSTER, F. D. and VISWANATHAN, S. (1990) A theory of interday variations in volume, variance, and trading costs in securities markets, *Review of Financial Studies*, 3, 593–624.

FRANK, M. and STENGOS, T. (1989) Measuring the strangeness of gold and silver rates of return, *Review of Economic Studies*, 56, 553–567.

FRANTZMANN, H. J. (1987) Der Montagseffekt am deutschen Aktienmarkt, *Zeitschrift für Betriebswirtschaft*, 57, 611–635.

GENNOTTE, G. and MARSH, T. (1986) Variations in *ex ante* risk premiums on capital assets. Working paper, University of California at Berkeley, Berkeley, CA.

GRANGER, C. W. J. (1992) Forecasting stock market prices: lessons for forecasters, *International Journal of Forecasting*, 8, 3–13.

GRASSBERGER, P. and Procaccia, I. (1983) Measuring the strangeness of strange attractors, *Physica*, 9D, 189–108.

HSIEH, D. A. (1989) Testing for nonlinear dependence in daily foreign exchange rates, *Journal of Business*, 62, 339–368.

HSIEH, D. A. (1991) Chaos and nonlinear dynamics: application to financial markets, *Journal of Finance*, 46, 1839–1877.

HSIEH, D. A. (1993) Implications of nonlinear dynamics for financial risk management. *Journal of Financial and Quantitative Analysis*, 28, 41–64.

JEGADEESH, N. (1990) Evidence of predictable behavior of security returns, *Journal of Finance*, 45, 881–898.

KENDALL, M. G. and STUART, A. S. (1977) *The Advanced Theory of Statistics*, Hafner, New York, Vol. 3.

LAMOUREUX, C. G. and LASTRAPES, W. D. (1990) Persistence in variance, structural change, and the GARCH model, *Journal of Business & Economic Statistics*, 8, 225–234.

LEHMANN, B. (1990) Fads, martingales and market efficiency, *Quarterly Journal of Economics*, 105, 1–28.

LIU, T., GRANGER, C. W. J. and HELLER, W. (1991) Using the correlation exponent to decide if an economic series is chaotic. Working paper, University of California at San Diego, San Diego, CA (1991).

MÖLLER, H. P. (1984) Stock market research in Germany: some empirical results and critical remarks. In BAMBERG, G. and SPREMAN, K. (eds.), *Risk and Capital*, Springer, New York.

NELSON, D. (1991) Conditional heteroskedasticity in asset returns: a new approach, *Econometrica*, 59, 347–370.

NERENBERG, M. and ESSEX, C. (1990) Correlation dimension and systematic geometric effects, *Physical Review A*, 42, 7065–7074.

RAMSEY, J. B., SAYERS, C. L. and ROTHMAN, P. (1990) The statistical properties of dimension calculations using small data sets: some economic applications, *International Economic Review*, 31, 991–1020.

RAMSEY, J. B. and YUAN, H.-J. (1989) Bias and error bars in dimension calculations and their evaluation in some simple models, *Physics Letters A*, 134, 287–297.

RAMSEY, J. B. and YUAN, H.-J. (1990) The statistical properties of dimension calculations using small data sets, *Nonlinearity*, 3, 155–176.

von ROSEN, R. (1988) Der DAX und die Deutsche Terminbörse DTB, *Kreditwesen*, 41, 743–745.

ROSSER JR, J. B. (1991) *From Catastrophe to Chaos: A General Theory of Economic Discontinuities*, Kluwer, Boston MA.

SCHEINKMAN, J. A. (1990) Nonlinearities in economic dynamics, *Economic Journal*, 100, 33–48.

SCHEINKMAN, J. A., and LeBARON, B. (1989) Nonlinear dynamics and stock returns, *Journal of Business*, 62, 311–337.

SIMS, C. A. (1984) Martingale-like behavior of prices and interest rates. Discussion paper No. 205, Department of Economics, University of Minnesota, Minneapolis, MN.

5

Complex and Random Appearing Stock Prices: A Chaotic Approach

EFI PILARINU AND GEORGE C. PHILIPPATOS

Introduction

There has recently been considerable interest in chaotic dynamics in a variety of disciplines. Extremely influential scientists emphasize disorder, instability, diversity, disequilibrium, nonlinear relationships, as those aspects of reality that characterize today's dynamic environment.[1]

Researchers are investigating pathways to chaos and erratic dynamics in economics. Benhabib and Day (1981) and Gaertner (1988) analyze consumer choice. Day (1983) and Dana and Montrucchio (1986) analyze a classical economic growth model and a dynamic oligopoly setting. Baumol and Benhabib (1989) and Shaffer (1991) consider models of firm behavior. Lorenz (1992) proves the existence of a strange attractor for a Kaldor-type business cycle model. The Santa Fe Institute Volume (1988) collectively presents the work of scientists from various disciplines in discussing the issue of the *Economy as an Evolving Complex System*.

Empirical research in finance, employing tools from chaos theory (correlation dimension estimates), examines whether additional structures exist above and beyond that captured by fitting linear models to log transformed, detrended/deseasonalized stock return series. Scheinkman and LeBaron (1989) examined daily and weekly returns from the VW CRSP index. The dependencies detected do not seem to be captured from an ARCH type specification. Brock (1987), examined subsets of the above data and also monthly returns of the VW and EW NYSE index. Genotte and Marsh (1986) examined subsets of the above monthly data and also adjusted for the January effect. Hsieh (1991) examined weekly returns of various portfolios and indices, daily returns and 15-minute returns of the S&P500. Willey (1992) tested for nonlinear dependencies in the daily prices of the Standard & Poor's 100 Stock Index and the NASDAQ 100 Stock Index. Eckmann *et al.* (1988) found two positive Lyapunov exponents for weekly returns of the VW CRSP index. All the above studies examined whether predictability exists over and above stochastic financial stock return models (e.g. random walk, martingale, ARCH, GARCH).[2]

In this chapter we do not search for evidence of incremental predictability in financial asset returns. Rather, we investigate whether chaos is a plausible alternative modeling approach to the complex and random appearing behavior of stock prices. The reason being that exceedingly complex time paths can be generated by simple nonlinear dynamic systems. Such trajectories can be misinterpreted as the outcome of random processes by standard statistical tests. Sakai and Tokumaru (1980) show that a modified version of the triangular recursion map generates the same autocorrelation coefficients as a first-order autoregressive process. Casti (1989) and Malliaris and Philippatos (1992) show that the trajectories produced by the tent map are indistinguishable from the sample path followed by flipping a fair coin. We examine short holding periods (daily) at various portfolio aggregation levels (individual stocks, indices), since the existing empirical evidence for the corresponding return series appears to be contradictory. Furthermore, we focus on examining whether the new modeling approach to complex and random appearing behavior leads to results that may not be obtained or may contradict those derived from a stochastic approach to randomness. We test the hypothesis of whether aggregation across assets, which exhibits low-dimensional type dynamic behavior, preserves the structure or order. In other words, we investigate whether dependencies vary across portfolio aggregation levels at the daily time aggregation level.

In the second section, we present an improved method of extracting the correlation dimension invariant from a single time series. The Grassberger–Procaccia algorithm (1983) for estimating the correlation dimension is used, based on the redundancy criterion for selecting the time delay in reconstructing the phase space, a method yet to be utilized in financial applications. In the third section, we discuss in detail the issue under consideration. We examine the static behavior (through the correlation integral) and the dynamic behavior (through the generalized mutual information) of daily prices of individual stocks from the DJIA versus daily index levels of the DJIA and the S&P500. The implications of the results are examined and the conclusions of this work are discussed in the final section.

Methods of Extracting Correlation Dimension Estimates from a Single Time Series

Various invariant measures exist that enable us to distinguish random from deterministic systems. Dimension invariants are static measures that describe spatial properties of the system. Entropic quantities and Lyapunov exponents are dynamic invariants that quantify the temporal properties of the system (i.e. properties related to the evolution of the system) . If one is mainly interested in establishing or rejecting the presence of chaos, then between the two dynamic invariant categories the entropic measures are preferred. The calculation of the Lyapunov exponents is complicated and since the sum of all positive Lyapunov exponents is equal to the Kolomgorov entropy, the latter suffices. Entropic and dimension measures can be calculated from the same information.

The correlation dimension D quantifies the average spatial correlation. It is the average information gained by increased resolution, by taking into account conditional probabilities[3]

$$D = \lim \lim \log C(\varepsilon)/\log \varepsilon, \text{ as } \varepsilon \to 0, N \to \infty$$

$$C(\varepsilon) = \{\text{the number of pairs } \|x_i - x_j\| < \varepsilon\}/N^2.$$

Since the true law of motion governing the system under examination is unknown and the only available information is a single observable of the system, we employ the time delay method for reconstructing the phase space (Takens, 1983). Assume that the only available measurement is a single variable x_i, $i = 1, 2, \ldots, N$. There exists a diffeomorphism between the n-dimensional true generating process and the reconstructed d-histories, if $d \geqslant 2n + 1$. Thus, by 'transforming' the single time series into vector series of various dimensions, we embed the reconstructed phase space into the true one

$$x_i^d = (x_i, x_{i+\tau}, x_{i+2\tau}, \ldots, x_{i+(d-1)\tau}), i = 1, 2, \ldots, N - (d - 1)\tau.$$

Having created the d-histories by coupling τ delayed values, we then calculate the correlation integral $C^d(\varepsilon)$

$$C^d(\varepsilon) = \{\text{the number of pairs } \|x_i^d - x_j^d\| < \varepsilon\}/N_n^2, N_n = N - (d - 1)\tau.$$

As ε changes the number of points included in the correlation integral also change. If a structure exists and not all the degrees of freedom are exploited by the system, then proportionally fewer new neighborhoods are included as ε increases. For example, consider a three-dimensional object embedded in a four-dimensional space. For any increase in the resolution parameter, the increase in the points included in the correlation integral is only due to three out of the four available directions. Grassberger and Procaccia (1983) have shown that there exists a scaling relationship between the correlation integral $C^d(\varepsilon)$ and the correlation dimension D as the resolution ε shrinks

$$C^d(\varepsilon) \approx \varepsilon^D.$$

In practice, since the true dimension is unknown we study the behavior of the correlation integral $C^d(\varepsilon)$ for increasing embedding dimensions d. We estimate D^d for each embedding dimension value d

$$D^d = \lim [\log C^d(\varepsilon)/\log \varepsilon], \varepsilon \to 0.$$

If as d increases so does D^d, then the system is viewed as being high dimensional. If D^d converges or saturates to some level D, then D is the estimated correlation dimension. Although the above algorithm appears to be a clear-cut procedure, there are considerable problems in applying this technique. The selection of the sample size N, the appropriate ranges of the embedding dimension d, the resolution parameter ε, and the time delay τ in reconstructing the phase space, must be discussed.

The minimum sample size to estimate the correlation dimension D has been 'calculated' as $N_{min} = 21.5^D$. Thus, in order to detect an attractor of dimension three, one needs at least 10,000 points. With less than 1000 observations (which is the case in many financial studies), the largest dimension that can be measured is between two and three. Ramsey et al. (1990) have studied the effect of the sample size and the embedding dimension on the estimated correlation dimension. In practice, given the expected scaling relationship $C^d(\varepsilon) \approx \varepsilon^D$, one estimates D^d for each embedding dimension d with an OLS regression model of the logarithm of the correlation integral $C^d(\varepsilon)$ against the logarithm of the resolution parameter ε. Ramsey and Yuan (1989) claim that the above relationship is highly nonlinear and they show that the bias in the estimated dimension increases with embedding dimension, but decreases with sample size. The estimated variance of the dimension estimate decreases with sample size, but increases very rapidly with embedding dimension. In fact, the actual variance can be as high as 64 times larger than that estimated by the

OLS procedure. Therefore, for one unit increase in the embedding dimension considered, one should dramatically increase the sample size in order to obtain reliable estimates. The choice of the appropriate range of the resolution parameter ε is also important, especially in the presence of noise in the observable examined. First, for scaling values below the noise level one should observe a nonscaling behavior of the correlation integral, and for values above the noise level the logarithmic plots of the correlation integral versus the resolution parameter (GP plots) should be straight lines with slopes that saturate. Ben-Mizrachi *et al.* (1984) propose a modified algorithm that also provides for an estimate of the noise level of the system. Second, even in the absence of noise because of the finite sample size, the GP plots will saturate for very low values of the resolution parameter (i.e. no points will be included). The same behavior will be observed for very high values of the resolution parameter since the attractor has a finite size (i.e. all points will be included).

The choice of the time delay in reconstructing the phase space is the most important issue, since it determines whether the reconstructed phase space actually resembles the true phase space or if their dimensions are equal. The dramatic effect of the time delay selection can be vividly understood in the case of a system which exhibits some periodicity. If one selects this period as the time delay, then the reconstructed phase space will be a single point. It is thus evident that the 'optimal' choice should be based on selecting the time delay that couples points of a single time series as independently as possible into vectors. Early suggestions for choosing the time delay and simultaneously reducing the effect of the noise level by Broomhead and King (1986) have proved unsuccessful. The authors propose a sophisticated linear analysis of time series called the *singular system approach*. It is based on the Karhunen–Loeve theorem in information theory. The basic idea is that the mean-squared distance between points on the reconstructed attractor should be maximized. The procedure proposed has a built-in filter for reducing noise and the Broomhead and King approach of reconstructing the phase space appears to have a striking advantage. However, Fraser (1989a) and Mees *et al.* (1987) do not find it successful, based on the fact that the notion of independence underlying the singular approach procedure is only that of linear independence. Thus, if the densities of the observable are nonGaussian, they show that the singular approach procedure is not optimal. Fraser and Swinney (1986) have proposed another approach that is based on general dependence, by choosing the time delay that produces the first local minimum of the mutual information.[4] Mutual information in a two-dimensional setting measures how many bits on average can be predicted about one dimension, given a measurement in the other direction. If one considers scalar measurements versus some lagged values (e.g. $(x(t), x(t - t))$) then mutual information measures the redundancy of the second axis of delayed values. The minimization is required in order to ensure that subsequent coordinates are as independent as possible and spanning the m-dimensional space to its full extent. Mutual information $I(Q, S)$ (for a two-dimensional case) is calculated from the entropy quantities $H(\cdot)$ as

$$I(Q, S) = H(Q) + H(S) - H(S, Q)$$

$$H(S) = -\Sigma_s p_s \log p_s$$

$$H(Q, S) = -\Sigma p_{sq} \log p_{sq}.$$

It quantifies the average bits of information that can be predicted about q, given a measurement of s. Fraser (1989b) generalized the algorithm from the two-dimensional case to an n-dimensional case (embedding), where mutual information measures the number of bits that are redundant in a vector measurement:

$$I(X_0, X_1, \ldots, X_n) = \Sigma_i H(X_i) - H(X_0, X_1, \ldots, X_n).$$

The intuition of the time delay selection criterion can be best understood if one evaluates the redundancy measure at two extreme cases. At a zero redundancy value, knowledge of some components of a vector cannot be used to predict anything about the remaining components, therefore implying total independence (thus, we seek to minimize I). If the system is completely deterministic (i.e. x determines exactly y, $y = f(x)$), then redundancy is equal to infinity.[5]

The algorithm (provided by A. M. Fraser) changes the floating point delayed vectors into integer representations in a fashion that preserves the orderings and then partitions the space in rectangular grids of 4^m elements by dividing the axis into 2^m equiprobable segments. A chi square test checks for structure in each 'box' based on the null hypothesis that the probability density function is flat. Since the base of the logarithms used in the calculations is two, the information is measured in bits. For example, if we partition a one-dimensional space in 64 equiprobable bins, then the probability of an isolated measurement being in any one of the 64 bins is 1/64 and thus $H = -\log_2 1/64 = 6$ bits. If the underlying distribution is Gaussian, then the singular approach and the redundancy method give the same results (Fraser, 1989a). In fact, mutual information (I) has an exact relation with the autocorrelation function (C)

$$I(X, Y) = -1/2 \log(1 - C^2(X, Y)).$$

The difference is that mutual information can detect nonlinear correlations. At each embedding dimension d and time delay τ the redundancy measure calculated $I_d(\tau)$ shows the degree of predictability. Thus, higher dimensions, that obviously have higher informational content, should show greater redundancy values at each time delay. *Ceteris paribus*, variables that are more independent, show smaller values of mutual information. Fraser (1989b) has also provided for a selection of the embedding dimension at the smallest value of d at which the information production saturates. Thus, in order to avoid the detrimental effect (bias of the estimate and its variance) we increase the embedding dimension for each series examined up to the point that mutual information values appear to converge.

Individual Daily Stock Prices and Index Daily Levels

The Issue

Empirical evidence supporting the presence of dependencies in stock returns that cannot be captured by linear nonstationary specifications has been well documented. Hinich and Patterson (1985) and Brockett *et al.* (1988) examined daily returns of individual stocks from the NYSE and the AMEX. Ashley and Patterson (1989) look at daily returns of the CRSP value weighted stock index. Hinich and Patterson (1988) examined a 15-minute return series of individual stocks from the Dow Jones Industrial Average Index. Overall, linearity and Gaussianity is rejected at the various aggregation levels examined (time-wise and portfolio-wise). Most importantly, the bispectral analysis tests employed in the above studies show that the dependencies detected cannot be captured by linear nonstationary specifications, thus *nonlinear structures exist in individual daily stock returns*.

Barnett and Chen (1986) present evidence consistent with the hypothesis that daily individual stock returns are pure white noise. The autocorrelation function of daily returns of IBM[6] for the first 807 observations closely resembles the delta function characterizing pure white noise. Their decision (not to calculate the correlation dimension for the IBM data) is further reinforced from the uniform cloud pattern of the phase portrait calculated from 2000 observations, also characteristic of Gaussian noise. However, this evidence of independence for daily stock returns can be due to the small sample size (807) and the arbitrary time lag chosen in the phase portrait construction (20 lags). Scheinkman and LeBaron (1989) find no evidence of additional structure for individual daily stock returns.

They examine the residuals of the daily and weekly stock returns for Abott Laboratories for embedding dimensions as high as 20 and observe similar behavior for their shuffled counterpart. Brock (1987) also concluded that no additional structure exists in monthly returns of individual stocks, by comparing the correlation integral behavior of Kodak with a shuffled counterpart at only one embedding dimension ($d = 10$). Based on these results, one can conclude that the currently employed linear, nonstationary, stochastic models are appropriate for daily and even weekly individual stock returns[7] (since no additional structure was found). However, Hinich and Patterson (1985, 1988) present evidence of nonlinearities for individual daily stock returns. These results lead to nonlinear model specifications for individual daily stock prices.

For daily holding periods the empirical findings for the dependencies in index returns are even more confusing. Ashley and Patterson (1989) present bispectral-based results for the daily returns of the CRSP value-weighted stock index (1981–1984) that reject linearity and Gaussianity. Hsieh (1991) in a thorough investigation of the power of the BDS statistic (Brock and Dechert (1986, 1989)) presented evidence of nonlinearities for daily returns of the S&P500 index from 1983 to 1989. Willey (1992) claims that (weak) evidence exists of a low correlation dimension (approximately 2) for the S&P100 index and the NASDAQ100 index for the period 1982–1988 (although the estimated correlation dimension values failed to stabilize at any single value). However, Scheinkman and LeBaron (1989) found very weak evidence of additional structure for the daily returns of the VW CRSP index (5200 observations). Thus, it appears that aggregation across assets may not preserve the structure, since individual stocks and indices seem to be described by different processes (linear and nonlinear, respectively), or have a different degree of predictability. The latter conclusion does not preclude that the nonlinear dependencies at the two different portfolio aggregation levels may vary. Both groups of studies are in agreement concerning the presence of nonlinear dependencies for high aggregation levels (indices) at higher than weekly holding periods.

Based on the above 'controversy' we investigate whether structure does exist in individual daily stock prices in the spirit of the bispectral based studies and compare their local spatial and dynamic behavior to that of an index which includes them as individual components. We implement the methodology described in the previous section for certain individual stock price series from the DJIA. This index is chosen because the relatively small number of stocks composing it enables us to construct a meaningful comparison of an index and its individual components. We examine only stocks for which data are available from 1962 to 1991 on the CRSP tapes: Bethlehem Steel, Boeing, Chevron, Woolworth, Westinghouse, Texaco, Alcoa, DuPont, Procter & Gamble, Eastman Kodak, American Tobacco, Chrysler, Coca Cola. These stocks were in the DJIA index for the whole period examined, except for American Tobacco that was eliminated in 1985, Chrysler in 1979, and Boeing and Coca Cola that entered the index in 1987.[8] We finally examine the S&P500 index, the second most frequently followed stock market indicator that also includes the industrials selected.[9]

Why Prices?

In finance, returns have received all the attention in empirical applications. Returns have been used because they appear to 'fit' some known distributions and thus can be analyzed easily through standard statistical theory. The Brownian motion process of independent Gaussian increments (the most common distributional assumption in finance) was 'borrowed' by economic modelers in the 1960s from physicists. The Efficient Market Hypothesis framework was developed to accompany it. Ever since, academics have been trying to empirically test the above setting. The results are contradictory and the arguments are perpetuated. A simple argument against the independent increment hypothesis was first developed by Mandelbrot (1967). The idea was based on the observation that prices are *not continuous* as are the sample functions of the Brownian motion. Furthermore, they differ from other physical observables in that price formation involves both the knowledge of the present and anticipation of the future. The *anticipatory nature* of the system results in prices that can wander anywhere. Mandelbrot (1982) states that: "without institutional constraint and inertia to complicate matters, a price determined on the basis of anticipation can crash to zero or soar out of sight; it can do anything." These ideas led to the development of a family of 'stable' distributions called the Levy or Pareto distributions. The logarithmic transformation of their characteristic functions is the well-known 'stable Paretian' distribution. The Gaussian distribution was only one member of this family. Another era, one of infinite variance distributions, emerged. However, in the 1970s Gaussian distribution assumptions were again favored over Levy distributions and Mandelbrot's (1967, 1971) principle of a scaling structure in price changes.

Returns, independent increments, finite variances, efficient markets, remain on the 'empirical stage'. Since the framework is stochastic, any conclusions concerning the properties of the distribution of returns can be transformed to the implied price distribution. For example, the assumption of normal returns implies lognormal prices or vice versa. In a stochastic framework there exists a one-to-one correspondence between price and return distributional assumptions. The latter validates the theoretical examination of return distributions instead of price distributions, but may not be valid from an empirical perspective. Return series may fit a specific distribution with a certain degree of accuracy, but price series may fit the implied price distribution with a substantially lower degree of accuracy.

In a chaotic framework, the above stochastic theoretical correspondence may not hold. If one assumes that prices do follow a chaotic process, then the transformation of prices to return series may not preserve the structure, and vice versa.[10] Prices are the actual outcomes produced from the system. Prices seem to exhibit *the complexity, the irregularities, the discontinuities, as well as the sudden ups and downs* that chaos theory attempts to describe. Deceptively simple mathematical equations of nonlinear dynamic systems exist in chaos theory, that seem capable of accounting for the above. In a chaotic framework it appears more appropriate to examine first prices. Obviously, if one finds that prices (returns) are stochastic then so are returns (prices). All previous studies have focused on rejecting specific stochastic return models, by presenting evidence of 'extra' structure. This is not our objective. Thus, we do not detrend our data, since we do not wish to detect any additional forecastible structure in the residuals of stochastic models. We use raw price data, since our objective is to model the observed complexity and randomness as if chaos was the only appropriate tool at our disposal. We avoid the bias in the correlation dimension estimation due to the presence of correlations, by reconstructing the phase space with an optimal time delay selection criterion. We do not employ any test that potentially distinguishes various modeling alternatives (bootstrap technique), since our objective is to use the new methodology in a nonparametric fashion that sheds light on issues in finance from a different perspective.

Results

The procedure that is followed for the analysis of each time series is as follows:

(a) Mutual information values are calculated for each time series for increasing time delay values ($\tau = 1, 2, 3, \ldots$) until the first local minimum is reached. The procedure is repeated for increasing embedding dimensions ($d = 2, 3, 4, \ldots$) up to the embedding dimension value at which the mutual information values appear to saturate.[11]

(b) The relevant ranges of the resolution parameter ε are determined by trial and error. The ranges selected are such that the correlation integral is different to 1 (i.e. all points included) and 0 (i.e. no points included). We chose ten different values.[12]

(c) For a given embedding dimension d the correlation integral was calculated for all ten resolution parameter values. The time delayed vectors at each embedding dimension are reconstructed based on the optimal time delay determined in the first step (by the redundancy criterion). Thus, at different embedding dimensions the 'coupling' of delayed values may vary.

(d) The logarithmic plot of the correlation integral values versus the resolution parameter values are constructed (GP plots) for each embedding dimension. We increase the embedding dimension values two or three units higher than the saturation level indicated from the mutual information increase rate.

(e) By examining the behavior of the slopes of the GP plots as the resolution parameter changes, we determine the appropriate linear scaling region (for each embedding dimension). This range of values is used in an OLS regression of the logarithm of the correlation integral values against the logarithm of the resolution parameter values.

(f) For our analysis we compare and contrast the mutual information values and the correlation dimension estimates among the price series examined.

The mutual information values of the individual stock price series and the indices examined are given in Tables 5.1–5.7 and Table 5.8, respectively. For each price series the mutual information values increase as the embedding dimension increases (as expected). The increase in the mutual information values, however, is at a decreasing rate with respect to the embedding dimensions and approximately converges at an embedding dimension of eight for all individual stocks. The information production rate of the series at embedding dimensions higher than eight is relatively small and stable. In fact, Fraser (1989b) claims that this 'saturating' embedding dimension can be viewed as a rough estimate of the degrees of freedom of the system. All individual stocks exhibit very similar dynamic behavior in that their mutual information values at each embedding dimension are of the same magnitude. For the indices, however, the dynamic behavior varies. An example of the difference in the mutual information values of one individual stock (Westinghouse) with the S&P500 index and the DJIA index and another individual stock (Procter & Gamble) can be clearly seen in Fig. 5.1 as a function of the embedding dimension for three different time delay values ($\tau = 1, 2, 3$).

TABLE 5.1 *Mutual Information Values of the Individual Stocks of the DJIA Index for an Embedding Dimension Equal to Two (Emboldened Values are the First Local Minima)*

$d = 2$	$\tau = 1$	$\tau = 2$	$\tau = 3$
Bethlehem Steel	**3.53**	5.57	4.08
Boeing	**3.37**	5.09	3.88
Chevron	**3.37**	5.39	3.82
Westinghouse	**3.83**	5.44	4.17
Woolworth	**4.06**	5.85	4.53
Texaco	**3.56**	5.09	3.71
Alcoa	**3.47**	4.41	3.67
Procter & Gamble	**2.01**	5.35	4.01
American Tobacco	**3.44**	5.41	3.88
Chrysler	**3.31**	4.68	3.62
Coca Cola	**4.57**	5.53	4.87
Eastman Kodak	**3.68**	4.90	4.73
DuPont	**3.59**	4.70	4.67

The S&P500 index levels show a 'saturation' of information production at an embedding dimension around 5 and moreover, substantially lower values at each embedding dimension and time delay than the individual stocks. Therefore, this index not only appears to be described by a system with less degrees of freedom (5) than that for individual stocks (8), but also exhibits higher predictability. These results are consistent with the existence of

TABLE 5.2 *Mutual Information Values of the Individual Stocks of the DJIA Index for an Embedding Dimension Equal to Three (Emboldened Values are the First Local Minima)*

$d = 3$	$\tau = 1$	$\tau = 2$	$\tau = 3$
Bethlehem Steel	**7.93**	9.58	7.51
Boeing	**7.54**	8.82	7.18
Chevron	**7.73**	9.09	7.03
Westinghouse	**8.18**	9.32	7.88
Woolworth	**8.75**	9.65	8.48
Texaco	**7.51**	8.99	7.03
Alcoa	**7.40**	8.80	6.90
Procter & Gamble	**8.20**	9.15	7.78
American Tobacco	**7.91**	9.34	7.33
Chrysler	**7.13**	8.76	6.63
Coca Cola	**9.01**	9.55	8.89
Eastman Kodak	**7.20**	8.18	7.74
DuPont	**7.04**	7.81	7.80

TABLE 5.3 *Mutual Information Values of the Individual Stocks of the DJIA Index for an Embedding Dimension Equal to Four (Emboldened Values are the First Local Minima)*

$d = 4$	$\tau = 1$	$\tau = 2$	$\tau = 3$
Bethlehem Steel	**10.92**	12.17	10.44
Boeing	**9.98**	11.12	9.55
Chevron	**10.41**	11.55	9.79
Westinghouse	**10.94**	11.94	10.97
Woolworth	**11.45**	12.53	11.17
Texaco	**10.10**	13.01	9.93
Alcoa	**10.00**	11.19	9.53
Procter & Gamble	**10.92**	11.83	10.27
American Tobacco	**10.95**	11.93	10.23
Chrysler	**9.55**	10.94	9.30
Coca Cola	**12.13**	12.54	11.77
Eastman Kodak	9.61	**8.18**	9.18
DuPont	9.47	9.36	9.34*

*The first local minimum occurs at a time delay equal to four, where the mutual information values are 8.98 ($\tau = 4$) and 13.04 ($\tau = 5$).

TABLE 5.4 *Mutual Information Values of the Individual Stocks of the DJIA Index for an Embedding Dimension Equal to Five (Emboldened Values are the First Local Minima)*

$d = 5$	$\tau = 1$	$\tau = 2$	$\tau = 3$
Bethlehem Steel	**13.57**	13.78	12.47
Boeing	**11.20**	12.38	11.19
Chevron	**12.12**	13.25	11.90
Westinghouse	**12.65**	13.89	12.75
Woolworth	**12.96**	14.23	13.16
Texaco	**11.55**	13.01	11.91
Alcoa	**11.67**	12.81	11.55
Procter & Gamble	**12.51**	13.63	12.38
American Tobacco	**12.80**	13.69	12.35
Chrysler	**10.94**	12.36	11.20
Coca Cola	**13.90**	14.52	13.69
Eastman Kodak	10.49	10.31	10.12*
DuPont	10.51	**10.15**	10.16

*The first local minimum occurs at a time delay equal to four, where the mutual information values are 9.55 ($\tau = 4$) and 14.82 ($\tau = 5$).

TABLE 5.5 *Mutual Information Values of the Individual Stocks of the DJIA Index for an Embedding Dimension Equal to Six (Emboldened Values are the First Local Minima)*

$d = 6$	$\tau = 1$	$\tau = 2$	$\tau = 3$
Bethlehem Steel	**13.93**	14.41	13.64
Boeing	**12.31**	12.85	12.43
Chevron	**13.43**	13.99	13.44
Westinghouse	**13.64**	14.68	14.20
Woolworth	**14.02**	15.10	14.48
Texaco	**12.58**	13.71	13.38
Alcoa	**12.94**	13.61	12.96
Procter & Gamble	**13.66**	14.45	13.83
American Tobacco	**14.10**	14.65	13.92
Chrysler	**11.88**	12.83	12.65
Coca Cola	**15.35**	15.85	14.91
Eastman Kodak	11.45	11.13	11.02*
DuPont	11.67	11.34	11.19†

*The first local minimum occurs at a time delay equal to four, where the mutual information values are 10.44 ($\tau = 4$) and 16.83 ($\tau = 5$).
†The first local minimum occurs at a time delay equal to four, where the mutual information values are 10.97 ($\tau = 4$) and 18.53 ($\tau = 5$).

TABLE 5.6 *Mutual Information Values of the Individual Stocks of the DJIA Index for an Embedding Dimension Equal to Seven (Emboldened Values are the First Local Minima)*

$d = 7$	$\tau = 1$	$\tau = 2$	$\tau = 3$
Bethlehem Steel	15.28	**15.11**	15.29
Boeing	12.92	**12.80**	13.73
Chevron	14.20	**14.18**	14.97
Westinghouse	**13.98**	14.49	15.72
Woolworth	**14.55**	15.15	15.87
Texaco	**13.21**	13.81	14.91
Alcoa	**13.71**	13.83	14.37
Procter & Gamble	**14.45**	14.85	15.43
American Tobacco	**14.87**	15.11	15.59
Chrysler	**12.36**	12.72	14.18
Coca Cola	**16.19**	16.57	16.15
Eastman Kodak	11.75	**11.60**	11.85
DuPont	12.31	12.18	12.05*

*The first local minimum occurs at a time delay equal to four, where the mutual information values are 11.62 ($\tau = 4$) and 20.64 ($\tau = 5$).

TABLE 5.7 *Mutual Information Values of the Individual Stocks of the DJIA Index for an Embedding Dimension Equal to Eight (Emboldened Values are the First Local Minima)*

$d = 8$	$\tau = 1$	$\tau = 2$	$\tau = 3$
Bethlehem Steel	15.47	**15.28**	16.46
Boeing	13.37	12.83	**14.96**
Chevron	14.98	14.32	**16.29**
Westinghouse	14.35	**14.21**	16.97
Woolworth	15.08	**14.90**	16.09
Texaco	13.87	**13.69**	16.05
Alcoa	14.38	**13.97**	15.60
Procter & Gamble	15.23	**14.93**	16.74
American Tobacco	15.57	**15.19**	15.56
Chrysler	**12.55**	12.59	15.47
Coca Cola	**16.86**	16.99	17.03
Eastman Kodak	11.95	**11.59**	12.27
DuPont	12.77	12.75	12.56*

*The first local minimum occurs at a time delay equal to four, where the mutual information values are 12.13 ($\tau = 4$) and 22.66 ($\tau = 5$).

TABLE 5.8 *Mutual Information Values of Indices*

	$\tau = 1$	$\tau = 2$	$\tau = 3$	$\tau = 4$	$\tau = 5$
DJIA					
$d = 2$	**2.90**	3.86	3.85	2.86	5.30
$d = 3$	**6.00**	6.65	6.57	5.77	9.47
$d = 4$	8.18	8.10	7.98	**7.87**	13.36
$d = 5$	9.45	9.42	9.29	**9.16**	16.36
$d = 6$	11.28	11.10	11.00	**10.83**	19.70
$d = 7$	**12.72**	12.76	12.48	12.07	22.90
$d = 8$	14.14	14.00	13.64	**13.35**	26.02
S&P500					
$d = 2$	2.19	1.65	**1.41**	1.42	1.54
$d = 3$	3.64	3.18	**2.68**	2.72	2.84
$d = 4$	4.53	4.23	4.11	**3.85**	3.98
$d = 5$	5.15	**5.07**	5.32	4.80	4.88
$d = 6$	5.40	**5.20**	6.21	5.11	5.30
$d = 7$	5.52	**5.24**	6.92	5.20	5.53
$d = 8$	5.66	**5.61**	7.54	5.74	5.91

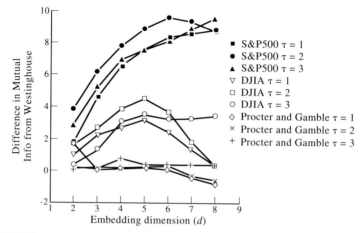

FIGURE 5.1 *Difference in Mutual Information Values at Various Portfolio Aggregation Levels*

diversification. They also support the use of different models for describing individual stock behavior and index behavior. The DJIA dynamic behavior is closer to that of the individual stocks with only slightly lower values at each embedding dimension but no difference in the information production rate. Although both indices examined include the stocks considered as individual components, they differ in two major respects. The DJIA is a price weighted index that has substantially less individual components (30/500) and is significantly less diversified since it includes only industrials. The S&P500 is a value weighted index with 80 percent approximately of industrials.

Next the static behavior of the various series is examined, through the behavior of the correlation integral at various embedding dimensions and resolutions values. The geometry of the series described through the behavior of the correlation integral (Packard *et al.*, 1980) is consistent with the observed dynamic behavior.[13] The resolution parameter ranges chosen in order to avoid the effect of the finite size of the sample and of the attractor are: 0.9^6, 0.9^8, 0.9^{10}, 0.9^{12}, 0.9^{14}, 0.9^{16}, 0.9^{18}, 0.9^{20}, 0.9^{22}, 0.9^{24}. The embedding dimension ranges for the individual stocks are from 2 to 11 and for the indices from 2 to 8. Figure 5.2 exhibits the GP plots for each time series. In order to draw any conclusions from inspecting the GP plots, we compare them with the two extreme cases of the GP plots from a completely random[14] series and from a completely deterministic series (Fig. 5.3).

Completely random series exhibit GP plots with curves for each embedding dimension which have slopes equal to the embedding

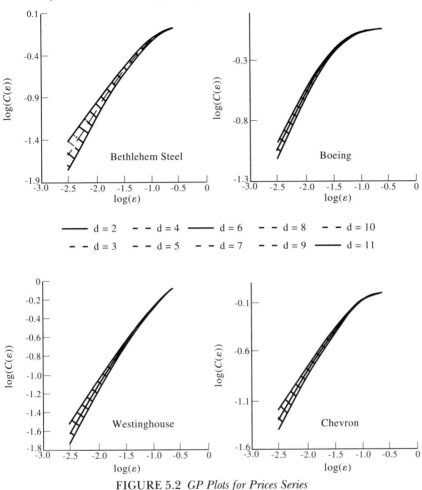

FIGURE 5.2 *GP Plots for Prices Series*

dimension. Completely random series exhibit GP plots with parallel straight lines[15] that a have a slope equal to the correlation dimension. Thus, by simply comparing the GP plots one concludes that structure does exist in all series. Although any differences in the slopes (i.e. correlation integral convergence) between individual stocks and indices may not be evident from simply examining the graphs, one clearly detects a difference in the displacement of the curves among the two groups. The GP plots of the individual stocks exhibit larger displacement from each other as the embedding dimension increases. The latter is a rough estimate of metric entropy (Procaccia, 1985). Thus, indices show lower values of metric entropy than individual

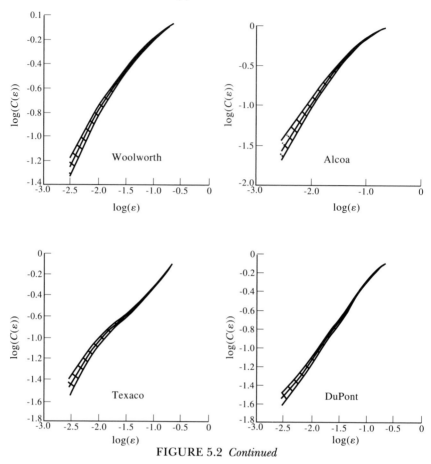

FIGURE 5.2 *Continued*

stock series. This is in complete agreement with their lower mutual information values. Overall, indices appear more predictable than individual stocks. All individual stocks exhibit similar nonlinear dependencies, which are different than those for indices. Table 5.9 displays the slopes at each embedding dimension. All individual stock prices exhibit similar behavior. The convergence of the correlation integral indicates weaker evidence of a low dimensional structure for individual stocks than for indices. The latter is consistent with the difference in the estimate of the degrees of freedom of the two series, observed above. For individual stocks the estimates do not converge at a single value, as for the indices, and also the standard error of the estimate increases as the embedding dimension changes.

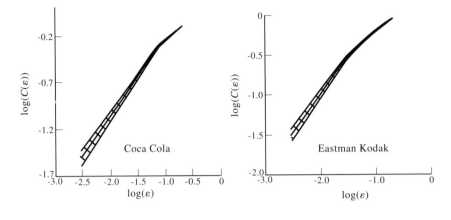

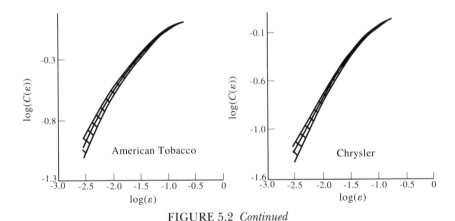

FIGURE 5.2 *Continued*

Conclusions and Implications

In summary, the dependencies at a daily time aggregation level vary between individual stocks and indices. Evidence of low dimensional structure as a plausible alternative in modeling complex and random appearing daily stock prices appears stronger at higher portfolio aggregation levels. The spatial characteristics of these groups are similar and it is only the dynamic characteristics that account for the differential behavior.

But why should we care about knowing whether financial data are generated (or can be modeled) by random or deterministic means? The implications of the alternate approaches to complex and random appearing behavior are immense. Even if at a certain aggregation

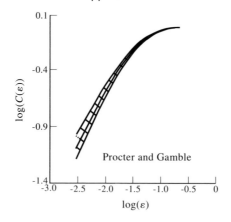

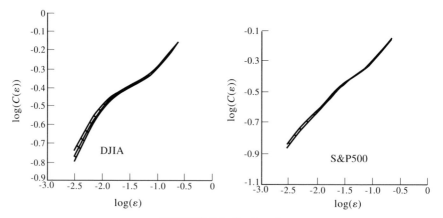

FIGURE 5.2 *Continued*

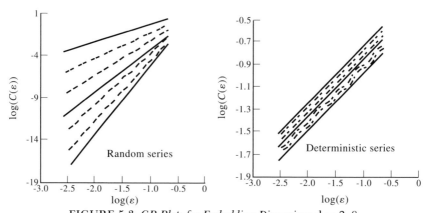

FIGURE 5.3 *GP Plots for Embedding Dimensions* d = 2–8

level (time-wise or portfolio-wise) deterministic models appear to be as good a fit as a stochastic specification, the implications are in many respects totally different.

Forecasting

Under a chaotic scenario, short-term predictability is possible. Long-term predictability is not possible. Thus, the above empirical results suggest that, given a daily holding period, short-term predictability appears more promising at higher portfolio aggregation levels. In other words, even though individual stocks and portfolios may depend nonlinearly on the same number of factors (as indicated by the magnitude of the correlation dimension), they differ substantially with respect to the form of the dependencies. At higher portfolio aggregation levels the evidence suggests that the implied nonlinear dependencies can be described by more simple relationships than those at the individual level.

Market Efficiency

Chaotic prices fully reflect all information, since sensitivity to initial conditions 'transmits' even an imperceptible change in the system. Thus, market efficiency may hold under a chaotic regime. Market efficiency may hold at a certain aggregation level and may well be rejected at another aggregation level, given the evidence of differential dynamic behavior (i.e. information diffusion). However, the current techniques used for testing the market efficiency paradigm by examining the significance of the coefficients of various lagged models may not be appropriate under a chaotic scenario. Arbitrage cannot persist under a semideterministic (chaotic) regime, because even if an individual investor had complete knowledge of the underlying structure at one point in time (the chaotic model), he or she could not take advantage of this 'proprietary' information. Such action would require complete knowledge of all the market participants' models and expectations. Chaotic complexity does not allow us to disentangle the information contained in the model. The dominant anticipatory nature of the system prohibits arbitrage.

Nonstationarity

Ad hoc nonstationary distributional assumptions are circumvented under a chaotic regime. Variability is endogenously produced even without any 'exogenous' effects (i.e. institutional constraints, macro-economic effects, etc.). The empirical results of this chapter, if

TABLE 5.9 Correlation Integral (Numbers in Parentheses are the Standard Error of the Estimates)

	$d = 2$	$d = 3$	$d = 4$	$d = 5$	$d = 6$	$d = 7$	$d = 8$	$d = 9$	$d = 10$	$d = 11$
Bethlehem Steel	0.76 (0.03)	0.79 (0.03)	0.80 (0.03)	0.82 (0.03)	0.84 (0.03)	0.85 (0.03)	0.86 (0.03)	0.87 (0.04)	0.89 (0.04)	0.90 (0.04)
Boeing	0.45 (0.05)	0.46 (0.05)	0.47 (0.05)	0.48 (0.05)	0.48 (0.05)	0.49 (0.05)	0.50 (0.05)	0.50 (0.05)	0.51 (0.06)	0.51 (0.06)
Chevron	0.76 (0.03)	0.78 (0.03)	0.79 (0.03)	0.80 (0.03)	0.81 (0.03)	0.82 (0.03)	0.83 (0.03)	0.84 (0.03)	0.85 (0.03)	0.86 (0.03)
Westinghouse	0.71 (0.02)	0.72 (0.02)	0.73 (0.02)	0.74 (0.03)	0.75 (0.03)	0.75 (0.03)	0.76 (0.03)	0.77 (0.03)	0.77 (0.03)	0.78 (0.03)
Woolworth	0.48 (0.02)	0.49 (0.02)	0.50 (0.02)	0.50 (0.02)	0.51 (0.02)	0.51 (0.02)	0.52 (0.02)	0.52 (0.02)	0.53 (0.02)	0.53 (0.02)
Procter & Gamble	0.48 (0.04)	0.50 (0.04)	0.51 (0.04)	0.52 (0.04)	0.53 (0.05)	0.54 (0.05)	0.55 (0.05)	0.56 (0.05)	0.57 (0.05)	0.58 (0.05)
Texaco	0.54 (0.01)	0.55 (0.01)	0.56 (0.01)	0.57 (0.01)	0.58 (0.01)	0.58 (0.02)	0.59 (0.02)	0.60 (0.02)	0.60 (0.02)	0.61 (0.02)
Alcoa	0.72 (0.03)	0.79 (0.03)	0.81 (0.03)	0.82 (0.03)	0.84 (0.03)	0.86 (0.03)	0.87 (0.03)			

TABLE 5.9 *Continued*

	$d=2$	$d=3$	$d=4$	$d=5$	$d=6$	$d=7$	$d=8$	$d=9$	$d=10$	$d=11$
American Tobacco	0.58 (0.02)	0.59 (0.02)	0.60 (0.03)	0.61 (0.03)	0.62 (0.03)	0.63 (0.03)	0.64 (0.03)	0.65 (0.03)	0.66 (0.03)	0.66 (0.03)
Chrysler	0.76 (0.02)	0.78 (0.02)	0.79 (0.02)	0.80 (0.02)	0.81 (0.02)	0.82 (0.03)	0.83 (0.03)	0.83 (0.03)	0.84 (0.03)	0.85 (0.03)
Coca Cola	0.78 (0.008)	0.79 (0.008)	0.81 (0.007)	0.82 (0.007)	0.83 (0.007)	0.83 (0.007)	0.84 (0.007)	0.85 (0.007)	0.86 (0.007)	0.87 (0.007)
Eastman Kodak	0.79 (0.02)	0.81 (0.02)	0.83 (0.03)	0.84 (0.03)	0.85 (0.03)	0.86 (0.03)	0.87 (0.03)	0.88 (0.03)	0.89 (0.03)	0.90 (0.03)
DuPont	0.79 (0.01)	0.80 (0.01)	0.81 (0.01)	0.82 (0.009)	0.82 (0.009)	0.82 (0.009)	0.83 (0.009)	0.84 (0.009)	0.85 (0.009)	0.85 (0.009)
DJIA	0.18 (0.01)	0.18 (0.01)	0.18 (0.01)	0.18 (0.01)	0.18 (0.01)	0.19 (0.01)	0.19 (0.01)	0.19 (0.01)	0.19 (0.01)	0.19 (0.01)
S&P500	0.39 (0.01)	0.39 (0.01)	0.39 (0.01)	0.40 (0.01)	0.40 (0.01)	0.40 (0.01)	0.40 (0.01)			

translated in a traditional stochastic setting, would imply that the nonstationarity assumptions employed should be different across various portfolio aggregation levels in order to account for their differential dynamic behavior.

Risk measurement

Under a chaotic regime, risk cannot be solely measured through variability of the (artificially) implied probability distribution of the chaotic model. In a stochastic setting, variability (measured through variance or any higher moments) is the only source of uncertainty. Variability of conditional distributions is considered a measure of relative risk. Chaos offers a dynamic framework and thus, risk is associated with the dynamic properties of the system. Entropic measures (absolute or conditional) can capture the uncertainty associated with the diffusion of information.[16] These measures can quantify average systematic and unsystematic risk. Lyapunov exponents measure the rate of information flow in various directions. Since these directions are the dimensions of the system, Lyapunov exponents can quantify the dynamic evolution of sources of risk through time.

The primary purpose of this chapter was to apply an improved technique from the diagnostic criteria of chaos theory. Mutual information values and correlation integral behavior are used as alternative nonparametric tools in examining random and complex appearing stock prices at various aggregation levels. The implications of the results obtained are contrasted to a stochastic alternative. As Lorenz (1989) has noted it is surely too early to declare that chaos is the essential characteristic of economic life. However, research towards this direction must continue since there is a need for a more informative framework than the linear Gaussian setting.

Acknowledgements

The present version of this chapter has benefited from comments by A. Malliaris and M. Hinich. The authors also wish to thank A. M. Fraser for providing the program that calculates the generalized mutual information values and T. Stengos for additional software supplied.

Notes

1. A detailed overview of the importance of this scientific change can be found in the two books of the 1977 Nobel Prize winner for his work in thermodynamics of nonequilibrium systems (Prigogine, 1980; Prigogine and Stengers, 1984).

2. Other studies have examined rates of return on silver and gold (Frank and Stengos, 1989), daily foreign exchange rates (Hsieh, 1989), and futures prices for commodities and for financial assets (Blank, 1991).

3. The correlation dimension is a lower bound to the information dimension that is based on the unconditional probability distribution constructed by embedding the true space in a probability space through an invariant probability measure.

4. The first local minimum is preferred to the second one, in order to avoid the contamination of information from stretching and folding.

5. Any positive mutual information value indicates some degree of dependence. Note that very large time delay values will result in independence due to the decay of correlation with time.

6. Beginning on July 2, 1962 the authors examined 2000 successive observations.

7. All studies dealing with the detection of additional structure in stock returns examine higher than weekly aggregation levels.

8. Boeing replaced International Nickel, and Coca Cola replaced Owens Illinois. American Tobacco was replaced by McDonalds, and Chrysler by IBM.

9. All the data is obtained from the CRSP tapes for the period 1962–1991, except for the DJIA levels that were purchased from Heizer Software Inc. The sample size of each series is 7421 observations.

10. If for example we assume that stock prices can be described by the logistic equation:

$$P_t = \mu\, P_{t-1}(P_{t-1} - 1)$$

then returns $R_t = (P_t - P_{t-1})/P_{t-1}$ are not described from the logistic equation.

11. All previous studies arbitrarily increase the embedding dimension and in some cases have used values as high as 20 for sample sizes of around 1000 observations.

12. Most studies use five resolution parameter values since the algorithm is very slow due to the large number of calculations.

13. In fact, the dynamic invariants of a system are related to the static invariants (Kaplan and Yorke, 1979), thus linking stability properties with information diffusion.

14. One can analyze a random series if the correlation dimension algorithm is applied on the output of a random number generator. The resolution parameter values must be such that the true deterministic form of the random number generator cannot be detected.

15. Given that there is no noise present in the series (which would show as 'knees' in the straight lines) and also no finite sample size or finite attractor size effects (which would show as saturated lines at very high and very low resolution parameter values).

16. Entropy has been used as a more dynamic measure of uncertainty than variance and in testing the martingale hypothesis with filter-type security-trading models, in which the trading rule changes (Philippatos and Wilson, 1972; Martell and Philippatos, 1974).

References

ASHLEY, A. R. and PATTERSON, D. M. (1989) Linear versus nonlinear macro-economics: a statistical test, *International Economic Review*, 30, No. 3.

BARNETT and CHEN (1986) The aggregation-theoretic monetary aggregates are chaotic and have strange attractors: an econometric application of mathematical chaos. In BARNETT, W. A., BERNDT, E. R. and WHITE H. (eds.), *Dynamic Econometric Modeling*.

BAUMOL, W. J. and BENHABIB, J. (1989) Chaos: significance, mechanism and economic applications, *Journal of Economic Perspectives*, 3, No. 1.

BENHABIB, J. and DAY, R. H. (1981) Rational choice and erratic behavior, *Review of Economic Studies*, 48.

BEN-MIZRACHI, A., PROCACCIA, P. and GRASSBERGER, I. (1984) Characterization of experimental (noisy) strange attractors, *Physical Review A*, 29.

BLANK, C. S. (1991) Chaos in futures markets? A nonlinear dynamical analysis, *The Journal of Futures Markets*, 11, No. 6.

BROCK, A. W. (1987) Nonlinearity and complex dynamics in economics and finance. In ANDERSON, P. W., ARROW, K. J. and PINES, D. (eds.), *The Economy as an Evolving Complex System*, Addison-Wesley.

BROCK, W. A. and DECHERT, W. D. (1986) Theorems on distinguishing deterministic from random systems. In BARNETT W. A., BERNDT, E. R. and WHITE, H. (eds.), *Dynamic Econometric Modeling*.

BROCK, W. A. and DECHERT, W. D. (1989) Statistical inference theory for measures of complexity in chaos theory and nonlinear science. In ABRAHAM, N. B., ALFONSO, A. M., PASSAMANTE, A. and RAPP, P. E. (eds.), *Measures of Complexity and Chaos*, NATO ASI Series.

BROCKETT, L. P., HINICH, M. J. and PATTERSON, D. M. (1988) Bispectral-based tests for the detection of Gaussianity and linearity in time series, *Journal of the American Statistical Association*, 83, No. 403.

BROOMHEAD, D. S. and KING G. P. (1986) Extracting qualitative dynamics from experimental data, *Physica D*, 20.

CASTI, L. J. (1989) *Alternate Realities. Mathematical Models of Nature and Man*, Wiley, New York.

DANA, R. A. and MONTRUCCHIO, P. (1986) Dynamic complexity in duopoly games, *Journal of Economic Theory*, 40.

DAY, R. H. (1983) The emergence of chaos from classical economic growth. *Quarterly Journal of Economics*, 98.

ECKMANN, J. P., KAMPHORST, S. O., RUELLE, D. and SCHEINKMAN, J. (1988) Lyapunov exponents for stock returns. In ANDERSON, P. W., ARROW, K. J. and PINES, D. (eds.), *The Economy as an Evolving Complex System*, Addison-Wesley.

FRANK, M. and STENGOS, T. (1989) Measuring the strangeness of gold and silver rates of return, *Review of Economic Studies*, 40.

FRASER, A. M. (1989a) Reconstructing attractors from scalar time series: a comparison of singular and redundancy criteria, *Physica D*, 34.

FRASER, A. M. (1989b) Information and entropy in strange attractors, *IEEE Transactions on Information Theory*, 35, No. 2.

FRASER, A. M. and SWINNEY, H. L. (1986) Independent coordinates for strange attractors from mutual information, *Physical Review A*, 33, No. 2.

GAERTNER, W. (1988) Periodic and aperiodic consumer behavior. Unpublished paper cited by Kesley, D. In The economics of chaos or the chaos of economics, *Oxford Economic Papers*, Vol. 40.

GENNOTTE, G. and MARSH, T. (1986) Variations in *ex ante* risk premium on capital assets. University of California, Berkeley, Business School, Unpublished.

GRASSBERGER, P. and PROCACCIA, I. (1983) Measuring the strangeness of strange attractors, *Physica D*, Vol. 9.

HINICH, J. M. and PATTERSON, D. M. (1985) Evidence of nonlinearity in daily stock returns, *Journal of Business & Economic Statistics*, 3, No. 1.

HINICH, J. M. and PATTERSON, D. M. (1988) Evidence of nonlinearity in the trade-by-trade stock market return generating process. In BARNETT, W. A., GEWEKE, J. and SHELL, K. (eds.), *Economic Complexity: Chaos, Sunspots, Bubbles and Nonlinearity*.

HSIEH, A. D. (1989) Testing for nonlinear dependence in daily foreign exchange rates, *Journal of Business*, 63, No. 3.

HSIEH, A. D. (1991) Chaos and nonlinear dynamics: application to financial markets, *The Journal of Finance*, XLVL, No. 5.

KAPLAN, J. and YORKE, J. (1979) In PEITGEN, H. O. and WALTHER, H. O. (eds.), *Functional Differential Equations and Approximation of Fixed Points*.

LORENZ, H. W. (1989), *Nonlinear Dynamical Economics and Chaotic Motion*, Springer.

LORENZ, H. W. (1992), Strange attractors in a multisector business cycle model, *Journal of Economic Behavior and Organization*, to be published.

MALLIARIS, G. A. and PHILIPPATOS, G. (1992) Random walk vs chaotic dynamics in financial economics, *Proceedings of the Conference on Chaos in the Social Sciences*, Springer.

MANDELBROT, B. (1967) The variation of some other speculative prices, *Journal of Business*, 40.

MANDELBROT, B. (1971) When can price be arbitraged efficiently? A limit to the validity of the random walk and martingale models, *Review of Economics and Statistics*, LIII.

MANDELBROT, B. (1982) The many faces of scaling: fractals, geometry of nature, and economics. In SCHIEVEM, W. C. and ALLEN, P. M. (eds.), *Self-organization and Dissipative Structures: Applications in Various Physical and Social Sciences*, University of Texas at Austin, TX.

MARTELL, T. F. and PHILIPPATOS, G. C. (1974) Adaptation, information, and dependence in commodity markets, *Journal of Finance*, XXIX.

MEES, A. I., RAPP, P. E. and JENNINGS, L. S. (1987) Singular value decomposition and embedding dimension, *Physical Review A*, 36.

PACKARD, N. H., CRUTCHFIELD, J. P., FARMER, J. D. and SHAW, R. S. (1980) Geometry form a time series, *Physical Review Letters*, 45, No. 9.

PHILIPPATOS, G. C. and WILSON, C. J. (1972) Entropy, market risk, and the selection of efficient portfolios, *Applied Economics*, 4.

PHILIPPATOS, G C. and WILSON, C. J. (1974) Information theory and risk in capital markets, *The Journal of Management Science*, 2, No. 4.

PRIGOGINE, I. (1980) *From Being to Becoming*, W. H. Freeman, New York.

PRIGOGINE, I. and Stengers, I. (1984) *Order Out of Chaos*, Bantan Books, New York.

PROCACCIA, I. (1985) The static and dynamic invariants that characterize chaos and relations between then in theory and experiments, *Physica Scripta*, 19.

RAMSEY, J. B., SAYERS, C. and ROTHMAN, P. (1990) The statistical properties of dimension calculations using small data sets: some economic applications, *International Economic Review*, 31, No. 4.

RAMSEY, J. B. and YUAN, H. (1989) Bias and error bars in dimension calculations and their evaluation in some simple models *Physics Letters A*, 134, No. 5.

SAKAI, H. and TOKUMARU, H. (1980) Autocorrelations of a certain chaos, *IEEE Transactions on Acoustics, Speech and Signal Processing*, I, ASSP-28 (5).

SCHEINKMAN, J. A. and LEBARON, B. (1989) Nonlinear dynamics and stock returns, *Journal of Business*, 62, No. 3.

SHAFFER, S. (1991) Structural shifts and the volatility of chaotic markets, *Journal of Economic Behavior and Organization*, 15.

TAKENS, F. (1983) Distinguishing deterministic and random systems. In BORENBLATT, G., IOOSS, G. and JOSEPH, D. (eds.), *Nonlinear Dynamics and Turbulence*, Pitman, Boston, MA.

WILLEY, T. (1992) Testing for nonlinear dependence in daily stock indices, *Journal of Economics and Business*, 44.

6

A Strong Case for the Arrow–Pratt Risk Aversion Measure

RAFIQ DOSSANI, SHAHID HAMID, ARUN J. PRAKASH AND
MICHAEL W. SMYSER

Introduction

An ongoing research problem in the theory of risk bearing is the development of a quantitative measure of risk aversion.[1] A suitable measure is one whose changes can be associated with predictable changes in the composition of a portfolio. Thus, in their pioneering works, Arrow (1971) and Pratt (1964) proposed $R \equiv -U''/U'$ as a measure of local risk aversion associated with a von Neumann–Morgenstern utility function U, and justified the usefulness of this measure by showing that in a market consisting of a riskless asset and a single risky asset, an increase in R at all levels of wealth results in an increased demand for the riskless asset and a lower portfolio mean rate of return.[2]

How suitable is R when individuals choose portfolios of many risky assets? Hart (1975) provided an important negative result by showing that a uniform increase in R need not increase the individual's demand for the riskless asset. The intuitive reasoning behind this assertion was provided by Cass and Stiglitz (1972), for, if we realize that investors evaluate only the terminal wealth that results from alternative portfolio choices and since increases in the holdings of some risky asset could actually reduce risk if returns to that asset were negatively correlated with other sources of uncertainty, more risk averse individuals could invest more in that risky asset and less in the riskless asset, thereby achieving a reduction in overall portfolio risk.[3]

Researchers have interpreted the Hart result as implying that the Arrow–Pratt measure is useful only in special cases, such as when the returns of risky assets are uncorrelated (see Kihlstrom *et al.* (1981) and Ross (1981)). An alternative measure of risk aversion has been proposed by Ross (1981); but his measure also only has special applications. More recently, attempts have been made to either extend the Arrow–Pratt measure to multivariate utility functions or develop global rather than local measures of risk aversion. However, these attempts impose additional constraints. Bardsley (1991) used a Fourier transformation, rather than Taylor series expansion, to first derive a global approximation of the utility function, and then develop a global measure of risk aversion that applies to the entire indifference curve. However, to ensure the existence of the Fourier transformation, this method requires restrictions on both the utility function and the probability distribution of returns. Levy and Levy (1991) extend the univariate analysis of Arrow and Pratt to multivariate utility functions involving several goods. However, comparisons of risk aversions of two or more utility functions is impossible without additional restrictions on the utility function.

The purpose of this study is to show that Hart's results do not invalidate the use of the Arrow–Pratt measure. Since investors evaluate only the terminal wealth of their portfolios, a suitable test of R in the multiasset case is to see whether terminal wealth (rather than investment in particular assets) changes in some predictable fashion with a change in R. Thus, R will be a valid measure if, in the example of the previous paragraph, an increase in the holding of a particular risky asset as a result of a uniform increase in R causes an increase in the portfolio's riskless future return.

We apply the procedure used in the two asset case to a multiasset case and find that a uniform increase in the Arrow–Pratt measure of risk aversion results in a rise in the portfolio's *riskless future return*, a fall in the portfolio's mean rate of return, and a fall in the portfolio's range of possible future returns. Our results, therefore, strengthen the case for the Arrow–Pratt measure of risk aversion.

The Equilibrium Distribution of Risk Across Investors

Using the Arrow–Pratt measure of risk aversion, we have argued above that a more risk averse investor purchases more riskless terminal wealth and accepts a lower expected return for the lower level of risk taken. But how risk averse must an investor be before accepting no risk at all? Arrow (1971) shows that any risk averse investor, choosing from a riskless and a risky asset, would purchase some amount of the risky asset if and only if its expected rate of return is greater than the riskless rate. Only an infinitely risk averse investor will hold only the riskless asset no matter what the expected return of the risky asset is. In this chapter, we contribute a direct, but nontrivial, corollary of Arrow's result for the two asset world, and extend the corollary to the case of many assets. In the two asset world, if all investors are risk averse and agree on expected returns, we show that each investor will purchase some amount of the risky asset and, thus, each investor bears risk. In the multiasset case, the necessary conditions for our result are stronger than in the two asset world, and include the assumption of homogeneous beliefs.

Consider an exchange economy with investors trading claims to terminal wealth in a complete market.[4] Each investor i maximizes expected utility of terminal wealth, subject to a budget constraint

$$\max_{\{q_{ij},\,\ldots,\,q_{iJ}\}} E\left(U_i\right) = \sum_j \pi_{ij} U_i(x_{ij}) \tag{1}$$

$$\text{subject to } \sum_j q_{ij} = 1,$$

where j represents the index states; $j = 1, \ldots, J$; U_i are individual i's with strictly increasing ($U'' > 0$) and concave ($U'' < 0$) von Neumann–Morgenstern utility functions; π_j is the probability of occurrence of state j held by each individual (i.e. homogenous beliefs); $x_{ij} \equiv q_{ij}\bar{M}_i/P_j$ is the equilibrium terminal wealth in state j for an individual i; $0 < \bar{M}_i$ is the current value of i's endowment; q_{ij} is the proportion of $\bar{M}_i$ invested in P_j; P_j is the current price of one dollar of terminal wealth in state j.

We assume that all investors are risk averse; $U''_i < 0 \; \forall \; i$. In the first proposition we make use of the following two definitions.

Definition. For any investor i, an *equilibrium portfolio* is said to be *risky* if there exists any two states j and k with positive associated likelihoods, π_j, $\pi_k > 0$, such that $x_{ij} \neq x_{ik}$.

Definition. The *economy's returns* are to be *uncertain* if there exist states j and k with positive associated likelihoods, π_j, $\pi_k > 0$, such that $\Sigma_i x_{ij} \neq \Sigma_i x_{ik}$.

Proposition 1. Every investors' equilibrium portfolio is risky if, and only if, the economy's returns are uncertain.

Proof. In equilibrium, expected marginal rates of substitution of state contingent wealth are equal for all states j and k and all investors

i and m

$$\frac{\pi_j U_i'(x_{ij})}{\pi_k U_i'(x_{ik})} = \frac{P_j}{P_k} = \frac{\pi_j U_m'(x_{mj})}{\pi_k U_m'(x_{mk})}. \tag{2}$$

Sufficiency is proved by noting that investor i's equilibrium portfolio is riskless if

$$x_{ij} = x_{ik} \tag{3}$$

for all states j and k ($j \neq k$). Equations (2) and (3) then imply

$$x_{mj} = x_{mk} \tag{4}$$

for all states j and k, and all investors m. Therefore

$$\Sigma_i x_{ij} = \Sigma_i x_{ik} \tag{5}$$

for all states j and k. Hence, equations (3) and (4) cannot hold simultaneously for all i and m when the economy's returns are risky.

Necessity is proved by contradiction. If investor i holds a risky portfolio, then there exist states j and k, with π_j, $\pi_k > 0$, such that $x_{ij} \neq x_{ik}$. Assume, without loss of generality, that

$$x_{ij} > x_{ik}. \tag{6a}$$

Suppose

$$\Sigma_i x_{ij} = \Sigma_i x_{ik} \tag{7}$$

then for some investor m, it must be that

$$x_{mj} < x_{mk}. \tag{6b}$$

Now, since $U''(x_{ij}) < 0 \; \forall \; i$, we have by equations (2) and (6a)

$$U_i'(x_{ij}) < U_i'(x_{ik}) \Rightarrow \pi_j/\pi_k > P_j/P_k \tag{8a}$$

and from equations (2) and (6b)

$$U_m'(x_{mj}) > U_m'(x_{mk}) \Rightarrow \pi_j/\pi_k < P_j/P_k. \tag{8b}$$

But when investors have homogeneous beliefs equations (8a) and (8b) cannot hold simultaneously in equilibrium. Therefore, equations (7) cannot hold when some investor's portfolio is risky which was to be proved.

Corollary 1.1, which we state without proof, follows directly from the first proposition.

Corollary 1.1. Every investors' portfolio is riskless if, and only if, the economy's returns are certain.

The first proposition and Corollary 1.1 have an interesting application. If preferences and beliefs are such that all investors choose combinations of a riskfree asset and a single risky asset, then all investors hold positive amounts of the risky asset and its expected rate of return exceeds the riskfree rate.

Corollary 1.2. If all investors agree on expected returns and choose from a riskfree asset and a single risky asset in positive supply, then:

(i) each investor invests positively in the risky asset, and
(ii) the expected rate of return of the risky asset exceeds the expected rate of return of the riskfree asset.

Proof. Each investor solves the following problem

$$\max_{\{q_i, \, q_{if}\}} E(U_i) = \sum_i \pi_j U_i(r_j \, q_i + r_f \, q_{if}) \qquad (9)$$

$$\text{subject to } \overline{M}_i = q_{if} + P \, q_i,$$

where q_{if} and q_i are, respectively, the equilibrium quantities of the riskfree and risky asset held by investor i, r_f and r_j are, respectively, the returns per unit of the riskfree and risky asset, and P is the current price of the risky asset which, unlike P_j, is assumed to have a nonnegative payoff in each state j. Notice that there is no loss of generality if we assume the price of the riskfree asset to be one. Equation (9) can be written as

$$\max_{\{q_i\}} E(U_i) = \sum_j \pi_j U_i\big(r_j \, q_i + r_f(\overline{M}_i - P \, q_i)\big). \qquad (9a)$$

The first-order conditions are

$$\Sigma_j \, \pi_j \, r_j \, U'_i \, (r_j q_i + r_f q_f) = P \, r_f \Sigma_j \, \pi_j \, U'_i \, (r_j q_i + r_f q_f). \qquad (10)$$

The proof is by contradiction. For any investor i, $q_i \leq 0$ if

$$\Sigma_j \, \pi_j \, r_j \, U'_i \, (r_f q_f) \leq P \, r_f \Sigma_j \, \pi_j \, U'_i \, (r_f q_f) \qquad (11)$$

i.e. expected marginal utility at $q_i = 0$ does not exceed price. Upon simplification, equation (11) can be written

$$1/P\Sigma_j \, \pi_j \, r_j \leq r_f \tag{12}$$

hence, the expected return of the risky asset, $1/P\Sigma_j \, \pi_j \, r_j$, does not exceed the riskfree rate r_f. Since equation (12) does not depend on investor i, $q_i \leq 0$ for all investors is impossible since there is a positive market supply of the risky asset. Therefore, equation (12) cannot be true and $q_i > 0$ for all investors i.

Effect of an Uniform Increase in the Arrow–Pratt Measure of Risk Aversion

In this section, we show that a uniform increase in an investor's Arrow–Pratt measure of risk aversion increases the minimum level of portfolio terminal wealth and lowers the portfolio's expected rate of return as well as the range of terminal wealth.

Definition. The expected rate of return of a single claim to one dollar of state contingent wealth is given by

$$\frac{\pi_j(1) + (1 - \pi_j)(0)}{P_j} = \frac{\pi_j}{P_j} \, \forall \, j.$$

Observe that the market equilibrium condition (2) and the concavity of $U_i(\cdot)$ implies

$$x_{ij} > x_{ik} \Rightarrow U_i'(x_{ij}) < U_i'(x_{ik}) \Rightarrow \pi_j/P_j > \pi_k/P_k \tag{13}$$

for any two states j and k $(j \neq k)$ with $\pi_j, \pi_k > 0$. The relationship expressed in equation (13) shows that any risk averse investor purchases more terminal wealth in states with higher expected rates of return, π_j/P_j, and given any change in the investor's risk aversion (except for the trivial case of infinite risk aversion) the ordering remains strictly unaltered.

Proposition 2. Let U_i and V_i be, respectively, the utility functions of investor i before and after a uniform increase in risk aversion, and let x_{ij}^u (x_{ij}^v) be i's equilibrium terminal wealth in state j given i's utility function $U_i(V_i)$. Then

$$\min x_{ij}^u < \min x_{ij}^v. \tag{14}$$

Proof. From equation (13), the minimum level of terminal wealth occurs in the same state independently of the utility functions U_i and V_i. Denote this state by $j = 1$, assuming for simplicity that the lowest expected rate of return occurs in state one only

$$\min_j x_{ij}^u = x_{i1}^u \tag{15a}$$

$$\min_j x_{ij}^u < x_{i1}^v. \tag{15b}$$

From equation (2) and Pratt (1964), Theorem 1

$$\frac{V_i'(x_{ij}^u)}{V_i'(x_{i1}^u)} < \frac{U_i'(x_{ij}^u)}{U_i'(x_{i1}^u)} = \frac{P_j \pi_1}{P_1 \pi_j}, \, j = 2, \ldots, J. \tag{16}$$

To restore equilibrium, either

$$x_{i1}^v > x_{i1}^u \text{ and } x_{ij}^v \gtreqless x_{ij}^u, j = 2, \ldots, J, \tag{16a}$$

which would complete the proof, or

$$x_{i1}^v \leqslant x_{i1}^u \text{ and } x_{ij}^v < x_{ij}^u, j = 2, \ldots, J. \tag{16b}$$

Since $\bar{M}_i$ is unchanged by a uniform increase in risk aversion, the investor must purchase additional terminal wealth in some state if purchases of terminal wealth are reduced in some other state. Consequently, equation (16b) is not possible, and equation (14) follows from equations (16a) and (15).

Corollary 2.1. Following a uniform increase in risk aversion

(i) the range of terminal wealth levels of the investor's portfolio is reduced:

$$\{\max_j x_{ij}^v - \min_j x_{ij}^v\} < \{\max_j x_{ij}^u - \min_j x_{ij}^u\}.$$

(ii) the expected rate of return in the investor's portfolio is also reduced.

Proof. (i) Consider any state $n \neq 1$ such that

$$x_{in}^v < x_{in}^u \tag{17}$$

From equation (14), and given $\bar{M}_i$, equation (17) is true for some state $n \neq 1$. Let

$$x_{ik} = \max_j x_{ij}. \tag{18}$$

From equation (13), k is identical under both utility functions U_i and V_i. For simplicity, k is assumed to be unique. If $k = n$, $x_{ik}^v < x_{ik}^u$. If $k \neq n$, Pratt (1964), Theorem 1 implies

$$\frac{V_i'(x_{ik}^u)}{V_i'(x_\varepsilon^u)} < \frac{U_i'(x_{ik}^u)}{U_i'(x_\varepsilon^u)}. \tag{19a}$$

From equation (17)

$$x_{ik}^u > x_{ik}^v. \tag{19b}$$

In both cases, $\max_j x_{ij}^v (= x_{ik}^v) < \max_j x_{ij}^u (= x_{ik}^u)$.

Since, by Proposition 2, $\max_j x_{ij}^v > \min_j x_{ij}^u$. Therefore, $\{\max_j x_{ij}^v - \min_j x_{ij}^v\} < \{\max; x_{ij}^u - \min; x_{ij}^u\}$,

(ii) The proof is by contradiction. Given equation (14), a necessary condition for a rise or constancy in the portfolio's expected rate of return associated with a uniform increase in risk aversion is that states c and d exist such that

$$x_{ic}^v > x_{ic}^u, \tag{20a}$$

and

$$x_{id}^v > x_{id}^u \tag{20b}$$

when

$$\frac{\pi_c}{P_c} > \frac{\pi_d}{P_d}. \tag{21}$$

Hence, state c offers a higher expected rate of return resulting in a transfer of invested endowment from state c to state d. We show that this is impossible. From equations (13) and (21)

$$x_{ic}^u > x_{id}^u \tag{22}$$

and

$$x_{ic}^v > x_{id}^v. \tag{23}$$

From equation (16)

$$\frac{V_i'(x_{ic}^u)}{V_i'(x_{id}^u)} < \frac{U_i'(x_{ic}^u)}{U_i'(x_{id}^u)}. \tag{24}$$

From equations (20a) and (24)

$$x_{ic}^{v} < x_{ic}^{u} \tag{25}$$

which contradicts equation (20a).

Summary and Conclusions

In this chapter we show that all investors bear risk if all are risk averse, have homogeneous beliefs, and there is economic risk. Furthermore, Proposition 1 has important implications concerning the indexing of financial securities to hedge against inflation. Indexed securities provide a guaranteed real return irrespective of the price level. If there is economic risk, Proposition 1 implies that no investor will hold a fully indexed portfolio; indexing all securities does too much, hedging against both the rate of inflation and economic risk. This may explain why indexed securities lack widespread popularity and may suggest a role for partial indexation to cover only inflation risk, in the manner suggested in the literature on wage indexation.[5]

The sharing of economic risk by all investors, as shown in Corollary 1.1, seems like a very plausible result. Such a sharing rule, however, does not depend on the degree of risk aversion as long as all investors are risk averse. Intuitively, a risk averse investor who bears no risk is approximately risk neutral for small amounts of risk, and will purchase risky returns from a risk averse investor who bears some risk. Homogeneity of beliefs is a less obvious assumption than positive risk aversion. However, with heterogeneous beliefs, the existence of economic risk may not be agreed upon by all investors. There may be some scope for expanding the proposition when beliefs are heterogeneous, provided all investors agree on the set of positively probable states, as this would allow for a common identification of the existence of economic risk.

In the third section of this chapter, we examine the applicability of the Arrow–Pratt measure of absolute risk aversion in a complete market. It was shown that the measure was susceptible to useful comparative statics analysis: a uniform increase in the measure resulted in a reduction in the portfolio's expected rate of return and range of terminal wealth, and a rise in the portfolio's minimum level of terminal wealth; i.e. the level of terminal wealth for an investor is guaranteed.

Notes

1. See Arrow (1971), Cass and Stiglitz (1972), Hart (1975), Kihlstrom *et al.* (1981), and Pratt (1964).

2. See Arrow (1971, p. 98).
3. See Cass and Stiglitz (1972, p. 335).
4. In a complete market, any contingent contract is tradeable and states must be appropriately defined. With homogeneous beliefs, the only relevant uncertainty is the future return of each investor's endowment. States of nature are thus defined by vectors of investors' (random) terminal wealth.
5. See Gray (1975).

References

Arrow, K. J. (1971) *Essays in the Theory of Risk Bearing*, Markham, Chicago.
Bardsley, P. (1991) Global measures of risk aversion, *Journal of Economic Theory*, 55, 145–160.
Cass, D. and Stiglitz, J. E. (1970) The structure of investor preferences and asset returns, and separability in portfolio allocation: A contribution to the pure theory of mutual funds, *Journal of Economic Theory*, 2, 122–160.
Cass, D. and Stiglitz, J. E. (1972) Risk-aversion and wealth effects on portfolios with many assets, *Review of Economic Studies*, 39, 331–354.
Gray, J. A. (1975) On indexation and contract length, *Journal of Political Economy*, 86, 1–18.
Hart, O. D. (1975) Some negative results on the existence of comparative statics results in portfolio theory, *Review of Economic Studies*, 42, 615–621.
Kihlstrom, R. E., Romer, D. and Williams, S. (1981) Risk-aversion with random initial wealth. *Econometrica*, 49, 911–920.
Levy, H. and Levy, A. (1991) Arrow–Pratt measures of risk aversion: The multivariate case, *International Economic Review*, 32, 891–898.
Pratt, J. W. (1964) Risk aversion in the small and the large, *Econometrica*, 49, 122–136.
Ross, S. A. (1981) Some stronger measures of risk aversion in the small and large with applications, *Econometrica*, 49, 621–638.
Yaari, M. E. (1969) Some remarks on measures of risk aversions and on their uses, *Journal of Economic Theory*, 1, 315–329.

7

The Role of Banks in Debt Restructuring

KOSE JOHN AND GOPALA K. VASUDEVAN

Introduction

In the 1980s there was a dramatic increase in the leverage of U.S. corporations accompanied by a high incidence of financial distress during the late 1980s. For academics, practitioners, and policy-makers an important question raised by these distressed firms is: Are these firms able to resolve their financial distress efficiently? Jensen (1989) argues that highly leveraged firms should be able to resolve their financial distress quickly and efficiently. There is a lot of value to these firms and it is in the interest of all parties to have an efficient reorganization. An alternative view is that asymmetric information, conflicts among creditors, and the effects of bankruptcy law can hinder an efficient restructuring and firms will incur large bankruptcy costs.

Banks are generally considered to be more sophisticated lenders than public debt holders and bank debt is relatively easier to restructure. Several papers have characterized the choice of bank debt as a case where the borrower considers the benefit of an efficient restructuring to dominate the monitoring costs which have to be paid to the bank (see, for example, Berlin and Loeys (1988) and Rajan (1992)). However, recent papers by Diamond (1993) and Gertner and Scharfstein (1991) demonstrate that when there is both public debt and bank debt outstanding there can still be inefficiencies in the restructuring process. All these papers assume that the firm has to choose between liquidation and a private restructuring without allowing for the possibility that firms have the choice of restructuring privately in a workout, restructuring formally in the court-adjudicated

Chapter 11 process or liquidation. In this study we allow the firm the choice between workouts, Chapter 11 and liquidation. We show that when the firm's debt is entirely bank debt, there will always be efficient resolution of financial distress where the firm will restructure privately without incurring the dead weight costs of Chapter 11 bankruptcy. However, when there is both bank debt as well as public debt there will be inefficiencies in the restructuring process since the bank has an incentive to lend to the firm in Chapter 11. By lending to the firm in Chapter 11 under the *'Debtor in Possession Financing'* the bank will have a new claim which is senior to the existing claims.

Our results explain the evidence in Asquith *et al.* (1991) who find that in the presence of public debt, banks almost never forgive principal on their loans and rarely provide new financing. The implications of our model is also consistent with their evidence which indicates that banks whose private and public debt is secured have a higher chance of filing for Chapter 11.

The remainder of the chapter is organized into three sections. The second section provides a review of the literature and a review of bankruptcy law. The third section provides a model that examines the reorganization decision of distressed firms and finally there is a concluding section.

Background

One of the earlier papers which has examined the conflicts between the different claimants of a distressed firm is that of Bulow and Shoven (1978). In the Bulow and Shoven model these conflicts can lead to inefficiencies when a firm is in financial distress and firms may not choose the optimal liquidation policy because the bank-equity coalition would benefit from continuation. Recently, Gertner and Scharfstein (1991) developed a more generalized version of the Bulow and Shoven model where they relax the assumption that the firm cannot renegotiate with public debt holders. They find that coordination problems among the public debt holders can still lead to inefficiencies in private restructuring. They also find that Chapter 11 can mitigate the underinvestment problem and lead to more efficient investment when the firm faces underinvestment; this would be more likely when the firm has shorter public debt, the bank debt is senior, or when the public debt has seniority covenants.

James (1993) examined the conditions under which bank lenders would agree to take equity positions in financially distressed firms. James found that the bank's decision to take equity positions would depend on the renegotiability of public debt and the presence of public debt. Banks would take equity positions only if the public debt holders also restructure their claims and when banks can hold a large equity stake. Firms with public debt outstanding lose much of the flexibility for renegotiation associated with private borrowing. The paper finds that firms where banks take equity stakes seem to perform better in the long run.

In the first systematic empirical study to examine the restructuring decision of financially distressed firms, Gilson *et al.* (1990) analyzed a sample of 169 publicly traded companies that experienced financial distress during 1978–1987. Their study found that the average direct cost of a private restructuring is much lower than the cost of a Chapter 11 restructuring.[1] They also found that financial distress is more likely to be resolved through a private restructuring when the firm has a greater fraction of bank debt, the firm has fewer distinct classes of debt and when the firm has a larger proportion of intangible assets.

Asquith *et al.* (1991) analyzed a sample of 102 junk bond issuers that were subsequently in financial distress. They found that banks rarely provide new financing outside Chapter 11 and they seldom agree to forgive the principal on the loans outside Chapter 11. They found that firms for which a greater proportion of the bank and private debt is secured have a greater chance of ending up in Chapter 11. They concluded that despite the common view that banks have a relationship with their borrowers and would be more willing to renegotiate privately, banks do not play much of a role in resolving financial distress. Asquith *et al.* concede that they do not have a satisfactory explanation as to why firms with larger amounts of secured debt have a greater chance of filing for bankruptcy. In our model we show that when the bank finances the firm in Chapter 11 the new bank claims will be senior to the existing claims. This transfer of wealth which would take place from public debt holders to the bank is the main reason why firms with larger amounts of secured debt file for Chapter 11.

Corporate Reorganizations

When a firm is in financial distress it has two options to restructure its debt contract. It can either restructure privately in a workout or it can reorganize in a formal Chapter 11 process. In this section we describe some of the features of bankruptcy law that can affect the reorganization decision of distressed firms. We argue that there are three features of the bankruptcy code that can affect the reorganization choice of distressed firms; these are the automatic stay, the voting procedure of plan approval, and the debtor-in-possession financing.

When a firm files for Chapter 11 there is an automatic stay that prevents creditors from any attempts to collect their debt until the firm emerges from Chapter 11.[2] Once a firm files for Chapter 11 it has to file a reorganization plan. Under the reorganization plan the different claimholders are classified under various classes where similar claimholders are grouped together in the same class, for example, trade debt, secured debt, preferred stock, etc. A separate exchange of securities is proposed for each class of claimholders and the value of the new securities issued to each claimholder class is based on absolute priority rules, i.e. each claimholder class receives claims only if all the senior claimholders have been paid in full. However, in practice, deviations from absolute priority are common (see Franks and Torous (1989); Eberhart *et al.* (1990)), and equity holders receive some claims even though senior classes have not been paid in full.

The debtor has the exclusive right to propose the first reorganization plan within 180 days and has an additional 60 days to get the plan approved by the creditors. In general, the court extends the exclusivity period several times. Acceptance of the plan requires approval by two-thirds majority in value and a simple majority in number for each class. If any class does not accept the plan, the judge can 'cram down' the plan provided that the dissenting class is paid in full or deviations from absolute priority are not violated.

Although Chapter 11 is considered to be more costly when compared to workouts (see note 1) there are several advantages to filing for Chapter 11. Firstly the automatic stay prevents the creditors from seizing the assets of the firm. Another incentive for firms to file for Chapter 11 is that a successful workout requires the consent of all debt holders while a successful reorganization requires the approval of a specified majority of each creditor class. The third reason why firms file for Chapter 11 is that the 'debtor in possession financing' enables firms to issue new debt claims in Chapter 11 which have priority over all existing claims. Macy's, for example, was able to raise more than $600 million dollars after it had filed for Chapter 11.

Recently firms have combined the advantages of Chapter 11 with the cost savings and lower time involved in a private restructuring by having 'pre-packaged' Chapter 11 filings. In a pre-packaged filing the terms of the reorganization are finalized before the bankruptcy filing and the reorganization plan is filed along with the Chapter 11 filing. This enables firms to avail of all the advantages of a Chapter 11 filing.

The Model

Our two-date single period model is designed to capture the essential aspects of the problem (see Fig. 7.1). At the initial date $t = 0$ the firm is in financial distress because it does not have the funds needed to make the current debt payment due and to make the investment needed to continue operations. All firms have bank debt with a face value B due at time $t = 0$ and they also have public debt with a total face value D consisting of D_1 and D_2 due at time $t = 0$ and $t = 1$, respectively. All firms have an uncertain cash flow V from the existing assets. This can be either h or l with a probability P and $(1 - P)$. Firms differ in the value of their investment opportunities. There are two types of firms. High-quality firms have an investment opportunity with a net present value of cash flows equal to $V_H - I$. Poor-quality firms have an investment opportunity with a net present value of cash flows $V_P - I$. Both firms need to invest I at $t = 0$ to obtain these cash flows at $t = 1$. We also assume that the high-quality firms are solvent but are illiquid. These firms have a present value of assets which is greater than the payments which have to be made to the public debt and the bank. However, they do not have the funds needed to make the payment B to the bank, the payment D_1 to the public debt and the investment I. The poor-quality firms are insolvent firms since the total value of their debt is higher than the present value of the cash flows from the existing assets and the investment opportunity V_P. Both the firms have positive net present value investment opportunities with V_H higher than V_P. When the firm files for bankruptcy it incurs a fixed cost C_F. The cost C_F can be viewed as the direct cost of a Chapter 11 filing which comprises the fees paid to lawyers, accountants, and other administrative expenses. We summarize the assumptions and notation below:

B = face value of bank debt due at time $t = 0$.
D_1, D_2 = public debt due at time $t = 0$ and $t = 1$, respectively.
V_H = value of the cash flows for the high-quality firm from investment I at $t = 0$.
V_P = value of the cash flows for the low-quality firm from investment I at $t = 0$.
C_F = Chapter 11 filing costs.
V = present value of the cash flows from the assets in place for all firms.
$V = Ph + (1 - P)l$
$h > B + D + I > l$
$V + V_H - I > B + D > V + V_P - I.$
$V_H > V_P > I.$

We assume that the bank is fully informed of firm value, while the public debt holders do not know the true value of the firm. We assume that renegotiations with the public debt are impossible and restructuring of the firm essentially involves renegotiations with the bank. Although, in some cases, it may be possible to renegotiate with public debt outside Chapter 11, these generally involve an exchange offer where new securities are issued in exchange for old or there is a cash for debt offer. In the model, firms also need an infusion of capital for investment, we assume that it is impossible for the firm to issue new public debt outside Chapter 11. This assumption would be valid when outsiders do not know the true value of the firm and there are sufficient numbers of poor-quality firms.[3] Since the bank and the firm share the same information set, we model the renegotiations between the firm and the bank as an *alternating offer bargaining game* under full information where the first offer is made by the firm.

We examine three different types of capital structure. In the first case the firm only has bank debt, in the second case the bank debt is senior and public debt is junior and in the third case the bank debt is junior and public debt is senior.

Case 1. *The firm has bank debt alone.* In the first case all firms have bank debt alone. We assume that the high-quality firm has sufficient assets to meet the full value of its debt claims, while the poor-quality firm is insolvent i.e. $(V + V_H - I > B \geqslant V + V_p - I)$. First we examine the restructuring decision of the high-quality firm. The restructuring decision would depend on the bank and the firm's payoffs in a private restructuring and in Chapter 11.

For the high-quality firm:

$$\text{Bank's payoff in Chapter 11 process} = B + I \qquad (1a)$$

$$\text{Bank's payoff in a workout} = B + I \qquad (1b)$$

$$\text{Equity's payoff in Chapter 11 process} = V + V_H - B - I - C_F \ (1c)$$

$$\text{Equity's payoff in a workout} = V + V_H - B - I. \qquad (1d)$$

When the firm has bank debt alone the restructuring decision depends on the bank and the equity's payoffs in Chapter 11 and workouts. In this case the bank is indifferent between workout and Chapter 11 because it will get the full value of its claim $B + I$ where B is the existing bank debt and I is the new funds provided for investment. However, the equity holders prefer restructuring in a workout because their payoff in a workout is higher than the payoff in a Chapter 11 filing by the cost of the Chapter 11 filing C_F. Hence, the high-quality firm will be able to restructure in a workout.

For the poor-quality firm:

Bank's expected payoff in Chapter 11 $= V + V_P - C_F - I$ (2a)

Bank's expected payoff in workout $= V + V_P - C_F - I$ (2b)

Equity's expected payoff in Chapter 11 $= 0$ (2c)

Equity's expected payoff in workout $= C_F$.   (2d)

In the renegotiations which take place between the firm and the bank, the equity holders make the first offer in the form of a plan of reorganization. Since the firm is insolvent the bank will not be paid in full. If the bank forces the firm into Chapter 11 the court will award the bank the full value of the firm $(V + V_P - C_F - I)$. However, the value of the firm has gone down by C_F, the direct costs of bankruptcy. In a workout the offer made by the equity will be structured so that the bank is indifferent between accepting the offer today or forcing the firm to file for Chapter 11 and having a claim over the entire assets of the firm. Thus equity would make the same offer $(V + V_P - C_F - I)$ in a workout. If the bank rejects this offer and forces the firm into Chapter 11 it ends up with the same payment $(V + V_P - C_F - I)$.[4]

We find that when there is bank debt alone we always have an efficient resolution of financial distress. This is consistent with the general view that bank debt is more easily negotiable. The high-quality firm which is liquidity constrained gets funds from the bank and restructures quickly in a private workout, the bank is paid the full value of its claim. The poor-quality firm also restructures in a workout where the bank forgives a portion of its existing claims. There are deviations from absolute priority and the equity holders save the court costs C_F. However, the dead weight costs of Chapter 11 are not incurred in either case. This is consistent with arguments made by Haugen and Senbet (1978) and Jensen (1989) who argue that it is always in the interest of all parties to avoid the large costs associated with financial distress and there would always be efficient restructuring. In the next section we will see that when there are two classes of debt outstanding the costs of financial distress will always be incurred by the insolvent firms. Banks would prefer to lend to the firm in Chapter 11 where they have a claim which has priority over all existing claims.

Case 2. Bank debt is senior and public debt is junior. In this section we examine the case where the firm has both bank debt and public debt and bank debt is senior. This type of capital structure is most commonly seen in practice because banks very rarely hold a junior claim.[5] When the firm has this type of capital structure we find that the high-quality firm always has an efficient restructuring where the bank will renegotiate its claims privately and finance the new investment to be made. The poor-quality firm will always file for Chapter 11 where the bank lends funds for investment. These new claims which the bank holds will have priority over all existing claims. The bank's strategy is to expropriate the wealth from the public debt. In the next two sections we assume that the high-quality firm has sufficient assets in place to pay the bank as well as public debt, while the poor-quality firm has sufficient assets to pay the bank, i.e. $V_H - I > B + D > V_P - I > B$.

For the high-quality firm:

$$\text{Bank's payoff in a workout} = B + D_1 + I \tag{3a}$$

$$\text{Bank's payoff in Chapter 11} = B + D_1 + I \tag{3b}$$

$$\text{Equity's payoff in a workout} = V + V_H - I - D - B \tag{3c}$$

$$\text{Equity's payoff in Chapter 11} = V + V_H - I - D - B - C_F. \tag{3d}$$

If the force is able to restructure in a workout the bank will have to provide the funds needed for investment I and to make the interim debt payment B. Equation (3a) denotes the bank's payoff in a workout and equation (3b) denotes the bank's payoff in Chapter 11. Since the bank gets the full value of its claims in a workout as well as in Chapter 11, the bank is indifferent between restructuring in a workout or in Chapter 11. Equation (3c) denotes equity's payoff in a workout and equation (3d) denotes their payoff in Chapter 11. Equity does better in a workout because the dead weight costs of bankruptcy C_F are not incurred and these savings go to the equity. In this case the bank is indifferent between filing for Chapter 11 and having a workout, while the equity strictly prefers a workout and the firm is always able to restructure privately.

For the poor-quality firm:

$$\text{Bank's payoff in a workout} = B + (V + V_P - I - B - D_2) \tag{4a}$$

$$\text{Bank's payoff in Chapter 11} = B + I + D_1 \tag{4b}$$

$$\text{Equity's expected payoff in a workout} = 0 \tag{4c}$$

$$\text{Equity's expected payoff in Chapter 11} = 0. \tag{4d}$$

The firm can either file for Chapter 11, have a workout, or file for liquidation. The firm would never file for liquidation because strict absolute priority rules are followed in liquidation and equity would get nothing. As long as there are risky cash flows from the assets in place the equity would prefer to continue even though their expected payoff from continuation is zero. The payoff to the bank in a workout is given in equation (4a). The bank will be paid the face value of its debt B in full because it has the senior claim and the bank also has a claim over the assets of the firm which remain after paying the public debt D_2. When the firm restructures in a workout the bank will have to restructure the claim so that the bank debt is due at $t = 1$ and it also provides the funds needed for the interim debt payment D_1 and the investment I needed. The bank will not reduce the face value of the debt B because bank debt is senior and the value of the firm is larger than the face value of bank debt. The equity holder's threat to file for Chapter 11 is not credible and equity would have to pay the full value of the bank debt B. Equation (4b) denotes the payoff to the bank in Chapter 11. If the bank provides funds for investment and the intermediate debt payment D_1 in Chapter 11, the new claim ($I + D_1$) would have priority over all existing claims; since equation (4a) is less than equation (4b) for ($V + V_P - I < B + D$) the bank would always prefer to lend to the firm in Chapter 11.[6] For equity holders the expected value of their claim is zero in workouts and Chapter 11. However, in the state when the firm realizes the cash flow h from the assets in place (with a probability P), the equity would realize a positive cash flow after settling all the existing claims. Since equity would get nothing in liquidation because strict absolute priority rules are followed, equity always has an incentive to continue. Since the only chance to continue is to file for Chapter 11 the firm would file for Chapter 11.

Our results for this section are consistent with the findings of Asquith *et al.* (1991). They analyzed a sample of junk bond issuers which were in financial distress, the firms had high leverage and low interest coverage ratios similar to the poor-quality firms in our model. The firms in their sample had a capital structure similar to the case we analyzed in this section with a combination of bank debt and public debt and bank debt senior to public debt. They documented that banks never (with one exception among the 102 firms in their sample) forgave principal on their loans and that they rarely provided new financing outside of bankruptcy. They also found that firms with larger amounts of secured debt had a greater chance of filing for Chapter 11. All their results are consistent with the model we have analyzed in this section.

Case 3. Bank debt is junior and there is public debt. In this section we examine the case where the firm has both bank debt and public debt and the bank debt is junior to the public debt. For the high-quality firm V_H the firm would be restructured in a workout because the bank would be paid the full value of its claims. For the poor-quality firm V_P the bank would prefer to lend in Chapter 11 where the new claims issued to the bank will have priority over all existing claims. If there are no seniority covenants restricting the issue of new debt which would be senior to the existing public debt the bank would be willing to lend outside Chapter 11.

For the high-quality firm:

Expected payoff for equity in Chapter 11 process
$$= (V + V_H - I - B - D_1 - D_2 - C_F) \tag{5a}$$

Expected payoff for the equity in a workout
$$= (V + V_H - I - B - D_1 - D_2) \tag{5b}$$

Payoff for the bank in Chapter 11 process $= B + I + D_1$ (5c)

Payoff for the bank in a workout $= B + I + D_1$. (5d)

If the firm restructures in Chapter 11 the equity holders would get the cash flows which remain after paying the bank debt B, the public debt D, and the costs of Chapter 11, C_F. If the firm is able to have a successful workout the equity holders have an expected payoff which is higher than the payoff in a workout by C_F. In this case the equity holders prefer restructuring in a workout rather than Chapter 11 because they save the deadweight costs of bankruptcy C_F. The bank is indifferent between lending in Chapter 11 and lending in a workout because in either case it will be paid the full value of its claims $B + I + D_1$. Hence for the high-quality firm there will always be an efficient restructuring where the claims are restructured in a workout.

For the poor-quality firm:

Payoff to bank in a workout $= V + V_P - I - D_2 - C_F$ (6a)

Payoff to bank in chapter 11 process $= V + V_P - I - D_2 - C_F + (I + D_1)$ (6b)

Payoff to equity in a workout $= C_F$ (6c)

Payoff to equity in Chapter 11 process $= 0$. (6d)

When the firm has a workout the bank has to provide funds $(I + D_1)$ and the bank has a claim over the cash flows which remain after paying the senior public debt minus the court costs C_F as given in equation (6a). The equity would only offer a claim which is given in equation (6a) because even if the bank refuses this offer the alternative for the bank is to file for Chapter 11 where the firm can

| | | | | |

FIGURE 7.1

seek a new lender to finance the claim $(I + D_1)$ the bank agrees. To finance the firm in Chapter 11 the bank has a claim over the firm's assets given by equation (6b). The new funds provided by the bank will have priority over all existing debt. Since equation (6b) is greater than equation (6a) by $(I + D_1)$ the bank would prefer to finance the firm in Chapter 11. Although the equity holders have a lower claim in Chapter 11 they would still prefer to file for Chapter 11 and continue. In the state where the firm has a cash flow h from the existing assets the cash flows will be sufficient to pay off all the claimholders and have something left for equity. This is better than allowing the firm to be liquidated and receive nothing. The poor-quality firm will always file for Chapter 11 when the bank debt is junior because by doing so the bank is able to expropriate wealth from the public debt.

Conclusions

We have examined the role of banks in the resolution of financial distress. Contrary to the general view that bank debt is more easily renegotiated, we find that this only holds when the firm has bank debt alone. When the firm has multiple classes of debt such as public debt and bank debt most of the flexibility associated with bank lenders no longer exists. Our model predicts that the incentive to file for Chapter 11 increases with the amount of secured debt in the capital structure. Banks prefer to provide new funds in Chapter 11 because the new funds provided by the bank will have priority over all existing claims. We find that when bank debt is senior, banks never reduce the value of their claims and these insolvent firms have to file for Chapter 11. This is consistent with the evidence in Asquith *et al.* (1991) who find that banks rarely reduce the value of their claims, and firms with larger amounts of secured debt have a higher chance of filing for Chapter 11. When bank debt is junior, banks would still agree to restructure their claims only in Chapter 11.

Acknowledgements

Helpful discussions with Ed Altman, Dilip Ghosh, Tony Saunders and Greg Udell are acknowledged. Kose John acknowledges support from a Bank and Financial Analysts Faculty Fellowship and G. K. Vasudevan, from a Suffolk University Summer Research Grant.

Notes

1. Gilson *et al.* (1990) found that in workouts the cost of an exchange offer is 0.65 percent of the book value of assets. Previous research has estimated the cost of a Chapter 11 filing to be between 2.8 and 7.5 percent of total assets.
2. When the firm defaults on the payments the creditors can also file for bankruptcy, this is called an "involuntary bankruptcy filing." If the firm does not want to continue it can also file for liquidation which is called Chapter 7.
3. In John and Vasudevan (1992) we show that information asymmetries prevent distressed firms from issuing claims outside Chapter 11. Khanna and Poulsen (1993) document evidence in support of this argument.
4. To make the offer in the workout even more attractive for the bank we can think that the equity holders would offer a dollar (or even a penny more) so that the bank agrees to settle in the workout.
5. See, for example, Asquith *et al.* (1991), James (1993) and James (1984) among others.
6. When the firm files for Chapter 11 there will be an automatic stay which prevents the public debt holders from collecting the interim payment D_1. Adding that feature does not change the results of the model.

References

ASQUITH, P., GERTNER, R. and SCHARFSTEIN, D. (1991) Anatomy of financial distress: an examination of junk bond issuers. Unpublished manuscript, MIT and University of Chicago.

BERLIN, M. and LOEYS, J. (1988) Bond covenants and delegated monitoring, *Journal of Finance*, 43(2), 397–412.

BROWN, D., JAMES, C. and MOORADIAN, R. (1993) The information content of distressed restructurings involving public and private debt claims, *Journal of Financial Economics*, 93–118.

BULOW, J. and SHOVEN, J. (1978) The bankruptcy decision, *Bell Journal of Economics*, 435–456.

DIAMOND, D. (1993) Seniority and the maturity of debt contracts, *Journal of Financial Economics*, 33, 341–368.

EBERHART, A. C., MOORE, W. T. and ROENFELDT, R. (1990) Security pricing and deviations from the absolute priority rule in bankruptcy proceedings, *Journal of Finance*, 45, 1457–1470.

FRANKS, J. R. and TOROUS, W. N. (1989) An empirical investigation of U.S. firms in reorganization, *Journal of Finance*, 44, 747–770.

GERTNER, R. and SCHARFSTEIN, D. (1991) A theory of workouts and the effects of reorganization law, *Journal of Finance*, 1189–1122.

GILSON, S. C., JOHN, K. and LANG, L. (1990) Troubled debt restructurings: an empirical study of private reorganization of firms in default, *Journal of Financial Economics* , 315–353.

HAUGEN, R. and SENBET, L. W. (1978) The insignificance of bankruptcy costs to the theory of optimal capital structure, *Journal of Finance*, 383–393.

JAMES, C. (1984) Some evidence on the uniqueness of bank loans, *Journal of Financial Economics*, 19, 217–236.

JAMES, C. (1993) When do banks take equity? An analysis of bank loan restructurings and the role of public debt. Unpublished manuscript, University of Florida.

JENSEN, M. C. (1989) Active investors, lbo's and the privatization of bankruptcy, *Journal of Applied Corporate Finance*, 35–44.

JENSEN, M. C. (1991) Corporate control and the politics of finance, *Journal of Applied Corporate Finance*, 13–33.

JOHN, K. and VASUDEVAN, G. K. (1992) Bankruptcy and reorganization: a theory of the choice between workouts and Chapter 11. Unpublished manuscript, New York University.

RAJAN, R. (1992) Insiders and outsiders: the choice between informed and arm's, length debt, *Journal of Finance*, 1367–1400.

8

Stock Prices, Merger Activity and the Macroeconomy

IKE MATHUR AND VIJAYA SUBRAHMANYAM

Introduction

Two quintessential areas of research in finance involve stock prices and mergers. The former is quite often viewed as a significant measure of the level of activity in the economy and in capital markets. The latter is representative of resource allocation and reallocation processes in the economy, arising out of changes in economic conditions and technological innovations affecting industries. While research on influence of microeconomic variables on stock prices and on wealth effects of mergers has been in progress for a number of years, only recently have researchers focused attention on the relationships between stock prices, merger activity and macroeconomic variables. The focus of this latter research primarily has been on examining whether the information conveyed by macroeconomic factors is reflected in stock prices. Little, if any, attention has been devoted to assessing the causal interdependencies among stock prices, mergers, and measures of economic activity. The purpose of this chapter is to provide empirical evidence on these interdependencies within a multivariate VAR framework.

Recent literature points to a revival of interest in the relationships between macroeconomic activity and financial markets. Gertler (1988) very aptly states, "Recently, interest has grown in exploring the possible links between the financial system and aggregate economic behavior." A significant contribution to the literature is by Chen *et al.* (1986), whose results imply that stock prices are driven by innovations in the economic state variables. Kim and Wu (1987) incorporate a multifactor return generating process in the traditional CAPM and find that their model is capable of directly utilizing macroeconomic variables in defining factors.

Chang and Pinegar (1989, 1990) examined different economic variables to study their interrelationships with the stock market. They found that the stock market seasonal coincided with seasonalities in industrial production. They used bivariate Granger tests of causality, which indicated that returns on large firms' stocks predict seasonal real growth at least six months in advance. Further, their research reveals that a risk premium exists for expected inflation and industrial production in non-January months.[1]

Darrat (1988, 1990) investigated the relationship between aggregate stock returns and a number of macrovariables, including monetary and fiscal policy. He used the FPE/multivariate, unidirectional Granger-causality modeling technique to test whether changes in Canadian stock returns are caused by economic variables (base money and fiscal deficits). His results demonstrated that lagged changes in fiscal deficits Granger-cause returns.

Melicher et al. (1983), Becketti (1986), and Clark et al. (1988) have shown that not only is aggregate merger activity closely related to macroeconomic factors, but also to capital market factors. The relationship between merger activity and macroeconomic variables such as industrial activity, business failures, stock prices and interest rates was analyzed by Melicher et al. (1983). They employed a time series approach to describe changes in the incidence of mergers relative to changes in macrovariables. They show a weak relationship between merger activity and economic conditions, with changes in industrial production and business failures lagging behind changes in merger activity. Their results indicate that changes in stock prices and bond yields can be used to forecast future changes in recorded merger activity. Since merger negotiations begin two quarters before consummation, increased merger activity may simply reflect the expectations of rising stock prices and declining interest rates.

Becketti (1986) also studied the linkages between mergers and the macroeconomy. His analysis measured the extent to which aggregate cyclical fluctuations accounted for variations in merger activity and identified those macroeconomic variables that have been most responsible for changes in merger activity. His results showed that past values of the stock price index, capacity utilization rates, and the stock of debt were positively correlated with current merger activity, while the past values of the T-bill rate and GNP were negatively correlated. Clark et al. (1988) used Granger's causality technique and Sim's technique to develop a bivariate model relating merger activity, stock prices and industrial production. They found a significant contemporaneous relationship between merger activity and stock prices.[2]

These above studies, while providing insights into stock prices and merger activity, suffer from two limitations. The first limitation relates to the approach used to specify and test relationships between stock prices, mergers and the macroeconomy. The research to date has been either multivariate and undimensional or bivariate and bi-directional. The interrelatedness of the variables is not fully explored as a multivariate system, thereby not providing richer insights into the interrelationships. The second limitation relates to the general emphasis on the effects of the macroeconomy on stock prices and on merger activity. Thus, generally, the linkages are prespecified with stock prices or mergers as the dependent variable and macro-economic variables as independent. Some, such as Becketti (1986) and Clark *et al.* (1988), have stated that a two-way relationship should be examined.[3] While a bidirectional bivariate model may provide more insights than a undimensional model, it still cannot provide the conceptual understanding gained from using a multivariate model that permits the evaluation of relative influences. The afore-mentioned limitations are addressed in this chapter by developing a multivariate bidirectional, causal vector autoregressive (VAR) model in which the interrelationships among stock prices, merger activity and macroeconomic variables are fully explored.

The results of this study show significant interdependencies among stock prices, merger activity, business failures, yields on long-term government bonds, and industrial production. It is shown that stock prices influence merger activity. Increasing stock prices also produce rising interest rates with a lag of two quarters. A feedback relationship is identified between stock prices and industrial production. The data and the VAR methodology are given in the second section, and the empirical results are given in the third section. The hypotheses are assessed in the light of the results and conclusions are drawn in the last section.

Data and Methodology

Data

Stock prices are represented by the Dow Jones Industrial Average. Quarterly data were obtained from the "Banking and Finance" section in *Basic Statistics*, Standard & Poor's Statistical Series. Data on merger activity—number of merger and acquisition transactions completed in a quarter—were obtained from the "Quarterly Profile of Merger and Acquisition Activity" in *Mergers and Acquisitions*.

Stock prices and merger activity are often used as a measure of the level of activity in capital markets. Similarly, bankruptcy is also viewed as reflective of expectations regarding general economic conditions. Bankruptcy avoidance has been advanced as a reason for merger activity. Shrieves and Stevens (1979) present reasons such as avoidance of legal and administrative costs, and possible loss of tax-loss carry-forwards for firms preferring mergers to bankruptcy. Pastena and Ruland (1986) show that distressed firms with high ownership rights reveal an increased propensity for merging rather than declaring bankruptcy. Data on number of business failures were compiled from Dun and Bradstreet's *Commercial Failures Index.*

Changes in nominal interest rates may influence rates of return required by investors and, therefore, affect stock prices. Also, cost of funds, both borrowed and equity, may influence the decision to acquire. Further, it may be conjectured that merger- and margin-fueled demand for credit might influence interest rates. Thus, causal linkages between stock prices, merger activity and nominal interest rates, as represented by long-term government bond yields, merit consideration. Data were obtained from the *Federal Reserve Bulletin.*

Changes in industrial production are frequently cited as affecting the feasibilities of engaging in investment opportunities. Becketti (1986) demonstrated that merger activity peaks before the peak of the business cycle expansion. Clark *et al.* (1988) showed that a rise in merger activity leads to a decrease in output with a two-year lag. These studies point to the need for including industrial production in the model. Data for industrial production were obtained from the "Income and Trade" section in *Basic Statistics.*

Quarterly data from 1967:I to 1990:I were utilized for all the time series. Log transforms for all series, except bond yields, were obtained prior to making them stationary through first differencing. Summary statistics for the variables are presented in Table 8.1.

The unemployment rate, the inflation rate and Tobin's Q were also considered in addition to the variables mentioned above. Partial correlation coefficients indicated that the unemployment rate was highly correlated with the number of business failures ($\rho = 0.64$, $P = 0.00$). The inflation rate had a partial correlation coefficient of 0.95 ($\rho = 0.00$) in relation to bond yields, while Tobin's Q was also highly related to bond yields ($\rho = -0.78$, $P = 0.00$). Bond yields and number of business failures were included in the analysis due to their *a priori* causal case and due to their use in related studies. Therefore, the unemployment rate, the inflation rate and Tobin's Q were excluded from analysis.

TABLE 8.1 *Summary Statistics for Data**

	Mean	Standard deviation	Minimum	Maximum
DJ industrial average	1,163.79	529.53	596.90	2,680.35
No. of mergers	506.10	268.51	135.00	1,626.00
No. of business failures	5,968.15	5,000.70	1,592.00	16,606.00
Bond yield	8.40	2.43	4.45	14.48
Industry productivity index	103.72	20.14	72.40	142.60

*Data are from 1967:I to 1990:I.

Methodology

A multivariate VAR system of equations, rather than the single equation approach, is used for modeling the system. This technique avoids the assumptions regarding the exogeneity of the variables. The Granger-causality definition, in conjunction with Akaike's final prediction error (*FPE*) criterion, is used in the VAR model.[4] This allows for each variable to depend on a subset or all other variables in the system and also provides for different lags for each variable in each equation. According to the definition of Granger causality (1980), if $\sigma^2(X_t|Z_{t-1}) \leq \sigma^2(X_t|Z_{t-1} - Y_{t-1})$, then Y is said to cause X if the information set that includes past data on Y, Z_{t-1}, gives a better prediction of X than the same information set without data on Y ($Z_{t-1} - Y_{t-1}$). If the inequality does not hold, then X is said not to cause Y. If $\sigma^2(X_{t-1}|Z_{t-1}) \leq \sigma^2(X_t|Z_{t-1} - Y_{t-1})$ and if $\sigma^2(Y_t|Z_{t-1}) \leq \sigma^2(Y_t|Z_{t-1} - X_{t-1})$, where Z_{t-1} is the information set containing past data on X, then feedback is said to exist between X and Y.

First, the own lag length of the variables is determined by varying lag lengths, in the autoregression $Y_t = a_0 + a_{11}(L)Y_t + e_t$, from 1 to m. Y_t is stationary, $a_{11}(L)$ is a distributed lag polynomial such that $a_{11}(L) = a_{11}{}^j L^j$. L is the lag operator so that $L^j Y_t = Y_{t-j}, \ldots, m$ is the highest order lag and e_t is the zero mean white noise error term. The *FPE* is calculated for each autoregression, and is defined for each lag $j, j = 1, \ldots, m$, as

$$FPE_{(j)} = [(T + j + 1)/(T - j - 1)][SSR_{(j)}/T], \qquad (1)$$

T is the number of observations used in estimating the auto-regression. The lag length minimizing the *FPE* is selected as the order of $a_{11}(L)$.

Once the lag for Y_t is fixed, the specific gravity method is used to determine the order in which other variables enter the equation, following Y, based on minimizing the FPE. If $Y_t = a_0 + a_{11}(L)Y_t + a_{12}(L)X_t + e_t$, then X_t is the relevant variable entering the equation, and $a_{12}(L)$ is a distributed lag polynomial defined in a manner similar to $a_{11}(L)$. $a_{11}(L)$ is fixed at its previously determined order (j) and the lags in $a_{12}(L)$ are varied over $k = 1, \ldots, m$. The FPEs are computed as

$$FPE_{(j,k)} - [(T + j + k + 1)/(T - j - k - 1)][SSR_{(j,k)}/T]. \qquad (2)$$

The lag length for X_t that gives the minimum FPE is selected as the lag order for that variable. If min $FPE_{(j,k)} \leq$ min FPE_j, then X is said to Granger cause Y. This can be extended to as many variables as required by the model.

When all five equations are specified, they combine to form a system. Considering the variables in the system, one might suspect the presence of contemporaneous correlation of the error terms across the equations. Thus, Zellner's seemingly unrelated regression estimation procedure is used to estimate the model.[5] The model specification is tested by carrying out likelihood ratio tests of the adequacy of the system against each proposed change. The likelihood ratio statistics are computed as $-2\log (L^R/L^U)$, where L^R is the maximum likelihood of the restricted system and L^U is the maximum likelihood of the unrestricted model. This statistic asymptotically follows a chi-square distribution with n degrees of freedom, where n is the number of restrictions. Using the causality relations arguments from the earlier part of this chapter and the concept of causality, the model is expressed in matrix form as

$$\mathbf{X} = \mathbf{AB} + \mathbf{e}, \qquad (3)$$

where

$\mathbf{X}^T = (X_{1t}\ X_{2t}\ X_{3t}\ X_{4t}\ X_{5t})$ is a 1×5 vector
$\mathbf{A} = (a^{(j)}_{pq}(L))$ is a 5×5 matrix of coefficients
$\mathbf{B}^T = (X_{1(t-1)}\ X_{2(t-1)}\ X_{3(t-1)}\ X_{4(t-1)}\ X_{5(t-1)})$ is a 1×5 vector of independent variables
$\mathbf{e}^T = (e_{1t}\ e_{2t}\ e_{3t}\ e_{4t}\ e_{5t})$ is a 1×5 vector of disturbances
X_{1t} = index of Dow Jones Industrial Average at time t
X_{2t} = number of mergers and acquisitions at time t
X_{3t} = number of business failures at time t
X_{4t} = yields on long term government bonds at time t
X_{5t} = industrial production at time t.

Empirical Results

The variables in the equation (3) were ranked in order of decreasing specific gravity with the own lagged values entering an equation first, followed by lagged values of the other four variables. The aggregated model in stacked form is given as

$$
\begin{bmatrix} X_{1t} \\ X_{2t} \\ X_{3t} \\ X_{4t} \\ X_{5t} \end{bmatrix} = \begin{bmatrix} a_{11}^{(1)}(L) & 0 & 0 & 0 & a_{15}^{(4)}(L) \\ a_{21}^{(6)}(L) & a_{22}^{(8)}(L) & 0 & 0 & 0 \\ 0 & 0 & a_{33}^{(10)}(L) & 0 & a_{35}^{(3)}(L) \\ a_{41}^{(2)}(L) & 0 & 0 & a_{44}^{(5)}(L) & 0 \\ a_{51}^{(2)}(L) & 0 & 0 & 0 & a_{55}^{(1)}(L) \end{bmatrix} \begin{bmatrix} X_{1(t-1)} \\ X_{2(t-1)} \\ X_{3(t-1)} \\ X_{4(t-1)} \\ X_{5(t-1)} \end{bmatrix} + \begin{bmatrix} e_1 \\ e_2 \\ e_3 \\ e_4 \\ e_5 \end{bmatrix}. \quad (4)
$$

Here $a_{pq}^{\ j}(L) = a_{pq1}L + \ldots + a_{pqj}L^j$.

Prior to analyzing the system of equations given above, it is essential to establish that the model represents the data adequately. These tests of hypotheses are presented in Table 8.2. The hypotheses 1, 5, 9, 13, and 17 test whether the model may be simplified by constraining the various nonzero off-diagonal lagged polynomials to be zero. For these hypotheses listed, the chi-square statistics are significant at the 1, 1, 5, 10, and 1 percent levels, respectively, indicating that the various lag polynomials being tested are significantly different from zero. The tests 2, 3, 4, 6, 7, 8, 10, 11, 12, 14, 15, 16, 18, 19, and 20 examine whether easing the zero restrictions for the appropriate off-diagonal elements improve the model. The various coefficients of the lag polynomials being tested do not differ significantly from zero. These results indicate that the model formulated above is adequate.

Conclusions regarding the direction of causality among the variables can be drawn from Table 8.2. Stock prices are observed to be influenced by industrial production only. Hypothesis 1 in Table 8.2 substantiates this causal relation. Equation (1) in Table 8.3 shows significant negative coefficients for industrial production, with lags of one and four quarters. The intermediate lags of two and three quarters are found to be insignificant. The results are similar to those obtained by vector autoregressive causality tests by James *et al.* (1985), who showed causality going from changes in industrial production to stock returns, with the three-month lag showing a negative coefficient. The coefficient for the one quarter own lag length for stock prices is not significant.

Hypothesis 5, Table 8.2, indicates that changes in stock prices cause changes in the number of mergers. Changes in business failures, interest rates, and industrial production do not cause changes in

TABLE 8.2 *Likelihood Ratio Tests*†

Hypotheses	χ^2 Statistics
1. $a_{15}^{(4)}(L) = 0$	14.47***
2. $a_{12}(L) \neq 0$	3.41
3. $a_{13}(L) \neq 0$	7.08
4. $a_{14}(L) \neq 0$	6.84
5. $a_{21}^{(6)}(L) = 0$	22.69***
6. $a_{23}(L) \neq 0$	4.31
7. $a_{24}(L) \neq 0$	1.27
8. $a_{25}(L) \neq 0$	1.24
9. $a_{35}^{(3)}(L) = 0$	9.98**
10. $a_{31}(L) \neq 0$	2.63
11. $a_{32}(L) \neq 0$	0.21
12. $a_{34}(L) \neq 0$	4.05
13. $a_{41}^{(2)}(L) = 0$	3.21*
14. $a_{42}(L) \neq 0$	6.95
15. $a_{43}(L) \neq 0$	3.38
16. $a_{45}(L) \neq 0$	1.43
17. $a_{51}^{(2)}(L) = 0$	23.83***
18. $a_{52}(L) \neq 0$	4.37
19. $a_{53}(L) \neq 0$	3.29
20. $a_{54}(L) \neq 0$	3.04

*Significant at the 0.10 level. **Significant at the 0.05 level. ***Significant at the 0.01 level.
†Tests results are with model hypotheses maintained, i.e. 1, 5, 9, 13, and 17 in null form and 2, 3, 4, 6, 7, 8, 10, 11, 12, 14, 15, 16, 18, 19, and 20 in alternate form.

mergers as anticipated. This is explicit from the SUR estimation of equation (2) in Table 8.3. A positive significant relationship is observed in equation (2) in Table 8.3 (at lags of two and three quarters), a negative significant relationship is observed at a lag of five quarters and a significant, positive relationship is seen at a lag of six quarters for merger activity. The own lag length for merger activity is eight quarters, with the one quarter lag showing a significant, negative coefficient, and the eight quarter lag showing a significant, positive coefficient.

Mergers do respond to past movements in stock prices. Table 8.3 shows that the second and third lags are statistically significant with positive coefficients, indicating that a rise (fall) in stock prices creates an impetus for a rise (fall) in merger activity. The fourth lag is insignificant. However, the fifth and sixth lags are significant with negative coefficients, implying that, with a lag of approximately one

TABLE 8.3 *Estimation of Parameters: Aggregated Model*
(t-*values are given in parentheses*)

Equation		1	2	3	4	5
Independent variables	Dependent variables	X_{1t}	X_{2t}	X_{3t}	X_{4t}	X_{5t}
	Lag	(DJ)	(NM)	(BF)	(BY)	(IP)
Constant	0	0.0275 (2.84)*	−0.0050 (−0.30)	0.0078 (0.78)	0.0013 (0.02)	0.0022 (1.18)
$X_{1(t-1)}$	1	0.0206 (0.20)	−0.0909 (−0.46)		0.2502 (0.27)	0.0971 (4.65)***
(Dow Jones industrial average)	2		0.4588 (2.37)**		1.6090 (1.83)*	0.0440 (1.96)*
	3		0.5983 (3.12)**			
	4		−0.1323 (−0.66)			
	5		−0.3487 (−1.73)*			
	6		0.3827 (1.93)*			
$X_{2(t-1)}$	1		−0.3079 (−3.06)***			
(Number of mergers)	2		−0.0431 (−0.41)			
	3		−0.1337 (−1.29)			
	4		−0.0399 (−0.38)			
	5		0.0870 (0.89)			
	6		−0.0450 (−0.47)			

TABLE 8.3 Continued

Equation		1	2	3	4	5
Independent variables	Dependent variables	X_{1t}	X_{2t}	X_{3t}	X_{4t}	X_{5t}
	Lag	(DJ)	(NM)	(BF)	(BY)	(IP)
	7		0.1170 (1.27)			
	8		0.3074 (3.50)***			
$X_{3(t-1)}$	1			0.0741 (0.73)		
(Number of business failures)	2			0.0220 (0.22)		
	3			0.0052 (0.05)		
	4			0.4509 (4.67)***		
	5			0.1169 (1.12)		
	6			0.0296 (0.28)		
	7			0.1781 (1.86)*		
	8			0.0415 (0.43)		
	9			0.0052 (0.05)		
	10			−0.4071 (−4.19)***		
$X_{4(t-1)}$	1				−0.0765 (0.77)	
(Bond yields)	2				0.0502 (0.50)	

TABLE 8.3 *Continued*

Equation		1	2	3	4	5
	Dependent variables	X_{1t}	X_{2t}	X_{3t}	X_{4t}	X_{5t}
Independent variables	Lag	(DJ)	(NM)	(BF)	(BY)	(IP)
	3				0.2025 (2.10)**	
	4				0.0972 (0.99)	
	5				−0.1804 (−1.91)*	
$X_{5(t-1)}$	1	−0.8226 (−1.87)*		−1.0300 (−2.32)**		0.3934 (4.57)***
(Industrial production)	2	−0.0243 (−0.05)		0.7553 (1.54)		
	3	0.3141 (0.65)		0.6614 (1.46)		
	4	−1.3807 (−3.21)***				

*Significant at the 0.10 level.
**Significant at the 0.05 level.
***Significant at the 0.01 level.

and one-half years, stock prices increases (declines) indicate declines (increases) in merger activity. Consistent with the results of Nelson (1959, 1966), Weston (1961) and Melicher *et al.* (1983), changes in industrial production do not appear to cause changes in mergers and acquisitions. Melicher *et al.* find a very weak correlation between mergers and prior bond yields, although any causality from bond yields to mergers is not evident in the present analysis. This is also the case for business failures.

Hypothesis 9, Table 8.2, indicates that changes in industrial production are leading indicators of business failures. Further, from Table 8.3, equation (3), the significant negative coefficient (at lag 1) implies that as industrial production increases, business failures decrease, one quarter later, which is consistent with prior expectations. Merger activity, bond yields and stock prices do not appear to be of significance in explaining business failures.

Hypothesis 13, Table 8.2, and equation (4), Table 8.3, show that changes in bond yields are influenced by changes in stock prices. In general, increases in stock prices result in increasing bond yields with a lag of two quarters. Rising stock prices may be reflective of an enhanced economic environment for firms, signalling improved profitability for them and, thereby, raising the demand for borrowed funds. This would in turn lead to excess demand pressure on loanable funds, resulting in increases in interest rates in the future (Melicher *et al.*, 1983). Equation (4), Table 8.3, shows a significant positive relation between the stock prices and bond yields.[6]

Hypothesis 17 in Table 8.2 and equation (5) in Table 8.3 indicate that industrial production is affected by stock prices with lags of one and two quarters. These results are consistent with observations by Fama (1981) that changes in the stock market are reflected in changes in industrial production. These results are also similar to those of Chang and Pinegar (1989), who conducted bivariate tests of Granger causality and found that returns on large firms' stocks unindirectionally cause changes in industrial production with a lag of at least six months.

Conclusions

Interdependencies among stock prices, merger activity and the macroeconomy have been the subject of recent studies. However, most of the prior research has been limited in scope due to a lack of either a multivariate model to explain stock prices, merger activity and the macroeconomy and/or a two-way causal model explaining relationships among all of the variables, without *a priori* assumptions regarding the direction of causality. This chapter is an attempt to overcome these deficiencies. Five variables—the Dow Jones Industrial Average, number of mergers, number of business failures, yields on long-term government bonds, and industrial production—are utilized in a VAR analysis of interdependencies.

The results show that an increase (or decrease) in stock prices produces rising (falling) interest rates two quarters later. A feedback relationship is found to exist between industrial production and stock prices with one causing the other with different lag lengths. Mergers are noted to be influenced by previous stock price movements. Increases (or decreases) in stock prices lead to increases (or decreases) in mergers in subsequent quarters. Although, conceptually, business failure, industrial production and bond yields could be expected to influence mergers, the results prove otherwise.

Results demonstrate causality going from industrial production to business failures. Increases (or decreases) in industrial production produce decreases (or increases) in the number of business failures. A relation between bond yields and mergers is not identified, although some literature shows a weak correlation between the two variables.

The attractiveness of the multidirectional, multivariate model is highlighted on the basis of the observed results. It is somewhat surprising that mergers do not have a great impact on the macroeconomy, especially on business failures and stock prices. Stock prices show significant influences on merger activity, bond yields, and industrial production. The feedback relationship observed among industrial production and stock prices indicates that identification of two-way lead–lag structures in a multivariate system is essential for studies of this nature.

Acknowledgements

The authors thank Marcia Cornett, Dave Davidson, Dilip Ghosh, and Stu Rosenstein for helpful comments on earlier drafts of this chapter.

Notes

1. Their results provide further credibility to the hypothesis that stock returns reflect real activity.
2. A number of other authors such as, for example, Chappel and Cheng (1984), Golbe and White (1987) and Shughart and Tollison (1984) have also studied relationships between merger activity and macroeconomic factors.
3. Clark *et al.* (1988) examine a lead–lag structure and utilize bidirectional models. However, their models are bivariate and mergers and stock prices and mergers and industrial production are examined as isolated relationships.
4. Hsiao (1981) has argued that prespecification of lag-lengths may influence test results. Further, Thornton and Batten (1985) show that Akaike's FPE criterion is superior to other criteria for lag-length selection.
5. Dhrymes (1971), among others, shows that iterating Zellner's procedure to convergence produces estimates equivalent to MLEs.
6. Since increasing stock prices produce declining yields for investors, one would expect to see a contemporaneous negative relationship between changes in stock prices and changes in bond yields. A regression utilizing contemporaneous observations for these two variables had the expected negative parameter, which was statistically significant.

References

Becketti, S. (1986) Corporate mergers and the business cycle, *Economic Review*, Federal Reserve Bank of Kansas City, 13–26.

CHANG, E. C. and PINEGAR, J. M. (1989) Seasonal fluctuations in industrial production and stock market seasonals, *Journal of Financial and Quantitative Analysis*, 24, 59–74.

CHANG, E. C. and PINEGAR, J. M. (1990) Stock market seasonal and prespecified multifactor pricing relations, *Journal of Financial and Quantitative Analysis*, 25, 517–533.

CHAPPEL, H. W. and CHENG, D. C. (1984) Firm's acquisition decisions and Tobin's Q ratio, *Journal of Economics and Business*, 36, 29–42.

CHEN, N. F., ROLL, R. and ROSS, S. A. (1986) Economic forces and the stock market, *Journal of Business*, 59, 383–403.

CLARK, J. J., CHAKRABARTI, A. K. and CHIANG, T. C. (1988) Stock prices and merger movements: interactive relations, *Weltwirtschaftliches Archiv*, 124, 287–300.

DARRAT, A. F. (1988) On fiscal policy and the stock market, *Journal of Money, Credit, and Banking*, 20, Part 1, 353–363.

DARRAT, A. F. (1990) Stock returns, money, and fiscal deficits, *Journal of Financial and Quantitative Analysis*, 25, 387–398.

DHRYMES, P. J. (1971) Equivalence of iterative Aitken and maximum likelihood estimators for a system of regression equations, *Australian Economic Papers*, 10, 20–24.

FAMA, E. F. (1981) Stock returns, real activity, inflation, and money, *American Economic Review*, September, 545–565.

GERTLER, M. (1988) Financial structure and aggregate economic activity, *Journal of Money, Credit, and Banking*, 20, Part 2, 559–588.

GOLBE, D. L. and WHITE, L. J. (1987) A time-series analysis of mergers and acquisitions in the U.S. economy (mimeo). Presented at *National Bureau of Economic Research Conference on Mergers and Acquisitions*.

GRANGER, C. W. J. (1980) Testing for causality: a personal viewpoint, *Journal of Economic Dynamics and Control*, 2, 329–352.

HSIAO, CHENG (1981) Autoregressive modeling and money-income causality detection, *Journal of Monetary Economics*, 7, 85–106.

JAMES, C., KOREISHA, S. and PARTCH, M. (1985) A VARMA analysis of the causal relations among stock returns, real output, and nominal interest rates, *Journal of Finance*, December, 1375–1384.

KIM, K. M. and WU, C. (1987) Macro-economic factors and stock returns, *The Journal of Financial Research*, 10, 87–98.

MELICHER, R. W., LEDOLTER, J. and D'ANTONIO, L. J. (1983) A time series analysis of aggregate merger activity. *Review of Economics and Statistics*, 65, 423–430.

NELSON, R. L. (1959) *Merger Movements in American Industry 1895–1956*, Princeton University Press, Princeton, NJ.

NELSON, R. L. (1966) Business cycle factors in the choice between internal and external growth. In ALBERTS, W. W. and SEGALL, J. E. (eds.), *The Corporate Merger*, University of Chicago Press.

PASTENA, V. and RULAND, W. (1986) The merger/bankruptcy alternative, *Accounting Review*, 61, No. 2.

SHRIEVES, R. and STEVENS, D. (1979) Bankruptcy avoidance as a motive for merger, *Journal of Financial and Quantitative Analysis*, 14, 501–515.

SHUGART, W. E. H. and TOLLISON, R. D. (1984) The random character of merger activity, *Rand Journal of Economics*, 15, 500–509.

THORNTON, D. L. and BATTEN, D. W. (1985) Lag-length selection and tests of granger causality between money and income, *Journal of Money Credit and Banking*, 17, 164–178.

WESTON, J. F. (1961) *The Role of Mergers in the Growth of Large Firms*, University of California Press, Berkeley, CA, Chapter 5.

WESTON, J. F., CHUNG, K. S. and HOAG, S. E. (1990) *Mergers, Restructuring, and Corporate Control*, Prentice-Hall, Englewood Cliff, NJ.

9

The Impact of the Type of Offering on the Underpricing of IPOs

DEV PRASAD

Introduction

The existence of the phenomenon of 'underpricing' has been well established for common stock initial public offerings (CSIPOs). Earlier empirical studies have found that the average firm goes public with an offering price that is lower than the price which prevails in the immediate after-market. However, the extent of underpricing varies from firm to firm. Most of the earlier empirical papers appear to have concentrated on examining the underpricing of CSIPOs without regard to the type of offering even though an examination of the prospectuses of different firms reveals that the mode of, and motivation for, going public varies from firm to firm.

Prasad (1990, 1994) points out that, in practice, there are three types of offerings. The first type is that of 'pure primary offerings' (which are also further referred to as 'primary offerings') where only the company offers shares to the public. In other words, funds are raised by the firm through the issue of new shares to outside investors, and all the funds from the issue go to the firm after adjusting for the floatation costs. The purpose of the offering may be to expand operations, pay off debt, etc. Many of the CSIPOs are observed to be primary offerings. The second type is that of 'pure secondary offerings' (further referred to as 'secondary offerings') where only some of the existing shareholders offer some or all of their shares to outside investors in the public offering. The motivation for the firm going public, in this case, appears to be 'harvesting' by these existing shareholders. In other words, such shareholders are cashing in their investments. Presumably, through divestment of their personal shares, the selling shareholders expect to make a profit by selling the offered shares at a price higher than the price paid by them at the time of their initial investment. In this case, no new funds become available to the firm through the public offering. This type of case, however, does not appear to be very common. The third type of offering is that of 'simultaneous primary and secondary offerings' (further also referred to as 'mixed offerings') where both new shares of the company and the shares of some existing shareholders are simultaneously made available for purchase by outside investors in the same public offering. This type of offering is also very common. A number of questions arise relating to whether investors will distinguish amongst the three types of offerings (namely primary offerings, secondary offerings, and mixed offerings) while making their pricing and investment decisions: Are investors indifferent between the choice of buying into a firm through the issuance of new shares by the firm, or, through the shares offered by existing shareholders (primary offerings versus secondary offerings)? Will the investors be indifferent to whether the shares are offered by the firm alone, or, by the firm and existing shareholders simultaneously (primary offerings versus mixed offerings)? While investors may consider the selling of stock by the firm as a necessary evil, the investors may consider the sale of shares by existing shareholders as a bad sign since the latter's harvesting reduces the proportion of equity retained by such shareholders. The investors may ask: Why are existing shareholders selling out if the prospects for the firm are so great? Has the value of the stock already reached its maximum?

This study is motivated to examine the above issues based on the results of some earlier studies (discussed further in the next section) which suggest that there may be differences in the pricing behavior of mixed offerings and primary offerings of CSIPOs. Accordingly, the null hypothesis for this study is

> The extent of underpricing is the same for all types of offerings of CSIPOs whether they are primary offerings or mixed offerings or secondary offerings.

Some other studies (also discussed in the next section) have suggested that there are differences in the underpricing behavior of IPOs based on where the shares are to be traded subsequently, i.e. whether the shares would be traded on the New York Stock Exchange (NYSE), the American Stock Exchange (AMEX) or the Over-The-Counter (OTC) market.[1] Thus, this study is also motivated to further examine separately the above null hypothesis for these three types of offerings for the NYSE firms only , and then, for the OTC firms only.[2] While it may be expected that the same pattern of underpricing for the different types of offerings would be found in each market segment, it may further be expected that the levels of underpricing would be lower for NYSE IPOs as compared to OTC IPOs.

The rest of the chapter is laid out as follows: In the next section, the earlier empirical works are reviewed. Further, the principal issues which provide the motivation for this study are discussed. Information on the data, sources of the data, methodology for data analysis, etc. are provided in the third section. The results of empirical testing are detailed in the fourth section. The final section summarizes the results and presents the conclusions, as well as discussing the implications of the results for the firm, selling stock holders and investors. This final section also provides suggestions for possible directions for further research in the area.

Literature Review

Earlier studies have firmly established the existence of underpricing. However, the extent of underpricing observed varies from study to study. The differences in the levels of underpricing may be due to differences in the data sets of the various studies such as the number of IPOs in the sample, the time periods over which the IPOs were issued, etc. There are also some variations in the methodology. One variation is in terms of the after-market period used in the calculations: the calculations of the extent of underpricing may be based on the first day returns, and/ or first week returns, and/or first month returns. Another variation is that in some studies, underpricing has been measured in terms of first day excess returns, and/ or first week excess returns, and/or first month excess returns. These may be seen from the results of some of these earlier studies summarized as follows: Reilly and Hatfield (1969) examine 53 CSIPOs over the 1963 –1965 period. They found the first week returns to be 9.00 percent and the first month returns to be 8.00 percent. Ibbotson (1975) examined 128 CSIPOs issued over the period 1960–1969. He found the first month return from the date of the offering to be 11.40 percent. However, when McDonald and Fisher (1972) examined 142 CSIPOs issued in 1969, they found the first week returns to be 28.50 percent and the first month returns to be 34.60 percent. Logue (1973) found the average first day published returns to be 30.00 percent when he examined 250 CSIPOs over 1965–1969. Neuberger and Hammond (1974) found for 816 CSIPOs over 1965–1969, that the first week and first month returns to be 17.10 percent and 19.10 percent, respectively. Ibbotson and Jaffe (1975) found the first month return average to be 16.83 percent for all CSIPOs issued during January 1, 1960 to October 31, 1970. Reilly (1977) examined 486 CSIPOs over the period 1972–1975 and found the first week returns to be 10.90 percent while the first month returns are 11.60 percent. Block and Stanley (1980) found lower returns for 102 CSIPOs issued over 1974–1978 with the first week returns and first month returns being 5.96 and 3.36 percent, respectively. In contrast, Neuberger and La Chapelle (1983) found higher average returns for 118 CSIPOs over 1975–1980 with the first week returns being 27.70 percent and the first month returns being 26.50 percent. However, when Ibbotson *et al.* (1988) examined 128 CSIPOs over 1960–1987, they found the first month return for the 1960s decade to be 21.25 percent, the 1970s decade to be 8.95 percent and for 1980–1987 to be 16.09 percent. Ritter (1984), while examining 1028 CSIPOs over the period 1977–1982, found the average first day returns to be 26.50 percent. Beatty and Ritter (1986) examined 545 CSIPOs issued during 1981–1982 and found the first day returns to be 14.10 percent. However, Chalk and Peavy (1987) found the first day returns to be 21.67 percent for 649 CSIPOs issued during 1975–1982. Miller and Reilly (1987) found the first day return to be 9.87 percent for 510 CSIPOs over the period 1982–1983.

A number of theoretical explanations have been offered to explain the observed phenomenon of underpricing. The explanations include: (a) favor to investors (Logue, 1973; Baron and Holmstrom, 1980); (b) information asymmetry and offering value uncertainty (Baron, 1982; Rock, 1986; Muscarella and Vetsuypens, 1989); (c) reduction of underwriter risk (Neuberger and La Chapelle, 1983); (d) regulations—ceilings (Brandi, 1985, 1987); (e) offering value uncertainty (Smith, 1986); (f) certification of insider information (Booth and Smith, 1986); (g) maintenance of underwriter reputation (Beatty and Ritter, 1986); and, (h) regulations—legal liability (Tinic, 1988; Alexander, 1993; Drake and Vetsuypens, 1993). Almost all the theoretical explanations are based on, or related to, the level of risk perceived by the potential investors. For example, Logue (1973) argued that an investment banker minimizes his costs and risks and gains favor with investors by underpricing. Investors tend to avoid issues which would make their *ex ante* returns normal or below normal. To assure a positive initial return to investors, the offering price is set below the expected market value. Thus, on an average, new issues would tend to rise to a premium and generate superior returns in the absence of any special factors. Smith (1986) implied that average underpricing is greater for issues with greater price uncertainty. Baron (1982) based his explanation of underpricing on the information asymmetry existing between investment bankers and issuers. He set up a theoretical model which implies that the amount by which the issue is underpriced is related to the uncertainty about

TABLE 9.1 *Descriptive Statistics*

	OTC offerings	NYSE offerings	Total offerings
Pure primary offerings			
Number of offerings	34	37	71
Mean offering price ($)	10.63	15.22	13.02
Standard deviation ($)	4.66	5.32	5.49
Minimum offering price ($)	4.00	7.00	4.00
Maximum offering price ($)	22.00	32.00	32.00
Pure secondary offerings			
Number of offerings	2	7	9
Mean offering price ($)	18.25	18.06	18.10
Standard deviation ($)	8.84	7.91	7.53
Minimum offering price ($)	12.00	8.25	8.25
Maximum offering price ($)	24.50	30.00	30.00
Mixed offerings			
Number of offerings	44	19	63
Mean offering price ($)	12.47	17.58	14.01
Standard deviation ($)	4.68	3.93	5.03
Minimum offering price ($)	5.00	12.00	5.00
Maximum offering price ($)	30.00	25.50	30.00
Total offerings			
Number of offerings	80	63	143
Mean offering price ($)	11.83	16.25	13.78
Standard deviation ($)	4.89	5.34	5.53
Minimum offering price ($)	4.00	7.00	4.00
Maximum offering price ($)	30.00	32.00	32.00

the value of the offering. The implication is that there would be a larger amount of underpricing if there is larger uncertainty about the market value of the issue. Rock (1986) set up a theoretical model which implied that the underpricing and the uncertainty about the value of the offering are related. Rock argued that a larger amount of underpricing would result from greater uncertainty about the issuer's market value. Rock bases his explanation on the information asymmetry existing between informed and uninformed investors. However, Rock also hypothesized that some investors become better informed about the true value of a new issue while others remain uniformed because it may be too costly or difficult for them to obtain more information.

As may be seen from the above, most of the earlier papers appear to have concentrated on underpricing in the case of CSIPOs as a whole without considering that the market may perceive pure primary offerings to be different from mixed offerings and secondary offerings. The Logue (1973) and Prasad (1994) studies appear to be the only ones to make some examination of pricing behavior for the different types of offerings. Logue found lower performance for higher proportions of secondary issues relative to the total issue. Logue theorized that the significance of the secondary variable could be due to a closer relationships with the secondary issuers. Prasad (1994) examined a small sample of 35 firms of OTC firms over 1984–1992. Prasad found no difference in the level of underpricing for primary offerings compared to mixed offerings based on first day excess returns. However, he found mixed offerings to be underpriced more than the primary offerings (although only at a 15 percent level of significance) based on first month excess returns. Prasad suggested expanding the study with a larger sample and including secondary offerings (which were excluded from his sample). He also suggested expansion of the study to NYSE and AMEX IPOs since these segments of the financial markets are not perfectly correlated with the OTC. In addition, a study of the signalling behavior of CSIPOs by Prasad (1990) found that greater level of promoter's retention of equity is required for mixed offerings compared to the level of promoter's retention of equity required in the case of pure primary offerings to convey the same value of the firm's equity. Prasad conjectured that the potential investors may be viewing mixed offerings as being more risky investments than pure primary offerings. Thus, this study is motivated by the Logue (1973) and Prasad (1990, 1994) results to examine further, using a larger sample, whether greater underpricing exists in the case of mixed offerings compared to primary offerings. The primary and mixed offerings are then also compared to secondary offerings in this study. The expected trend would be for secondary offerings to be underpriced the most (viewed as most risky type of offering by investors), followed by a lower underpricing for mixed offerings, and, the least underpricing for primary offerings (viewed as the least risky type of offering by the investors). Such an expectation may be due to outside investors' perception of higher risk in the case of firms with offerings in which the promoters of the firm reducing their own holdings. Such dilution of ownership by the promoters may be viewed as being beyond any action required by the firm to continue its operations and grow.

This study is further motivated by the Affleck-Graves et al. (1993) and the Prasad (1995) studies which examined the impact of the trading system on the pricing behavior of CSIPOs. Both Affleck-Graves et al. (1993) and Prasad (1995) compared the extent of underpricing in different segments of the capital market. Affleck-Graves et al. found significant underpricing on all four trading systems: NYSE

(4.82 percent), AMEX (2.16 percent), NASDAQ/NMS (5.56 percent) and NASDAQ/Non-NMS (10.41 percent) using data for 55 NYSE firms, 41 AMEX firms, NASDAQ/NMS firms and 824 NASDAQ/Non-NMS firms over the 1983–1987 period, respectively. While they did not find any significant differences in the average levels of underpricing for CSIPOs amongst the NYSE, the AMEX and the NASDAQ/NMS trading systems, they did find significant difference in the levels of underpricing for all these trading systems when compared with the NASDAQ/Non-NMS. Prasad (1995), using data for 46 NYSE firms and 54 OTC firms which went public over the 1983–1992 period, also found the OTC firms to be significantly underpriced on average. However, in contrast to the Affleck-Graves *et al.* study, Prasad (1995) found that the NYSE firms are not significantly underpriced on average. Further, he found that there is a significant difference in the levels of underpricing of OTC firms when compared to the NYSE firms. Thus, the behavior of initial public offerings appear to differ depending on which market segment the shares are to be subsequently traded. Thus, this study also examines the impact of the trading system on underpricing for primary offerings compared to mixed offerings (and secondary offerings); that is, the underpricing for these three types of offerings based on whether the stock is to be subsequently traded on the NYSE or on the OTC market. The same trend may be expected in each market (the NYSE or OTC), i.e. for secondary offerings to be under-priced the most, followed by a lower underpricing for mixed offerings, and, the least underpricing for primary offerings. However, it may also be expected that these three types of offerings for NYSE firms will be less underpriced than the corresponding offerings for OTC firms. In other words, primary offerings of NYSE firms may be expected to be less underpriced than the primary offerings of OTC firms, and so on.

Data and Methodology

The data relates to CSIPOs of various firms which went public for the first time during the period starting from 1983 up to the middle of 1992 for which prospectuses could be obtained from the firms themselves directly or from investment bankers and brokers. A number of firms could not be included in the study due to various reasons such as—only the 'red herrings' (preliminary prospectuses) could be obtained, the offerings involved common stock and warrants simultaneously, etc. The final sample relates to the data for 143 firms. From the prospectuses of the different firms, information is drawn relating to the date of issue of the CSIPO, the offering price for each

CSIPO, etc. Some of the descriptive statistics of the sample are summarized in Table 9.1. The table provides information regarding the average offering prices of the IPOs ($13.78), the standard deviations of the offering prices ($5.53), the minimum offering price ($4.00) and the maximum offering price ($32.00) for the sample as a whole. Also, a break-up is provided in terms of the three types of offerings, namely, pure primary offerings (71 firms with an average offering price of $13.02), pure secondary offerings (9 firms with an average offering price of $18.10), and mixed offerings (63 firms with an average offering price of $14.01). Table 9.1 also details the break-up for each type of offering based upon where the secondary trading would take place. In other words, a break-up is provided based on whether the CSIPO is listed for sale after the offering on the NYSE or the OTC (63 firms and 80 firms, respectively). Firms whose stock would be traded on the American Stock Exchange (AMEX) could not be included in the study since very few prospectuses could be obtained for such firms. As may be seen from Table 9.1, only nine of the 143 offerings involve pure secondary offerings. Thus, for the purposes of testing the null hypotheses, the study concentrates mainly on primary and mixed offerings. However, even though the sample for secondary offerings is too small for rigorous testing of hypotheses, some preliminary tests are conducted for comparison purposes.

The basic methodology followed in this study is similar to those in earlier studies by McDonald and Fisher (1972), Reilly (1977), Neuberger and La Chapelle (1983), Brandi (1985, 1987), Prasad (1994, 1995), etc. In this study, in the first instance, the returns for each firm (for all the firms in the sample) are calculated for the one-day period from the date of the issue using equation (1) based on the pricing data for each firm

$$R_{j,1} = (P_{j,1} - P_{j,0})/P_{j,0}. \tag{1}$$

where $R_{j,1}$ is the the one-day return from the date of the issue, for firm j, $P_{j,1}$ is the closing stock price of the firm j on the issue date itself, and $P_{j,0}$ is the offering stock price of the firm j.

Data for the after-market prices for each of the firms are drawn from various issues of the Standard and Poor's *Daily Stock Price Record*.

Corresponding one-day 'market returns' are calculated using values of the Wilshire 5000 as the market index. The Wilshire 5000 is chosen for this study as the base for comparisons since it is the broadest index available and formed from stocks listed on the NYSE, the AMEX, as well as the OTC. Wilshire Associates provided the daily data for the Wilshire 5000. The basic equation for calculating the market returns is given in equation (2)

$$R_{Mj,1} = (P_{Mj,1} - P_{Mj,0})/P_{Mj,0}, \qquad (2)$$

where $R_{Mj,1}$ is the one-day return for the market index corresponding to the offering by firm j, $P_{Mj,1}$ is the value of the market index corresponding to the offering by firm j (for the first day returns, this is the closing value on the issue date itself), and $P_{Mj,0}$ is the value of the market index corresponding to the offering stock price of the firm j (the closing value of the index on the day prior to the issue date for firm j—noting that this is also the opening value of the index on the issue date which corresponds to the fact that the offering price for firm j is the opening price on the date of the issue).

Corresponding excess returns are then calculated for each firm using equation (3)

$$ER_{j,1} = R_{j,1} - R_{M,1}, \qquad (3)$$

where $ER_{j,1}$ is the one-day excess return corresponding to the issue by firm j, $R_{j,1}$ is the one-day return for firm j, and $R_{Mj,1}$ is the one-day return for the market index corresponding to the offering by firm j.

The average excess returns are then calculated using equation (4)

$$AER_1 = [(\Sigma ER_{j,1})/n], \qquad (4)$$

where AER_1 is the average one-day excess return, $ER_{j,1}$ is the one-day excess return corresponding to the issue by firm j, and n is the number of firms.

The average excess returns for each type of offering are then calculated after breaking up the sample into primary offerings, mixed offerings and secondary offerings irrespective of where the stocks are listed. The same process is further repeated to calculate average excess returns for the all offerings of stocks to be listed on the NYSE; followed by calculations for the NYSE primary offerings, the NYSE mixed offerings and the NYSE secondary offerings as sub-groups. Finally, similar calculations are made for the OTC stocks as a whole and sub-groups of primary offerings, mixed offerings and secondary offerings.

Results

As may be seen from Table 9.1, there appear to be differences in the average offering prices of primary, secondary and mixed offerings. There appear to be further differences in average offering prices of these types of offerings depending on whether the stocks are to be traded on the NYSE or the OTC. These average offering

prices and the associated levels of underpricing (along with their
differences) are examined further based on the results provided in
Tables 9.2–9.9.

Table 9.2 lays out the levels of underpricing for all the primary
offerings and all the mixed offerings irrespective of where the stocks
are to be traded. As may be seen from Table 9.2, primary offerings
are, on average, underpriced by 3.89 percent which is significant at
the 1 percent level. On the other hand, mixed offerings are underpriced at a higher level of 6.86 percent which is also significant at the
1 percent level. However, the difference in underpricing of 2.97 percent is only significant at the 10 percent level. While mixed offerings
appear to go to the market at a higher average price of $14.01
compared to the average offering price of $13.02 for primary

TABLE 9.2 *Mean Excess Returns: Primary versus Mixed Offerings (OTC and NYSE)*

	Primary offerings first day (percent)	Mixed offerings first day (percent)	Difference in offerings first day (percent)
Mean	3.89	6.86	–2.97
Standard deviation	9.00	9.17	
n	71	63	
Degrees of freedom	70	62	133
t-value	3.642 ****	5.940****	–1.888*

Notes: n = number of observations.
For each group: degrees of freedom = $(n - 1)$

$$t\text{-value} = \frac{\bar{x}}{\sqrt{\{s^2 / n\}}}$$

where x = average excess returns for the offerings; s = standard deviation
of excess returns. For differences between groups: degrees of freedom = $(n_1 + n_2 - 1)$

$$t\text{-value} = \frac{\bar{x}_1 - \bar{x}_2}{\sqrt{\{(s_1^2 / n_1) + (s_2^2 / n_2)\}}},$$

where x_1 = average excess returns for primary offerings; x_2 = average excess
returns for mixed offerings; s_1 = standard deviation of excess returns for primary
offerings; s_2 = standard deviation of excess returns for mixed offerings; n_1 =
number of primary offerings; and n_2 = number of mixed offerings.
Level of significance: ****1 percent, ***2 percent, **5 percent, *10 percent.

offerings, the difference of $0.99 is found to be statistically insignificant (refer to Table 9.3).

As may be seen from Table 9.4, primary offerings, which are to be subsequently traded on the NYSE, are underpriced by 1.78 percent on average. However, this level of underpricing is statistically insignificant. In contrast, mixed offerings are underpriced at level of 2.23 percent which is significant at the 5 percent level. While the mixed offerings appear to be underpriced at a higher level than primary offerings in this case also, the difference in underpricing of 0.45 percent is not found to be statistically significant this time.[3]

In this case also, mixed offerings appear to go to the market at a higher average price ($17.58) compared to the average offering price of primary offerings ($15.22). However, in contrast to the result for

TABLE 9.3 *Mean Offering Prices: Primary versus Mixed Offerings (OTC and NYSE)*

	Primary offerings first day ($)	Mixed offerings first day ($)	Difference in offerings first day ($)
Mean	13.02	14.01	−0.99
Standard deviation	5.490	5.026	
n	71	63	
Degrees of freedom			133
t-value			−1.090

Notes: n = number of observations.

For each group: degrees of freedom = $(n - 1)$

$$t\text{-value} = \frac{\bar{x}}{\sqrt{\{s^2 / n\}}}$$

where x = average excess returns for the offerings; s = standard deviation of excess returns. For differences between groups: degrees of freedom = $(n_1 + n_2 - 1)$

$$t\text{-value} = \frac{\bar{x}_1 - \bar{x}_2}{\sqrt{\{(s_1^2 / n_1) + (s_2^2 / n_2)\}}},$$

where x_1 = average excess returns for primary offerings; x_2 = average excess returns for mixed offerings; s_1 = standard deviation of excess returns for primary offerings; s_2 = standard deviation of excess returns for mixed offerings; n_1 = number of primary offerings; and n_2 = number of mixed offerings.

Level of significance: ****1 percent, ***2 percent, **5 percent, *10 percent.

TABLE 9.4 *Mean Excess Returns: Primary versus Mixed Offerings (NYSE)*

	Primary offerings first day (percent)	Mixed offerings first day (percent)	Difference in offerings first day (percent)
Mean	1.78	2.23	−0.45
Standard deviation	8.06	3.91	
Number of observations	37	19	
Degrees of freedom	36	18	53
t-value	1.343	2.420**	−0.281

Notes: n = number of observations.
For each group: degrees of freedom = $(n - 1)$

$$t\text{-value} = \frac{\bar{x}}{\sqrt{\{s^2 / n\}}}$$

where x = average excess returns for the offerings; s = standard deviation of excess returns. For differences between groups: (Smith–Satterthwaite test)

$$df = \frac{\{(s_1^2/n_1) + (s_2^2/n_2)\}^2}{\{(s_1^2/n_1)^2/(n_1 - 1) + (s_2^2/n_2)^2/(n_2 - 1)\}}.$$

The degrees of freedom are rounded off to the next lowest whole number.

$$t\text{-value} = \frac{\bar{x}_1 - \bar{x}_2}{\sqrt{\{(s_1^2/n_1) + (s_2^2/n_2)\}}},$$

where x_1 = average excess returns for primary offerings; x_2 = average excess returns for mixed offerings; s_1 = standard deviation of excess returns for primary offerings; s_2 = standard deviation of excess returns for mixed offerings; n_1 = number of primary offerings; and n_2 = number of mixed offerings.
    Level of significance: ****1 percent, ***2 percent, **5 percent, *10 percent.

the offerings taken irrespective of the market for subsequent trading (Table 9.3), Table 9.5 shows that the difference of $2.36 for the NYSE offerings is found to be statistically significant at the 10 percent level only.
    Table 9.6 lays out the levels of underpricing for all the primary and mixed offerings where the stocks are to be traded on the OTC. As may be seen from Table 9.6, primary offerings are underpriced, on average, by 6.18 percent which is significant at the 1 percent level. Similarly, mixed offerings are underpriced at a level of 8.86 percent which is higher than the underpricing level for primary offerings.

TABLE 9.5 *Mean Offering Prices: Primary versus Mixed Offerings (NYSE)*

	Primary offerings first day ($)	Mixed offerings first day ($)	Difference in offerings first day ($)
Mean	15.22	17.58	−2.36
Standard deviation	5.317	3.927	
Number of observations	37	19	
Degrees of freedom			47
t-value			−1.880*

Notes: n = number of observations.
For each group: degrees of freedom = $(n-1)$

$$t\text{-value} = \frac{\bar{x}}{\sqrt{\{s^2/n\}}}$$

where x = average excess returns for the offerings; s = standard deviation of excess returns. For differences between groups: (Smith–Satterthwaite test)

$$df = \frac{\{(s_1^2/n_1)+(s_2^2/n_2)\}^2}{\{(s_1^2/n_1)^2/(n_1-1)+(s_2^2/n_2)^2/(n_2-1)\}}.$$

The degrees of freedom are rounded off to the next lowest whole number.

$$t\text{-value} = \frac{\bar{x}_1 - \bar{x}_2}{\sqrt{\{(s_1^2/n_1)+(s_2^2/n_2)\}}},$$

where x_1 = average excess returns for primary offerings; x_2 = average excess returns for mixed offerings; s_1 = standard deviation of excess returns for primary offerings; s_2 = standard deviation of excess returns for mixed offerings; n_1 = number of primary offerings; and n_2 = number of mixed offerings.
Level of significance: ****1 percent, ***2 percent, **5 percent, *10 percent.

This level of underpricing of 8.86 percent is also significant at the 1 percent level. However, the difference in underpricing of 2.68 percent is not statistically significant.

Table 9.7 shows that once again mixed offerings appear to go to the market at a higher average price of $12.47 compared to the average offering price of $10.62 for primary offerings. Here also the difference of $1.85 is found to be statistically significant at the 10 percent level only.

As mentioned earlier, only nine of the 143 offerings are secondary offerings. Out of these nine, seven of the secondary offerings were to

TABLE 9.6 *Mean Excess Returns: Primary versus Mixed Offerings (OTC)*

	Primary offerings first day (percent)	Mixed offerings first day (percent)	Difference in offerings first day (percent)
Mean	6.18	8.86	−2.68
Standard deviation	9.52	10.06	
n	34	44	
Degrees of freedom	33	43	77
t-value	3.785 ****	5.842 ****	−1.203

Notes: n = number of observations.
For each group: degrees of freedom = $(n - 1)$

$$t\text{-value} = \frac{\bar{x}}{\sqrt{\{s^2 / n\}}}$$

where x = average excess returns for the offerings; s = standard deviation of excess returns. For differences between groups: degrees of freedom = $(n_1 + n_2 - 1)$

$$t\text{-value} = \frac{\bar{x}_1 - \bar{x}_2}{\sqrt{\{(s_1^2 / n_1) + (s_2^2 / n_2)\}}},$$

where x_1 = average excess returns for primary offerings; x_2 = average excess returns for mixed offerings; s_1 = standard deviation of excess returns for primary offerings; s_2 = standard deviation of excess returns for mixed offerings; n_1 = number of primary offerings; and n_2 = number of mixed offerings.
Level of significance: ****1 percent, ***2 percent, **5 percent, *10 percent.

be traded on the NYSE with the other two to be traded on the OTC. These samples are too small to make detailed comparisons. However, the seven NYSE secondary offerings are analyzed and compared to the NYSE primary and mixed offerings to see if there are any preliminary conclusions that may be drawn with regard to the pricing behavior of secondary offerings. As may be seen from Tables 9.4 and 9.8, the extent of underpricing of 7.88 percent for secondary offerings is significant only at the 10 percent level. Further, though the secondary offerings are underpriced more than the primary offerings by 6.10 percent, the same is significant only at the 20 percent level. Similarly, secondary offerings are underpriced more than mixed offerings by 5.65 percent, but the same is also significant only at the 20 percent level. Probably these results have been influenced by the small sample sizes.

As may be seen from Tables 9.5 and 9.9, the average offering price of secondary offerings is $18.06, which is higher than the average offering price of primary offerings by $2.84 and higher than the

TABLE 9.7 *Mean Offering Prices: Primary versus Mixed Offerings (OTC)*

	Primary offerings first day ($)	Mixed offerings first day ($)	Difference in offerings first day ($)
Mean	10.62	12.47	−1.85
Standard deviation	4.663	4.679	
n	34	44	
Degrees of freedom	77		
t-value			−1.735*

Notes: n = number of observations.
For each group: degrees of freedom = $(n - 1)$

$$t\text{-value} = \frac{\bar{x}}{\sqrt{\{s^2/n\}}}$$

where x = average excess returns for the offerings; s = standard deviation of excess returns. For differences between groups: degrees of freedom = $(n_1 + n_2 - 1)$

$$t\text{-value} = \frac{\bar{x}_1 - \bar{x}_2}{\sqrt{\{(s_1^2/n_1) + (s_2^2/n_2)\}}},$$

where x_1 = average excess returns for primary offerings; x_2 = average excess returns for mixed offerings; s_1 = standard deviation of excess returns for primary offerings; s_2 = standard deviation of excess returns for mixed offerings; n_1 = number of primary offerings; and n_2 = number of mixed offerings.
Level of significance: ****1 percent, ***2 percent, **5 percent, *10 percent.

average offering price of mixed offerings by $0.48. However, these differences are statistically insignificant. Again it is likely that these preliminary results may have been influenced by the small sample sizes. Even though the preliminary results appear to be in line with the expected trends, examination of a larger sample of secondary offerings is required to judge the extent of support for the above results.

Summary, Conclusions and Implications

The results appear to provide support for the expectation that secondary offerings would be underpriced the most, followed by a lower underpricing for mixed offerings, and the least underpricing for primary offerings. For the total sample, the average underpricing for mixed and primary offerings is 6.86 and 3.89 percent,

TABLE 9.8 *Mean Excess Returns: Comparison with Secondary Offerings (NYSE)*

| | Secondary offerings first day (percent) | Difference with | |
		Primary offerings first day (percent)	Mixed offerings first day (percent)
Mean	7.88	−6.10	−5.65
Standard deviation	8.685		
Number of observations	7		
Degrees of freedom	6	8	6
t-value	2.401*	−1.725	−1.681

Notes: n = number of observations.
For each group: degrees of freedom = $(n - 1)$

$$t\text{-value} = \frac{\bar{x}}{\sqrt{\{s^2/n\}}}$$

where x = average excess returns for the offerings; s = standard deviation of excess returns. For differences between groups: (Smith–Satterthwaite test)

$$df = \frac{\{(s_1^2/n_1) + (s_2^2/n_2)\}^2}{\{(s_1^2/n_1)^2/(n_1 - 1) + (s_2^2/n_2)^2/(n_2 - 1)\}}.$$

The degrees of freedom are rounded off to the next lowest whole number.

$$t\text{-value} = \frac{\bar{x}_1 - \bar{x}_2}{\sqrt{\{(s_1^2/n_1) + (s_2^2/n_2)\}}},$$

where x_1 = average excess returns for primary offerings or mixed offerings; x_2 = average excess returns for secondary offerings; s_1 = standard deviation of excess returns for primary or mixed offerings; s_2 = standard deviation of excess returns for secondary offerings; n_1 = number of primary or mixed offerings; and n_2 = number of secondary offerings.
Level of significance: ****1 percent, ***2 percent, **5 percent, *10 percent.

respectively. For the NYSE firms, the average underpricing for secondary, mixed, and primary offerings is 7.88, 2.23 and 1.78 percent, respectively. For the OTC firms, the average underpricing for mixed and primary offerings is 8.86 and 6.18 percent, respectively. The differences in the mean first day excess returns (the level of underpricing) may lead to an initial conclusion that the market considers secondary offerings to be more risky than mixed offerings, and mixed offerings to be more risky than primary

TABLE 9.9 *Mean Offering Prices: Comparison with Secondary Offerings (NYSE)*

	Secondary offerings first day ($)	Difference with Primary offerings first day ($)	Difference with Mixed offerings first day ($)
Mean	18.06	−2.84	−0.48
Standard deviation	7.913		
Number of observations	7		
Degrees of freedom	6	7	7
t-value	6.039	−0.911	−0.154

Notes: n = number of observations.
For each group: degrees of freedom = $(n - 1)$

$$t\text{-value} = \frac{\bar{x}}{\sqrt{\{s^2/n\}}}$$

where x = average excess returns for the offerings; s = standard deviation of excess returns. For differences between groups: (Smith–Satterthwaite test)

$$df = \frac{\{(s_1^2/n_1) + (s_2^2/n_2)\}^2}{\{(s_1^2/n_1)^2/(n_1 - 1) + (s_2^2/n_2)^2/(n_2 - 1)\}}.$$

The degrees of freedom are rounded off to the next lowest whole number.

$$t\text{-value} = \frac{\bar{x}_1 - \bar{x}_2}{\sqrt{\{(s_1^2/n_1) + (s_2^2/n_2)\}}},$$

where x_1 = average excess returns for primary or mixed offerings; x_2 = average excess returns for secondary offerings; s_1 = standard deviation of excess returns for primary or mixed offerings; s_2 = standard deviation of excess returns for secondary offerings; n_1 = number of primary or mixed offerings; and n_2 = number of secondary offerings.
Level of significance: ****1 percent, ***2 percent, **5 percent, *10 percent.

offerings. However, the *t*-values show mixed support for this conjecture. For the total sample, the difference in the underpricing of mixed and primary offerings (2.97 percent) is significant only at the 10 percent level even though both mixed offerings are significantly underpriced at the 1 percent level (6.86 and 3.89 percent, respectively). The implication is that it may be advisable for promoters to consider separating the raising of funds for the firm through public offerings from the sale of their personal holdings in order to reduce the level of underpricing. For the NYSE firms, the differences in the underpricing of secondary and mixed offerings, and of secondary and primary offerings are only at the 20 percent level of significance. Further, the difference in the underpricing of mixed and primary offerings is insignificant. This result should not be considered as a major surprise since, on average, NYSE firms are not significantly underpriced. The interesting result is that the underpricing of secondary offerings of NYSE firms is 7.88 percent significant at the 10 percent level, and the underpricing of mixed offerings is 2.23 percent significant at the 5 percent level, while the primary offerings are not significantly underpriced (1.78 percent underpricing). In the case of OTC firms, the difference in the underpricing of mixed and primary offerings (2.68 percent) is not significant even though, here too, both mixed offerings are significantly underpriced at the 1 percent level (8.86 and 6.18 percent, respectively). Thus, investors into OTC firms do not appear to consider mixed offerings as being more risky than primary offerings. This underpricing behavior appears to be in contrast to the signalling behavior of CSIPOs where a higher promotor's retention of equity is required to convey the same value of the firm's equity in the case of mixed offerings compared to primary offerings (Prasad, 1990). It is also observed from the results of the study that each type of offering has a higher level of underpricing for OTC firms compared to NYSE firms. The OTC primary offerings are underpriced 6.18 percent compared to 1.78 percent for the NYSE firms. Similarly, the OTC mixed offerings are underpriced 8.86 percent compared to 2.23 percent for the NYSE firms. Thus, both mixed and primary offerings of OTC firms appear to be considered more risky than the corresponding offerings of the NYSE firms.

Overall, it would appear that if existing shareholders wish to harvest their investment it may be advisable for them to do so at the time the firm is going public to raise additional funds for expansion, etc. They may realize relatively less, due to the higher underpricing, if the firm goes public specifically for the purpose of harvesting. Both the firm and the selling shareholders are likely to benefit the most if the firm goes public with a pure primary offering with the shareholders harvesting in the after-market. Further, it appears that if firms and shareholders have a choice of going public with shares to be traded on the OTC or the NYSE, the latter option may be preferable as they are likely to face little or no underpricing.

For future research, further examination is required using larger samples specially for secondary offerings. Also the research could be extended using a one month period from the date of the offering since Brandi (1987) suggests that it may take four weeks or more for the IPO to reach market equilibrium. This study also suggests that the Prasad (1990) study could be extended to examine the impact of the trading system on the signalling behavior of CSIPOs as a whole, as well as for these three types of offerings.

Acknowledgement

The author wishes to thank the anonymous referees and the editor (Dilip Ghosh) for helpful comments and suggestions. The author also wishes to thank Bradley Ge for research assistance.

Notes

1. While IPOs are offered in the primary market (OTC) and subsequently traded in the secondary market (OTC, NYSE, AMEX, etc.), this study examines underpricing in the case of IPOs which are to be listed on the NASDAQ and for IPOs which are to be listed on the NYSE. For convenience, in this study, such IPOs are sometimes loosely referred to as OTC IPOs and NYSE IPOs, or as OTC offerings and NYSE offerings, or as OTC stocks and NYSE stocks; and the firms correspondingly as OTC firms and NYSE firms.
2. In this study, the terms OTC and NASDAQ are used interchangeably even though this is not strictly true.
3. The significance of the difference is tested using the Smith–Satterthwaite test which is appropriate in the case of smaller samples since the sample size for the mixed offerings is only 19 in this case.

References

AFFLECK-GRAVES, J., HEGDE, S. P., MILLER, R. E. and REILLY, F. K. (1993) The effect of the trading system on the underpricing of initial public offerings, *Financial Management*, 22, 99–108.

ALEXANDER, J. C. (1993) The lawsuit avoidance theory of why initial public offerings are underpriced, *UCLA Law Review*, 41, 17–73.

BARON, D. P. (1982) A model of the demand for investment bank advising and distribution services for new issue, *Journal of Finance*, 37, 955–976.

BARON, D. P. and HOLMSTROM, B. (1980) The investment bank contract for new issues under asymmetric information: delegation and the incentive problem, *Journal of Finance*, 35, 1115–1138.

BEATTY, R. P. and RITTER, J. R. (1986) Investment banking, reputation, and the underpricing of initial public offerings, *Journal of Financial Economics*, No. 15, 213–232.

BLOCK, S. and STANLEY, M. (1980) The financial characteristics and price movement patterns of companies approaching the unseasoned securities market in the late 1970s, *Financial Management*, 9, 30–36.

BOOTH, J. R. and SMITH II, R. L. (1986) Capital raising, underwriting and the certification hypothesis, *Journal of Financial Economics*, No. 15, 261–281.

BRANDI, J. T. (1985) Securities practitioners and blue sky laws: a survey of comments and a ranking of states by stringency of regulations, *The Journal of Corporation Law*, 10, 689–710.

BRANDI, J. T. (1987) Merit securities regulation, market efficiency, and new issue stock performance, *The Journal of Corporation Law*, 12, 699–712.

CHALK, A. J. and PEAVY, J. W. (1987) Initial public offerings: daily returns, offering types, and the price effect, *Financial Analysts Journal*, 43, 65–69.

DRAKE, P. D. and VETSUYPENS, M. R. (1993) IPO underpricing and insurance against legal liability, *Financial Management*, 22, 64–73.

IBBOTSON, R. G. (1975) Price performance of common stock new issues, *Journal of Financial Economics*, 2, 235–272.

IBBOTSON, R. G. and JAFFE, J. (1975) 'Hot issue' markets, *Journal of Finance*, 30, 1027–1042.

IBBOTSON, R. G., SINDELAR, J. L. and RITTER, J. R. (1988) Initial public offerings, *Journal of Applied Corporate Finance*, 1, 37–45.

LOGUE, D. (1973) On the pricing of unseasoned equity issues, 1965–69, *Journal of Financial and Quantitative Analysis*, 8, 91–103.

McDONALD, J. and FISHER, A. K. (1972) New issue stock price behavior, *Journal of Finance*, 27, 97–102.

MILLER, R. E. and REILLY, F. R. (1987) An examination of mispricing, returns, and uncertainty for initial public offerings, *Financial Management*, 16.

MUSCARELLA, C. J. and VETSUYPENS, M. R. (1989) A simple test of Baron's model of IPO pricing, *Journal of Financial Economics*, 24, 125–136.

NEUBERGER, B. M. and HAMMOND, C. T. (1974) A study of underwriters' experience with unseasoned new issues, *Journal of Financial and Quantitative Analysis*, 9, 165–177.

NEUBERGER, B. M. and LA CHAPELLE, C. A. (1983) Unseasoned new issue price performance on three tiers: 1975–80, *Financial Management*, 12, 23–28.

PRASAD, D. (1990) An asymmetric information approach to forecasting project quality. Ph.D. dissertation, University of Oklahoma.

PRASAD, D. (1994) Is underpricing greater for mixed offerings as compared to pure primary offerings in the OTC market?, *Journal of Financial and Strategic Decisions*, 7, 25–34.

PRASAD D. (1995) 'Underpricing' of IPOs on the OTC versus the NYSE. In GHOSH, D. K. and KHAKSARI, S. (eds.), *New Directions in Finance*, Routledge & Kegan Paul, London, pp. 170–182.

REILLY, F. K. (1977) New issues revisited, *Financial Management*, 6, 28–42.

REILLY, F. K. and HATFIELD, K. (1969) Investor experience with new stock issues, *Financial Analysts Journal*, 25, 73–78.

RITTER, J. (1984) The 'hot' issue market of 1980, *Journal of Business*, 57, 215–240.

ROCK, K. (1986) Why new issues are underpriced, *Journal of Financial Economics*, 15, 187–212.

SMITH JR, C. W. (1986) Investment banking and the capital acquisition process. *Journal of Financial Economics*, No. 15, 3–29.

TINIC, S. M. (1988) Anatomy of initial public offerings of common stock, *The Journal of Finance*, XLIII, 789–822.

10

Assessment of Investment Quality of Securities: A Fuzzy Set Theory Approach

RAMAKRISHNAN S. KOUNDINYA

Introduction

Assessment of investment quality of securities, the core function of a security analyst's profession, has undergone some dramatic changes since the proposition of market efficiency and the formulation of capital asset pricing models. The low point of the profession was the seeming inevitability of market efficiency and the consequent futility of active management of investments as a worthwhile effort. The profession has however survived, and thrives by reorienting its approaches to selectivity. New approaches blend fundamental analysis with the newer techniques and technologies. The underlying theme in the search for selectivity is the lack of precision in the financial information relevant to the determination of investment quality. Traditional models and methods of finance are mathematical and rigorous. However, they fail to cope with the lack of precision in the determination of performance of the firm and the future course of the economic environment. Furthermore, they fail to provide the means to incorporate vagueness in judgments both in regard to evaluation of information, and reasoning as to their implication to future performance.

The notion of fuzzy sets introduced by Zadeh (1965), and further advances in dealing with vagueness through the use of linguistic variables as vehicles to summarize information contained in the mass of data, offer a methodological framework for alternative approaches to the assessment of investment quality of securities. Facility to incorporate the imprecision in information and vagueness in the judgmental process enables a personalized approach to quality assessment.

The purpose of this chapter is to examine the problem of investment quality assessment, and propose a model based on the calculus of fuzzy sets for grouping securities into varying grades of investment quality.

Fuzzy Set Theory: A (Re)Statement

Zadeh in his seminal 1965 paper conceptualized the notion of fuzzy set as a "class of objects with a continuum of grades of membership. Such asset is characterized by a membership (characteristic) function that assigns each object a grade of membership varying between zero and one."

Mathematically, a fuzzy set K of the universe E is defined by

$$K = \{U_K(X)/E\}, \tag{1}$$

where $U_K(X)$ is the membership or compatibility function that associates with each member X in the universe E a number in the interval $[0, 1]$. This number represents the grade of compatibility of X with the fuzzy set K. The compatibility value is a measure of the degree of association rather than the probability of occurrence.

The notion of fuzzy set(s), and membership or compatibility functions are rooted in the uncertainties associated with information. According to Kangari and Boyer (1989), probability methods deal with uncertainty related to precise but incomplete information. Fuzzy set theory helps to deal with imprecise information. Often subjective reasoning of imprecise information is characterized by the usage of words; linguistic characterizations to express the degree of association, compliance, belonging, etc. of elements into criterion groups as determined by relevant features. In such situations fuzzy set theory enables translation of verbal assessments to a numerical scheme. Such a scheme while preserving the imprecision in the information, offers an ability for numerical manipulations of such information. For example, a security might be considered to be of investment grade if the firms are well managed, have a record of earnings growth, and low, financial risk. The calculus of fuzzy set theory enables transformation of the above reasoning on investment quality to a numerical scaling or scoring system.

The core of the analytical framework of fuzzy set theory is the membership or compatibility function. The membership or compatibility value of an element with the fuzzy set conveys the degree of 'belonging'. For example, average earnings' growth of 30 percent per year over the past five years may be viewed as having a compatibility value of 0.7 with the fuzzy set excellent record of earnings' growth, but growth rate of 5 percent would be viewed as having a compatibility value of only 0.05. The determination of the compatibility functions is subjective and based on expert knowledge of the problem or decision situation. Once membership or compatibility functions are determined subjectively or otherwise, the calculus of fuzzy sets based on several operations such as union, complementation, etc. provide the tools to manipulate fuzzy information in a decision context.

Assessment of Investment Quality

Benjamin Graham is a household name to the community of investment professionals in the North American continent. He is acclaimed by his admirers as the innovator of the art and science of security analysis. He was a consistent believer in the idea of investment quality as determined by fundamental analysis. Graham's last message to his friend Rea was "invest in financially sound companies whose earnings and dividends' yields are high" (see Rea (1987)). This message brings out clearly the fuzzy nature of the process of investment quality assessment. All through the investment literature fuzzy notions such as high return, low risk, low PE, high growth, well diversified, highly liquid, above the market, well managed, etc. are pervasive. Clearly, identifying relevant factors however vaguely perceived as related to investment quality and defining them as fuzzy sets would provide an alternative approach to the search for selectivity that reflect the process of human reasoning. The model proposed here will serve to illustrate the scope for personalizing a subjective and qualitative approach to grading investment quality.

Prior Studies

Publications in the relatively young area of fuzzy set theory have been explosive in the past decade. However, application of these ideas to financial decision-making is still in its infancy. Zebda (1984) applied these techniques to the study of cost variances and Gutierrez and Carmona (1988) discussed a fuzzy set approach to financial ratio analysis.

In the area of security analysis Hammerbacher and Yager (1981) modeled personalization of security selection to meet a preferred set of objectives. They solved the problem of choosing an investor specific security based on fuzzy financial criteria such as low price earnings ratio, short-term stability, etc. The proposed research is distinct from the above application in its focus and methodology. This paper develops a classification scheme for grouping securities graded by the order of investment quality. This procedure facilitates formation of portfolios of securities that are likely to show performances in the order of quality as determined by the investor. The computational procedure used by Chen-Ling and Pen-Guezhong (1987) is adopted.

Model Structure and Investment Grade Measure

The notion of investment quality is subjective and as such cannot be directly related to a base variable that is numerically defined. Investor could however define this as a linguistic variable, whose values are not numbers but words such as very high, high, etc. These in turn can be viewed as fuzzy restrictions in the values of financial performance variables considered as relevant base variables. For this preliminary model a simpler but more direct approach relating investment quality and financial performance is adopted. The investment quality measure is structured as a composite index dependent on indexes defined by the set of the three representative factors: growth potential, financial flexibility, and managerial record. The composite index value is evaluated as a weighted average of the values of these three indexes. A set of financial variables is selected as the set of base variables to define the fuzzy sets corresponding to the component indexes. Membership or compatibility functions for the fuzzy sets defined are chosen from a class of functions specified by

$$\text{membership/compatibility value} = 1/[(1 + a * (V - L)^2)], \quad (2)$$

where a determines the rate of decline of the membership value relative to the limiting value L. The function(s) is (are) evaluated for different values V of the financial performance variable(s) used as base variable(s). At $V = L$, membership equals one. The limiting value is either the maximum or minimum as appropriate among the observations (securities).

Variables and Membership/Compatibility Functions

Financial performance variables selected for this preliminary analysis are from the value line/screen plus database (1987). The variables used as base variables for grading growth potential are: current EPS, 12 month EPS percentage change, current PE ratio, estimated percentage change EPS—current fiscal year, 5-year EPS growth rate, projected EPS growth rate, projected 3–5-year price appreciation, and projected 3-year average return. Debt-to-capital ratio is used as base variable to grade financial flexibility. Managerial record is graded using base variables of return on net worth, price stability, and projected book value growth rate.

The membership/compatibility functions that relate the securities to the fuzzy sets corresponding to the above selected variables and membership charts are as follows.

1. Current EPS (R8). Membership value = $1/[(1 + 0.02 * (R8-30)^2)]$. The limiting value of \$30 per share is the maximum for a selected sample of securities. The choice of 0.02 for a reflects the author's subjective view that current EPS as a measure of growth potential is not significant unless the relative performance of the firm is very high. This is consistent with the view that significant current earnings will set firms apart in their ability to fund future growth internally compared to the multitude of firms generating moderate current EPS.

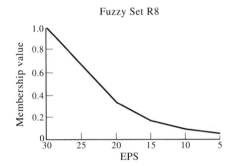

Fuzzy Set R8

2. Twelve-month EPS percent change (H7). Membership value = $1/[1 + 0.05 * (H7-240)^2]$. The limiting value of 12-month EPS percentage change in the sample was a high 240 percent. Even with a low rate of decline ($a = 0.05$) the membership value for most commonly occurring growth values drop significantly.

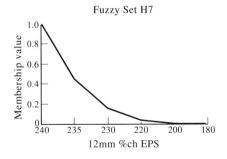

Fuzzy Set H7

3. Five-year EPS growth (H8). Membership value = $1/[1+ 0.01 * (H8-70)^2]$. The limiting value of 70 percent growth is about five times the average growth for the sample and the membership values drop quickly for most securities.

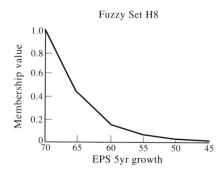

Fuzzy Set H8

4. Current PE ratio (M4). Membership value = $1/[1 + 0.5 * (M4-4)^2]$. The limiting value of four is the lowest PE ratio in the sample. Membership values decline for higher PE ratios. This membership function reflects the investor view that growth potential is higher for securities with lower PE ratios. This is consistent with the notion of possible undervaluation of stocks with low PE ratios.

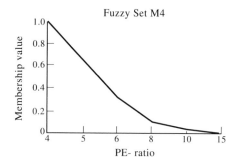

Fuzzy Set M4

5. Estimated percentage change EPS (FY) (G3). Membership value = $1/[1 + 0.1 * (G3-320)^2]$. The limiting value in the sample is a very high 320 percent. The rates of change in EPS for most securities are well below the limiting value. Corresponding compatibility values are also low.

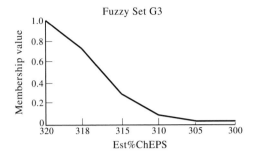

6. Projected EPS growth (G5). Membership value = $1/[1 + 0.05 \ (G5-40)^2]$. Values of projected EPS growth rates for most securities in the sample are lower than the maximum of 40 percent. However, there were a significant number of securities with 20 percent growth rates. The membership values in the sample exhibited a reasonable distribution.

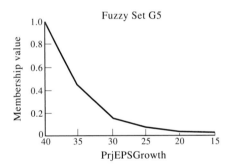

7. Projected 3–5-year principal appreciation (G4). Membership value = $1/[1 + 0.02 * (G4-275)^2]$. While the limiting value was as high as 275 percent, the sample had a perceptible distribution of membership values.

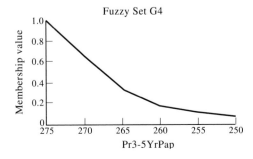

8. Projected 3–5-year return (G8). Membership value = $1/[1 + 0.10 * (G8-40)^2]$. The average projected return in the sample was 15 percent. But there were clusters of securities in ranges of 5–10 percent below the limiting value and around the mean value. The membership values reflected such clustering in the sample.

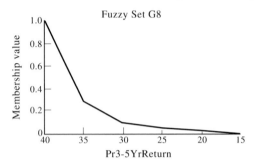

9. Debt-to-capital ratio (H5). Membership Value = $1/[1 + 0.01 *(H5)^2]$. Debt-to-capital ratio is the only measure used to assess financial flexibility index. A membership value of 1 is assigned to an all equity firm with declining compatibility values for increasing leverage.

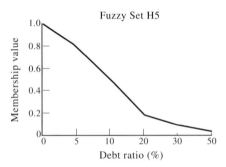

10. Return on net worth (H2). Membership value = $1/[1 + 0.02 * (H2-50)^2]$. Average return on net worth was 17 percent, with a median value of 16 percent. The membership values exhibited a wide dispersion in the sample.

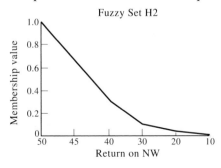

11. Price stability (R6). Membership value = $1/[1 + 0.01 * (R6-100)^2]$. The average index of price stability of 70 percent compared favorably with the maximum value of 100 percent. However, the values were clustered around different ranges in the sample. The membership values reflected such clustering.

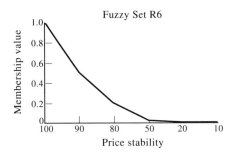

12. Projected book value growth(G7). Membership value = $1/[1 + 0.01 * (G7-30)^2]$. The limiting value of 30 percent growth is about three times the average value. The sample exhibited clusters of growth rates.

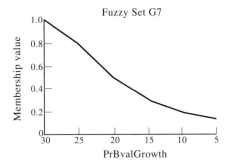

The class of membership functions discussed reflect a relatively conservative perception of investment quality grades. To qualify for high compatibility value, securities must perform well above the average on base variables. To be graded as an acceptable investment quality the firm's performance must be close to the maximum at least in one or two base variables. Membership functions with higher *a* values tend to weight higher performance much more than lower performance levels. As a class, these functions tend to cluster the average and below average performances together at the lower end of the membership scale. The above fuzzy quality grading process is more likely to have a lower risk of type 2 error of classifying a low-quality investment as acceptable, at the cost of a higher risk of type 1 error of assigning a low grade to a high-quality investment.

The membership values for the fuzzy indexes of growth potential, financial flexibility, and managerial record are obtained by averaging the membership values of respective base variables. The composite fuzzy index of investment quality is obtained by weighing the above three measures with weights 0.5, 0.3, and 0.2, respectively.

Analysis of Results

Fuzzy indices, and the composite fuzzy index of investment quality were computed for a sample of stocks that satisfied the conditions.

Current EPS > 0, 5 year book values growth > 0,
5-year EPS Growth > 0, PE ratio $\leq$ 20,
market value $\geq$ $500 million and no 'NA' values.

The selected sample included 476 stocks. The observations were sorted in the descending order of fuzzy index of investment quality for analysis. To analyze the pattern of classification for this preliminary study, the corresponding value line measures of timeliness and safety ranks were used. These range from one to five in descending order of quality. As a benchmark, securities that had the selected combinations of timeliness and safety ranks are assumed to be of higher investment quality. These combinations are (1,1), (1,2) (1,3), (2,1), (2,2), (2,3), (3,1), and (3,2).

In the total sample, 51 percent of the securities had one of the above combination rankings. Selected percentiles of the securities ordered (descending) by the fuzzy index of investment quality revealed the following pattern: The top 10 percent group had 66 percent of securities having one or the other of the combination rankings used as a benchmark. In the top 20 percent group, 72 percent were from the benchmark security combinations. In the top 30 percent group, 75 percent were from the benchmark group. Analysis of the bottom 10 percent showed that only 30 percent of it belonged to the benchmark group. These preliminary results indicate that the fuzzy classification procedure could logically order investment quality of securities.

Conclusions

This chapter discussed the application of fuzzy set theory to classify securities in the order of investment quality. An investor determined fuzzy index of membership in the investment quality group is used for the ranking of securities. Preliminary results indicate that the ordering of securities is logically consistent with the ordering by value line rank combinations. This approach enables an investor to personalize the process of investment quality assessment.

References

CHEN-LING and PEN-GUEZHONG (1987) A predictive method of teachers' structure in China's university (1985–2000), *Management Science,* 33, 738–749.

GUTIEREZ, I. and CARMONA, S. (1988) A fuzzy set approach to financial ratio analysis, *European Journal of Operations Research,* 36, 78–84.

HAMMERBACHER, M. I. and YAGER, R. R. (1981) The personalization of security selection: an application of fuzzy set theory, *Fuzzy Sets and Systems,* 5, 1–9.

KANGARI, R. and BOYER, L. T. (1989) Risk management by expert systems, *Project Management Journal,* XX, 40–48.

REA, B. J. (1987) Remembering Benjamin Graham—teacher and friend. In BERSTEIN, P. I. (ed.), *Security Selection and Active Portfolio Management,* Institutional Investor, New York.

VALUE LINE (1987) *Value/Screen Plus,* Value Line, Inc., New York.

ZADEH, L. A. (1965) Fuzzy sets, *Information and Control,* 8, 338–353.

ZEBDA, A. (1984) The investigation of cost variances: a fuzzy set theory approach, *Decision Sciences,* 15, 359–388.

11

Equity Markets with Frictions: An Examination

ABRAHAM MULUGETTA AND GILLES DUTEIL

Introduction

Many of the complexities that besiege securities trading emanate from the uncertainty of what price investors are going to receive when they place their orders in the market. The timing of order placement, the price of the order, the number of shares in the order, and the mechanism of the trading process all have bearing on whether an order will be executed or not and at what transaction price. The operational organization structure of an equity exchange influences the time interval of order placement and order execution, the supply of immediacy, and the level of transaction price uncertainty which in turn together affect the strategic decision of investors when they place orders.

The question of uncertainty in immediacy of security trading and transaction price is a result of market imperfection. In a perfect market, where there are no impediments to trade, problems of price discovery and immediacy of trade are nonexistent. However, the equity markets are full of frictions or impediments. Frictions in the form of bid–ask spreads, commissions, taxes, nontransparencies of orders, costs of information, circuit breakers, trade suspensions, costs of order placement and withdrawal, costs of order execution, and other hindrances abound the equity market making it a nonfrictionless one. The extent to which an exchange has alleviated these frictions through its organizational arrangements of equity trading process indicates the level of its attempt to increase the operational efficiency of the market.

In general, the major function of equity market is to efficiently allocate financial resources from ultimate savers to ultimate borrowers. In this function, it has to gain the trust of the market participants that not only will the primary, but also the secondary markets operate efficiently. To assure participants of its dedication to accomplish this mission, it has taken upon itself the necessary supportive functions of dissemination of quote and transaction prices and volumes information, implementation of priority rules of trading, surveillance of trading process, stabilization of prices, facilitation of small- and large-order transactions, among others. Therefore, to examine the operational efficiency of the market the following questions must be addressed: (1) How and why does a market operate inefficiently? (2) How do investors act toward the inefficiencies? (3) How might an exchange market be restructured and regulated to be responsive to competitive pressure while at the same time raising the level of its efficiency. Attempts to answer these questions will ultimately lead to the understanding of the function of security exchange through a market microstructure analysis.

Schwartz (1988) states that microstructure analysis focuses on the detail of the trading process whose major elements include the generation and dissemination of information, the arrival of orders, the rules, institutions and other design features of the market that determine how orders are transmitted into trades. Cohen *et al.* (1985) have also indicated that microstructure analysis considers the interplay among the market participants, trading mechanisms, and the dynamic behavior of security prices when trading is impeded by friction. The very consideration of existence of friction markedly differentiates studies that entertain microstructure analysis from those that adopt the frictionless market exposition. The recent availability of intraday data on quotes and transactions in terms of orders, prices and volumes of different size stocks and the disclosure of at least five (sometimes four) of the best quotes lends itself to a systematic study of equity market. In addition, the transparency of market information on trade reservation, suspension and remission and other reasons thereon on computer tapes and visualization of all these data in real time on computer screens give substance to the market data making it opportunistic to study equity market with due consideration to existing frictions. There are several approaches to investigate the operational efficiency of a security market that have evolved from market microstructure. The approach used in this study focuses on institutional description and examination as it relates to the French equity market.

The French equity market has been subjected to a number of major changes over the last ten years. The changes were a result of competitive pressure that emanated in foreign security markets, such as U.S. and U.K. as well an internal desire to modernize the process of security trading. The Act of May 1, 1975 that eliminated fixed commission on security trading in the United States became the fore-bearer of reform in several money market centers of the world. The 'Big Bang' of London in 1986 is a good example of the impact of the May Day Act of the United States. The major reforms since 1988 in the French security market that removed fixed commission, opened brokerage/or dealership services to domestic and foreign entities, among others, are also reactions to competitive stimuli as well as to technological transformation that infused the industry.

The stated mission of the Ministry of Economics and Finance, the Bank of France and the Commission des Operations de Bourse to make Paris the hub of the financial market center can be analyzed (demonstrated) by studying the evolution of the equity market. The change in the equity market, besides outmoding the central exchange—the Palais Des Bourse in Paris, has computerized order receipt, quotes, transactions disclosure, executions and settlements of trans-actions—making the French equity market the first paperless market.

Overall, the study is divided into four sections. The first part will give a bird's-eye view of the global financial market's changing environment. The second part will discuss reforms in the French equity market. The third section will explore the equity market based on real time observation from the trading room at ISEFI (CESIB) Marseille, France for about three months to understand the operational efficiency of the market *vis-à-vis* the stated regulations that govern it. The fourth section, based on apparent, less apparent and irregular operations in contrast to the rules of the market, will investigate some of the anomalies observed on the real time data feed and seek explanations through personal interviews. It is the belief of the researchers that the four-stage investigation will give a better understanding of the current status of the French equity market with policy implications both at home and abroad.

Changing Environment and Competitive Pressure

The last 20 years has witnessed a number of significant changes in national and international financial markets. The change from fixed to managed exchange rate systems, the oil price increases and the aftermath of recycling the surplus oil revenues, the cropping up of tax-haven financial centers, the debt burden of developing nations and the restructuring of these debts and interest, the proposed unification of Europe and the implication to European financial markets, the economic democratization of Eastern Europe and the required capital for the process as well as the North America Free Trade Agreement, have brought a host of regulatory metamorphoses. The changing process has accelerated the globalization of financial markets with a resultant competition among the industrialized nations to make their own financial markets the center of exchange.

As a result, the financial security markets have been subjected to a battery of regulations and deregulations to cope with the dynamism of global economic environments. Poser (1991) states that deregulation refers to the removal of restraints on competition within particular markets and between different markets and as such, it is better labeled as economic regulation rather than deregulation. The economic regulations or the removal of restraints that deal with financial securities can be classified into three areas: (1) rules requiring stockbrokers to charge their customers a minimum commission rate on securities transactions; (2) restrictions on access to the market, such as rules excluding certain types of persons or institutions from stock exchange membership; and (3) restrictions on the types of activities that may be performed by market participants. Whereas acts that are generally designed to protect investors, such as corporate information disclosure, competence and honesty of dealers and brokers, insider trading, etc. are referred to as regulations. These economic regulations and deregulations in the past ten years have been the hallmark of the French security market.

Institutional investors, such as pension funds, mutual funds, and insurance corporations, have become the major players in equity markets in the last 30 years, not only in the United States but in many developed countries as well. They often trade in large blocks of securities, increasing the level of activities in the market. While this is true, the charges of the brokerage firms that handle exchange trading remain fixed irrespective of volume and contrary to the benefits that are said to accrue from economy of scale. For example, if the commission is set for 100 shares, a person who buys 10,000 shares will pay 100 times the commission paid on 100 shares. The services given in security trading and the cost of handling the transaction by brokers do not proportionately increase with the size of the security traded. Thus, unless this fixed commission per certain number of shares or per certain dollar value is removed, it will constitute benefiting the broker at the expense of institutional investors. As such, it can be subjected to antitrust law. It is this setting that brought about the Security Act of May 1, 1975, in the United States that removed fixed commission on brokerage activities. It is also this Act that paved the way for exchange membership reform in the United States and acted as a catalyst for the 'Big Bang' of London and the monumental overhaul of the French security market.

While the change in the United States is driven by the intent to reduce the cost of commission charged to institutional investors, the cases of the U.K. and France are not in the same vein. The regulatory reforms in the U.K. were first and foremost implemented to recapture the decreasing securities trading in the London stock exchange and Eurobond markets, attract international banks and security firms and make London the center of international securities trading (Poser, 1991; Pagano and Roehl, 1990). The case in France is similarly motivated. It is mainly the force of international competition, particularly from that of London, which has attracted some of the highly valued French stocks from the Paris Bourse and the internal desire of the Bourse to excel in the competitive environment that propelled governmental institutions to take a sweeping action of reform.

Reforms in the French Security Market

In terms of size, the French equity market is the fourth largest in the world after New York, Tokyo, and London. Its size dramatically increased in the 1980s—the volume of shares traded between 1981 and 1988 increased more than eight times, while the value of shares traded on the official market increased by more than five times. There are several factors that contributed to the explosive growth of the market. Among them, the following factors are given prominence: (1) The governmental competitive posture, in particular, the 1983 Treasury Department deregulatory program of the stock exchange; (2) the privatization of the banking and other industries; (3) the relaxation of foreign exchange control; (4) the creation of future and option markets; and (5) the establishment of a competitive spirit of the regulatory institutions and members of the exchange.

The evolution in the French equity market makes it an intriguing one to research, for it epitomizes a combination of various characteristics of different types of equity market organizations. Currently it is continuous and batch, dealership and auction, fragmented and nonfragmented markets at the same time. As such, it embodies the general characteristics manifested by each market within the framework of the French financial market environment. It captures to a large extent their efficiencies and inefficiencies and since 1988, has been working on their peculiarities *vis-à-vis* its own environment to improve the soundness and operational effectiveness of the stock market.

The January 22, 1988 Act was a turning point for it overhauled the structure and the processes of security trading. Structure-wise, it created four institutions with different but complimentary tasks to assist in organizing, regulating, and overseeing functions of la Commission des Operations de Bourse (COB is similar to the Security Exchange Commission of the United States).

Before the change, one of the major players of the security markets were the members of the Bourse (about 100), known as agents de change, that had a history of about 200 years (originally started in 1807 by Napoleon). It was only through these agents that security trading was performed. For their services, the agents were paid a fixed regulated commission. Order handling (receipts and withdrawals), transactions, executions, and settlements were their exclusive domain. However, the agents were only a go-between for sellers and buyers. The growing French security market and the changes in foreign security markets made it clear that these agents needed to be well capitalized and active intermediaries to efficiently and effectively handle the different demands generated in the markets. It is the realization of the suspended demand and the implication if no reform is undertaken that brought about the 1987 and 1988 reforms. These reforms opened up the capital of the agents to outsiders—domestic and foreign enterprises. The newly incorporated members under the name of Sociétés de Bourse are permitted to handle not only brokerage service but also dealership, future and option tradings among others.

Operational Structure of the Paris Bourse

The Paris Bourse uses a centralized automated system for displaying and processing orders, the CAC system (Cotation Assistée en Continue). This system is inspired from the Toronto CATS system and was implemented in Paris in 1986. Since then, trading in all securities has been transferred from the trading floors of Palais Brongnard onto the CAC system.

The French equity market is segmented into three divisions. These divisions arose because of listing requirements and volume traded:

1. 'La Cote Officielle' which is divided into two categories. 'Le Règlement Mensuel' where the most active stocks, whose settlement is done once a month, are traded. 'Le Marché comptant' is where less active stocks are traded on immediate settlement basis. Stocks are designated to be traded in one of the above categories by Société des Bourses Françaises.
2. 'Le Second Marché'. This division was created in 1983 and was inspired by the London Unlisted Securities Market. The requirements for being listed on 'Second Marché' are less stringent than those needed for the 'Cote Officielle', allowing medium-sized companies access to financial market. But as only 10 percent of the

company's capital has to be put into public hands, the average number of shares outstanding in the market is rather low.

3. 'Le marché Hors-cote' is a nonregulated market where no special requirement is needed for trading. Some stocks are actively traded and others do not even have one trade per term. This market is not considered as an official exchange but rather like an over-the-counter market. This 'marché Hors-cote' is not well thought of by the public because it lacks an adequate supervisory body and minimum requirements, which lead it to become the theater of financial scandals, discouraging small individual investors.

Since December 2, 1991, trading categories were implemented in the CAC system, defining specific trading mechanisms for each of them.

Stocks are assigned to a category by Société des Bourses Françaises upon the following criteria.

Category 1. A firm needs to satisfy at least one of the three criteria to be traded in Category 1:

(a) more than 250,000FF volume per working day;
(b) more than 20 trades per working day;
(c) average market spread equal or lower than 1 percent.

Stocks in Category 1 are traded on a continuous market from 10:00 to 17:00. Trades are put on hold ('Réservation') for 15 minutes if price changes are higher than $\pm$ 10 percent compared to last closing price, then two more price variations of $\pm$ 5 percent (in the same trend) are allowed.*

Category 2. A firm needs to satisfy at least one of the three criteria to be traded in Category 2:

(a) more than 50,000FF volume per working day;
(b) more than five trades per working day;
(c) average market spread equal or lower than 2 percent.

Stocks in Category 2 are traded on a continuous market from 10:00 to 17:00. Trades are put on hold for 30 minutes if price changes are higher than $\pm$ 5 percent compared to last closing price, then two more price variations of $\pm$ 2.5 percent (in the same trend) are allowed.

Category 3. Equities that do not meet the requirements of Categories 1 and 2 are traded in Category 3. Stocks in Category 3 are traded in

*The 'Réservation' process will be explained further later.

batch auctions which are held twice a day at 11:30 and 16:00. 'Réservation' occurs if the price changes over 5 percent compared to the previous batch auction.

Even before being implemented, these Categories were published by the Bourse, through financial papers as Categories indirectly establishing the 'liquidity' of stocks. The announcement of the official categorization has therefore led to a *de facto* liquidity rating by investors, as predicted by Duteil (1991) and Duteil and Mulugetta (1992), with constant influence on stocks' activity, which are traded in Categories 2 and 3.

In order to 'reverse' this *de facto* rating, the Bourse authorities have, since May 1, 1993, changed the denomination of the trading Categories which have become:

• 'Continu A' for Category 1;
• 'Continu B' for Category 2;
• 'Fixing A' for Category 3, except for marché Hors-cote;
• 'Fixing B' a new category in which all stocks listed in marché Hors-cote are traded through a single fixing at 16:30.

Continuous Market

Every working day at 10:00, the market opens with a batch auction where all eligible orders are filled at a common market clearing price. From 09:00 to 10:00, the pre-opening phase, orders are accumulated in the order book without any transaction. At 10:00 sharp, the CAC system computes for each stock, regarding only limit-orders which have been in the book before the opening, the equilibrium price at which the greatest number of shares can be exchanged (see Fig. 11.1).

When the opening price is set by the system, all limit-orders to buy at a better price, and all limit-orders to sell at a lower price than the opening price, are fully executed in priority. In the meantime, the system transform orders 'au prix du marché' (market-orders) into limit-orders at the opening price and are ranked given strict time priority, then limit-orders at the opening price, entered into the system before the opening, are respectively ranked. All these orders will receive equal treatment and are attributed with one 'quotité' (a round lot of 5–100 shares for Règlement Mensuel) given the rank priority, and so on until no more share is available. A slight priority is given to market-orders as they are ranked before limit-orders; this is mainly true for stocks which are traded in very thin markets.

After the opening batch auction, the system turns automatically to a

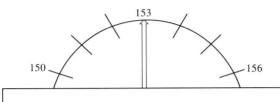

CUMUL	QUANTITÉ	PRIX	PRIX	QUANTITÉ	CUMUL
	400	marché	marché	400	
200	200	165	150	250	250
450	+250	155	151	+400	650
950	+500	154	152	+500	1150
1800=	+850	153	153	+600	=1700
2800	1000	152	154	1250	3000
5800	3000	151	155	1700	4700

FIGURE 11.1

continuous trading session to 17:00, where transactions are executed when matching orders are entered in the system. Continuous trading is available only for stocks classified into Categories 1 and 2 (Continu ·A and Continu B).

The CAC system accepts only two types of orders: market-orders and limit-orders.

Market-orders

Only the quantity to be traded is to be specified by these types of orders. Generally, market-orders are executed during the opening batch auction and if a broker is given market-orders by a client during a trade session, he enters it into the system to be executed at the next opening. But if specified by the client, a market-order can be submitted at any time to the market for immediate execution at the best price available. It should be noted that if the quantity asked (bid) by the market-order is higher than the quantity available to the best ask (bid) limit, then the remaining part of the order is automatically transformed into a limit-order at the transaction price. Thus, on Paris Bourse, a market-order does not walk up (or down) the order book. While this may be advantageous on one hand, it may be disadvantageous on the other for it entails partial execution risk to the investor. In order to circumvent this mechanism, a trader willing to immediately trade a large fixed number of shares can place a limit-order at a very favorable price, given that this price would not trigger the circuit breaker due to 'réservation' limit.

Limit-orders

Limit-orders should specify the quantity of shares to be bought or sold, a required price and a date for automatic withdrawal if not executed at submission (placement) of the order. By default, the order is good until cancelled ('à révocation'). Orders entered on the immediate settlement market are then valid until the end of the month, and those which are entered on Règlement Mensuel are valid until the next monthly settlement date.

Limit-orders cannot be submitted at arbitrary prices because there are minimum 'tick' sizes regarding the stock's price:

- 0.01FF for prices less than 5FF;
- 0.05FF for prices less than 100FF;
- 0.10FF for prices less than 500FF;
- 1.00FF for prices over than 500FF.

For orders at the same price limit, strict time priority for execution applies.

In practice, the order book can be observed on screens by any market participant, but the depth of the markets in which active stocks are traded may not be transparent on the TOPVAL screen display due to undisclosed orders (hidden-order). In general, traders who are involved in large trades are reluctant to reveal their positions to other participants. As a result, they may choose to display only a part of their limit-order. For example, a trader can enter a limit-order to sell 1000 shares of stock 'ABC' by 100 lots at 250FF. In this case, only 100 shares will appear on the ask side and when these 100 shares are filled, another 100 shares will be displayed on the screen, and so on until the order is fully executed. It should be noted that the hidden part of the order loses execution time priority to existing and incoming disclosed limit-orders at the same price.

Large orders can be pre-arranged between members at a price in between the current 'fourchette' (i.e. the best bid and ask prices) and can be executed through the market. This type of transaction is known as 'applications'.

Since 1989, brokers are entitled to trade for their own account so that brokers, banks, and authorized members can act as principals. When the market is open, these traders, based on mutual agreements (Operation de Contrepartie), can undertake 'application'. After closing, 'application' can be done at a price lying at the prevailing spread at closing time ± 1 percent.

On certain stocks, block trades are permitted at a price negotiated between the dealer and the client, even if this price is outside the current spread during the trading hours. In this case, the 'Société de

Bourse' is supposed to report the block trade to the market within five minutes and to fill all the limit-orders existing on the market whose prices are superior (inferior) for buy (sell) orders to the price at which the block was negotiated. But as there is no strict enforcement of this rule, it is not certain that all block trades fulfill these requirements.

Circuit Breakers

The market is monitored by 'Cellule de Surveillance', which may temporarily suspend trades on a stock if deemed necessary. Suspension happens when new market perturbating information on a security (take-over announcements, unexpected financial results, frauds, etc.) hits the market. At such moments, trades are put on hold (suspension) until further notice of trade remission. On the other hand, trades can be momentarily suspended if the price of a stock fluctuates over the allowable limits specified in each trading category. For example, in Category 1 (Continuous A), the allowable price variation before a stock is put on hold for 15 minutes is ± 10 percent then ± 5 percent (with a maximum of two more limits in the same upward or downward direction). Thus, on a basis of a closing price of 100FF, the price limitations as shown in Fig. 11.2 will kick in during temporary suspension.

These trading suspensions due to excessive price changes are known as 'réservations'. If a stock was 'réservé' all trading day long, then the reference price for the following day is the would have been price, at the maximum variation allowable.

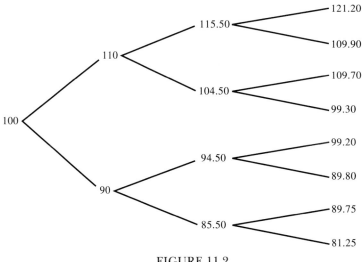

FIGURE 11.2

Explicit Costs to Members

A flat fee of 3.50FF is due each time a member enters or withdraws an order. Hidden parts of an order can be included in the same order for the same flat fee. Similarly, transactions are subject to a flat fee of 17.50FF each. It should be pointed out that each order filled into a trade is computed as one transaction; for example, if a member enters a market-order to buy 1000 shares of stock 'ABC' when the order book shows the following:

XXX ABC Cat.1

# Orders	Qty	Bid	Ask	Qty	No. of orders
2	500	100.00	100.60	1000	10
5	1000	100.10	100.70	1800	2
1	900	100.20	100.80	500	1
1	600	100.30	100.90	3000	1
8	1000	100.40	101.00	5000	3

then the market-order will be totally filled at 100.60FF, absorbing the 10 orders at the sell side. Thus, the transaction cost for the buy will be 10 (orders) $\times$ 17.5 = 175FF. Before January 1, 1993, this transaction fee (17.5FF times the number of orders to satisfy the quantity to be transacted) had to be paid regardless of the value of the transaction. For instance, in the above example, if on the ask side, the first row has only one order, the transaction fee would have been only 17.50FF. If, on the other hand, the number of orders in the first row for the 1000 shares were 100, the transaction fee would then have been 1750FF. This system penalizes small value stocks and therefore, starting January 1, 1993, maximum transaction fees are limited to 0.1 percent of the value of the transaction.

Some Anomalies or Market Irregularities Observed

Hidden-orders

Discussion of this part of the chapter strictly relies on observations from TOPVAL real time data feed. Orders can be placed and withdrawn at any time during the trading session and also within the first hour before the market opens. Understanding the motive of withdrawal of an order or placing of more orders can highlight the probable direction of price movement and the volume of hidden-orders.

Placing or withdrawing an order seems to be encouraged in the French equity market for it carries an explicit fixed cost of only 3.5FF irrespective of the value of the order. This placing or withdrawing of an order by traders before the opening hour of the market may act as a feeler of what the market can take in terms of volume and price. Indeed, it can be construed as a reconnaissance strategy with minimal cost before the actual action (trading) starts.

The TOPVAL feed gives on screen five of the best quotes of each security traded in terms of number of order, price, volume on both buy and sell sides during the pre-opening time (09:00–10:00). After 10:00, the screen also includes five of the latest transactions. The transparency of the pre-opening prices and volumes as well as the transactions at the opening lends itself to simultaneous comparison of prices and volumes. This comparison of prices and volumes can reveal the possible existence of hidden-orders. The example below depicts the batch opening price computation of the TOTAL company and the five best bid-and-ask quotes on December 2, 1992.

The prices shown below are in the best buy and the best sell sequences. From the illustrations, the best opening price that will clear most of the volume of orders is 236FF. On the transaction side— where the time of transaction is shown in hour, minute, and second— there was a transaction at 10:00 of 16,000 shares at 236FF per share. From the screen shown, the maximum number of shares at 236FF is 9800 on the buy side and 6200 shares on the sell side. Since exactly 16,000 shares were traded, there must have been a market of hidden-order of (16,000–9800) at least 6200 shares on the buy side and (16,000–6200) at least 9800 shares on the ask side. Hidden-order, in this instance, can be determined by using the illustration above and assuming the 650 shares on the bid side and the 1450 shares on the ask side, where prices are not indicated, as market-orders. If they are market-order, then 6200 shares on the buy side and 9800 on the sell side are hidden-orders. Thus, in this particular example (6200/9150), more than half on the buy side and (9800/4750) more than twice on the sell side were hidden-orders.

The example in Table 11.1, although it may not be representative of the level of hidden-orders at all times, may be indicative of the level of market nontransparency even in the highly proclaimed trans-parent security market.

Similarly, on the same date, EuroDisney opened at the expected opening price, but the volume of shares traded was 4800 and 200 shares higher on the bid and ask sides, respectively, at 58.50FF revealed in the quote shown in Table 11.2.

This again seems to be a hidden-order. On the same date, there was a discrepancy of 3825 shares between quote and traded volume for

TABLE 11.1 *Pre-opening Quotations and Opening Price Determination*

Pre-opening Quotation at 09:57

012027   Total Cat. B

	Bid			Ask	
3	650	OUV	OUV	1450	13
10	8650	236.0	236.0	4750	11
1	500	235.1	236.7	3000	1
1	500	235.0	237.0	1500	1
1	500	234.1	237.5	800	2

Opening Price Determination

Volume	Bid Price		Value	Price	Ask Volume		Value
650			OUV			OUV	1450
8650	×	236 =	2,041,400	236	×	4750 =	1,121,000
500	×	235.1 =	117,550	236.7	×	3000 =	710,100
500	×	235 =	117,500	237	×	1500 =	355,500
500	×	234 =	117,000	237.5	×	800 =	190,000
10150			2,393,450	10,050			2,376,600
	Average price bid				Average price ask		
	236.80FF				236.50FF		

Pre-opening Quotation at 09:58:18

012027   Total Cat. B

	Bid			Ask	
3	650	OUV	OUV	1450	13
11	9150	236.0	36.0	4750	11
1	500	235.2	236.7	3000	1
1	500	235.1	236.9	250	1
1	500	235.0	237.0	1500	1

Opening Trade at 10:00

012027   Total Cat. B

	Bid			Ask			Transaction	
1	500	235.2	236.0	1400	13		16K	236.0 10:00
1	500	235.1	236.7	3000	11			
1	500	235.0	236.9	250	1			
1	500	234.1	237.0	1500	1			
1	1000	234.0	237.5	800	1			

TABLE 11.2

Pre-opening Quotation at 10:00

012587   EuroDisney S.C.A.

Bid			Ask		
10	2900	OUV	OUV	200	2
18	16300	58.50	58.50	23600	10
3	800	58.40	58.90	100	1
1	4000	58.20	59.00	100	1
2	400	58.10	59.40	2500	1

Opening Trade at 10:01

012587   EuroDisney S.C.A.

Bid			Ask			Transaction		
3	800	58.40	58.50	600	1	24K	58.50	10:01
1	4000	58.20	58.90	100	1			
2	400	58.10	59.00	100	1			
9	3100	58.00	59.40	2500	1			
1	200	57.80	59.50	400	1			

the Peugeot Corporation. On December 4, 1992 at 10:00, there was a transaction of 16,000 shares of the Michelin Corporation at 182FF per share. The maximum number of shares that was revealed at 18FF were 13,500 on the bid and 5800 on the ask sides. What this again indicates is that there were hidden- or market-orders of 2500 shares on the bid side and 10,200 shares on the ask side.

Such examples are numerous during the observation months of October, November, and December, 1992, which may be indicative of the price volatility fear of traders. The Price of risky assets does not remain constant over time. Therefore, although the intent of hidden-order may be to minimize the volatility of price as a result of large order placement, still a trader will face price volatility as a result of passage of time (priority trading rule) inherent in hidden-orders. Yet the price volatility as a result of passage time in hidden-orders may be more than compensated for by a decrease in price volatility in a thin market where all the orders are not transparent.

Trading Over the Highest Price Limit and Trade Extension

Securities in Category 3, depending on their nature, are traded at 11:30 or 12:00 and 16:00 or 16:30. In general, trading of SITA, which is in Category 3, will occur at 11:30 and 16:00 given that the price change is not above or below 5 percent of the reference price at each session. SITA was traded on December 2, 1992 at 12:00 at 32FF per share. Therefore, the maximum price at which it should trade is 32 × 1.05 = 33.05FF. Interestingly, there were a number of trades at 16:30 (second session) at 35.00FF; 35FF is 5.9 percent higher than the limit price. This seems to violate the limit price rule. However, it should be pointed out that price limit is not applicable on derivative securities. Moreover, the number of SITA shares traded at this time was 1538. On the buy side, the most that could be traded was 1168 shares and on the sell side, 973 shares. In fact, the number of shares that can be crossed is limited by the lower number of shares that is available on either side. In this case, the 973 shares on the sell side became the determinant number unless there was a market-order or hidden-order.

It is interesting to observe that although trades in Category 3 are supposed to occur at two discrete times, 11:30 and 16:00, trade of securities in this category can occur between 11:30 and 12:00, not only at 11:30, and between 16:00 and 16:30, not only at 16:00. If a trader submits a quote one minute before the batch at 11:30 or 16:00, then the batch quote for that stock is moved to 10 minutes later trade and again if a trader submits a quote one minute before the ten minutes expires, then another ten minutes extension for the stock will be given. This process will continue up to 12:00 when the last transaction on the 11:30 will occur. But if one minute before 12:00 a quote is submitted, then the transaction has to wait until the second batch opening at 16:00.

Trade 'Réservation'

One of the anomalies which cannot be easily understood is the mechanism that set the circuit breaker into effect. The circuit breaker kicks in when a security quoted price rises or falls below a certain percentage of the reference price. However, during the three-month observation period (October, November, and December, 1992), the computation shown on the TOPVAL screen for setting the circuit breaker often does not match the actual price change that kicks in the circuit breaker. A trader who relies on the TOPVAL system alone can therefore be misled regarding the status of the activity of a security. The main reason for the confusion regarding the status of activity of a security that has been reserved is the reference price used for computation.

Technomed International opened for trade on October 29, 1992, with a reference price of 13.95FF. Technomed is classified in Category 2. Therefore, if the quoted price of Technomed increases by more than 5 percent from the reference price, then trade of this security will be reserved (suspended) for 30 minutes. After 30 minutes, if quoted prices are above 7.62 percent of the reference price, the circuit breaker will set in for another 30 minutes. Again, if after 30 minutes, the quoted price is above 10.32 percent of the original reference price, trade of this security will completely halt for the day. Surprisingly, there were eight different transactions of Technomed stock at 16.85FF. When 16.85FF is compared to the reference price of 13.95FF, it is higher by more than 20 percent, which contradicts the maximum allowable price increase of 10.32 percent for trade to halt.

Pre-opening reference price, as stated in the Bourse literature, is the last transaction price of the previous trading day. Yet the pre-opening price of Technomed on October 30 was 18.25FF rather than the last transaction price of 16.85FF of October 29. Through telephone interviews of the Surveillance Department of the Bourse, it was found that if trade for a particular stock is reserved and the quoted price increase was much higher than the maximum allowable price increase, then the highest quote at the close of the previous day will be used as a reference price and this quote will correspond to quotes in financial newspapers. The 18.50FF price seems to be set by taking into consideration that Technomed was reserved for most of the previous day and, if it had been traded, the maximum price at which its last transaction would have occurred would have been 18.50FF. Yet there appears that there is a degree of subjectivity involved in setting reference prices for suspended (reserved) stocks. It is not clear whether this 18.50FF best bid or ask was at the time of suspension, during suspension, or at the close of the trading day. Clear knowledge of this reference price determination may be an important consideration for traders in terms of timing of order placement and pricing quotes.

Even when reference prices on the TOPVAL screen correspond to quotes in financial newspapers on a stock, there still seems to be a violation of circuit breaker rules. For example, on November 5, 1992, SDR Picardi had a reference price of 27.20FF that exactly corresponded to financial newspaper quotes. However, in the first hour of trading, it was traded at 29.90FF, which was about 9.9 percent higher than the reference price without any suspension. Actually, there should have been two suspensions given. SDR Picardi belongs in Category 2.

Another irregularity observed that clearly requires close supervision by exchange officials are cases like Technomed. Technomed (TMI) stock had not been traded since October 29 at 11:57, up to November 3, at 18:00, because its quoted price had increased over and above the allowable maximum increase. During this period, its reference price was 18.25FF, but there were peculiar single orders to sell 300 shares at 50FF, 225 shares at 56FF, and 60 shares at 60FF. These single orders seems to be placed in the market by traders to intentionally create quote imbalances so that no trade on this particular stock would occur. Given that the cost of order placement and withdrawal is a minuscule 3.5FF, trade disruption by unscrupulous traders can make the market inefficient unless strong action is taken by the Bourse. As yet, there have been no publicly acknowledged actions on traders by the Bourse. During the three-month observation period, a large number of securities, in particular those classified in Category 3, had been, it looked, subjected to unscrupulous actions of some traders.

Conclusion

Equity markets are full of frictions or impediments. Frictions in the form of bid–ask spreads, commissions, taxes, nontransparencies of orders, costs of information, circuit breakers, trade suspensions, costs of order placement and withdrawal, costs of order execution, and other hindrances abound the equity market making it a nonfrictionless one. The extent to which an exchange has removed these frictions through its organizational arrangements of equity trading process indicates the level of its attempt to increase the operational efficiency of the market. The exchange has to gain the trust of market participants that both the primary and the secondary markets will operate efficiently. To assure participants of its dedication to accomplish this mission, the exchange has to take upon itself the necessary supportive functions of dissemination of quote and transaction prices and volumes information, implementation of priority rules of trading, surveillance of trading process, stabilization of prices, etc.

The French security market has been undergoing changes to increase its operational efficiency. The automation of the quote, transaction, execution, and settlement has made the French security market not only the first paperless market, but also one of the most efficient. The exchange officials' ever-readiness to make the market operationally efficient can be exemplified, among many others, by the recent change of security categorization, which heretofore might have been construed as official liquidity classification of security. The change in categorization suppressed any *de facto* official liquidity classification of security. In addition, the instant adjustment of reference prices on the TOPVAL screen, which previously would have taken at least a day, is another illustration of the commitment of the exchange to facilitate the ease of pricing quotes and timing of order placement. However, the exchange has to pay close attention to some traders' activities, such as placing a quote at a price—with clear intentions—to kick in the circuit breaker, thereby disrupting trade in security.

References

COHEN, J. C., MAIER, S., SCHWARTZ R. A. and WHITCOMB, D. K. (1985) *The Microstructure of Security Markets*, Prentice Hall.

DUTEIL, G. (1991) French equity markets: does liquidity exist? Working paper 91/10, Les Travaux du CETFI, Université d'Aix-Marseille III, June.

DUTEIL, G. and MULUGETTA, A. (1992) An analysis of equity markets of quotation systems. In GHOSH, D. K. (ed.), *The Changing Environment of International Financial Markets: Issues and Analysis*, Macmillan Press, London, Chapter 18.

PAGANO, M. and ROELL, A. (1990) Trading system in European stock exchanges: current performance and policy options. Discussion paper No. 75, L.S.E. Financial Market Group Discussion Paper Series.

PLUMMER, T. (1989) *Forecasting Financial Markets: The Truth Behind Technical Analysis*.

POSER, N. S. (1991) *International Security Regulation*, Little, Brown and Company, Boston, MA.

SCHWARTZ, R. A. (1988) *Equity Markets: Structure, Trading, and Performance*, Harper & Row.

SOCIÉTÉ DES BOURSES FRANÇAISES (1992). La Bourse de Paris: Organisation et Fonctionnement.

12

Using Real Options Analysis in Capital Budgeting: The Opportunity Cost of Excess Capacity

ROBYN MCLAUGHLIN AND ROBERT A. TAGGART, JR

The Opportunity Cost of Using Excess Capacity

A common problem in capital budgeting arises when a new project proposal calls for the use of existing, but currently idle, equipment or facilities. The issue is whether there is any opportunity cost to diverting these facilities to the new project. For example, the firm will incur an opportunity cost if diversion of capacity to the new project precludes its future use by other projects or causes production facilities to be replaced sooner than they otherwise would have been.[1] Although the new project may be worthwhile on a stand-alone basis, the firm should recognize that its adoption may impose externalities on existing projects. Any such effects should be measured and included in the calculation of the new project's net present value.

Methods for estimating this opportunity cost are available, but they focus exclusively on the firm's future investment and make very strong assumptions about the predictability of that investment. In doing so they fail to recognize the option elements of the problem, and in some circumstances this may result in seriously misleading estimates.[2] Our aim in this chapter is to analyze these option elements explicitly. We show that when uncertainty disappears the option elements become unimportant, and the true opportunity cost collapses to the solution given by existing methods. However, as uncertainty grows, these option elements come to dominate the problem, and existing methods can substantially underestimate or overestimate the true opportunity cost.

The essence of our option framework is as follows: Capacity in place gives the firm an option to produce. Thus, if a firm diverts capacity from Product A to Product B, it forgoes the option to produce A immediately, but it acquires an option to replace the diverted capacity. The true opportunity cost of using the excess capacity is the change in value of the firm's options. By focusing on the state-contingent nature of optimal future decisions, this framework recognizes that the opportunity cost is not necessarily equal to the present value of specific investment or production decisions.

The next section describes the problem and presents the real options analysis in general terms. Existing approaches to measuring opportunity cost are then contrasted with the options approach. The third section in this chapter presents a specific numerical example in which the cost of diverting excess capacity is calculated for different values of variables such as investment cost, the interest rate, product price uncertainty, and unit production cost. We show that the true opportunity cost can vary widely under these conditions in ways that are not captured by existing approaches. The final section briefly summarizes our results and offers conclusions.

The Opportunity Cost of Diverting Capacity

The Problem

Consider a firm with a unit of capacity, such as a plant, which is currently devoted to the production of Product A. Each year, the firm observes the prevailing market price for A, compares that with its unit operating cost, and produces A if it is profitable to do so. The existing plant has a remaining life of N years. By investing E, the firm can build a new plant with an economic life of L years, which will become operational immediately.[3]

Suppose that the current price of A is such that the firm has just decided not to produce this year and thus to let the plant stand as excess capacity until at least next year. Suppose further that a new opportunity suddenly arises: by investing in some renovations, the firm could refit the plant to produce an alternative product, B. For simplicity, we assume that once the renovation is complete, it is prohibitively expensive to switch back to the production of A and that the salvage value of the plant is zero throughout its useful life.[4]

On a stand-alone basis, the NPV of producing B is simply the present value of profits from B for the N years remaining in the life of the plant, minus the cost of renovating the plant, plus any change in value of the options associated with this first unit of B-capacity.[5]

However, this stand-alone NPV is reduced by the opportunity cost of diverting the plant away from Product A.

The Real Options Framework

Following Pindyck (1988), we can view plants as being installed sequentially in order of decreasing value to the firm.[6] This allows us to focus on the plant that currently produces A. Since we are only concerned with measuring the opportunity cost of diverting the marginal unit of capacity, we can ignore the effect on firm value of any other units.[7]

When a firm installs a plant, it acquires two types of options: a strip of production options, one for each year of the plant's useful life, and a replacement option, which is equivalent to a future investment option. The production options are European; for example, the option to produce in year 3 matures in that year when the firm learns the price of A. The exercise price of each production option is the unit operating cost times the level of production. The firm will exercise its production option in year 3 if that year's unit price of A exceeds unit cost. In addition to its production options, a firm that has a plant in place has the option to replace that plant at the end of its useful life.[8] The replacement option, which is a future investment option, is American since it can be exercised either at that time or later.

If the firm does not have a plant in place in a given year, it has no production options, but it does have an immediate investment option. This option is American, since it can be exercised either now or later, and the exercise price is E, the cost of building a new plant. The investment option is a compound option, or an option on options. If the firm exercises its investment option, building a new plant, it acquires in turn the strip of production options that allow it to choose whether or not to produce in each year of the plant's life. By building a plant, the firm also acquires an American option to replace that plant, beginning L years after the plant is built.

In this framework, the opportunity cost of diverting excess capacity to a new product is the change in the value of the firm's options which is caused by diverting the capacity. If the firm does not divert capacity, it has the option to produce A any year between now and the end of the plant's useful life. If the plant will wear out in year N, the firm also has the option to replace it in year N (or later). On the other hand, if the firm does divert capacity, it acquires an option to invest immediately in a new plant to produce A. By diverting capacity now, the firm loses its options to produce A and its option to replace a unit of A-capacity in year N. However, it gains the option to acquire the unit of A-capacity immediately.[9] Thus the opportunity cost, C, of diverting capacity from A to B can be represented as

$$C = \sum_{t=0}^{N} P_t + I_N - I_0,$$ (1)

where P_t is the current value of the option to produce A in year t, and I_0 and I_N are the current values of the options to invest in a unit of A-capacity effective immediately and effective in year N, respectively.

Existing Approaches to Opportunity Cost Measurement

The most plausible existing method for calculating this opportunity cost calls for charging the new project with the equivalent annual cost (EAC) of a plant for each year that diversion of capacity is estimated to cause a capacity shortage for the original product.[10] With a plant life of L years, for example, the EAC is the annual payment on an L-year annuity whose present value is equal to the plant's initial investment outlay. If diverting capacity to B is expected to cause a shortage of A-capacity beginning in year S, opportunity cost under this method is the present value of these EAC charges from year S to year $N - 1$:[11]

$$C = \sum_{t=S}^{N-1} \frac{\text{EAC}}{(1+r)^t}.$$ (2)

One could interpret EAC as the annual rental payment a lessor would need to charge in order to recoup the initial cost of the plant plus interest over the plant's useful life. If a rental market actually existed, a company that diverted its plant to Product B could restore the lost capacity to produce A by renting a similar plant. It would then face the decision of whether or not to build a replacement plant in year N, just as it would have if the capacity had never been diverted.

An alternative interpretation is that charging the EAC for $(N - S)$ years is equivalent to moving up not only the first plant replacement from year N to year S, but all future replacement cycles as well.[12] Thus, the opportunity cost is the present value of moving up the plant investment from year N to year S, again from year $N + L$ to year $S + L$, again from year $N + 2L$ to year $S + 2L$, etc.

This latter interpretation highlights the fact that the EAC method relies on stringent assumptions about the timing of future investment expenditures. By assuming that all future investment will take place with certainty at particular dates, it ignores the option component of the investment decision. In the next section, we show that these option components become unimportant only when uncertainty disappears and the timing of future investments can be accurately predicted today. Even if the EAC method is implemented with a risk-adjusted discount rate, it cannot capture this option component, since risk-adjusted discounting at a constant rate is ill-equipped to handle situations in which decisions will be postponed until more uncertainty is resolved.[13] In contrast, an option framework recognizes that the investment options need not be exercised at the first possible moment.

Valuation of the Firm's Production and Investment Options

In this section, we construct examples in which the firm's production and investment options can be valued explicitly. The economic environment assumed in these examples is intentionally simplified and may not capture all the features of an actual decision-making situation. Nevertheless, the examples do serve to illustrate the basic determinants of the opportunity cost of using excess capacity. In the next subsection, we illustrate our solution technique with two simplified, one-cycle examples. Results from more general examples are discussed in the subsequent subsection.

Examples With Only One Investment Cycle

The economic horizon ends when the existing plant wears out. If the economic horizon ends in year N, the replacement option for the existing plant, I_N, is worthless. In that case, the opportunity cost of diverting capacity can be illustrated with a standard option diagram, as shown in Fig. 12.1. V represents the value of the options to produce A between now and year N. If the firm diverts capacity to B, it obtains an option, I, to invest in A-capacity at a cost E. Since the economic horizon is too short to allow any replacement decisions, I is simply a call option on V with exercise price E, and, from equation (1), the opportunity cost of diverting capacity is equal to $V - I$.

Figure 12.1 illustrates two different upper bounds on the opportunity cost. First, the value of I is at least $V - E$, so the opportunity cost is at most E. This is also true in more general cases to which the standard diagram does not apply, because no matter how valuable the forgone production options are, the firm could always replace them immediately by investing amount E. After that, it could make all future decisions as it would have done anyway. Figure 12.1 also indicates that V is an upper bound on the opportunity cost, since the value of the investment option is always nonnegative. Even in more general settings, the opportunity cost can never exceed the value of the lost production options, since the firm can always postpone any investment until it would have occurred anyway.

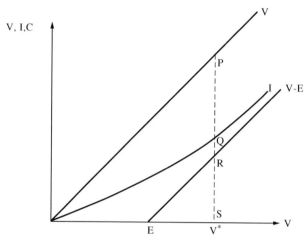

FIGURE 12.1 *Opportunity Cost Measurement When the Economic Horizon* = N *(The Remaining Life of the Existing Plant)*

V = value of production options from now to time N. E = cost of building a new plant. I = value of option to invest in a new plant immediately (I is a call option on V with exercise price E). C = opportunity cost of using excess capacity = $V - I$. Given $V = V^*$, distance $RS = V^* - E$, distance $PR = E$, distance $PQ = I$.

Figure 12.1 also illustrates the circumstances in which either of the two upper limits is likely to be binding. As V grows large, the firm becomes more likely to invest immediately to restore its lost production options, and the opportunity cost approaches E. For this special case in which the economic horizon ends in year N, this is analogous to the EAC solution. That is because the plant would never need to be replaced if capacity were not diverted, so the opportunity cost is the value of any additional investment expenditures the firm makes if it does divert capacity. When V is small, on the other hand, the firm is unlikely to invest, preferring instead to simply forgo the production options.

The economic horizon coincides with the useful life of a new plant. In our second simplified example we assume that a new plant has a useful life of six years, and that the economic horizon also ends six years from now. Since a new plant becomes operational immediately (i.e. in year 0), the product price revealed in year 5 is the last one before the horizon date. The plant's capacity is 1 million units of A with a unit operating cost of $10.5.[14] The current price of Product A is $10 and in each future year this price will move up (down) by a multiple of

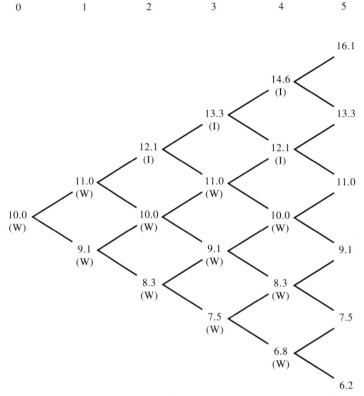

0	1	2	3	4	5

FIGURE 12.2 *Tree of Possible Product Prices with a Six-year Horizon*
At each node the optimal investment decision for a firm that reaches that node
without a plant already in place for the next period is shown in parentheses
below the price. The optimal decision is to either invest (I) or wait (W).

1.10 (1/1.10). This gives rise to the 'tree' of possible future prices
illustrated in Fig. 12.2. We assume that the 'risk-neutral probability'
of either a price increase or decrease in a given year is equal to 0.5.[15]
    The current plant will wear out after four years ($N = 4$), and a new
plant with a useful life of six years can be built then, or at any later
date until the end of the horizon, for an investment expenditure of $3
million ($E = \$3$ million). The riskless interest rate, r, is 5 percent per
year. For this one-cycle example, all activity ceases at the end of six
years, so any plants built after the current year will cease production
before their useful lives are finished.
    If a firm has capacity in place, it will exercise its production option
in any given year if the price of A exceeds $10.5, the unit operating

cost. The current value of that year's production option is simply the present value of its 'expected' cash flow, where state-contingent cash flows incorporate the optimal exercise decision and expected values are computed using the risk-neutral probabilities. Since the current price of A is $10, for example, year 0's production option is worthless, but the current value of year 1's production option is given by

$$P_1 = \frac{0.5(11 - 10.5)(1 \text{ million}) + 0.5(0)}{1.05} = \$0.238 \text{ million}. \qquad (3)$$

Note that the production option will be exercised if the price moves up, but not if the price moves down. Similarly, the value of year 2's production option is

$$P_2 = \frac{(0.5)^2(12.1 - 10.5)(1 \text{ million}) + 2(0.5)(0.5)(0) + (0.5)^2(0)}{(1.05)^2} = \$0.363 \text{ million}.$$

$$(4)$$

Valuing the investment options is more complex, since two questions must be answered. The first is whether investing in a plant at any given time yields a positive NPV. Because of the short economic horizon, any plant built now or in the future in this example will not be replaced, so the first question can be answered by subtracting the $3 million cost of the plant from the value of the production options gained by building it. Valuing the production options for years 0–5 with the risk-neutral probabilities as described above, the NPV of investing in a new plant immediately is $–0.788 million.[16] Thus, in this example, it will not be worthwhile for the firm to invest immediately.

Even if the NPV of investing immediately were positive, however, the firm would still have to consider the second question, raised by McDonald and Siegel (1986), which is whether it is better to wait before investing. The value of waiting is equal to the 'expected' present value of waiting until year 1, observing the product price at that time and then following the optimal investment strategy contingent on that price. By waiting, the firm forgoes the production option in year 0, but it also gains information about the future price of A. This information is valuable, because it enables the firm to avoid investing in capacity in situations where future production is unlikely to be profitable.

The optimal strategy at each price node, which consists of either investing (I) or waiting (W) further, is in turn found by working backward through the price tree from the economic horizon to that node, evaluating all future production options as of the time of that node, and then comparing the net present values of investing at that time versus the discounted expected value of waiting one more year. The optimal strategy for a firm that reaches a given node without a unit of capacity already in place for the next period is shown in parentheses below the relevant price in Fig. 12.2. In the case at hand, the optimal strategy is to wait in year 0, wait again in year 1, and then invest in year 2 only if the price is $12.1. In year 1, the NPV of investing if the price is $11 is $1.112 million, but it is even more profitable ($1.694 million) to wait another year, because the firm can then avoid committing capital until there is a greater likelihood that the future path of prices will be favorable.

The opportunity cost of diverting the plant to the production of B is given by equation (1) as

$$C = \sum_{t=0}^{3} P_t + I_4 - I_0. \tag{5}$$

Using the valuation technique described above, the sum of the forgone production options is 1.066, the current value of the option to invest in year 4 is 0.301, and the value of the option to invest immediately or later is worth 0.816, so the opportunity cost of diverting capacity is $.551 million.

Note that the opportunity cost measure given by equation (5) is substantially below either of the two lower bounds described in in Fig. 12.1. It is less than E (which equals three in this case), because the firm would not choose to replace the diverted capacity immediately, and even when it does, it saves the replacement expenditure that might otherwise have been made in year 4. Likewise, the true opportunity cost is less than the sum of the forgone production options (1.066 in this case), because, if the path of prices is sufficiently favorable, the firm will find it economical to invest in year 2 and recover some of these lost options.

The EAC method is not applicable in this example, since it is predicated on an infinite economic horizon. However, the difference in present value of investment outlays, depending on whether capacity is diverted or not, would represent a single-replacement-cycle analogue to the EAC method. In the example at hand, the firm would never replace the diverted capacity immediately, since the nearest production option is out of the money. If the price of A rises, however, there is a state of nature in year 1 in which the firm would want to produce A. Thus, we could calculate the opportunity cost of diverting capacity as the present value of moving the $3 million investment up from year 4 to year 1, or $C = 3[(1/1.05) - (1/1.05)^4] = \$0.389$ million. This technique underestimates the true opportunity cost for this example, because it assumes that future replacement expenditures are certain, rather than state-contingent. In particular, it assumes that the firm would necessarily replace the existing plant in year 4, whereas in fact this replacement is highly uncertain.

Results from the General Example

In general, the opportunity cost measure produced by the real options approach will vary with all of the standard determinants of option values: the exercise prices of the production and investment options, the interest rate, the degree of uncertainty in product prices, and the time periods over which the options can be exercised. This in turn can produce wide variations in opportunity cost both in absolute terms and relative to the measures provided by the EAC technique.

To get some idea of the sensitivity of the true opportunity cost to variations in its underlying determinants, we performed a series of simulations. For the most part, our base case assumes the same parameter values as in the example above: a unit operating cost of $10.5, and a plant production capacity of one million units of A per year; a time-to-replacement for the existing plant of two years; an investment cost of $3 million, and a useful plant life of six years. We did, however, assume an economic horizon of 50 years to get a better idea of the effect of a whole sequence of future replacement decisions. In an attempt to represent the effect of uncertainty less crudely than in the example above, we also assumed that product price follows a lognormal process with a mean of zero and a standard deviation of 10 percent per year. To better approximate this distribution, we estimated all option values with a grid consisting of 10 steps per year.[17] As a result of these changes, the results in the simulations are of the same order of magnitude, but not strictly comparable with the results given earlier.

There are some factors, such as the cost of investment and the interest rate, that affect opportunity cost as measured by either the real options or the EAC methods, but they do so in different ways. Moreover, since the EAC method focuses entirely on investment expenditures, there are several additional factors that have a significant impact on the valuation of options but do not enter into the calculation of the EAC (e.g. output price, standard deviation of output price and production cost).

Factors affecting both option and EAC estimates of opportunity cost. Figure 12.3 shows how opportunity cost varies with the cost of building a new plant. If the investment cost is zero, the diverted capacity is replaced costlessly and the opportunity cost of diverting capacity is zero for both the real options method and the EAC

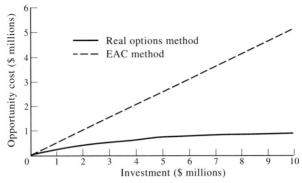

FIGURE 12.3 *Investment Cost and the Opportunity Cost of Diverting Capacity*

method. For both methods, the opportunity cost rises with the cost of a new plant, but it does so much more gradually under the options method. As investment cost increases, the firm becomes less and less likely to exercise its investment option before year 4 and thus changes in investment cost become less significant. Since the firm can always simply choose not to replace the capacity to produce A, the value of the lost production options represents an upper bound on the opportunity cost. The EAC method however, assumes that the firm always invests at the earliest opportunity, whether or not that is the best action for the firm and whatever the cost of building a plant. Thus, the EAC estimate increases at a constant rate with the cost of investment and quickly overstates the true opportunity cost.[18]

The effects of changes in the riskless rate of interest are shown in Fig. 12.4. The opportunity cost calculated using the options method

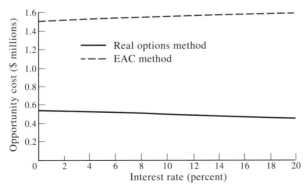

FIGURE 12.4 *Riskless Interest Rate and the Opportunity Cost of Diverting Capacity*

decreases slightly as the interest rate increases, but it is relatively insensitive to changes in the rate. The cost calculated using the EAC method increases with the riskless rate and always overestimates the true opportunity cost. Under the EAC method, increasing the interest rate increases the cost of moving forward the sequence of replacement investments. Under the real options method, by contrast, an increase in the interest rate also reduces the present value of any future production profits. Although it may be more expensive to move the sequence of investments forward, it may also be less compelling to do so.

Figure 12.5 shows the relationship between opportunity cost and time-to-replacement for two different plant lives, six and ten years. In general, the longer the time to initial replacement, the higher the opportunity cost, because the firm is giving up a longer strip of production options when it diverts capacity. For a given time to initial replacement, though, the opportunity cost is lower the longer the useful life of a newly-built plant. This is because the same initial investment buys more production options, so the firm is more likely to invest. Costs estimated with the EAC method also increase with the time-to-replacement since there are more periods to the annuity. Again, the method overstates the true value of the opportunity cost because it ignores the option components of the problem.

Factors that affect option but not EAC estimates of opportunity cost. Figure 12.6 shows what happens to the opportunity cost of using excess capacity when all other parameters are as in our base case, but the standard deviation of the price process (that is, the size of the yearly up and down moves) is allowed to vary. When the yearly variation in price is very small, the opportunity cost goes to zero. This is because

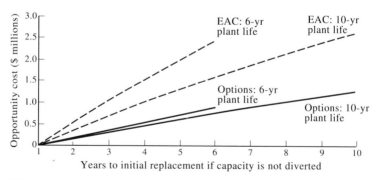

FIGURE 12.5 *Time to Initial Replacement, Plant Life and the Opportunity Cost of Diverting Capacity*

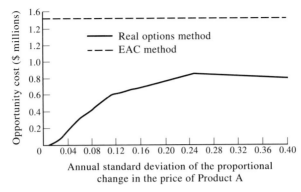

FIGURE 12.6 *Standard Deviation of Product Price and the Opportunity Cost of Diverting Capacity for Production Cost = 10.5*

the production options are out of the money at the start, and there is insufficient price variation for them to be in the money any time in the next four years. The opportunity cost then rises as price variability rises, because this increases the value of both the production and investment options. However, I_0, the value of the option to invest immediately, is more sensitive to changes in standard deviation than I_4, the value of the option to invest beginning in year 4. At high standard deviation levels, as Fig. 12.6 illustrates, increases in I_0 can dominate the increases in I_4 and in the value of the production options, and the opportunity cost can turn down.

Since the initial production option is out of the money in our base-case example, the option and EAC measures of opportunity cost do not coincide, even when uncertainty disappears. If the initial production option were in the money, however, and the standard deviation of the price process were zero, a firm that diverted capacity would always want to invest immediately in order to capture all of the valuable options to produce A. It would thus move up the first replacement investment from year 4 to year 0, and it would move up all future replacements as well. If the economic horizon were infinite, then the option and EAC methods should produce identical opportunity cost measures. This is illustrated approximately in Fig. 12.7, in which all other base-case parameters are kept the same but the unit operating cost is reduced to six, putting the initial production option into the money. At low standard deviations, the firm is virtually certain to invest in year 0 if capacity is diverted versus year 4 if it is not, in year 6 if capacity is diverted versus year 10 if it is not, etc. Thus the option calculation nearly coincides with the EAC calculation.[19] As the standard deviation increases, however, the true opportunity cost

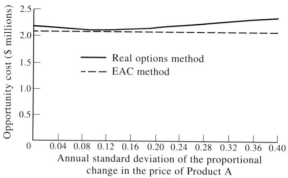

FIGURE 12.7 *Standard Deviation of Product Price and the Opportunity Cost of Diverting Capacity for Production Cost = 6*

rises above the EAC measure. This is because, while the firm might still invest in year 0 when it diverts capacity, there is a greater likelihood that it would choose not to replace the capacity in year 4 had it not diverted in the first place.

Figure 12.8 shows the variation in opportunity cost for different levels of unit production cost. At low production costs, such that the initial production option is deep in the money, the options calculation coincides with the EAC calculation, except for the small discrepancy caused by the finite horizon. As production cost increases initially from these levels, the true opportunity cost rises above the EAC. As in Fig. 12.7, this is because the firm will still invest in year 0 if it diverts capacity, but it becomes increasingly likely not to invest in year 4 if it does not divert capacity now. For higher levels of production cost, the firm no longer invests immediately if it diverts capacity, and the opportunity cost turns down, sharply at first and then more gradually. The EAC measure, by contrast, makes a single, downward jump when production cost reaches 10. Beyond that level, production in year 0 is no longer profitable, so the EAC is charged only in years 1–3, rather than 0–3. However, the EAC measure does not reflect the fact that, as unit cost reaches high levels, neither investment nor production are likely to occur in the future, so that the true opportunity cost becomes negligible.

Finally, the effect of lengthening the economic horizon is shown in Fig. 12.9. If the horizon is only one year, the opportunity cost is zero, because the first production option is worthless, and if the firm diverts capacity it loses nothing. As the horizon lengthens, the opportunity cost initially rises, but then begins to ratchet up and down. This is because the life of the last plant built may be prematurely terminated, and the degree of premature termination

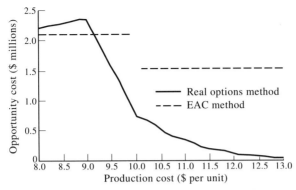

FIGURE 12.8 *Production Cost and the Opportunity Cost of Diverting Capacity*

differs under the diversion strategy or the alternative strategy with the length of the horizon. However, as the economic horizon becomes very long, this ratchet effect is dampened, and the opportunity cost converges to a value of approximately $0.526 million. While the true opportunity cost varies somewhat for different horizons here, the EAC technique always produces an overestimate, because it does not account for the uncertainty inherent in the firm's future production and investment decisions.

It is clear from these examples that the true opportunity cost of diverting excess capacity to another use can vary widely, even in the context of a simplified economic environment. What general statements can be made, then, that might serve as a guide to managerial decision-making? First, there are a number of plausible circumstances in which there will be no opportunity cost at all. This occurs either

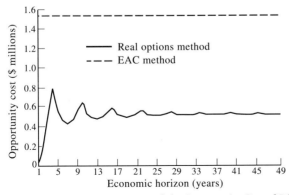

FIGURE 12.9 *Economic Horizon and the Opportunity Cost of Diverting Capacity*

when the production options the firm sacrifices by diverting capacity have little value or when they can be cheaply replaced. Second, as shown above, two upper bounds on the opportunity cost can be identified in any situation. The first is the cost of replacing the diverted capacity immediately, and the second is the value of the forgone production options. It is particularly important to recognize both of these upper bounds, since one of them may be considerably different from the other. In all of the examples above, the first upper bound, the cost of immediately replacing the diverted capacity (plant cost is $3 million in our example), is a gross overestimate of the true opportunity cost. The decision-maker would be better advised in such cases to try to estimate the value of the lost production options.

Summary and Conclusions

Existing methods for estimating the opportunity cost of diverting a unit of excess capacity to some other use focus on the cost of replacing that unit. However, these approaches ignore the option elements of the problem, and as a result they may produce estimates that are seriously distorted. By contrast, a real options perspective includes changes in the values of both production and investment options that are affected by diverting capacity. In actual practice, it may be difficult to precisely estimate the value of all of the production and investment options in equation (1). Nevertheless, the analysis above can help to identify situations in which the true opportunity cost is likely to be high or low, and it can alert the decision-maker to conditions under which existing measurement techniques may give misleading results.

Acknowledgements

We are grateful to Alan J. Daskin, Timothy Mech, Nalin Kulatilaka, Alexandros Prezas and Hassan Tehranian for helpful comments and suggestions on an earlier draft.

This chapter appeared originally in *Financial Management*, Summer 1992.

Notes

1. An example occurs in the classic 'Super Project' case in Butters *et al.* (1987), in which a General Foods Corporation proposal for a new instant dessert product, 'Super', entails the use of facilities that were previously installed for the existing product, Jell-O. Company managers in the case argue over whether the Super project should be charged an opportunity cost for using these Jell-O facilities.

2. The option components of real assets have been the subject of a growing literature, which has recently been surveyed by Sick (1989). See also Kensinger (1987), Trigeorgis and Mason (1987) and Bjerksund and Ekern (1990).

3. A lag between investment and production could also be introduced without changing the essential nature of the results. The absence of such a lag facilitates comparison of our opportunity cost measure with that produced by the Equivalent Annual Cost method, as described further in the second section of this chapter.

4. If production could be switched back to A, additional options would be created that would tend to reduce the opportunity cost of diverting capacity. Similarly, a positive salvage value for the plant would create an abandonment option, as in Myers and Majd (1990). However, including these additional option elements would not add significant insights into the problem of opportunity cost, but would substantially complicate the analysis, since the various options may interact. See Trigeorgis (1990, 1991) for further analysis of such interactions.

5. In an options framework, for example, stand-alone NPV would include the value forgone by obtaining a unit of B-capacity immediately, since this kills the option to wait until a future year before obtaining that unit. See McDonald and Siegel (1986).

6. The total number of plants the firm can install profitably is thus limited, which rules out the possibility of infinite investment (perhaps because the firm operates under increasing long-run average costs).

7. To see this, let the current plant be unit J. Since capacity is installed sequentially in order of decreasing value, investment in unit J is at least as attractive as investment in unit $J + 1$. Thus, the decision of whether or not to invest in unit $J + 1$ is unaffected by the decision to divert, because if the firm chooses to invest in unit $J + 1$, it will do so whether or not it has diverted capacity to product B. For example, if the firm has diverted capacity, and if it still wishes to invest in unit $J + 1$, it will also be optimal to invest in unit J. Thus, we can ignore unit $J + 1$ in our analysis.

8. For simplicity, it is assumed that plants wear out all at once at the end of their useful lives and that replacement plants are identical to plants in place. Thus, an option to replace the plant before the end of its useful life would have no value.

9. As explained in note 7, opportunity cost is calculated using only the investment and production options for the current plant, since that is the only capacity unit affected by the decision to divert.

10. The EAC method is described in Brealey and Myers (1991). Two other common methods make rather implausible assumptions about useful plant life. One sets opportunity cost equal to the replacement cost of the facilities used, but this implicitly assumes that a new plant will last only as long as the existing plant (to year N). A second method calculates the change in the present value of investment when plant replacement is moved up from year N to year S. This implicitly assumes that the new plant will last as long as the replacement of the existing plant would have (to year $N + L$). Otherwise, the future sequence of plant replacements would depend on whether capacity is diverted today.

11. Because we assume no lag between investment and production, we compute the EAC annuity payment using the beginning-of-period timing convention

and charge the EAC from years S to $N - 1$. However, the results would be identical if we calculated EAC using the end-of-period convention and made the EAC charges from years $S + 1$ to N.

12. The cost of an unending series of plants with the first built at $t = S$ is equivalent to paying the EAC every year forever, beginning in year S. The cost of an unending series of plants with the first built at $t = N$ is equivalent to paying the EAC in perpetuity, beginning in year N. The difference in the present values of these two streams, which is the present value of an $(N - S)$-year annuity with payments equal to the EAC, thus represents the cost of moving all future replacement cycles ahead by $(N - S)$ years.

13. See Brealey and Myers (1991).

14. For simplicity, fixed costs and taxes are ignored, and unit production costs are assumed constant over both the plant's useful life and the level of capacity utilization. In any given year during its life, then, the plant will be either fully used or completely idle. In a realistic setting, the firm would have to face additional decisions, such as whether to expand or contract capacity. This additional complexity will not add any insights to the problem of opportunity cost measurement *per se*, however, so the focus here will be on a single plant.

15. If Product A were a security, these risk-neutral probabilities would have to be such that the 'expected' return on Product A equaled the risk-free rate. For a manufactured product, however, there is no reason to assume that an investor will expect to earn the risk-free rate from simply holding the product for a year. We assume that the expected change in the price of A is determined in an equilibrium asset pricing model, such as Merton's (1973) Intertemporal Capital Asset Pricing Model, and that this expected change is zero in a risk-neutral world. This price process is analogous to that of a stock paying a proportional dividend, δ, at a rate equal to the risk-free rate. See McDonald and Siegel (1984) for further discussion of this point.

16. Specifically, the current values of the production options for years 3–5, respectively, are (in $ millions) 0.465, 0.542, and 0.604.

17. The option values were estimated using a binomial lattice technique, as described in Cox et al. (1979). With ten steps per year and an annual standard deviation of 0.10, the size of each upward move is $e^{(0.1\sqrt{0.1})} - 1 = 0.032$, or 3.2 percent, and the size of each downward move is $e^{(-0.1\sqrt{0.1})} - 1 = -0.031$, or −3.1 percent.

18. Specifically, using the beginning-of-year payment convention, EAC is calculated as

$$\text{EAC} = \frac{rE(1+r^5)}{\left[(1+r)^6 - 1\right]},$$

and assuming that investment is moved up from year 4 to year 1, this EAC is charged for years 1, 2, and 3, so

$$C = \frac{\text{EAC}}{(1+r)} + \frac{\text{EAC}}{(1+r)^2} + \frac{\text{EAC}}{(1+r)^3}.$$

19. As above, the EAC is \$0.563 for $E = 3$, and charging this amount for years 0–3 gives an opportunity cost measure of 2.096. In the options calculation with zero standard deviation, investment is moved up from year 4 to 0, from 10 to 6 and so on. However, because of the 50-year horizon, the last investment occurs in year 48 under the diversion strategy, versus year 46 if the firm does not divert capacity. Since there is one more investment under the diversion strategy, the 50-year analogue to the EAC calculation is slightly higher than the infinite-horizon EAC calculation. The exact present value of the difference in the investment expenditure streams is 2.183.

References

BJERKSUND, P. and EKERN, S. (1990) Managing investment opportunities under price uncertainty: from 'last chance' to 'wait and see' strategies, *Financial Management*, 65–83.

BREALEY, R. A. and MYERS, S. C. (1991) *Principles of Corporate Finance*, McGraw-Hill, New York, 4th edn.

BUTTERS, J. K., FRUHAN Jr, W. E., MULLINS Jr, D. W. and PIPER, T. R. (1987) *Case Problems in Finance*, Irwin, Homewood, IL, 9th edn.

COX, J. C., ROSS, S. A. and RUBINSTEIN, M. (1979) Option pricing: a simplified approach, *Journal of Financial Economics*, 229–263.

KENSINGER, J. W. (1987) Adding the value of active management into the capital budgeting equation, *Midland Corporate Finance Journal*, Spring, 31–42.

McDONALD, R. L. and SIEGEL, D. R. (1984) Option pricing when the underlying asset earns a below-equilibrium rate of return: a note, *Journal of Finance*, March, 261–265.

McDONALD, R. L. and SIEGEL, D. R. (1986) The value of waiting to invest., *Quarterly Journal of Economics*, 101, 707–727.

MERTON, R. C. (1973) An intertemporal capital asset pricing model, *Econometrica*, 867–887.

MYERS, S. C. (1987) Financial theory and financial strategy, *Midland Corporate Finance Journal*, Spring, 6–13.

MYERS, S. C. and MAJD, S. (1990) Abandonment value and project life, *Advances in Futures and Options Research*.

PINDYCK, R. S. (1988) Irreversible investment, capacity choice and the value of the firm, *American Economic Review*, December, 969–985.

SICK, G. (1989) Capital budgeting with real options. Monograph 1989-3, *Salomon Brothers Center for the Study of Financial Institutions Monograph Series in Finance and Economics*, New York University.

TRIGEORGIS, L. (1990) Option interactions and the valuation of investments with multiple real options. Boston University Working Paper.

TRIGEORGIS, L. (1991) A log-transformed binomial numerical analysis method for valuing complex multi-option investments, *Journal of Financial and Quantitative Analysis*, 309–326.

TRIGEORGIS, L. and MASON, S. P. (1987) Valuing managerial flexibility, *Midland Corporate Finance Journal*, Spring, 14–21.

13

Is the Real Interest Rate Stable?

O. DAVID GULLEY

Introduction

In recent years, new methods to examine the time-series properties of macroeconomic variables have been developed. These methods allow researchers to better understand economic growth, business cycles, financial markets, consumption and saving behavior, among others. Given its crucial roll in economic activity, the behavior of the real interest rate is of particular interest. In a recent paper, Rose (1988) examines the time-series properties of the *ex ante* real interest rate in the United States. He finds evidence that this rate is non-stationary and notes that this result is puzzling since, among other reasons, consumption capital asset pricing models suggest that the real interest rate and the growth rate of consumption should have similar time-series properties. Rose shows that the growth rate of consumption is stationary, which calls into question the validity of the CCAPM.

These results warrant further investigation. Rose bases his conclusion that the real interest rate is nonstationary on the finding that the inflation rate is stationary. In this chapter, the time-series properties of several inflation rates are found to vary across sample periods. Further, direct tests indicate that the time-series properties of the *ex post* real interest rate also vary across sample periods.

The chapter is organized as follows. The next section reviews Rose's methodology and results. The subsequent section presents empirical findings concerning the time-series properties of inflation and real interest rates. There is then a concluding section.

A Review of Rose's Results

Rose begins with the standard approximation to the Fisher equation:

$$i_t = r_t^e + p_t^e \tag{1}$$

where i_t is the one-period nominal interest rate on some asset, r_t^e is the *ex ante* real interest rate, and p_t^e is the expected inflation rate. While p_t^e cannot be observed, the *ex post* inflation rate, p_t, can be observed. The relationship between p_t and p_t^e can be given by $p_t = p_t^e + u_t$, where u_t is the inflation forecast error. Assuming u_t is a stationary series, p_t^e and p_t will have the same time-series properties. For example, both series might be difference-stationary, denoted $I(1)$, or stationary, denoted $I(0)$.[1] Using annual, quarterly, and monthly data for various sample periods, Rose shows that several measures of p_t (the percent change in the GNP/GDP deflator, the CPI, the implicit price deflator, the PPI, and the WPI) are generally stationary. This finding implies that the corresponding, unknown, measures of p_t^e are also stationary because a linear combination of two $I(0)$ series (in this case, p_t and u_t) will yield another $I(0)$ series.[2] Next, he shows that several measures of i_t (long-term corporate bond rates, commercial paper rates, three-month Treasury-bill rates, one-month CD rates, one-month Eurodollar deposit rates, and one-month finance paper rates) are $I(1)$ series. He argues that since nominal rates are $I(1)$ and expected inflation is $I(0)$, r_t^e is $I(1)$ because the right-hand side of equation (1) must contain a nonstationary process if the left-hand side does as well. This is the major result of his paper: The *ex ante* real interest rate must be non-stationary because the inflation rate is stationary. Thus, Rose infers the behavior of r_t^e from the behavior of i_t and p_t. He also demonstrates that this finding may hold for other countries as well.

These findings are unappealing in several ways. First, as mentioned above, the CCAPM implies that the real interest rate and the growth rate of consumption should have the same time-series properties. Rose shows that the growth rate of consumption is station-ary. Thus, his results call into question the validity of CCAPMs.[3] Second, a nonstationary real interest rate possesses an intuitively un-appealing property. A nonstationary series does not have a population mean to which it tends to return. If the *ex ante* rate is non-stationary and also happened to be negative, there would be every reason to believe that this negative rate would persist. This, after all, is one of the hallmarks of a nonstationary series: It has no 'normal' value to which it tends to return. However, as Barro and Sala-i-Martin (1990) point out, persistent negative real interest rates make little economic sense.[4] For illustrative purposes, Fig. 13.1 shows the

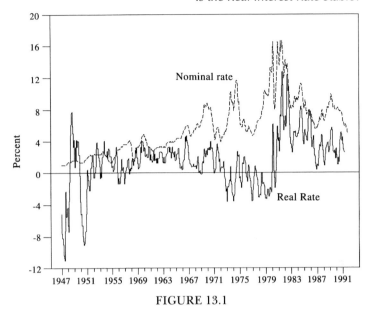

FIGURE 13.1

nominal and *ex post* real rates for six-month commercial paper over the period 1947:1–1991:5. The *ex post* real rate is computed using

$$r_t = (i_t - p_t)/(1 + p_t), \tag{2}$$

where p_t is the annualized seasonally unadjusted CPI inflation rate over the appropriate six-month period. The behavior of this particular *ex post* real rate is typical of others. Notice that *ex post* rates were negative in the mid-1970s. Again, if this series is nonstationary, these negative rates would tend to persist. No economic force would tend to move the rates toward positive values.

There is also some empirical evidence that contradicts Rose's findings. Fama (1975) examines the 1953–1971 period and finds that the *ex ante* real interest rate is stable. More recently, Litterman and Weiss (1985) and Thoma (1992) find the *ex ante* rate is generated by a stationary AR(1) process. These and other papers that examine real interest rates do not use the recently developed unit-root methodology to examine the time-series properties of real rates. Rose (1988) is one of the first to do so. Evans (1992) also uses unit-root methodology and finds the *ex post* real commercial paper rate to be an $I(0)$ series over the 1877–1988 period. Further, Hallman *et al.* (1991) find that inflation is an $I(1)$ series from 1955–1988. Likewise, Bonham (1991) finds the inflation rate to be an $I(1)$ series from 1955:1 to 1990:3. Barsky (1987) argues that "Inflation evolved . . . to a highly persistent, nonstationary ARIMA process in the post-1960 period" (p. 3). Finally, Rose finds the inflation rate to be an $I(1)$ series over the 1959:1–1979:9 and 1979:10–1986:6 periods. Thus, the time-series properties of inflation appear to be sensitive to the choice of the sample period.

However, other authors find evidence that the *ex ante* rate is generated by a nonstationary process. See Nelson and Schwert (1977), Garbade and Wachtel (1978), Fama and Gibbons (1982), and Mishkin (1984).[5] Clearly, there is disagreement over the time-series properties of real interest rates. As this variable is crucial to the functioning of an economy, more study of Rose's results is warranted.

Empirical Results

As previously discussed, Rose infers the properties of the *ex ante* real rate from the properties of the inflation rate. He reports that with the exception of the 1959:1–1979:9 and 1979:10–1986:6 periods, various inflation rates are stationary. If it can be shown that inflation is not stationary over other sample periods, then Rose's results are called into question. This study will concentrate on the monthly results reported by Rose. Table 13.1 presents augmented Dickey–Fuller unit-root tests for seasonally unadjusted monthly CPI and PPI inflation rates over various time periods.[6] The inflation rate is defined as the difference of the log of the index. For a majority of the periods, including many that Rose examines, the null hypothesis of a unit root cannot be rejected. Also note that relatively small changes in sample periods can produce quite different results. For example, inflation appears to be stationary over the 1948:3–1972:12 sample period. However, the inflation rate appears to be nonstationary over the 1953:1–1971:12 period. Rose examines the time-series properties of nominal interest rates for the 1971:3–1979:9 and 1971:3–1986:11 periods and finds them to be nonstationary. However, he does not test the time-series properties of inflation over these same two periods. Table 13.1 clearly indicates that inflation appears to be nonstationary during these time periods. Thus, the type of inference Rose makes concerning the time-series properties of the *ex ante* real rate (i.e. that if the nominal rate is nonstationary and the inflation rate is stationary, then the real rate must be nonstationary) cannot be made if inflation is nonstationary. While the reported unit-root tests use 12 lags, the results are not sensitive to the choice of the lag structure. The seasonally adjusted CPI and PPI inflation rates were also tested for unit roots. The results are nearly identical to those reported in Table 13.1.[7]

Another possible way to discern the time-series properties of *ex ante*

TABLE 13.1 *Unit-root Tests of Inflation and Real Interest Rates*

Period	CPI	PPI	r_t	Used in Rose
1948:3–1972:12	−4.120*	−4.642*	−4.982*	Yes
1948:3–1986:6	−3.003*	−3.481*	−3.647*	Yes
1951:4–1958:12	−4.119*	−3.988*	−2.647	Yes
1953:1–1971:12	−1.465	−2.801	−2.509	Yes
1959:1–1979:9	−0.360	−1.438	−0.743	Yes
1971:3–1979:9	−1.022	−1.629	−1.349	Yes
1971:3–1986:11	−1.443	−1.437	−0.955	Yes
1973:1–1986:6	−1.600	−1.185	−0.866	Yes
1979:10–1986:6	−1.167	−0.622	−2.214	Yes
1948:3–1991:11	−3.270*	−3.966*	−4.075*	
1953:1–1991:11	−2.093	−2.728	−2.277	
1971:3–1991:11	−1.911	−1.975	−1.519	
1973:1–1991:11	−1.918	−1.915	−1.531	
1979:10–1991:11	−2.201	−2.071	−2.708	
1982:10–1991:11	−2.961*	−2.554	−2.696	

*Statistically significant at the 5 percent level.

Both price levels are seasonally unadjusted. Each inflation rate is the first difference of the log of the series. r_t is the *ex post* six-month commercial paper rate constructed using equation (2). Unit-root tests are conducted using the augmented Dickey–Fuller regression:

$$x_t = \alpha + \rho x_{t-1} + \sum_{i=1}^{12} \gamma_i \Delta x_{t-1} + \varepsilon_t.$$

The null hypothesis is $\rho = 1$. Box–Ljung Q-statistics indicate that the residuals for all regressions are white noise. In all cases where the null hypothesis is not rejected, the difference of the variable is found to be stationary. Thus, these variables follow $I(1)$ processes during these periods.

real interest rates is to examine the properties of *ex post* real rates, as in Evans (1992). An *ex post* real rate is calculated from equation (2) using the six-month commercial paper rate and the seasonally unadjusted CPI inflation rate. The resulting *ex post* real rate is subjected to unit-root tests over the same sample periods as above and the results are shown in Table 13.1.[8] As with the inflation rates, the time-series properties of real rates vary across sample periods. Only during the 1951:4–1958:12 period are the findings consistent with the findings of Rose: A stationary inflation rate and a nonstationary real interest rate. Note that the properties of the inflation rate and *ex post* real rate are almost always the same within a given sample period. For several of the periods, both rates are stationary. This

TABLE 13.2 *Unit-root Tests of Foreign Inflation Rates*

Country	Test statistic
Canada	−2.620
France	−0.872
Germany	−1.423
Italy	−1.285
Japan	−1.873
U.K.	−1.573
U.S.	−2.045

*Statistically significant at the 5 percent level.

All data are from the IMF's *International Financial Statistics*, various issues. The sample period is 1970:1–1991:4. Unit-root tests are conducted using the augmented Dickey–Fuller regression

$$x_t = \alpha + \rho x_{t-1} + \sum_{i=1}^{12} \gamma_i \Delta x_{t-1} + \varepsilon_t.$$

The null hypothesis is $\rho = 1$. Box–Ljung Q-statistics indicate that the residuals for all regressions are white noise. In all cases where the null hypothesis is not rejected, the difference of the variable is found to be stationary. Thus, these variables follow $I(1)$ processes during these periods.

finding is interesting since the nominal interest rate is universally found to be nonstationary. From equation (1), it would seem that if the nominal rate is nonstationary, then the inflation rate and/or the real interest must be nonstationary. There are several possible explanations for this finding. First, a nonstationary inflation forecast error could generate the nonstationary nominal rate. This is unlikely given the findings of Keane and Runkle (1990) who find that price level forecast errors follow the rational expectations model. The implication is that price level, and therefore, inflation, forecast errors are stationary. Second, as Bonham (1991) and others have pointed out, the Fisher equation describes the long-run relationship between the relevant variables. Deviations from this relationship could also generate the nonstationary nominal interest rate.

Rose also performed the same analysis on 18 OECD countries using quarterly data over 1957–1984 and found results similar to those for the United States. Table 13.2 presents unit-root test results on the inflation rates of the G-7 countries for the 1970:1–1991:4 period. As can be seen, the null hypothesis of a unit root cannot be rejected for any of the inflation rates. Thus, it appears that Rose's results are sensitive to the choice of the sample period.

Finally, Perron (1989) has developed unit-root tests that account for one-time shifts in the mean and/or trend of a time series. He shows that failure to account for these shifts biases standard unit-root tests in favor of the null hypothesis. He finds that such shifts occurred at 1973:1 for many series. Since a majority of the unit-root tests reported in Table 13.1 fail to reject the null hypothesis of a unit root and include 1973:1 as part of the sample period, there is potential bias. Using Perron's methodology, the relevant unit-root tests were redone to account for a one-time shift in the mean and/or trend at 1973:1. The results are not qualitatively affected.[9]

Summary and Conclusions

The purpose of this study was to demonstrate that inferring the time-series properties of the *ex ante* real interest rate from those of the nominal interest and inflation rate is fraught with difficulty. The empirical evidence on which the inferences are based (the time-series properties of the inflation rate) is fragile across sample periods. Combining the findings of this chapter with those of Rose (1988) and Barsky (1987), the time-series properties of inflation seem to have changed sometime during the 1960s and/or 1970s in that inflation rates are more likely to be nonstationary in sample periods limited to the 1970s and 1980s. Why this is so remains to be discovered. Further, direct tests on *ex post* real interest rates found that the time-series properties varied across sample periods.

As always, the limitations of the unit-root methodology must be noted. The tests are known to have low power in rejecting the null hypothesis when the true root is close to one or when the sample size is small and/or spans a time period that is not long enough to bring out the true properties of the series.

The differences in the findings between this chapter and Rose (1988), as well as the general disagreement within the literature, indicate that additional work needs to be undertaken to understand the behavior of *ex ante* real interest rates. Various attempts have been made to generate *ex ante* interest rates, such as in Huizinga and Mishkin (1985). The recently developed unit-root and cointegration methodologies offer potentially useful tools for the investigation of this question because they can help determine the behavior of the real rate as well as its relationship with other variables.

Acknowledgement

The author would like to thank Scott Sumner for helpful discussions.

Notes

1. In general, if a series must be differenced d times to achieve stationarity, the series is called an $I(d)$ series.
2. Keane and Runkle (1990) provide convincing evidence that price-level forecast errors are stationary. This implies that inflation forecast errors (u_t) are stationary as well.
3. Of course, Rose it not the first to document problems with the CCAPM. For a recent discussion of this topic, see Evans and Hasan (1992).
4. Many authors derive estimates of the *ex ante* rate which are negative in the mid-1970s and behave quite similarly to *ex post* rates. See Huizinga and Mishkin (1985) as an example.
5. The type of process generating r_t^e is not agreed on. Some authors argue that r_t^e is generated by a random walk. Others argue that it is generated by its own past and other variables. Thoma (1992) provides references to many of these papers.
6. Various nominal interest rates are also subjected to unit-root tests for the sample periods discussed below: The six-month commercial paper rate, three-month T-bill rates, the one-month rate on Finance Paper, the one-month CD rate, and the one-month Eurodollar rate. The commercial paper rate and the T-bill rate are available from 1947 on CITIBASE. The other three rates are available from 1970. In all cases, the rates are $I(1)$ and are consistent with the findings of Rose (1988) and the rest of the literature.
7. All data are from the CITIBASE tapes. The four price indexes used here correspond to those used in Rose (1988). It should be pointed out that the seasonally adjusted PPI is only available from 1967 in CITIBASE. In addition, Table 13.1 only reports the '*t*-like' unit-root test statistics. The $T^*(\rho - 1)$ unit-root test statistics yield similar results.
8. *Ex post* real rates were also constructed using the nominal rates discussed in note 5 and then subjected to unit-root tests. The results are not qualitatively different from the results reported in Table 13.1.
9. Perron's technique adds dummy variables to the augmented Dickey–Fuller unit-root equation to model the possible shift in the mean and/or trend of the series. He calculates critical values for the test statistics assuming a trend variable is included in the regression. The coefficient on the trend was usually not significant in the modified Dickey–Fuller regressions.

References

BARRO, R. J. and SALA-I-MARTIN, X. (1990) World real interest rates. In BLANCHARD, O. J. and FISCHER, S (eds.), *NBER Macroeconomics Annual*, The MIT Press, Cambridge, MA, pp. 15–61.

BARSKY, R. B. (1987) The Fisher hypothesis and the forecastability and persistence of inflation, *Journal of Monetary Economics*, 19, 3–24.

BONHAM, C. S. (1991) Correct cointegration tests of the long-run relationship between nominal interest and inflation, *Applied Economics*, 23, 1487–1492.

EVANS, P. (1992) Finite horizons, infinite horizons, and the real interest rate, *Economic Inquiry*, 30, 14–28.

EVANS, P. and HASAN, I. (1992) Finite horizons and the consumption capital asset pricing model: theory and evidence. Manuscript, Ohio State University.

FAMA, E. F. (1975) Short-term interest rates as predictors of inflation, *American Economic Review*, 65, 269–282.

FAMA, E. F. and GIBBONS, M. R. (1982) Inflation, real returns and capital investment, *Journal of Monetary Economics*, 9, 297–323.

GARBADE, K. and WACHTEL, P. (1978) Time variation in the relationship between inflation and interest rates, *Journal of Monetary Economics*, 4, 755–765.

HALLMAN, J. J. *et al.* (1991) Is the price level tied to the M2 monetary aggregate in the long run? *American Economic Review*, 81, 841–858.

HUIZINGA, J. and MISHKIN, F. S. (1985) Monetary policy regime shifts and the unusual behavior of real interest rates. NBER Working Paper No. 1678.

KEANE, M. P. and RUNKLE, D. E. (1990) Testing the rationality of price forecasts: new evidence from panel data, *American Economic Review*, 90, 714–735.

LITTERMAN, R. B. and WEISS, L. (1985) Money, real interest rates, and output: a reinterpretation of postwar U.S. data, *Econometrica*, 53, 129–156.

MISHKIN, F. S. (1984) The real interest rate: a multi-country empirical study, *The Canadian Journal of Economics*, 17, 284–311.

NELSON, C. R. and SCHWERT, G. W. (1977) Short-term interest rates as predictors of inflation: on testing the hypothesis that the real rate of interest is constant, *American Economic Review*, 67, 478–496.

PERRON, P. (1989) The great crash, the oil price shock, and the unit root hypothesis, *Econometrica*, 57, 1361–1401.

ROSE, A. K. (1988) Is the real interest rate stable? *Journal of Finance*, 43, 1095–1112.

THOMA, M. A. (1992) Some international evidence on the exogeneity of the *ex-ante* real rate of interest and the rationality of expectations, *Journal of Macroeconomics*, 14, 33–45.

14

Agency Costs and Employee Stock Ownership Plans

K. THOMAS LIAW

Introduction

Employee stock ownership plans were introduced by the Employee Retirement and Income Security Act of 1974. Employee stock ownership plans consist of a stock bonus plan or stock bonus plan combined with a money purchase pension plan. Specifically, an employee stock ownership plan (ESOP) is an employee benefit plan in the form of a trust fund that invests primarily in the company stock. There are leveraged ESOPs and nonleveraged ESOPs. To set up a leveraged ESOP, a trust fund is developed with new company shares or cash being contributed to it. Different classes of stocks may exist, but the ESOP will often concentrate upon those with voting right. The company continues to make contributions to the ESOP, allowing the plan to make payments on its loan. Finally, as the loan is retired, the company stock is allocated to employees in proportion to their earnings. These are held in accounts for the employees. Note that there are two basic differences between an ESOP and a non-ESOP stock bonus plan. First, an ESOP must be primarily invested in its employer's stock, while a non-ESOP plan may or may not be so. Second, ESOPs may be leveraged and may receive credit from the sponsoring company, which is not permitted to other types of qualified plans (Conte and Kruse, 1991).

ESOPs have become popular not only for tax reduction reasons. They are able, if implemented correctly, to bring a number of benefits. Among these are increased employee productivity, increased growth, efficient financing, further takeover defense, and, as mentioned, tax benefits.[1]

Some studies have provided evidence that the adoption of an ESOP will increase productivity (Rosen, 1987; Rosen and Quarrey, 1987). As well as increased productivity, companies with ESOPs tend to grow at a faster rate (Rosen and Quarrey, 1987). Other studies produce mixed results (see for example, Chang (1990), Chaplinsky and Niehaus (1990), and Scholes and Wolfson (1990)).

ESOPs will also affect the employees. There is first the somewhat intangible but still important psychological effect that the status of 'owner' brings to the employee. He or she now has a stake in the company, and this affects his or her outlook on work. This could lead employees toward value-increasing activities, including (a) less likely to sabotage or harm the company, (b) more careful in not leaking company secrets, (c) suggest value-increasing ideas, (d) more concerned about shirking or perquisite taking, (e) less likely to bad-mouth the company, and (f) more likely to support issues that benefit the company, etc. There are also financial benefits available to the ESOP participants. Tax-free rollovers of proceeds from sales to ESOPs are available under certain circumstances and there can also be benefits to a taxpayer's estate. Of course, the appreciation of the stock price (better corporate performance) will bestow financial rewards on employees as well.

This chapter focuses on the impact of an ESOP on corporate investments. The approach employed is a principal-agent dynamic game (Grossman and Hart, 1983; Rogerson, 1983; Lancaster, 1973; Kamien and Schwartz, 1981). Without an ESOP, the divergent interests of shareholders and employees lead to a suboptimal investment path (an optimal investment path maximizes shareholders and employees' welfare). It is shown that the adoption of an ESOP will improve corporate investments and hence reduce agency costs. As a result, both stockholders and employees are better off.

The chapter is organized as follows. The next section presents model formulation and basic assumptions. The second and third sections examine corporate investments without and with the ESOP. Finally, the last section concludes the study.

Model Formulation and Assumptions[2]

In a principal–agent framework, the stockholders are the principal (or the owner) and the employees are the agent. The employees are assumed to determine the ratio of consumption to total output,[3] between the given upper (j) and lower (h) limits. The objective of employees is to maximize the total discounted consumption.

The stockholders can determine the proportion of total output not consumed by the employees to be invested and the rest for their own consumption. It is assumed that there is no depreciation on capital stock.

The assumptions are summarized as: (1) Total output $= R(K(t))$, (2) Employee's consumption $= c(t)R(K)$, (3) Stockholder's consumption $= s(t)R(K)[1 - c(t)]$, and (4) Investment $= i(t)R(K)[1 - c(t)]$. $R(K(t))$ is the total output and is an increasing function of K, $K(t)$ is the capital stock, $s(t)$ is the proportion of output consumed by the stockholders, $c(t)$ is the proportion consumed by employees, and $i(t)$ is the rate of investment at time t ($i = 1 - s$). Hence, the net investment or the change in capital stock is $\dot{K} = R(t)i(t)[1 - c(t)]$. The time horizon is $0 \leqslant t \leqslant T$.

The employees determine the value of $c(t)$ through wage bargaining and other means. Under this setting, the employees may demand a high $c(t)$ if they believe the owners will consume all the remaining earnings and put nothing for investment. On the other hand, the employees will choose a low $c(t)$ now if they believe the owners will use the remaining earnings to make profitable investment for the company.

The owners are also assumed to aim at maximizing total discounted consumption within the time horizon. Like employees, the stockholders will make decisions on investment based on their belief about employees' choices.

The best interest of the owners may not be the same as that of the employees, i.e. there are conflicts between principal and agent. With the employee stock ownership plan, the employees also own a share of the company. The objective of the employees and that of the stockholders could coincide.

Corporate Investments Without ESOPs

There are two separate maximization problems: one for stockholders and another for employees (or capitalists and workers as in Lancaster, 1973). Each group devises a strategy to maximize its own objective, but the outcome depends on the other group's choice as well. The equilibrium concept is similar to that of a Cournot equilibrium. Employees have control over the rate of consumption (or saving) and stockholders have control over the rate of investment.

Employee's optimization problem is to choose $c(t)$ to maximize the total discounted consumption up to time T[4]

$$\max \int_0^T e^{-rt} R(K)c(t)\, dt \qquad (1)$$

$$\text{subject to } \dot{K} = R(t)i(t)[1 - c(t)]$$
$$0 < c(t) < 1$$

and anticipated choice of $i(t)$ by the stockholders.

i.e. the employees maximize the total discounted consumption subject to the anticipated choice of stockholders and other stated constraints. The Lagrangian can be expressed as:

$$SL = e^{-rt} R(K)c(t) + \lambda_1 R(K)i(t)(1 - c(t)) + \delta_1(1 - c) + \delta_2(c), \quad (2)$$

where λ_1 represents the marginal value to the employees of an increase in capital stock. An optimal solution satisfies

$$\partial SL/\partial c = e^{-rt} R(K) - \lambda_1 R(K) i - \delta_1 + \delta_2$$
$$= R(K)[e^{-rt} - \lambda_1 i] - \delta_1 + \delta_2$$
$$= 0 \quad (3)$$

$$\delta_1, \delta_2 \geq 0, \delta = 0, \delta_2 c = 0 \quad (4)$$

$$\dot{\lambda}_1 = -\partial SL/\partial K = -[e^{-rt}R'(K)c(t) + \lambda_1 R'(K)i(t)(1 - c(t))] \quad (5)$$

$$\lambda_1(T) = 0. \quad (6)$$

The first-order conditions imply that

$$c = h \text{ whenever } i\lambda_1 > e^{-rt} \quad (7)$$

$$\text{or } c = j \text{ whenever } i\lambda_1 < e^{-rt}. \quad (8)$$

This is part of the solution. In order to obtain a complete solution, we need to solve the stockholder's problem simultaneously. The optimization problem for stockholders is

$$\max \int_0^T e^{-rt} R(K)[1 - c(t)][1 - i(t)]dt \quad (9)$$

$$\text{subject to } \dot{K} = R(t)i(t)[1 - c(t)]$$

$$0 \leq i(t) \leq 1$$

and anticipated choice of $c(t)$ by the employees.

The stockholders maximize the objective function by choosing the optimal path of investment and by taking into account the possible choices of $c(t)$ by employees. The Lagrangian is

$$SL = e^{-rt}R(K)(1 - c)(1 - i) + \lambda_2 R(K)i(t)(1 - c(t)) + \lambda_1(1 - i) + \lambda_2(i) \quad (10)$$

where λ_2 can be interpreted as the marginal value of investment to the stockholders. Note that this could be different from the marginal value of investment to employees, i.e. λ_1 is not equal to λ_2 in general. The necessary conditions are

$$\partial SL/\partial i = e^{-rt} R(K)(1 - c) + \lambda_2 R(K)(1 - c) - \lambda_1 + \lambda_2 = 0 \quad (11)$$

$$\gamma_1 \gamma_2 \geq 0, \quad \gamma_1(1 - i) = 0, \quad \delta_2 i = 0 \quad (12)$$

$$\dot{\lambda}_2 = -\partial ML/\partial K = -[e^{-rt}R'(K)(1 - c)(1 - i) + \lambda_2 R'(K)i(t)(1 - c(t))] \quad (13)$$

$$\lambda_2(T) = 0. \quad (14)$$

Equations (11)–(14) imply that

$$i = 0 \text{ whenever } i\lambda_2 > e^{-rt} \quad (15)$$

$$\text{or } i = 1 \text{ whenever } i\lambda_2 < e^{-rt}. \quad (16)$$

The illustration above suggests that there are four possible solutions. These are

$$(I) \quad c = h, i = 0 \text{ if } \lambda_1 i > e^{-rt} \text{ and } \lambda_2 < e^{-rt} \quad (17)$$

$$(II) \quad c = h, i = 1 \text{ if } \lambda_1 i > e^{-rt} \text{ and } \lambda_2 > e^{-rt} \quad (18)$$

$$(III) \quad c = j, i = 0 \text{ if } \lambda_1 i < e^{-rt} \text{ and } \lambda_2 < e^{-rt} \quad (19)$$

$$(IV) \quad c = j, i = 1 \text{ if } \lambda_1 i < e^{-rt} \text{ and } \lambda_2 > e^{-rt}. \quad (20)$$

Equations (17)–(20) suggest that there are four possible situations at any point in time: (I) employees choose a minimum consumption and stockholders choose a minimum investment; (II) employees choose a minimum consumption and stockholders choose a maximum investment; (III) employees choose a maximum consumption and stockholders choose a minimum investment; and (IV) employees choose a maximum consumption and stockholders choose a maximum investment. These situations are summarized in Table 14.1.

An examination of equations (17)–(20) reveals that (I) is not optimal since the employees will not accept minimum consumption if the owners are not investing, i.e. $i = 0$ and $\lambda_1 i > e^{-rt}$ (> 0) are incompatible.

The boundary condition is $\lambda_2(T) = 0$. Also, λ_2 is continuous in t. This implies that $\lambda_2 < e^{-rt}$ for some period before the terminal time T. Let $\underline{t}$ denote the time such that $\lambda_2(\underline{t}) = e^{-rt}$ and $\lambda_2(t) < e^{-rt}$ for $\underline{t} < t \leq T$. In this phase, we have stage (III). In this phase, we have

$$\dot{K} = 0 \quad (21)$$

$$\dot{\lambda}_1 = -e^{-rt}R'(K)j \quad (22)$$

TABLE 14.1 *Four Possible Situations*

	Employees	
	Maximum consumption	Minimum consumption
Stockholders — Maximum investment	Situation (IV)	Situation (III)
Stockholders — Minimum investment	Situation (II)	Situation (I)

$$\dot{\lambda}_2 = -e^{-rt}R'(K)(1-j). \tag{23}$$

since both λ_1 and λ_2 are declining in t. We must have $\lambda_2(t) > e^{-rt}$ for $0 \leqslant t < \underline{t}$. This phenomenon can be observed during stages (II) and (IV). As indicated by equations (18) and (20), i is equal to one. Hence $\lambda_1(\underline{t}) > e^{-rt}$ and λ_1 is declining faster than λ_2 prior to the last phase if the maximum rate of consumption $j > 0.5$.

Thus the solution consists of two phases, beginning at (III) and then switching to (II) at $\underline{t}$. In other words, both the principal and agent accumulate up to $\underline{t}$; then both groups will switch to maximum consumption. The results here will be compared to those of the next section. In so doing, the benefits of an ESOP become obvious.

Corporate Investments With ESOPs

Employees have a share of the company with the adoption of an ESOP. The interests of employees and that of the shareholders now coincide. They would choose the optimal investments to maximize their welfare. This is formulated as follows:

$$\max \int_0^T e^{-rt}R(K)\{c(t)+[1-c(t)][1-i(t)]\}\,dt \tag{24}$$

$$= \int_0^T e^{-rt}R(K)[1-(1-c(t))i(t)]\,dt$$

$$= \int_0^T e^{-rt}R(K)[1-v]\,dt,$$

where $v = i(1-c)$ is the ratio of investment and is now the strategic variable for stockholders and employees. The Lagrangian is

$$L = e^{-rt} R(K)(1 - v) + \lambda R(K)v + \alpha_1 (1 - c - v) + \alpha_2 v, \qquad (25)$$

where λ is the marginal value of investment to the society. The first-order conditions are

$$\partial L/\partial v = -e^{-rt}R(K) + \lambda R(K) - \alpha_1 + \alpha_2 = 0 \qquad (26)$$

$$\dot{\lambda} = -\partial L/\partial K = -[e^{-rt} R'(K)(1 - v) + \lambda R'(K)v] \qquad (27)$$

$$\lambda(T) = 0. \qquad (28)$$

In the last phase, maximum consumption or minimum investment is optimal, i.e. $v = 0$. Hence

$$\dot{\lambda} = e^{-rt}R'(K). \qquad (29)$$

Comparing equation (29) with equations (22) and (23), it is obvious that λ is declining faster than λ_1 and λ_2. Therefore, we obtain

$$\lambda(t^*) = e^{-rt}, t^* > \underline{t}, \qquad (30)$$

i.e. the time of switching from maximum investment to maximum consumption with an ESOP (t^*) is later than that without an ESOP ($\underline{t}$). As indicated in Lancaster (1973), this is sufficient to show that the separation of saving and investment decisions is suboptimal.

Conclusions

The benefits of an ESOP are examined in a principal-agent setting. There exist 'agency costs' if the objectives of shareholders and employees are divergent. When a company adopts the ESOP, there is firstly the somewhat intangible but still important psychological effect that the status of 'owner' brings to the employee. He or she now has a stake in the company, and this affects his or her outlook on work. Therefore, both stockholders and employees will pursue the same objective after the adoption of an ESOP. The problem is solved by the bang–bang control technique (Kamien and Schwartz, 1981). It is shown that the adoption of an ESOP improves corporate investments and hence increases social welfare.

Notes

1. There are four major tax benefits associated with an ESOP. These are: (i) when an ESOP borrows to buy stock, not only are the interest payments tax

deductible, so are the repayments of principal; (ii) a commercial lender may exclude from taxable income 50 percent of the interest earned from loans to an ESOP; (iii) dividends paid on stock that is held by an ESOP can be deducted from corporate payable; and (iv) owners of privately held corporations who sell their shares to an ESOP can defer the capital gains tax if they reinvest the gains in the stock of a US corporation within a year.

2. The setting of the model is similar to the one in Lancaster (1973) and Kamien and Schwartz (1981). Lancaster models capitalism as a dynamic conflict. Lancaster shows that there is a dynamic welfare loss due to the separation of saving (by workers) and investment (capitalists) decisions. Similar settings, bang–bang control, can be found in Kamien and Schwartz (1981).
3. See Lancaster (1973) for justification of this assumption.
4. See, for example, Kamien and Schwartz (1981) for techniques to solve this type of maximization problem.

References

CHANG, S. (1990) Employee stock ownership plans and shareholder wealth, *Financial Management*, Spring, 48–58.

CHAPLINSKY, S. and NIEHAUS, G. (1990) The tax and distributional effects of leveraged ESOPs, *Financial Management*, Spring, 29–38.

CONTE, M. A. and KRUSE, D. (1991) ESOPs and profit-sharing plans: do they link employee pay to company performance? *Financial Management*, Winter, 91–100.

GROSSMAN, S. and HART, O. (1983) An analysis of the principal-agent problem, *Econometrica*, 51, No. 1.

JONES, D. F. (1987) Estate tax deduction for sales to ESOPs still beneficial despite RA '87 restrictions, *Journal of Taxation*, February.

KAMIEN, M. I. and SCHWARTZ, N. L. (1981) *Dynamic Optimization: The Calculus of Variations and Optimal Control in Economics and Management*, North Holland.

KLIEGMAN, M. J. (1989) Obtaining a tax-free rollover of proceeds from sales to ESOPs, *Journal of Taxation*, January.

LANCASTER, K. (1973) The dynamic inefficiency of capitalism, *Journal of Political Economy*, 1092–1109.

PEIREZ, D. H. (1988) ESOPs popularity on the ride, *Pension World*, October.

ROGERSON, W. P. (1983) The first-order approach to principal-agent problems. Mimeo.

ROSEN, C. (1987) The growing appeal of the leveraged ESOP, *Journal of Business Strategy*, January/February.

ROSEN, C. and QUARREY, M. (1987) How well is employee stock ownership working. *Harvard Business Review*, September/October 1987.

SCHOLES, M. and WOLFSON, M. (1990) Employee stock ownership plans corporate restructuring: myths and realities, *Financial Management*, Spring, 12–28.

STRUGATCH, W. (1988) Banking ESOPs are no longer fables, *Bankers Monthly*, May.

TAPLIN, P. T. (1988) Sharing information with employee-owners improves firms' productivity and profitability, *Employee Benefit Plan Review*, August.

Part II

15

Innovations in Currency Markets: Rolling Spot™ Contracts

IRA G. KAWALLER

When a bank foreign exchange trader decides to take a view on a particular currency, he or she typically will make a spot market transaction to take a position. Then, when the view no longer holds, the position is terminated or offset; and gains or losses are realized. But there's more to it than that.

Consider the case of a trader who makes the determination that the Deutschemark is likely to strengthen in the near term. A long spot Deutschemark position traded in the United States today would be scheduled to settle in two business days. In other words, two business days later, German marks would be credited to the original trader's German bank and debited from the German bank designated by the counterparty. These adjustments would take place during the time frame in which the Bundesbank is open. Later, on that same calendar date when the Fed is operating, U.S. dollars would be debited from the trader's U.S. bank and credited to the counterparty's bank.

Looking closer at this long Deutschemark position, it should be clear that the trader has the capacity to earn mark-denominated interest income on the marks now held. At the same time, he bears an interest expense or opportunity cost on the dollars required to buy the marks. Thus, the spot position will generate some net income or expense, depending on the respective daily investment and financing rates available in the market, for as long as the trade is maintained. This income or expense is commonly referred to as 'positive' or 'negative carry'.

In practice, this outcome is realized using a somewhat different market mechanism. That is, instead of borrowing and lending *per se*, traders use currency swap transactions. The cost (or benefit) associated with the swap would match the net interest income or expense referred to above. Swaps are just a more convenient way to get to the same place. They work like this: Again, returning to the long mark exposure, if U.S. overnight interest rates are higher than German overnight rates, the swap fosters a daily expense; and conversely with U.S. interest rates lower, the swap generates income. The reverse would be the case for a short Deutschemark position. Mechanically, this carry is realized either by trading a 'spot/next' swap on the same day as the original spot market trade or waiting until the following day and then trading a 'tomorrow/next', or 'tom/next' swap. Either way, the swap offsets the starting spot position on the original value date and re-imposes the same position with a value date on the subsequent business day.

Like all markets, markets for both spot currencies and currency swaps are quoted with bids and offers, where position takers (as opposed to dealers) typically buy at the offered price and sell at the bid. As a consequence, the respective bid/offer spreads should be viewed as transactions costs. While the magnitudes differ by currency, varying somewhat with market conditions, the spot market bid/ask spreads on the major currencies run in the range of ten points (e.g. $0.0010/£ or DM0.0010/$) or so. Spreads for daily swaps are generally less than 0.5 points (e.g. 0.00005), and perhaps even as small as 0.1 point, depending on the currency and prevailing circumstances. In addition to these costs, those who trade through the broker market will have commission charges of $8–15 per million (per side) for spot trades and about a quarter of that for each daily swap transaction.

Aside from these direct costs, traders will also be sensitive to one additional important consideration: Business of this nature is typically constrained by credit lines, due to the timing risk associated with the nonsimultaneous currency flows. In this example, for instance, the payer of marks runs the risk of counterparty default, as a gap exists between the time when marks are paid (e.g. when the Bundesbank operates) and when dollars are received (e.g. when the Federal Reserve wire operates). As a consequence of this risk, bankers must clearly know their counterparty, evaluate the credit standing of that institution, and impose some limitation to the activities—even for top-rated financial institutions.

A Better Way

For the segment of the interbank market that requires the physical exchange of currencies, the existing practices and conventions for spot trading are perfectly appropriate and viable. For example, the corporate treasurer who needs the actual foreign exchange to pay for goods and services would see the traditional spot market trade as the only reasonable mechanism. For those who have more of a discretionary approach or a trading perspective, however, the Chicago Mercantile Exchange's Rolling Spot contracts are likely offer considerable advantages over the traditional market.

Rolling Spot contracts have a number of similarities to their forebearers, traditional currency futures. Both are exchange traded; both are standardized instruments in terms of size and settlement date; and both are accessed using the same brokers or futures commission merchants who service all other CFTC regulated futures and options activities. At the same time there are some important differences between the new instruments and the traditional futures. While traditional currency futures are designed with pricing in U.S. terms (i.e. the non-U.S. dollar currency is the base currency and prices are expressed in U.S. dollars), this practice does not hold universally for Rolling Spot contracts. Rather, Rolling Spot contracts follow interbank conventions. For the pound Sterling and Australian dollars, Rolling Spot contracts prices are quoted in U.S. terms (i.e. in dollars), while for all the other CME currencies, the dollar is the base currency and prices are quoted in European terms (e.g. marks per dollar or yen per dollar, etc.).

As with traditional futures contracts, the Rolling Spot contracts are marked-to-market, daily, reflecting the change in the contract price from settlement-to-settlement (or if the trade were just initiated, from the entry price to the settlement price on that day). In addition to this traditional marking-to-market, however, the exchange also *automatically* makes a daily adjustment to position holders in Rolling Spot, designed to reflect the spot/next swap points. To determine the magnitude of this adjustment, the CME surveys the interbank swap market makers and assesses the market condition as of 11:00 a.m. central time. The mid-market swap price (found by averaging the bid and offer prices from a sample of swap dealers) is designated as the 'IMM swap points'. These points are then used in the adjustment of the daily settlements, paying or receiving in a manner consistent with bank practices. For example, suppose the 11:00 Deutschemark spot/next swaps market conditions were 1.70–1.80, reflecting the fact that the next day forward price was trading at a premium to spot. IMM swap points would be 1.75 and the CME would adjust its variation margin by the size of the contract[1] multiplied by this mid-point price. In this case, as the size of the DM Rolling Spot is $250,000, the secondary adjustment is $250,000 × DM0.000175/\$ = DM43.75 per contract—paying to the short and collecting from the long.[2]

One technical aspect of this contract deserves special mention: The swap market is dynamic and responsive to changing market conditions throughout the day. It is reasonable to expect that if these swap prices remain at the IMM swap point value for the remainder of the CME's trading day, Rolling Spot prices would likely be equal to traditional spot prices. Otherwise, arbitrageurs would enter the market and ultimately foster an adjustment to this equilibrium. In the event that swap conditions vary from the IMM swap points, Rolling Spot and traditional spot prices will likely differ. The magnitude of this difference should reflect the discrepancy between the market swap conditions and the IMM swap points. In similar fashion, if these discrepancies were not offsetting, again, an arbitrage opportunity would be present.

Rolling Spot contracts cannot be maintained indefinitely. Like their traditional futures' cousins, they have a similar quarterly expiration. That is, trading terminates two business days before the third Wednesdays of March, June, September and December. Thus, prior to expiration, the maintenance of an open position simply requires that the trader be positioned to make a single cash adjustment, just as is the case with a traditional futures position, until either the position is liquidated (offset) or the contract expires; but again, all swap adjustments are handled automatically and included in this daily cash settlement. Upon expiration, remaining open positions are required to make or take physical delivery on the third Wednesday of the quarterly month.

For those interested in maintaining their open positions beyond the quarterly delivery dates, the CME has a mechanism available. That is, one week prior to the expiration of Rolling Spot, a new Rolling Spot is listed for trading—one with the next quarterly expiration date. For example, if the Rolling Spot were scheduled to stop trading on September 13, a new Rolling Spot would begin trading coincidentally, starting on September 6. Both, incidentally, should trade at identical prices, as each is adjusted by identical IMM spot/next swap points. Thus, during the week of September 6–13, anyone who wanted the capacity to extend their open position beyond the September 13 expiration would spread out of the expiring Rolling Spot into the new one, probably for the price of a tick. At this time, one round-turn would be completed and a commission charge would be generated.

In contrast to the known (and fixed) commission charges for the Rolling Spot contracts, the traditional spot market transaction costs grow over time, due to the charges associated with the daily rolls. The longer the holding period, the greater the number of swap transactions required, and thus the more expensive the trade.

Aside from direct commission costs, traders should also be sensitive to less tangible fixed costs associated with time, effort, and the possibility of just plain making errors. For traditional spot trading, traders and back office support spend time every day, trading, executing and processing the daily rolls; and depending on the number of counterparties with which one is involved, this time requirement could be considerable—and so could the mistakes. For the Rolling Spot contract, these adjustments are automatic, so these costs are virtually eliminated.

Even beyond these comparative cost advantages, perhaps the largest benefit of the Rolling Spot contract is that counterparty credit risk becomes a nonissue. As a consequence, substitution of Rolling Spot contracts for traditional spot transaction frees lines of credit, which all too often are scare recourses.

While many will appreciate the Rolling Spot contract for their advantages as trading vehicles, at least some players will ultimately want to exchange currencies physically. This objective, however, poses no problem. Beyond simply maintaining the contracts to their expiration (typically two business days before the third Wednesday of each quarterly month[3]) and exchanging currencies on the third Wednesday, two alternative procedures are available. Either the original Rolling Spot position can be offset and then a traditional spot trade can be instituted; or the Rolling Spot contract can be liquidated with an 'Exchange for Physicals' (EFP) transaction. An EFP establishes opposite simultaneous trades in the Rolling Spot contract and the traditional spot market.

And There's More

Along with the Rolling Spot contract, the CME has also introduced an innovative short-term option on Rolling Spot. The design of this contract is a dramatic departure from existing instruments. These options have a term or tenor limited to five business days. At the start of trading each week, a series of puts and calls will be listed with a range of strike prices above and below the most recent Rolling Spot settlement price. At least ten strike prices will be available. As with other options, a movement of the underlying Rolling Spot price would foster the introduction of new strike prices, time permitting. The options will expire at the close of trading on Friday (or Thursday if Friday is a holiday). The options are European in design, so they may be exercised only at expiration. Notice must be received by the Clearing House by 7:00 p.m. Chicago time, on that day. Exercise (and assignment) will result in the establishment of the Rolling Spot contract, as of the following Monday morning at the option's strike price. Importantly, no physical exchange of currencies will occur with exercise or assignment.

For those who want to exercise these options but don't want to bear the exposure of the price variability between Friday's close and Monday's open, an offsetting trade should be executed during business hours on *Friday*. For example, assume you own a call option with a strike price of $1.4000/£ while the Rolling Spot contract is trading at $1.5000/£, and also assume that you'd like to exercise. If you short the Rolling Spot at $1.5000 on Friday, the exercise of the call will necessarily result in an offset. You are, of course, subject to the effects of the IMM swap point adjustment on the short position held over the weekends, but you'll lock in the $0.1000 differential between the Rolling Spot price and the strike price of the call.

As is the case for those with Rolling Spot positions, those with option positions who want physical currencies have a number of choices, which generally include the following:

1. liquidate your options and make your desired trade in the traditional spot market;
2. exercise your options, liquidate the resulting Rolling Spot position, and again trade traditional spot; or
3. exercise your option and arrange an EFP transaction which, as noted earlier, simultaneously liquidates your Rolling Spot position and enters an offsetting spot market trade.

Once each quarter, yet another possibility exists. That is, for the option expiring immediately prior to the third Wednesday of the quarterly cycle (March, June, September and December), exercise at the end of the week will result in a Rolling Spot contract that, if held through the termination of trading on the next business day, will result in a physical exchange with a value date of the third Wednesday.

Conclusion

These Rolling Spot contracts offer some rather attractive features. Designed in a manner consistent with spot market pricing conventions, they will be easy to assimilate by the interbank trading/dealing community; the automatic daily swap adjustments will save time and money and significantly reduce the prospect of costly errors; and the exchange mechanism will virtually eliminate credit risk. While the full impact of these new instruments is yet to be realized, with these attributes, Rolling Spot contracts have the capacity to foster important institutional changes in the nature of currency trading.

Notes

1. A listing of all current and proposed contracts and their respective contract sizes is provided in the Appendix.
2. If the swap points were 1.80–1.70, reflecting a forward discount, the adjustment would pay to the long positions and collect from the shorts.
3. The Canadian dollar Rolling Spot offers an exception to this timing convention. It expires one day prior to the third Wednesday.

Appendix

Currency	Size of contract	Tick size (value)
Australian Dollar	A$250,000	$0.0001/A$ ($25.00)
British Pound Sterling	£250,000	$0.0001/£ ($25.00)
Canadian Dollar	$250,000	C$0.0001/$ (C$25.00)
French Franc	$250,000	FF0.0001/$ (FF25.00)
German Mark	$250,000	DM0.0001/$ (DM25.00)
Japanese Yen	$250,000	¥0.01/$ (¥2,500)
Swiss Franc	$250,000	SF0.0001/$ (SF25.00)

16

The Pricing of Forward and Futures Contracts with Heterogeneous Consumers

LLOYD P. BLENMAN

This chapter derives and contrasts forward and futures contract prices in a setting where traders have differential endowments and price expectations. General-equilibrium models of futures and forward prices are related to the single-goods models of Lucas (1978), Woodward (1980) and McCulloch (1980). These models demonstrate the role of marginal utility over time when pricing assets and in establishing the relation between forward and future spot interest rates (Woodward, 1980; McCulloch, 1980).

In a continuous-time framework, Richard and Sundaresan (1981), and Cox *et al.* (1981, 1985 a, b) develop general contingent-claims pricing models as well as models for futures and forward contracts. Contract prices are related to the expected future spot price at contract expiration as well as the covariation of marginal utility at the expiration date with the maturity price of the contract.

A different approach, employing continuous-time processes, is that of Garbade and Silber (1983), who develop pricing equations for futures contracts in terms of the movement of the underlying asset, utilizing a Black–Scholes methodology. These models are analogous to term-structure theory in the work of Woodward (1980). In an extension of McCulloch (1980), Woodward develops a series of propositions linking the existence of liquidity and solidity premiums to the covariation of future interest rates and the marginal utility of consumption.

225

In this study generalized pricing formulas for forward and futures contracts and their relation to each other are the focal issues address-ed. In the identical-consumers frictionless markets usually assumed, no contracts are traded, and all market participants have zero-valued wealth positions in forward and futures contracts. Not surprisingly, these prices are posited to be essentially forward processes of interest rates, future spot prices, and marginal utility of wealth. However, considerable evidence exists that current asset prices are systematic-ally linked to past prices. This is evident in the current dominance of GARCH modeling in finance. For a full examination of the importance of this development see the review by Bollerslev *et al.* (1992).

This knowledge leads logically to the question of what are the implications for the pricing relations when prices are allowed to evolve through time in a market setting. This relaxation necessitates the assumption of consumer heterogeneity as well as randomly varying prices to meet minimal conditions for the trading of contracts. The basic Richard and Sundaresan (1981) model is extended, adding two different consumer groups. Consumer heterogeneity is achieved by differential goods endowment and rate of time preference. In this model, equilibrium must not be characterized by the optimal number of contingent claims being forced to zero and hence contract holders' wealth is not necessarily held in goods only.

The generalized pricing relations that are developed indicate that both forward and futures contract prices can be treated as prices for the delivery of random quantities of goods even when interest rates are nonstochastic. This uncertainty derives from the assumption of consumer heterogeneity. However, the model extension clearly shows that the current prices of both forward and futures contracts depend not only on expected future spot prices at contract maturity, the future interest rate structure and marginal terminal utility of wealth, but also on past contract prices, expected net profits and the un-certainty over the quantity of goods to be delivered.

Replicable strategies that generate the derived pricing relations are presented. It is also shown that under the maintained assumptions, forward and futures prices for contracts on identical goods need not be equal, even when interest rates are nonstochastic. Finally, sufficient conditions for the equivalence of the results derived here and those in the extant literature are presented.

The next section develops the model and derives the partial differential equations which emanate from the solutions to the consumer's optimizing problems. The solutions of these partial differential equations provide the generalized pricing relations sought. The subsequent section discusses the issues of forward and futures valuation under current settlement procedures and details the solutions of the partial differential equations of the earlier section. The general nonequivalence of forward and futures prices is also demonstrated, even when interest rates are deterministic. The third section details the arbitrage strategies that replicate the pricing relations derived earlier and the final section summarizes these findings.

The Model

A general-equilibrium continuous-time, rational-expectations model of a multigoods economy, formulated by Richard and Sundaresan (1981), in which individuals act to maximize expected utility is used. Individuals hold contingent-claim contracts in a frictionless environment with explicitly costless market guarantees. The existence of traded contracts is assured by postulating the presence of two groups of consumers differentiated via their endowments and risk preferences. It is shown in Blenman (1986) that the marginal utility of wealth for each type of representative consumer is equal in equilibrium. Moreover, the general form of the partial differential equations that must be solved to derive the pricing formulas is identical for each consumer class in our optimization problem.

The equilibrium prices that are derived are consistent with Pareto-optimality. It is assumed that each individual of type k, $k = 1, 2$, tries to maximize expected utility in the form[1]

$$E\left[\int_0^T e^{-\rho t} u(c(t)) \, dt\right]. \tag{1}$$

There are n goods in this economy and the rate of net production of goods is governed by a net vector stochastic differential equation

$$dq = (h - c)dt + G \, dz, \tag{2}$$

where dq is an $n \times 1$ vector of the rate of change of net output of goods, G is an $n \times (k + n)$ diffusion matrix, dz is a $(k + n) \times 1$ vector of independent Weiner processes, h is the vector of expected instantaneous rates of output and c is the vector of instantaneous rates of consumption. Each consumer has a proportional share of the initial stock of goods $Q(0)$ and is able to invest in all productive processes. All goods are used as inputs in the production of goods i, $i = 1, 2, \ldots, n$. The total amount of j invested in production at time t is

$$q_j = \sum_{i=1}^n k_{ij}, \quad j = 1, 2, \ldots, n, \tag{3}$$

where k_{ij} represents the amount of the jth goods used in the production of goods i, $i = 1, 2, \ldots, n$. Additionally, $G = G(k_i, Y)$ and $h_i(k_i, Y)$, where k_i is the vector of goods used in the production of goods i and Y is the vector of technological state variables which influence productive activity. These technological state variables are governed by a stochastic differential equation

$$dY = \mu(Y, t) + S(Y)dz, \tag{4}$$

where Y is a $k \times 1$ vector and S is a $k \times (n + k)$ matrix. Stocks of output $Q(t)$ are subject to change via a diffusion process

$$dQ = B \, dt + D \, dz, \tag{5}$$

where Q is an $n \times 1$ vector, D is an $n \times (n + k)$ diffusion matrix, B is an $n \times 1$ vector and the summation of all endowments at time t equals the stock $Q\{t\}$. Finally, the stochastic differential equations governing the two types of contracts and the prices of the n goods associated with the two types of contracts are specified. Even though the processes governing the evolution of the prices of goods and contractual claims are specified in an *ex ante* fashion, the actual forms of these processes are determined endogeneously, since all processes and valuation formulas are functions of the underlying state variables Y and Q. In particular $V_k = V_k(Q, Y, t)$, $k = 1, 2$. V is an n element vector of the values of type k contracts on all n goods. By Itô's lemma the following relation for the jth element of V_k is obtained.

$$dV = \left[\sum_{i=1}^{n} V_{Q_i} B_i + \sum_{i=1}^{k} V_{Y_i} \mu_i + \frac{1}{2} \sum_{i=1}^{n} \sum_{j=1}^{n} V_{Q_i Q_i} (DD')_{ij} \right.$$

$$+ \sum_{i=1}^{k} \sum_{j=1}^{n} V_{Q_i Y_i} S_i D_i' + \frac{1}{2} \sum_{i=1}^{k} \sum_{j=1}^{k} V_{Y_i Y_j} (SS)_{ij}' \left. \right] dt$$

$$+ \left[\sum_{i=1}^{n} V_{Q_i} D_i + \sum_{i=1}^{k} V_{Y_i} S_i \right] dz. \tag{6}$$

This implies that $dV_k = (\alpha_k - \varphi_k)dt + H_k dz_k$ by restricting $(\alpha_k - \varphi_k)$, and H_k to be the analogue of the terms in brackets above. It is to be noted at this stage for future reference that the differential operator L, defined in equation (14) is such that $LV_k = (\alpha_k - \varphi_k)$, $k = 1, 2$. For purposes of simplicity equation (6) is represented as

$$dV_k = (\alpha_k - \varphi_k)dt + H_k \, dz, \tag{7}$$

where V_k is the vector of values of type k contracts, and $k = 1$ and 2, respectively, for forward and futures contracts. Prices of goods are described by the vector of stochastic differential equations $dp = \alpha_p\,dt + \sigma_p\,dz$. $\alpha_k - \varphi_k$ and α_p are the respective instantaneous rates of change of the values of contracts of type k and prices of goods of type k contracts. H_k and σ_k are their respective diffusion matrices. Each consumer is also assumed to be able to borrow and lend at the riskless rate of interest $r(t)$ and to hold goods and contingent claims. Each individual therefore has an equation of wealth such that,

$$p'q + \sum_{k=1}^{2} M_k V_k + \lambda = W, \qquad (8)$$

where λ is the amount invested in riskless lending and borrowing, M_k is an N-vector of the number of type k contracts held on each type of goods and V_k is an n-vector of the values of each type of contract held on each type of goods. By an application of Itô's lemma to the wealth equation

$$dW = p'q + q'dp + dp'dq + \sum_{k=1}^{2} M_k dV_k + \lambda r dt. \qquad (9)$$

This implies that

$$dW = \left[p'(h-c) + q'\alpha_p + tr\sigma_p G' + \sum_{k=1}^{2} M_k(\alpha_k - \varphi_k - V_k r) + (w - p'q)r \right] dt$$

$$+ \left[p'G + q'\sigma_p + \sum_{k=1}^{2} M_k H_k \right] dz. \qquad (10)$$

Let $dW = \beta_W\,dt + \sigma_W\,dz$; β_W and σ_W being the terms in square brackets in equation (10). The consumer's problem is to maximize expected utility for appropriate choice of the control variables M_k, c_k and k_{ij} subject to the wealth equation and the state variables Q and Y. Merton (1969, 1971) showed that the consumer's problem can be reduced to

$$\max E_t \left[\int_t^T e^{-\rho t} u(c(t))\,dt + I(Y(T),\ Q(T),\ W(T),\ T) \right] \qquad (11)$$

subject to the budget constraint

$$dW = \beta_W\,dt + \sigma_W\,dz. \qquad (12)$$

and $c(t) \geq 0$, $W(t) > 0$, and $W_0 = W_0 > 0$.

$I(Y(T), Q(T), W(T), T)$ in this context is simply a measure of the value function at the expected terminal time T. A transformation $J(Y, Q, W) = e^{\rho t} I(Y, Q, W, t)$ is used to eliminate the explicit dependence on the time variable. J is assumed to be concave in the wealth variable and the utility function is a von Neumann–Morgenstern utility function. The stochastic Bellman equation is then derived. Fleming and Rishel (1975) prove that if the control variables satisfy the Bellman equation then those control variables constitute optimal consumer decisions and J is the optimum value function. This condition is assumed to be met. The requisite Bellman equation is[2]

$$0 = \max_{c_i, m_k, k_{ij}} [LJ + u(c(t)) - \rho J], \tag{13}$$

where L is a differential operator such that

$$LJ = \beta_W J_W + \sum_{i=1}^{k} \mu_i J_{Y_i} + \sum_{i=1}^{n} B_i J_{Q_i} + \frac{1}{2} J_{WW} \sigma_W \sigma_W' + J_t$$

$$+ \sum_{i=1}^{k} \sum_{j=1}^{n} J_{Y_i Q_i}(S_i D_j') + \frac{1}{2} \sum_{i}^{k} \sum_{j}^{k} J_{Y_i Y_j}(SS')_{ij}$$

$$+ \sum_{i=1}^{k} J_{WY_i} \sigma_W S_i' + \sum_{i=1}^{n} J_{WQ_i} \sigma_W D_i' + \frac{1}{2} \sum_{i=1}^{n} \sum_{j=1}^{n} J_{Q_i Q_j}(DD')_{ij}. \tag{14}$$

Let

$$\psi = \max_{k_{ij}, c_i, M_k} LJ + U(c(t)) - \rho J = 0. \tag{15}$$

The first-order conditions derived from maximizing equation (15) subject to the control variables are

$$\psi_{c_i} = u_i(c(t)) - \rho J_W = 0, \, i = 1, 2, \ldots, n, \tag{16}$$

where u_i is the marginal utility of consumption of the ith good.

$$\psi_{M_k} = J_W\left[(\alpha_k - \phi_k) - V_k r\right] + J_{WW} H_k \sigma_W' + \sum_{i=1}^{k} J_{WY_i} H_k S_i'$$

$$+ \sum_{i=1}^{n} J_{WQ_i} H_k D_i' = 0; \, i = 1, 2 \tag{17}$$

and

$$\psi_{k_{ij}} = P_i + \frac{\partial h_i}{\partial k_{ij}} + \alpha_{p_j} - rP_j + \sigma_{p_j} \frac{\partial G_i}{\partial k_{ij}} + p_j \frac{\partial G_i}{\partial k_{ij}} + \sigma_{p_j}$$

$$+ J_{WW}\sigma'_W + \sum_{i=1}^{k} J_{WY_i}S'_i + \sum_{i=1}^{N} J_{WQ_i}H_k D'_i = 0; \ i, j = 1, \ldots, N. \quad (18)$$

By taking the total derivative of the stochastic Bellman equation with respect to W and using the differential operator L it can be shown that

$$0 = (r - \rho)J_W + LJ_W. \quad (19)$$

Additionally, repeated differentiation of equation (17) with respect to M_k shows that it can be expressed as

$$J_W[(\alpha_k - \varphi_k) - V_k r] = 0, k = 1, 2. \quad (20)$$

Equation (20) is the fundamental valuation equation that must be solved for current forward and futures prices. These solutions are derived in the next section after an analysis of the pricing characteristics of the contracts is presented.

Forward and Futures Contract Valuation

First the different treatment of forward and futures contracts is discussed and then solutions of equation (20) for the pricing formulas for futures and forward prices of goods j are presented. Futures contracts are continuous-payoff contracts, that have zero value to new contract holders after each payoff since the price of the contract is marked-to-market value at the end of every day. Hence, the change in value of a futures contract on goods j between payoffs is $dV_{2j} = df_j$. Here $df_j = f_j(t, T) - f(t_0, T), 0 \leqslant t_0 < t < T$.

Forward contracts are maturity-payoff contracts that are generally not zero-valued except at the time of issuance. The change in the value of a forward contract on the jth goods is $dV_{ij} = \beta_1(t, T)dF_j$. Here $dF_j = F_j(t, T) - F_j(t_0, T)$ and $0 \leqslant t_0 < t$. $\beta_1(t, T)$ is the present value of a dollar to be received with certainty at time T, and $0 \leqslant t_0 < t < T$. Goods type 1 is a numeraire good and its price is set at one identically for all times $t \in [0, T]$. Hence $\beta_1(t, T) \exp \int_t^T r(t, s)ds = 1$ defines the structure of spot and forward interest rates. $r(t, t) = r(t)$ is the current spot rate of interest.

The following notation is used: $F(t_0, T)(f(t_0, T))$ is the price at time t_0

of a forward (futures) contract entered at t_0 with maturity date T. $F(t, T)$ $(f(t, T))$ is the time-t price of a forward (futures) contract that has been held from time t_0 with maturity date T. $V_{ij}(t) = V_{ij}(t_0, t, T)$ is the value of the position held in a type i contingent claim contract on the jth goods from time t_0 to time t. $V_{ij}(T) = V_{ij}(t_0, T, T)$ is the value of the position held in a type i contingent claim on the jth goods from time t_0 to time T. $\gamma(t) = \gamma(t_0, t, T)$ is the percentage change in the price of a forward contract from time t_0 to time t. $\gamma(T) = \gamma(t_0, T, T)$ is the percentage change in the price of a forward contract from time t_0 to time T. $\gamma^*(t) = \gamma^*(t_0, t, T)$ is the percentage change in the price of a futures contract from time t_0 to time t. $\gamma^*(T) = \gamma^*(t_0, T, T)$ is the percentage change in the price of a futures contract from time t_0 to time T.

Forward Contracts

It is assumed that these contracts have been held from some arbitrary time t_0 such that $0 \leq t_0 < t$. The value of a single forward contract on goods j at time t is $V_{ij}(t) = \beta_1(t, T)(F(t, T) - F(t_0, T))$. $V_{1j}(t)$ therefore represents the cumulative change in the value of the contract to its holder since the contract was written. Since $V_{ij}(t) = \beta_1(t, T)(F(t, T) - F(t_0, T))$, this implies that

$$V_{1j}(t) = \left[1 - \frac{F_j(t_0, T)}{F_j(t, T)}\right] R_j(t, T) = \gamma(t)R_j(t, T), \qquad (21)$$

where $R_j(t, T)$ is defined to be equal to $\beta_1(t, T)F_j(t, T)$ and $\gamma(t)$ is as previously defined. The jth element of equation (20) $J_W[(\alpha_1 - \varphi_1) - V_1 r] = 0$ can be expressed as

$$L(J_W V_{1j}) - V_{1j}LJ_W - V_{1j}rJ_W = 0. \qquad (22)$$

By substituting for $V_{ij}(t)$, equation (22) is equivalent to

$$L(J_W \gamma(t)R_j(t, T)) - \rho\gamma(t)R_j(t, T)J_W = 0. \qquad (23)$$

On the assumption that all the continuity conditions are satisfied, by Theorem 5.2 of Friedman (1975), the solution of equation (23) is

$$J_W \gamma(t)R_j(t, T) =$$

$$E_t\left(J_W(T)\gamma(T)\beta_1(T, T)\theta_j(W(T), Y(T), Q(T), T)\exp\int_t^T -\rho ds\right), \qquad (24)$$

where $\theta_j(W(T), Y(T), Q(T), T) = \tilde{F}_j(T, T)$ is the boundary condition at time T on the jth contract whose time-t price is $F_j(t, T)$. Since $\beta_1(T, T)$ $= 1$ and $\tilde{F}_j(T, T) = \tilde{P}_j(T)$, the general solution of equation (23) can be simplified as follows:

$$F_j(t, T) = E_t\left(\frac{J_W(T)}{J_W(t)}\,\tilde{P}_j(T)\,\frac{\gamma(T)}{\gamma(t)}\exp\int_t^T(r(t, s) - \rho)\mathrm{d}s\right). \qquad (25)$$

Next we utilize the relation that $u_1(c(t)) = \rho J_W$ to show that equation (25) implies

$$F_j(t, T) = E_t\left\{\frac{(u_1(c(T))\gamma(T)}{(u_1(c(t))\gamma(t)}\,\tilde{P}_j(T)\exp\int_t^T(r(t, s) - \rho)\mathrm{d}s\right\}$$

$$= F_j(t_0, T) + E_t\left\{\frac{J_W(T)}{J_W(t)}(\tilde{P}_j(T) - F_j(t_0, T))\exp\int_t^T(r(t, s) - \rho)\mathrm{d}s\right\}.$$

$$\qquad (26)$$

This relation holds for $n - 1$ goods in the economy. Richard and Sundaresan (1981) in their derivation demonstrate that the forward price of the jth good $F_j(t, T)$ is the present value of a known number $\exp\int_t^T r(t, s)\mathrm{d}s$ of the goods to be delivered at time T. In their formulation $\gamma(T)/\gamma(t) = 1$. Based on their analysis, they assert, as does French (1983) that holding a guaranteed forward contract is in essence only a gamble on the expected future spot price. This formulation of the general pricing relation indicates that the forward price of a contract can be shown to be the present value of a random quantity of goods to be delivered at time T.

$\gamma(T)/\gamma(t)$ contains an implicit assumption about the behavior of prices from t to the maturity of the contract, relative to its past price behavior. It should be noted that there is no inherent contradiction between the results derived here and those obtained by Richard and Sundaresan (1981). Here the consideration is for the prices of forward contracts when such contracts are held by market participants from some arbitrary time t_0 until at least time t. As a result of the explicit assumptions that the values of the contracts were influenced by Weiner processes, a logical implication is that forward prices are also functions of the particular Weiner processes Z_i that have been specified implicitly. This formulation admits that of Richard and Sundaresan (1981) under the explicit assumption that $F_j(t_0, T) = 0$ or $F_j(t, T) = F_j(t_0, T)$. Hence there is explicit allowance for the possibility that the sequence of forward prices did not originate at time t.

An interpretation of the general pricing relation for forward prices shows that the mere uncertainty introduced by having to consider the expected movement of prices relative to their past history may possibly make a forward contract a *de facto* contract for a random quantity of goods. However, this does not indicate the full extent of the uncertainty and risks faced by forward contract holders. A complete treatment of those risks would then include the possibility of nonperformance.

Futures Contracts

From equation (20) it is noted that $J_W((\alpha_{2j}\varphi_{2j}) - V_{2j}r) = 0$ is the equation that must be solved to derive the pricing relation for the jth good. This can be expressed as

$$L(J_W V_{2j}) + (r - \rho)V_{2j}J_W = 0. \tag{27}$$

By applying Theorem 5.2 of Friedman (1975), the derived solution is

$$V_{2j} = E_t\left\{\frac{J_W(T)}{J_W(t)}V_{2j}(T)\exp\int_t^T (r(t,\,s) - \rho)ds\right\}$$

where $V_{2j}(t) = f_j(t,\,T) - f_j(t_0,\,T)$

and $V_{2j}(T) = \tilde{P}_t(T) - f_j(t_0,\,T). \tag{28}$

This implies that

$$f_j(t,\,T) = f_j(t_0,\,T) + E_t\left\{\frac{J_W(T)}{J_W(t)}(\tilde{P}_t(T) - f_j(t_0,\,T))\exp\int_t^T (r(t,\,s) - \rho)ds\right\}. \tag{29}$$

Equation (29) generates the standard Richard and Sundaresan (1981) pricing relation under the assumption that $f_j(t_0,\,T) = 0$ or $f_j(t_0,\,T) = f_j(t,\,T).$[3]

Strategies Replicating the General Pricing Relations

Forward Prices

Assume that the time-t price of a forward contract for goods j is $F_j(t, T)$, and that no implicit or explicit investment is required. Take a position in $\gamma(t)^{-1}\exp\int_t^T r(t, s)ds$ forward contracts and invest $F_j(t, T)$ in riskless long-term bonds maturing at time T. The current value of the bond holdings is $F_j(t, T)\exp\int_t^T r(t, s)ds$. The time-$T$ payoff on each contract is $\tilde{P}_j - F_j(t, T)$. The payoff at time T on all forward contracts on goods j is $\gamma(t)^{-1}\exp\int_t^T r(t, s)(\tilde{P}_j(T) - F_j(t, T))$. Hence the terminal value of the combined holdings of bonds and forward contracts is

$$F_j(t, T)\exp\int_t^T r(t, s)\,ds + \gamma(t)^{-1}\exp\int_t^T r(t, s)\,ds(\tilde{P}_t - F_j(t, T))$$

$$= F_j(t, T)\exp\int_t^T r(t, s)\,ds\left\{1 + \frac{\tilde{P}_t(T) - F_j(t, T)}{F_j(t, T) - F_j(t_0, T)}\right\}. \tag{30}$$

Note that

$$\gamma(t)^{-1} = \frac{F_j(t, T)}{F_j(t, T) - F_j(t_0, T)}. \tag{31}$$

The value of the combined holdings at time T simplifies to

$$F_j(t, T)\exp\int_t^T r(t, s)\,ds\left\{\frac{\tilde{P}_t(T) - F_j(t, T)}{F_j(t, T) - F_j(t_0, T)}\right\}. \tag{32}$$

However

$$\frac{\gamma(T)}{\gamma(T)} = \left\{\frac{\tilde{P}_t(T) - F_j(t, T)}{F_j(t, T) - F_j(t_0, T)}\right\}\frac{F_j(t, T)}{\tilde{P}_t(T)} \tag{33}$$

since $\tilde{P}_j = \tilde{F}_j(T, T)$ by definition. This result shows that equation (32) is equivalent to

$$\frac{\gamma(T)}{\gamma(T)}\exp\int_t^T r(t, s)\,ds\,\tilde{P}_t(T). \tag{34}$$

Since an investment of $F_j(t, T)$ at time t leads to the payoff shown in equation (34), $F_j(t, T)$ is its present value. However, equation (34) is an uncertain payoff, since perfect knowledge is not assumed. The investor is assumed to have a rate of time preference of ρ. The utility weighted value of the initial investment must therefore equal the expectation of the discounted utility-weighted value of the terminal payoff. This generates equation (26) which was derived as the solution to the general model.

Futures Prices

The arbitrage strategy presented here is a variant of the 'forward plan' strategy in proposition 2 of Cox *et al.* (1981). Assume that the time-*t* price of a futures contract with maturity at time T is $f(t, T)$ and that no implicit or explicit investment is required to hold a contract. Invest the sum of $f(t, T) - f(t_0, T)$ in first period bonds and continually roll over the end of period sum in further first period bonds until time T. In each investment period $j = t, t + 1, \ldots, T - 1$, buy $\Pi_j^{k=t} R_k$ futures contracts, liquidating the position at the end of the investment period. Invest the proceeds in first period bonds until time T.

The payoff that derives from this strategy is the sum of the proceeds from the initial investment of $f(t, T) - f(t_0, T)$ plus the proceeds generated by investing the cash flows from the futures market strategy. Therefore

$$(f(t, T) - f(t_0, T))\prod_{j=t}^{T-1} R_j + \sum_{j=t}^{T-1}\left(\prod_{k=t}^{j} R_k\right)(f(j+1, T) - f(t, T))\left(\prod_{k=j+1}^{T-1} R_j\right) \quad (35)$$

is the terminal value of all the invested cash flows plus the initial investment. $R_k, k = t, \ldots, T - 1$ equals one plus the rate of interest for the kth investment period. Equation (35) can be reduced to

$$\Pi_{j=t}^{T-1} R_j(\tilde{f}(T, T) - f(t_0, T)) = \Pi_{j=t}^{T-1} R_j(\tilde{P}(T) - f(t_0, T)). \quad (36)$$

assuming the convergence between futures market prices and cash market prices at contract maturity. The continuous-time analogue of equation (36) is

$$\exp\int_{t}^{T} r(s) \, ds(\tilde{P}(T) - f(t_0, T)). \quad (37)$$

The payoff characterized by equation (37) is uncertain and

assuming a rate of time preference of ρ, the utility-weighted value of the initial investment must equal the expectation of the discounted utility-weighted terminal payoff. This leads to the pricing relation derived earlier in equation (29). At this juncture it is appropriate to emphasize that the particular relations developed for forward and futures prices appears to depend on the choice of arbitrage strategies. Implicitly at least this seems to be the essential fact to be gleaned from the work of Cox *et al.* (1981) who develop a series of propositions on forward and futures prices in discrete and continuous-time analyses.

The next issue that is addressed here is that of the equivalence of forward and futures prices in a deterministic interest-rate setting. Under an assumption of nonstochastic interest rates, future spot rates equal forward rates implicit in the term structure. However, the generalized pricing relations in equations (26) and (29) suggest that even under these assumptions $F_j(t, T) \neq f_j(t_0, T)$ unless, in our model, (1) $F_j(t_0, T) = f_j(t_0, T)$ or (2) $F_j(t, T) = F_j(t_0, T)$ and $f_j(t, T) = f_j(t_0, T)$ are conditions that prevail.

Conclusion

This chapter has addressed the issues of forward and futures contract pricing in a heterogeneous consumer framework. In such a framework the possibility of nonzero-valued contract positions must not be excluded. It is found that even in a frictionless environment, with deterministic interest rates, the prices of forward and futures contracts that cover equivalent quantities of goods need not be equal.

Uncertainty forces a wedge between the prices of the two contract types unless the risks in each market are identical. Both forward and futures contracts can be characterized as essentially contracts for the delivery of random quantities of the underlying goods. The generalized pricing formulas reduce under specified restrictions to those derived by Richard and Sundaresan (1981) and Cox *et al.* (1981). Arbitrage strategies that generate these results are derived and presented.

The current price of a forward contract reflects the fact that the contract holder has contracted for the delivery or receipt of $\gamma(T)/\gamma$ $(t)\exp\int_t^T r(t, s)\, ds$ units of the underlying goods. In the homogeneous-consumer model, $\gamma(T)/\gamma(t)$ converges to one and the results of Richard and Sundaresan are derived. The current price of a futures contract reflects the fact the contract holder has made a bet on $\gamma^*(T)/\gamma^*(t)\exp\int_t^T r(t, s)\, ds$ units of the underlying goods, where $\gamma^*(T)$ and $\gamma^*(t)$ are the analogues for futures prices of equation (33). Unlike the case of the forward contract holder, the futures contract holder has no obligation to make or accept delivery on the contract unless the position is held to maturity. Typically a losing futures position is eliminated by taking an offsetting position in the contract.

Interest-rate uncertainty can preserve the Richard and Sundaresan
(1981) and Cox *et al.* (1981) results, but the relations presented here
suggest that another element is vitally important. Pricing uncertainty,
which does not need to be linked to interest-rate uncertainty, also
affects the quantity of goods ultimately delivered against a futures
contract. This result for futures prices can be easily verified by
inspection of (29). If $\gamma^*(T)/\gamma^*(t) = 1$, the general relation in equation
(29) is the same as that derived by the cited authors. However,
$\gamma^*(T)/\gamma^*(t)$ need not equal one and risk can be linked directly to
uncertainty over the quantity of goods delivered if the contract is to
be held to maturity.

Hence the risk in a futures contract, like a forward contract, is
linked to pricing uncertainty impact on the quantity of goods to be
delivered. However, the interest-rate element adds to the overall risk
unless nonstochastic interest rates are assumed. The results that are
generated in this general equilibrium model in a very real sense beg
the question of why individuals with different endowments and
wealth levels would take the opposite sides of contract positions. The
expectations of these individuals and their motives for contract
holding are therefore not explicitly modeled.

It is simply postulated that each individual is trying to maximize
utility of wealth at the terminal time T and each utilizes a
differentiated rate of time discount ρ. It is believed that richer pricing
models can be generated if these considerations are addressed.
However, our model extension clearly shows that the current prices
of both forward and futures contracts depend not only on expected
future spot prices at contract maturity, the future interest rate
structure and marginal utility of terminal wealth, but also on past
contract prices, expected net profits and the uncertainty over the
quantity of goods to be delivered.

Notes

1. In reality all the consumer specific variables E, ρ and μ should be indexed for
   consumer type. However, this notation is suppressed for ease of exposition.
2. For a rigorous derivation of the stochastic Bellman equation, see Dreyfus (1965).
   Merton (1969) shows that the resulting Bellman equation is valid $\forall t \in [0, T]$.
3. If $f_j(t_0, T) = 0$, then the equivalence of the general result and that of Richard
   and Sundaresan (1981) is obvious. If $f_j(t_0, T) = f_j(t, T)$ then result (A.16) in their
   study must be utilized to establish the equivalence of the two specifications.

References

BLACK, F. (1976) The pricing of commodity contracts, *Journal of Financial
Economics*, 5, 167–176.

BLENMAN, L. P. (1986) Implicit forward and futures relations in the T-bill market, Ohio State University.

BOLLERSLEV, T., CHOU, R. Y. and KRONER, K. F. (1992) ARCH modeling in finance: a review of the theoretical and empirical evidence, *Journal of Econometrics*, 52, 5–59.

COX, J .C., INGERSOLL, J. E. and ROSS, S. A. (1981) The relation between forward and futures prices, *Journal of Financial Economics*, 9, 321–346.

COX, J .C., INGERSOLL, J. E. and ROSS, S. A. (1985a) An intertemporal general equilibrium model of asset prices, *Econometrica*, 53, 363–384.

COX, J .C., INGERSOLL, J. E. and ROSS, S. A. (1985b) A theory of the term structure of interest rates, *Econometrica*, 53, 385–407.

DREYFUS, S. E. (1965) *Dynamic Programming and the Calculus of Variations*, Academic Press, New York.

FLEMING, W. H. and RISHEL, W. R. (1975) *Deterministic and Stochastic Optimal Control*, Springer, New York.

FRENCH, D. R. (1983) A comparison of forward and futures contracts, *Journal of Financial Economics*, 12, 311–342.

FRIEDMAN, A. (1975) *Stochastic Differential Equations and Applications*, Academic Press, New York, Vol. 1.

GARBADE, K. D. and SILBER, W. L. (1983) Futures contracts on commodities with multiple varieties: an analysis of premiums and discounts, *Journal of Business*, 56, 249–272.

JARROW, R. A. and OLDFIELD, G. S. (1981) Forward contracts and futures contracts, *Journal of Financial Economics*, 9, 373–382.

KANE, E. J. (1980) Arbitrage pressure and divergence between forward and futures interest rates, *Journal of Finance*, 35, 221–234, 1980.

LUCAS, R. (1978) Asset prices in an exchange economy, *Econometrica*, 46, 1429–1445.

MCCULLOCH, J. A. (1980) A static theory of the liquidity premium. Ohio State University.

MERTON, R. C. (1969) Lifetime portfolio selection under uncertainty: the continuous time case, *Review of Economic and Statistics* 51, 247–257.

MERTON, R. C. (1971) Optimal consumption and portfolio rules in a continuous time model, *Journal of Economic Theory*, 7, 373–413.

MORGAN, G. E. (1981) Forward and futures pricing of treasury bills, *Journal of Banking and Finance*, 5, 483–496.

RICHARD, F. S. and SUNDARESAN, M. (1981) A continuous time equilibrium model of forward and futures prices in a multigood economy, *Journal of Financial Economics*, 9, 347–371.

SAMUELSON, P. A. (1965) Proof that properly anticipated prices fluctuate randomly, *Industrial Management Review*, 6, 198–199.

WOODWARD, S. A. (1980) The liquidity and solidity premium, *American and Economic Review*, 73, 348–361.

17

Exchange Rate Determination in the Forward Exchange and Foreign Currency Futures Markets

ALI M. PARHIZGARI AND ROSWELL E. MATHIS, III

Introduction

Contracts which call for the delivery of a specific currency on a specified date in the future at a set price are traded in both forward exchange and foreign currency futures markets. These markets function to reduce the risk associated with the purchase and delivery of foreign currency in the future. The markets are also popular for exchange rate speculation and covered interest arbitrage.

Since the participants in the two markets are different and may be exposed to different information, one market may lead the other. In this study, tests are employed to detect the nature of the relationship between the forward and futures foreign currency markets. The currencies studied are the British pound, German mark, Japanese yen, and Swiss franc.

The remainder of this chapter is organized as follows. The next section addresses very briefly the two markets considered and reviews the prior work in this area. The ensuing sections discuss the methodology employed, the data, the application of the methodology, and the empirical results obtained. The final section contains the summary and conclusions.

Forward and Futures Currency Markets

Forward and futures currency markets differ in several ways. Foreign currency futures contracts are traded on organized exchanges which determine the terms of the contracts, whereas the terms of forward contracts, which are not traded on organized exchanges, are negotiable. For example, both the delivery date and contract size are specified by the futures exchanges. In addition, the clearinghouse and margining system of the futures market reduce the exposure of futures market participants to credit risk.

Forward and futures markets also differ in that they appeal to different market participants. The participants in the forward exchange market are typically foreign exchange brokers and institutional traders, while the participants in the foreign currency futures markets include businesses, financial firms, and individual investors.

A third difference between the forward and futures currency markets involves the intentions of the participants. Forward market participants usually take delivery of the currency upon maturity, whereas the participants in the futures market typically reverse their positions prior to maturity so that delivery of the currency does not occur.

The function and use of forward exchange and foreign currency futures markets depend upon the relationship between the forward and futures exchange rates and the spot or cash exchange rates. Forward and futures contract exchange rates are determined by the market participants in each market and, thus, reflect their collective expectations as to the future spot exchange rate. Therefore, the forward and futures currency markets are likely to be integrated. Garbade and Silber (1979) suggest that the price adjustment process in an imperfectly integrated market can occur in one of two ways. The first is a symmetrical adjustment in which the prices in one market adjust to the prices in another market as rapidly as the prices in the other market adjust to the prices in the first market. The second is that of a dominant-satellite market in which the adjustment is one-sided, that is, the prices in the satellite market almost always adjust to reflect those in the dominant market. A pure satellite market is one which always follows the dominant market.

The relationship between forward exchange and foreign currency futures markets has not been thoroughly investigated empirically, although the price adjustment process has been examined for other markets. A few studies have examined the relationship between the stock index cash and futures markets. Silber (1985) found evidence of continuous competition for leadership between cash and futures markets. Herbst *et al.* (1987) show that the index futures tend to lead the cash indices for both the Value Line and S&P500; however, they found that the cash indices usually reacted in less than a minute.

Dandapani *et al.* (1989) explored the relationship between the futures markets and the S&P500 and NYSE Stock Indices. They showed that a strong simultaneity between the types of markets exists and bidirectional feedback between them occurs. Their results pertaining to causality suggest that neither market is dominant in price determination when contracts are aggregated over contract months, but a unidirectional causality that runs from cash to futures prices was found to exist when contract months are considered separately.

Methodology

The methodology employed in this chapter to detect causal relationships replicates the procedures used by Parhizgari *et al.* (1994). The procedures, which are based on the work of Granger (1969), specify that a causal relationship exists if the prices in one market are determined by the prices in another market. If there is no causality, then lagged values of the prices in the first market should be of no use in predicting the prices in the second market once the past history of prices in the second market has been considered and vice versa. Granger's definition of causality implies that:

1. Forward exchange rates (*FE*) unidirectionally determine futures rates (*FR*), if *FE* cause *FR* and *FR* do not cause *FE*.
2. *FR* unidirectionally determine *FE* if *FR* cause *FE* and *FE* do not cause *FR*.
3. Feedback exists between forward and futures markets if *FE* cause *FR* and *FR* cause *FE*. Neither market is dominant in this case.
4. Forward and futures markets are statistically independent if *FE* do not cause *FR* and *FR* do not cause *FE*.

The empirical usage of Granger's method involves the estimation of the following equations

$$FE(t) = \alpha + \sum_{j=1}^{m} a(j)FE(t-j) + \sum_{k=1}^{n} b(k)FR(t-k) + U(t) \qquad (1)$$

and

$$FR(t) = \delta + \sum_{k=1}^{n'} c(k)FR(t-k) + \sum_{j=1}^{m'} d(j)FE(t-j) + Z(t). \qquad (2)$$

The lagged values of the dependent variables in equations (1) and (2) are used to eliminate serial correlation from the residuals $U(t)$ and $Z(t)$. If *FR* do not Granger-cause *FE* then the joint significance of the

the $b(k)$s should equal zero, and if FE do not cause FR then the joint significance of the $d(j)$s should equal zero.

The tests of the joint significance of the $b(k)$s and $d(j)$s involve the estimation of equations (1) and (2) in constrained forms, without the causal variables, and in unconstrained forms, with the causal variables. The test statistics are calculated as follows:

$$F = \frac{SSR_c - SSR_u}{df_c - df_u} \bigg/ \frac{SSR_u}{df_u}, \tag{3}$$

where SSR_c and SSR_u are the error sum of squares and df_c and df_u are the degrees of freedom for the constrained and unconstrained regressions, respectively.

The optimal length of the lags in equations (1) and (2) are determined using Akaike's minimum final prediction error (FPE) criterion as determined by Hsiao (1981). This procedure is employed because, as noted by Hsiao, the arbitrary choice of the lag lengths may bias the estimates of the coefficients for the autoregressive processes. The FPE is defined as:

$$FPE = \frac{NO + P + 1}{NO - P - 1} \bigg/ \frac{NO}{SSR}, \tag{4}$$

where

SSR = sum of squared residuals of the autoregressive process incorporating P autoregressive terms;

NO = number of observations;

P = m in the one-dimensional autoregression of FE;
$m + n$ in the autoregression incorporating m lagged FE and n lagged FR;
n' in the one-dimensional autoregression of FR;
$n' + m'$ in the autoregression incorporating n' lagged FR and m' lagged FE.

A sequential procedure is employed to determine the lag lengths which minimize equation (4).

Empirical Analysis

The relationship between the forward exchange and foreign currency futures markets is empirically investigated for four currencies, namely: the British pound, German mark, Japanese yen, and Swiss franc. Since there are four futures contract maturities traded for each security (i.e. March, June, September, and December), each contract maturity is considered separately. The data used in the analysis consists of the daily exchange rates for the period beginning in January, 1984 and ending during the middle of December, 1989. OLS is the method of estimation employed throughout this chapter.

As there exists a serial correlation when daily data is used, the first step in the analysis is to 'whiten' the time series by converting the data into the first difference of the natural logarithm. The next step is to determine the optimal lag length for equations (1) and (2) in the constrained form (i.e. determine m in equation (1) and n' in equation (2)) using the minimum *FPE* criterion. After m and n' have been determined, n and m' are determined using the minimum *FPE* criterion for equations (1) and (2) in the unconstrained form (i.e. including the causal variables).

If the minimum *FPE* of an equation in the unconstrained form is less than the minimum *FPE* of that equation in the constrained form then there is the possibility of a causal relationship that runs from the causal variable to the dependent variable. The *F*-test described in equation (3) is employed to determine if the causal relationship is statistically significant. However, if the minimum *FPE* of an equation in the constrained form is less than the minimum *FPE* of that equation in the unconstrained form then it can be concluded that there is not a causal relationship between the causal variable and the dependent variable.

Tables 17.1–17.4 show the results of the analysis for the four currencies. Column 1 of the tables gives the maturity of the futures contract which is being compared to the forward rates in the analysis. The second column designates the dependent variable, while the fifth column names the causal variable. The minimum *FPE*s without and with the causal variable are given in columns 4 and 7, respectively. The final column provides the *F*-values for the null hypothesis of no causality.

The results indicate, for all four currencies and for all four contract maturities, that significant causal relationships exist at the 1 percent level or below. In all cases, *FE* are shown to Granger-cause *FR* and *FR* are shown to Granger-cause *FE* at the 1 percent level. Thus, it appears that bidirectional feedback is taking place between the foreign currency futures and forward exchange markets with neither market assuming a dominant role.

Conclusions

In conclusion, the nature of the relationship between the forward exchange and foreign currency futures markets is investigated using

TABLE 17.1 Analysis of Causality from Futures Rates (FR) to Forward Rates (FE) and from Forward Rates to Futures Rates for the British Pound

Futures contract maturity	Dependent variable	Optimum lag of dep. var.	Minimum FPE of the one-dimensional auto-regressive process	Causal variable	Optimum lag of causal variable	Minimum FPE with the causal variable	F-value
March	FR	16	$4.881E-4$	FE	3	$4.277E-4$	32.974*
June	FR	16	$4.324E-4$	FE	2	$4.043E-4$	24.851*
September	FR	16	$3.623E-4$	FE	2	$3.332E-4$	31.155*
December	FR	16	$5.189E-4$	FE	3	$4.885E-4$	16.403*
March	FE	5	$2.524E-4$	FR	3	$1.996E-4$	61.151*
June	FE	6	$2.048E-4$	FR	3	$1.743E-4$	41.099*
September	FE	7	$1.482E-4$	FR	3	$1.227E-4$	49.082*
December	FE	6	$1.667E-4$	FR	3	$1.396E-4$	47.609*

*Significant at the 1 percent level or below.

TABLE 17.2 *Analysis of Causality from Futures Rates (FR) to Forward Rates (FE) and from Forward Rates to Futures Rates for the German Mark*

Futures contract maturity	Dependent variable	Optimum lag of dep. var.	Minimum FPE of the one-dimensional auto-regressive process	Causal variable	Optimum lag of causal variable	Minimum FPE with the causal variable	F-value
March	FR	16	4.929E – 4	FE	2	4.314E – 4	48.808*
June	FR	16	4.331E – 4	FE	2	4.049E –4	24.852*
September	FR	16	3.744E – 4	FE	3	3.499E – 4	17.605*
December	FR	16	5.352E – 4	FE	3	5.057E – 4	15.082*
March	FE	6	2.535E – 4	FR	3	1.992E – 4	62.750*
June	FE	6	2.049E – 4	FR	3	1.745E – 4	40.834*
September	FE	6	1.479E – 4	FR	3	1.224E – 4	49.047*
December	FE	6	1.722E – 4	FR	3	1.444E – 4	45.957*

*Significant at the 1 percent level or below.

TABLE 17.3 *Analysis of Causality from Futures Rates (FR) to Forward Rates (FE) and from Forward Rates to Futures Rates for the Japanese Yen*

Futures contract maturity	Dependent variable	Optimum lag of dep. var.	Minimum FPE of the one dimensional auto-regressive process	Causal variable	Optimum lag of causal variable	Minimum FPE with the causal variable	F-value
March	FR	16	$4.951E-4$	FE	3	$4.288E-4$	37.548*
June	FR	16	$4.928E-4$	FE	3	$4.553E-4$	20.042*
September	FR	16	$4.192E-4$	FE	3	$3.681E-4$	33.036*
December	FR	16	$5.012E-3$	FE	2	$4.758E-3$	19.926*
March	FE	6	$2.683E-4$	FR	3	$2.095E-4$	67.524*
June	FE	6	$2.086E-4$	FR	3	$1.803E-4$	37.008*
September	FE	6	$1.851E-4$	FR	3	$1.522E-4$	51.096*
December	FE	7	$1.939E-4$	FR	3	$1.587E-4$	52.390*

*Significant at the 1 percent level or below.

TABLE 17.4 *Analysis of Causality from Futures Rates (FR) to Forward Rates (FE) and from Forward Rates to Futures Rates for the Swiss Franc*

Futures contract maturity	Dependent variable	Optimum lag of dep. var.	Minimum FPE of the one dimensional auto-regressive process	Causal variable	Optimum lag of causal variable	Minimum FPE with the causal variable	F-value
March	FR	16	4.937E − 4	FE	2	4.321E − 4	48.747*
June	FR	16	4.292E − 4	FE	3	4.025E − 4	16.537*
September	FR	16	3.524E − 4	FE	3	3.268E − 4	19.491*
December	FR	16	5.480E − 4	FE	3	5.184E − 4	14.795*
March	FE	6	2.539E − 4	FR	3	1.995E − 4	62.639*
June	FE	5	2.041E − 4	FR	3	1.746E − 4	39.678*
September	FE	6	1.472E − 4	FR	3	1.222E − 4	48.381*
December	FE	6	1.707E − 4	FR	3	1.434E − 4	45.312*

*Significant at the 1 percent level or below.

daily data. The tests for causality are carried out according to Granger's method while employing Hsiao's final prediction error (*FPE*) criterion to determine the optimal lag structure. The results imply that a strong bidirectional feedback exists between the two markets, since, in all cases, *FR* are shown to cause *FE* and *FE* are shown to cause *FR*. Thus, neither market is dominant and it does not appear that the participants in either of the markets possess better information than the participants in the other market. Future research needs to address the simultaneity relationship between the two markets in order to further explore the feedback mechanism that exists between the two markets.

References

DANDAPANI, K., PARHIZGARI, A. M. and BHATTACHARYA, A. K. (1989) Price determination in the stock index and futures markets. Working paper, Finance Department, FIU.

GARBADE, K. and SILBER, W. (1979) Dominant and satellite markets: a study of dually-traded securities, *Review of Economics and Statistics*, 61, 455–460.

GRANGER, C. W. J. (1969) Investigating causal relations by economic models and cross spectral methods, *Econometrica*, 37, 424–438.

HERBST, A. F., McCORMACK, J. P. and WEST, E. N. (1987) Investigation of a lead–lag relationship between spot indices and their futures contracts, *Journal of Futures Markets*, 7, 373–382.

HSIAO, C. (1981) Autoregressive modeling and money-income causality detection, *Journal of Monetary Economics*, 7, 85–106.

PARHIZGARI, A. M., DANDAPANI, K. and BHATTACHARYA, A. K. (1994) Global market place and causality, *Global Finance Journal*, 5, 121–140.

SILBER, W. (1985) The economic role of financial futures. In PECK, A. (ed.), *Futures Markets: Their Economic Role*, American Enterprise Institute for Public Policy Research, Washington, DC, pp. 83–114.

18

Evidence on Market Efficiency in the Term Structure of Currency Futures Prices

MICHAEL A. SULLIVAN

Futures markets are organized for the convenience of speculators. A limited number of contracts are offered, enhancing liquidity and facilitating the closing of positions before the maturity date of a contract. However, the standardized contracts pose a challenge for empirical analysis. In particular, if futures prices are interpreted as forecasts of spot prices on contract maturity dates, then only a limited number of observations on forecast errors are available. For example, active trading in foreign currency futures is concentrated in contracts which mature on a quarterly cycle.

This inconvenient feature explains why most investigations of market efficiency in foreign exchange markets focus on forward contracts. Representative forward exchange rates with a fixed time to maturity are available on a daily basis, although the number which are used is smaller in order to get nonoverlapping forecast periods. For example, Lai and Lai (1991) use one-month forecast periods to investigate cointegration between forward and spot exchange rates.

However, futures markets do have some advantages for empirical study. They are centralized markets with explicit entry requirements and detailed transactions data, allowing a more complete picture of market operations and a more consistent assessment of price behavior. However, if the same approach used for forward markets is carried over to futures markets, as in Chowdhury (1991), then most observations will be excluded. Over the 18 years of his sample he uses only 64 of the available futures prices to conduct his tests because he analyzes three-month holding periods.

In fact, most futures positions are closed before a contract's maturity date, and the clearinghouse which organizes the market enforces daily settlement of profits and losses. Futures traders are more likely to focus on short-term changes during the life of the contract rather than the longer-term changes over its life. If market participants have this perspective, then it seems natural for the empirical analyst to test efficiency using more frequent sampling of the data.

As an example of the benefits of adapting the method of analysis to the market under investigation, Hodrick and Srivastava (1987) use daily data for currency futures to find evidence that futures prices contain a risk premium. They contrast the results with those from forward exchange markets and conjecture that daily risk premiums are highly positively correlated. This is based on their finding that current futures prices are biased predictors of subsequent futures prices and that the bias increases with the length of the forecast horizon.

This chapter directly exploits the fixed maturity dates of futures contracts to develop tests of market efficiency. A sequence of futures prices in a given contract may be interpreted as a sequence of forecasts of the spot price at a fixed future date. Absent a risk premium, the law of iterated expectations implies that changes in this series should be unpredictable. That is, the time series of futures prices for a particular contract should be nonstationary. While there have been many studies of futures prices, this chapter develops several new perspectives and applies new test methods.

Cavanaugh (1987), among others, assumes that futures prices in levels are nonstationary and tests for serial correlation of their changes. It is difficult to determine whether any observed pattern in the changes in futures prices is due to inefficiency or to a time-varying risk premium. This chapter focuses on testing implications of the market efficiency hypothesis which are robust in the face of such a premium. Doukas and Rahman (1987) directly test whether currency futures prices are stationary, but they look at series with a fixed time to maturity, so a sequence of prices in different contracts. It is fairly easy to show the link between prices in the same contract as it approaches maturity, and it is this series which is analyzed here. The tests benefit from using the entire sample of daily prices over the period.

Besides missing the opportunity to investigate the behavior of daily futures prices, previous studies have not dealt with the full range of prices available on a given day. Usually only the prices in the contract nearest to its maturity date are used. The volume of trades in contracts very far from maturity is spotty, at best. However, there is enough activity in the next term contract to warrant further study. The difference between prices observed on the same date in contracts with different maturity dates may be interpreted as forecasts of the change in the spot price over a fixed period in the future, and should likewise be nonstationary. More generally, the two prices should not be cointegrated, as this would imply that changes in forecasts are expected to be subsequently revised, contrary to the efficient markets hypothesis.

Granger (1986) mentions this property of prices determined in a jointly efficient speculative market, having in mind prices for two different commodities. But the same reasoning applies to prices for the same commodity distinguished by the time for delivery. Allowing for a bias in futures prices associated with a risk premium, the same characteristic is obtained when the risk premium follows a stationary stochastic process. Engle and Granger (1987) present a cointegration test using the term structure of interest rates, which tests for market efficiency while allowing for a stochastic term premium.

In fact, the fixed maturity dates of futures contracts facilitates study of the term structure of exchange rates. Havenner and Modjtahedi (1988) sample at weekly intervals the differences between forward rates of various maturities to analyze the characteristics of 'price revisions', changes in forecasts over time. But the fixed time to maturity of the contracts induces lengthy moving average components in the series which complicate statistical inference. For currency futures prices, in given contracts the forecast period remains fixed, and across contracts the periods do not overlap.

The plan of this chapter is as follows. The next section develops the implications of the efficient markets hypothesis for the behavior of the term structure of futures prices. This is followed by a section outlining the appropriate statistical tests, and describing the data and presenting the results. The final section provides a brief summary and indicates directions for further inquiry.

Implications of the Efficient Markets Hypothesis

In an efficient financial market prices reflect all easily available information and do not allow for extraordinary profits. Currency futures contracts allow traders to fix today the terms for purchase or sale of a foreign currency at a fixed future date. The payoff to a futures position at the maturity date of the contract depends on the spot price for the currency on that date. Assuming that the risk associated with that payoff requires no premium in order to induce traders to commit themselves to futures positions, today's futures price should be equal to the expected spot price at maturity, where the expectation is with respect to information available today. Tomorrow's price in the same contract may change to incorporate new information. However, if both are optimal forecasts given available information, then the expected change is zero and past changes will not help to predict future changes.

Of course, when traders set a futures price by taking opposite positions in a contract they think of the prospective cash flows. Financial theory provides the perspective to relate the observed price to forecasts of future prices. Cox *et al.* (1981) show how a futures price can be interpreted as the price of an asset, even though the contract itself has no value at the time it is initiated. Their derivation is useful to explain the source of a risk premium in futures prices while also tying together futures prices separated by a trading period.

Let $F_{t,t+m}$ be the time t price in a futures contract which matures at time $t + m$. Suppose that at time t a trader deposits $F_{t,t+m}$ earning a riskless interest rate of r_t over one day, and takes a long position in $1+r_t$ futures contracts. At time $t + 1$ the value of the holdings would be $(1 + r_t)F_{t,t+m} + (1 + r_t)(F_{t+1,t+m} - F_{t,t+m})$, that is, $(1+r_t)F_{t+1,t+m}$. Therefore, the time t futures price and the time $t + 1$ price, adjusted by the time t one-day interest rate, are the values of an asset on adjacent dates.

The connection between these prices can be analyzed using a simple but fairly general asset pricing model. In equilibrium, investors are indifferent toward an asset when the loss in time t utility associated with its purchase equals the gain associated with the random future payoff. Following the notation in Hodrick and Srivastava (1987), let $Q_{t,t+1}$ be the marginal rate of substitution of wealth, that is, the ratio of marginal utilities between time t and time $t + 1$. In equilibrium, futures prices on adjacent dates are related as follows:

$$F_{t,t+m} = E_t[Q_{t,t+1}(1 + r_t)F_{t+1,t+m}],$$

where E_t indicates an expectation conditional on information available at time t. This relation can be restated as

$$F_{t,t+m} = E_t[F_{t+1,t+m}] + (1 + r_t)\text{COV}_t[Q_{t,t+1}, F_{t+1,t+m}].$$

using the definition of the covariance operator indicated by COV_t to show that it is conditional on time t information, and noting that the time t value of a time $t + 1$ payoff of $1 + r_t$ is equal to one, the cost of the investment.

Today's futures price will be a biased forecast of next period's futures price when the covariance term is not zero. Consider a trader who commits at time t to buy the commodity at time $t + m$ for the time

t futures price. The expected profit at the end of the next trading day, denoted $y_{t,m} = E_t[F_{t+1, t+m}] - F_{t,t+m}$, measures the risk premium of the position. If on average the time $t + 1$ futures price is higher when the trader's wealth is lower, and so the marginal utility of wealth is higher, then the covariance term is positive and $y_{t,m} < 0$. The negative risk premium implies the position produces losses on average but makes profits when the trader needs it most. In equilibrium, this hedging benefit exactly offsets the expected loss.

Market efficiency implies that the time t futures price is partly a conditional expectation of the time $t + 1$ price. This leads to a testable hypothesis about the properties of futures prices in a given contract. With respect to a time series representation

$$F_{t+1, t+m} = \beta F_{t,t+m} + y_{t,m} + \varepsilon_{t+1}, \tag{1}$$

the efficient markets hypothesis asserts that $\beta = 1$, so that there is a unit root. The random component of the change in futures rates, ε, will have a persistent effect on the levels of subsequent rates. When market prices properly react to new information they eliminate any systematic tendency for those reactions to be subsequently revised. Therefore, futures prices accumulate these random changes and the series will not be stationary.

A test for a unit root checks one implication of market efficiency. A way to design other tests is to assume characteristics of the risk premium. The validity of the tests depends on the accuracy of the assumptions. For example, if the daily risk premium is constant, then it should show up as a drift term in futures prices and changes in futures prices should be uncorrelated. However, evidence from studies of forward exchange markets indicates that the risk premium varies over time. In that situation there may be serial correlation which reflects that variation, and changes in futures prices may be predictable in part.

While the interpretation of any apparent serial correlation is ambiguous, market efficiency has unambiguous consequences for the term structure of futures prices. The difference between futures prices observed on the same date in contracts with different maturity dates contains a forecast for the change in spot prices between those dates, and changes in that forecast will be unpredictable. Let $D_t = F_{t,t+n} - F_{t,t+m}$ be the difference between time t futures prices in contracts which mature at times $t + n$ and $t + m$. Based on equation (1), the time series representation

$$D_{t+1} = \beta D_t + (y_{t,n} - y_{t,m}) + \eta_{t+1}$$

will have $\beta = 1$ if the two markets are jointly efficient. The effect of the risk premium should be smaller here, since it is the difference between the premiums in the two contracts. For example, if the premium varies over time but is equal at any given date for the two contracts, then it would drop out altogether.

While the two prices are negotiated in the same market, they should behave as distinct prices, in the sense that one price should not help to predict the other. If that is the case, then Engle and Granger (1987) show that no linear combination of the variables should be stationary. So besides checking whether there is a unit root in the time series of D_t, the hypothesis of market efficiency can be tested by checking whether any other combination results in a stationary series. The unit root and cointegration tests proceed on the assumption that the risk premium in futures prices follows a stationary stochastic process, or is a constant. This reduces the possibility that an efficient market will be found inefficient because an incorrect process for the premium is imposed. With such a broad category of premiums included, the tests focus on market efficiency.

Statistical Tests

The data for this study consists of daily futures prices from the International Money Market of the Chicago Mercantile Exchange from December 1978 through March 1993[1] for five currencies: British pound (BP), Canadian dollar (CD), Japanese yen (JY), German mark (DM), and Swiss franc (SF). On each trading day of the sample period, settlement prices, in logs, for the contract nearest to maturity and the contract next closest to maturity are used. In all, there are 3847 observations on contracts which mature on the quarterly cycle of March, June, September, and December. The data were obtained from the Futures Industry Institute.

The problem in testing for a unit root is that the usual test statistics have unusual properties. Specifically, when the series does have a unit root the ratio of the estimate to its standard deviation does not have a t-distribution. Fuller (1976) and Dickey and Fuller (1979) analyze the time series regression model

$$\Delta x_t = a + (\beta - 1)x_{t-1} + \varepsilon_t,$$

where Δ is the first difference. The hypothesis of a unit root corresponds to $\beta = 1$, and the test statistic is $(b - 1)/s(b)$, where b is the ordinary least-squares estimate of β, and $s(b)$ is the usual estimate of the standard error of b. Dickey and Fuller show that when the errors in the regression are independently and identically distributed this ratio has a limiting distribution different from the usual t-distribution. They also use simulations to tabulate critical values for a test of $\beta = 1$ for various sample sizes.

For futures prices, the presence of a time-varying risk premium may cause the residuals in the regression model to be serially correlated. In such a situation, Dickey and Fuller suggest the regression be augmented to include lagged differences. Said and Dickey (1984) give some justification for this approach, showing that if the number of lagged differences included is an increasing function of the sample size, then the test statistic's asymptotic distribution is unaffected by linear dependence in the errors. Unfortunately, this does not give a clear guide for choosing that number in finite samples. Said and Dickey use standard F-tests and t-tests for the differenced series to get an indication of the proper lag length.

As another complication, several studies find nonlinear dependence among innovations in spot and futures prices, specifically, changes in their conditional variance. Hsieh (1989) successfully fits a GARCH model for spot prices; Fujihara and Park (1990) present similar evidence for changes in futures prices. To accommodate more general error processes in unit root tests, Phillips and Perron (1988) derive a statistic which has the same asymptotic distribution as the Dickey–Fuller statistic even when the errors are serially correlated and heteroscedastic. Their Z statistic uses the residuals from the simple regression model above to get a consistent estimate of the true error variance and adjust the Dickey–Fuller statistic.

Table 18.1 shows the results of unit root tests for the near-term contract prices in levels and first differences, and for the difference between next- and near-term prices. For F_t in levels no evidence against market efficiency appears, and all the currencies seem to have a unit root. The table reports calculated augmented Dickey–Fuller statistics using four lags of the dependent variable as additional regressors. Likewise, the Phillips–Perron Z statistic has been reported using four lags of the residuals. Variation in the number of lags affected the test statistics but not enough to change the test results.

In the futures price regression in levels, the coefficients on lagged differences reflect serial correlation of changes in futures prices. For some studies this is the main point of inquiry; however, conflicting results have been found. Cavanaugh (1987) presents evidence of autocorrelation at low lags, while Fujihara and Park (1990) find that few are significant using standard errors adjusted for heteroscedasticity. That characteristic is not under investigation here, but it has implications for unit root tests. The table contents test statistics for a lag length of four. Changing the lag length had no significant effect.

The hypothesis of market efficiency does not specifically restrict the

TABLE 18.1 *Unit Root Tests*

				Regression model: $\Delta x_t = a + (\beta - 1)x_{t-1} + \varepsilon_t$, $H_0: \beta = 1$ vs $H_1: \beta < 1$		
x	Currency	b	DW	DF	ADF	Z
F_t	BP	1.00	1.93	−1.36	−1.41	−1.40
	CD	1.00	1.88	−2.16	−2.17	−2.17
	DM	1.00	1.97	−0.35	−0.40	−0.39
	JY	1.00	1.99	0.16	0.13	0.16
	SF	1.00	1.96	−0.91	−0.97	−0.95
ΔF_t	BP	0.03	2.00	−59.99*	−27.46*	−59.99*
	CD	0.06	2.00	−58.30*	−27.26*	−58.22*
	DM	0.01	2.00	−61.20*	−27.39*	−61.21*
	JY	0.00	2.00	−61.76*	−26.77*	−61.76*
	SF	0.02	2.00	−60.72*	−27.53*	−60.72*
D_t	BP	1.00	2.38	−2.24	−1.12	−1.45
	CD	1.00	2.35	−1.49	−0.56	−0.66
	DM	1.00	2.40	−0.46	0.58	0.30
	JY	1.00	2.49	−1.56	−0.28	−0.28
	SF	1.00	2.39	0.02	1.54	1.11

*Reject H_0 at 5 percent level; b, OLS estimate of β; DW, Durbin–Watson statistic; DF, $(b - 1)/s(b)$, ratio of $b - 1$ to its estimated standard error; ADF, $(b - 1)/s(b)$ in model with four lags of dependent variable added as regressors; Z, Phillips–Perron Z statistic using four lags of residuals.

characteristics of first differences of futures prices. Rather, assumptions about the behavior of the risk premium could be tested using that series. However, cointegration tests are only appropriate when the candidate series achieve stationarity after the same order of differencing. As a preliminary for the cointegration tests, the results of tests for a unit root in the time series of first differences of near-term futures prices are reported. As Table 18.1 shows, the null hypothesis of a unit root is rejected.[2] The same regressions were run for next-term futures prices, in levels and first differences. Since the results were so similar, they are not reported.

In contrast, the difference between two futures prices on the same date appears to have a unit root, further evidence that currency futures markets are efficient. Tests for a unit root in the D_t series do not reject the null. However, the Durbin–Watson statistic indicates substantial negative serial correlation of the residuals. While this could reflect variation in the risk premium, it is more likely due to changes in volume during the life of a contract. Prices in the more

TABLE 18.2 *Cointegration Tests*

Cointegrating regression: $F_{t,t+n} = \delta + \gamma F_{t,t+m} + \varepsilon_t$			
Currency	d	g	DW	R^2
BP	−0.01	1.00	0.01	1.00
CD	−0.00	1.00	0.01	1.00
DM	0.01	0.98	0.01	1.00
JY	0.01	0.99	0.01	1.00
SF	0.02	0.98	0.01	1.00

Cointegration test: $\Delta e_t = (\beta - 1)e_{t-1} + \eta_t$				
$H_0: \beta = 1$ vs $H_1: \beta < 1$				
Currency	b	DW	DF	ADF	Z
BP	1.00	2.38	−2.27	−1.16	−1.48
CD	1.00	2.35	−1.47	−0.53	−0.64
DM	1.00	2.39	−1.13	−0.09	−0.36
JY	1.00	2.49	−2.03	−0.07	−0.66
SF	1.00	2.37	−0.74	0.61	0.21

Note. The null is not rejected by any of the statistics at a 5 percent level. *d* and *g*, OLS estimates of δ and γ; R^2, regression R-squared; *e*, residuals from cointegrating regression; other statistics, as indicated in the note to Table 18.1.

actively traded near-term contract will reflect all the information arriving during a given day, while next-term contract prices will often include some of that information the following day because the settlement price is set by trades farther from the close of the market. This lagged effect would manifest itself in negative serial correlation of changes in D_t. The unit root tests which directly adjust for such dependence allow a test of market efficiency even though the data is not perfectly aligned in timing.[3]

The last test presented relies on the concept of cointegration, developed in Engle and Granger (1987). As a brief review of the essential ideas, if a variable is nonstationary in levels but stationary in first differences then it is called integrated of order one, I(1). Two variables which are individually I(1) are called cointegrated when some linear combination of them is stationary. Cointegration implies a long-run relation between the variables. And, as Engle and Granger demonstrate, it implies that deviations from that relation are expected to be corrected in the future. With respect to the term structure of futures prices, the finding of cointegration would imply anticipated revisions of current changes in forecasts, in conflict with the hypothesis of market efficiency.

Engle and Granger suggest a two-step procedure for testing for cointegration between two I(1) variables, say x and y. First, the cointegrating regression is run

$$x_t = d + \gamma y_t + \varepsilon_t$$

and then the residuals are tested for a unit root. If the two variables are not cointegrated then no linear combination of them will be stationary and a unit root should appear in the residuals. Table 18.2 reports the results of this cointegration test. Statistics from the cointegrating regression have the classic characteristics of a 'spurious' regression, a high R-squared and a low Durbin–Watson statistic.[4] Based on the estimated coefficients, the residuals are almost the same as the difference between the next- and near-term contract prices. Therefore, it is not surprising that the hypothesis of a unit root in the residuals is not rejected.[5] There is no evidence that the term structure of futures prices is cointegrated, further support of the hypothesis of market efficiency.

Summary and Conclusions

There have been many tests of market efficiency in foreign exchange markets over the years. Inevitably, testable hypotheses require some assumption about the market value of risk associated with uncertainty about future currency prices. From the study of forward exchange markets, evidence has accumulated that there is a time-varying risk premium. Currency futures markets differ in terms from forward markets and offer different perspectives on the issue of market efficiency, as long as those unique characteristics are incorporated in the design of statistical tests.

This study uses a sequence of futures prices in a contract with fixed maturity date as the data to test market efficiency. By confining attention to changes in prices before the maturity date, it develops three implications of market efficiency which hold for a broad class of possible risk premiums. Therefore, it sharply focuses on tests of efficiency. Unit root and cointegration tests provide substantial support for the proposition that currency futures markets are efficient.

No amount of evidence will settle the debate over the efficiency of financial markets. What some interpret as a risk premium, others will characterize as inefficiency. Further study of futures markets which exploits their standardized terms and centralized trading may help sharpen the debate. Daily settlement prices can reveal some important characteristics of the risk premium. And the large body of transactions data would give a more realistic picture of the 'extra-ordinary' profits which some believe the market offers.

Acknowledgement

The author would like to thank Jon Ingersoll, Phil Dybvig, and Vittorio Grilli for helpful comments on an earlier draft of this chapter. Any remaining errors or omissions are the responsibility of the author.

Notes

1. The IMM began trading in 1972 but the early years had low and spotty volume.
2. Apparently, if there is a risk premium, then it follows a stationary process. Otherwise, first differences would contain a unit root.
3. Phillips and Perron (1988) mention that negatively correlated errors distort the size of tests based on the Z statistic, and, to a lesser degree, on the ADF statistic. Using the 5 percent critical values, Type I errors occurred in more than 5 percent of the simulations. But this would bias the results against finding market efficiency.
4. Phillips (1986) describes and explains these characteristics in detail. A 'spurious' regression is one between two unrelated variables. Phillips shows why a 'significant' relation may appear when the variables are I(1).
5. The critical values differ due to the two-step estimation process and are tabulated in Engle and Granger (1987) and Phillips and Ouliaris (1990).

References

CAVANAUGH, K. L. (1987) Price dynamics in foreign currency futures markets, *Journal of International Money and Finance*, 6, 295–314.

CHOWDHURY, A. R. (1991) Futures market efficiency: evidence from cointegration tests, *Journal of Futures Markets*, 11, 577–589.

COX, J. C., INGERSOLL, J. E. and ROSS, S. A. (1981) The relation between forward and futures prices, *Journal of Financial Economics*, 9, 321–346.

DICKEY, D. A. and FULLER, W. A. (1979) Distribution of the estimators for autoregressive time series with a unit root, *Journal of the American Statistical Association*, 74, 427–431.

DOUKAS, J. and RAHMAN, A. (1987) Unit root tests: evidence from the foreign exchange futures market, *Journal of Financial and Quantitative Analysis*, 22, 101–108.

ENGLE, R. F. and GRANGER, C. W. J. (1987) Cointegration and error correction: representation, estimation, and testing, *Econometrica* 55, 251–276.

FUJIHARA, R. and PARK, K. (1990) The probability distribution of futures prices in the foreign exchange market: a comparison of candidate processes, *Journal of Futures Markets*, 10, 623–642.

FULLER, W. A. (1976) *Introduction to Statistical Time Series*, John Wiley, New York.

GRANGER, C. W. J. (1986) Developments in the study of cointegrated economic variables, *Oxford Bulletin of Economics and Statistics*, 48, 213–228.

HAVENNER, A. and MODJTAHEDI, B. (1988) Foreign exchange rates: a multiple currency and maturity analysis, *Journal of Econometrics*, 37, 251–264.

Hodrick, R. J. and Srivastava, S. (1987) Foreign currency futures, *Journal of International Economics*, 22, 1–24.

Hsieh, D. A. (1989) Modeling heteroskedasticity in daily foreign exchange markets, *Journal of Business and Economic Statistics*, 7, 307–317.

Lai, K. S. and Lai, M. (1991) A cointegration test for market efficiency, *Journal of Futures Markets*, 11, 567–575.

Phillips, P. C. B. (1986) Understanding spurious regressions in econometrics, *Journal of Econometrics*, 33, 311–340.

Phillips, P. C. B. and Ouliaris, S. (1990) Asymptotic properties of residual based tests for cointegration, *Econometrica*, 58, 165–193.

Phillips, P. C. B. and Perron, P. (1988) Testing for a unit root in a time series regression, *Biometrika*, 75, 335–346.

Said, S. E. and Dickey, D. A. (1984) Testing for unit roots in autoregressive moving average models of unknown order, *Biometrika*, 71, 599–607.

19

A Theory of International Takeover Bidding

VIHANG R. ERRUNZA, ARTHUR F. MOREAU AND S. NAGARAJAN

Introduction

A major stylized fact in the takeover literature involves the substantial premiums paid to the target stockholders in successful takeovers. Most studies (see Jensen and Ruback (1983) and Jarrell and Poulsen (1989) for surveys), estimate these premiums to be between 20 and 30 percent of the target's pre-takeover value, the lower figures usually corresponding to 'friendly' mergers and the higher figures to 'hostile' takeovers. In contrast, the bidding firms show hardly any gains. Various theories have been advanced to explain the rather high premiums received by the target firms. For instance, competitive bidding is suggested by Bradley *et al.* (1984), who find that target premiums increase with the number of bidders. However, nearly half the takeovers involve only one bidder, seriously reducing the competition from the demand (bidding) side (Jarrell, 1985). Fishman (1988) suggests a strategic pre-empting motive for the high premiums. While these explanations are undoubtedly important, they do not fully explain the magnitude of the premiums observed.

An often overlooked evidence in the takeover literature is the significant participation of foreign firms in the market for corporate control in the United States. For instance, foreign firms were involved in nearly 23 percent (by dollar value) of all takeovers in the United States in 1987 (Grimm, 1988). According to Harris and Ravenscraft (1989), foreign acquirers pay over 50 percent higher premiums than domestic bidders. Hence, an understanding of the takeover process

263

involving foreign bidders is essential to further our understanding of the overall takeover activity in the United States.

Our insights from the existing literature on domestic takeovers do not fully carry over to the case of international takeovers for the following reason: Given the imperfections in the global market for financial and real assets, differential tax treatment and regulatory environments, foreign firms are likely to value the U.S. target firms differently from the domestic firms. Hence, differential valuation across domestic and foreign bidders may have important impact on their bidding behavior, and need to be explicitly taken into account. Note that even if foreign bidders value U.S. target firms more than the domestic bidders (as suggested in the popular press), it is not clear why the foreign firms must pay such high premiums, especially since barely topping the highest domestic bid would do just as well. This chapter is an attempt to rigorously model such differential valuation across domestic and foreign bidders, and study their implications for the outcome and efficiency of the takeover process. We derive testable implications regarding the target premiums and share tendering strategies and discriminatory provisions against foreign bidders.

Following Myerson (1981) and Myerson and Satterthwaite (1983), we model the takeover situation as a mechanism design problem facing the target stockholders, who decide their optimal tendering strategies in response to takeover bids by a domestic and a foreign firm under asymmetric information. It is shown that the optimal takeover mechanism for the target stockholders discriminates between the domestic and the foreign bidders. If the foreign bidder is likely to value the target more than the domestic firm *on average*, then it favors the domestic firm over the foreign firm in an attempt to induce the foreign firm to bid higher. It awards only a slim majority of shares to the winner, which, interestingly enough, is *not* always the highest bidder. Thus, the target's optimal takeover mechanism is not *ex post* efficient.

The chapter is organized as follows: In the next section we present the model and discuss the valuation asymmetry across domestic and foreign bidders. The optimal takeover mechanism for the target stockholders is then derived. We close by discussing the implications and extension of our model. All the proofs can be found in the Appendix.

The Model

Consider a firm T targeted for a takeover by two bidders—one domestic (D) and the other foreign (F).[1] The target's status quo value under the current management is v_T and is assumed to be common knowledge. Let the initial holdings of these three players in the target firm be $\{\alpha_i\}_{i \in N}$, where $N = \{T, F, D\}$ and $\Sigma_{i \in N}\alpha_i = 1$. Throughout the chapter, we assume that a simple majority ownership of shares is sufficient to gain control. Thus, $\alpha_T = 1 - \alpha_F - \alpha_D > 1/2$. All agents are assumed to be risk-neutral. The value of the target firm under bidder i's control is v_i, and will be referred to as the valuation of i. The valuation v_i is known only to bidder i ($i = D, F$) at the beginning of the takeover game, but it is common knowledge that the valuations are *independently and uniformly* distributed over the support $[0, \bar{v}_i]$. [2]

It is assumed that $\bar{v}_F > \bar{v}_D$. The interpretation is that the foreign bidder may value the target more (in the probabilistic sense) than the domestic bidder. This may be due to the fact that many foreign countries allow more favorable tax and accounting treatments for acquisitions relative to the United States. The asymmetry in valuation between the domestic and the foreign bidder may also arise from transaction cost differences (see Stulz, 1981a; Dumas, 1989; Senbet, 1979), market completion (see Errunza and Senbet, 1981, 1984) or other international segmentation factors (see Stulz, 1981b; Adler and Dumas, 1975; Dumas, 1989; Errunza and Losq, 1985, 1989; Eun and Janakiramanan, 1986). Essentially, the presence of explicit and implicit barriers to the flow of financial and real assets across national borders implies that the foreign bidder may obtain a greater value from investing in the same target firm, *ceteris paribus*, than the domestic bidder.

The problem for the target stockholders is to design an optimal takeover (auction) mechanism that will maximize its expected profit. Such a takeover mechanism should determine not only who wins control, but also their share allocations as well as their monetary payments for the transaction. Invoking the *revelation principle* (see Dasgupta *et al.*, 1979; Myerson, 1979; Harris and Townsend, 1981 or others), we can consider, without loss of generality, only equivalent *direct revelation* mechanisms, where each bidder confidentially reports its valuation to the target which then determines the outcome of the takeover game according to an appropriately chosen (*ex ante*) *direct revelation takeover* mechanism. Accordingly, define a *takeover mechanism* $\tau = \langle x(v), p(v), 1_{\{x\}}(v) \rangle$, where $v = \{v_D, v_F\}$ and $x_i(v)$ is the *share* allocation of i for all $i \in N$ subject to $\Sigma_{i \in N}x_i(v) = 1$; $p_i(v)$ is the *price* paid by bidder i to the target stockholders, where $i \in \{D, F\}$; $1_{\{x_i\}}(v)$ is an indicator function that determines who wins *control*, subject to

$$1_{\{x_i\}}(v) = \begin{cases} 1 & \text{if} \quad x_i > 1/2 \\ 0 & \text{else} \end{cases}$$

for all $i \in N$ and $\Sigma_{i \in N} x_i(v) = 1$. Note that τ is also a function of the initial shares α_i, but we shall suppress it for notational brevity. The profit to bidder i, conditional on the valuations $\{v_D, v_F\}$ from the mechanism τ, can be written as

$$\Pi_i[v_i, v_j \mid \tau] = v_i 1_{\{x_i\}}(v) x_i(v) + v_j 1_{\{x_j\}}(v) x_i(v) + v_T [1_{\{x_T\}}(v) x_i(v) - \alpha_i] - p_i(v) \tag{1}$$

where $i \neq j \in \{D, F\}$. The expected profit to i conditional on its valuation v_i is then

$$\Pi_i[v_i \mid \tau] = \left[v_i \int_0^{\bar{v}_j} 1_{\{x_i\}}(v) x_i(v) \, dv_j + \int_0^{\bar{v}_j} v_j x_i(v) 1_{\{x_i\}}(v) \, dv_j \right.$$

$$\left. + v_T \int_0^{\bar{v}_j} 1_{\{x_T\}}(v) x_i(v) \, dv_j - \int_0^{\bar{v}_j} p_i(v) \, dv_j \right] \frac{1}{\bar{v}_j} - \alpha_i v_T. \tag{2}$$

For notational ease, redefine the integrals as follows:

$$X_i[v_i \mid x] = \int_0^{\bar{v}_j} [1 - 1_{\{x_i\}}(v)] \frac{x_i(v)}{\bar{v}_j} \, dv_j$$

$$Y_i[v_i \mid x] = \int_0^{\bar{v}_j} 1_{\{x_i\}}(v) \frac{x_i(v)}{\bar{v}_j} \, dv_j$$

$$Z_i[v_i \mid x] = \int_0^{\bar{v}_j} (v_j - v_T) 1_{\{x_j\}}(v) \frac{x_i(v)}{\bar{v}_j} \, dv_j$$

$$P_i[v_i \mid p] = \int_0^{\bar{v}_j} \frac{p_i(v)}{\bar{v}_j} \, dv_j. \tag{3}$$

Using equation (3) and the fact that $1_{\{x_T\}} = 1 - 1_{\{x_i\}} - 1_{\{x_j\}}$, the conditional expected profit in equation (2) can be rewritten as

$$\Pi_i[v_i \mid \tau] = v_i Y_i(v_i) + Z_i(v_i) + v_T[X_i(v_i) - \alpha_i] - P_i(v_i) \quad \forall i \in \{D, F\}, \tag{4}$$

where $Y_i(v_i)$ can be interpreted as firm i's expected share allocation in the target firm if it gains control, $X_i(v_i)$ as its expected share allocation conditional only on v_i, $Z_i(v_i)$ as its expected profit (net of v_T) if j gains control and i becomes a minority stockholder in the target firm, and finally, $P_i(v_i)$ represents the payment i is expected to make to the target given its own valuation v_i.

A takeover mechanism is defined to be *incentive feasible* if it is *interim* (Bayesian) *incentive compatible* as well as *interim individually rational* (Myerson, 1979). The takeover mechanism is incentive compatible if honest reporting of each bidder forms a Bayesian Nash equilibrium. Formally, incentive compatibility is satisfied if, for each bidder, $i \in \{D, F\}$

$$\Pi_i[v_i \mid \tau] \geqslant v_i Y_i(\hat{v}_i) + Z_i(\hat{v}_i) + v_T[X_i(\hat{v}_i) - \alpha_i] - P_i(\hat{v}_i) \qquad (5)$$

for all v_i, $\hat{v}_i \in \{0, \bar{v}_i\}$. The following lemma characterizes the conditions for incentive compatibility.

Lemma 1

A takeover mechanism $\tau = \langle x, p, 1_{\{x\}} \rangle$ is Bayesian interim incentive compatible if and only if $Y_i[v_i \mid \tau]$ is nondecreasing and $\Pi_i[v_i \mid t]$ is convex with $\Pi_i'[v_i \mid \tau] = Y_i[v_i \mid \tau]$ a.e. for all $i \in \{D, F\}$. Moreover, if τ is incentive compatible

$$\Pi_i[v_i \mid \tau] = \int_0^{v_i} Y_i(u_i) \, \mathrm{d}u_i + \Pi_i[0 \mid \tau] \quad \forall \, v_i \in [0, \bar{v}_i], \, i \in \{D, F\}. \qquad (6)$$

Proof: See the Appendix.

That is, incentive compatibility holds if the marginal benefit from reporting a higher valuation under the takeover mechanism exactly offsets the marginal incentive for the bidders to lie and report a lower valuation. Essentially, the incentive compatible mechanism bribes the bidders to tell the truth. In order to induce the potential bidders to make a bid, the following individual rationality constraints must be satisfied

$$\Pi_i[v_i \mid \tau] \geqslant 0 \quad \forall \, v_i \in [0, \bar{v}_i], \quad i \in \{D, F\}. \qquad (7)$$

Since $\Pi_i[\cdot \mid \tau]$ is nondecreasing for an incentive compatible τ, condition (7) is satisfied if

$$\Pi_i[0 \mid \tau] \geqslant 0 \quad \forall \, i \in \{D, F\}. \qquad (8)$$

Clearly, profit maximizing target shareholders would set equation (8) to equality. Hence, in what follows, the individual rationality condition will be implicitly satisfied. The target's expected profit, given the mechanism τ, is given by

$$\Pi_T[\tau] = \left[v_T \int_0^{\bar{v}_F} \int_0^{\bar{v}_D} 1_{\{x_T\}}(v) x_T(v) \, dv_D \, dv_F \right.$$

$$+ \sum_{i \in \{D, F\}} \int_0^{\bar{v}_F} \int_0^{\bar{v}_D} v_i 1_{\{x_i\}}(v) x_T(v) \, dv_D \, dv_F$$

$$\left. + \int_0^{\bar{v}_F} \int_0^{\bar{v}_D} [p_D(v) + p_F(v)] \, dv_D \, dv_F \right] \frac{1}{\bar{v}_D \bar{v}_F} - \alpha_T v_T. \tag{9}$$

The following lemma simplifies the target shareholders' optimization problem.

Lemma 2

The target stockholders choose the incentive feasible takeover mechanism $\tau = \langle x, p, 1_{\{x\}} \rangle$ to maximize $\Pi_T[\tau]$, where

$$\Pi_T[\tau] = \sum_{i \in \{D, F\}} \int_0^{\bar{v}_F} \int_0^{\bar{v}_D} \{(1 + x_i(v)) v_i - v_T - \bar{v}_i x_i(v)\} \frac{1_{\{x_i\}}(v)}{\bar{v}_D \bar{v}_F} \, dv_D \, dv_F.$$

Proof: See the Appendix.

Note that the prices paid by the bidder do not appear in the target stockholders' objective function. This is because, as will be seen, the mechanism design technique directly determines the equilibrium allocations. We are now ready to characterize the optimal takeover mechanism for the target stockholders.

Proposition 1

The optimal takeover mechanism for the target stockholders $\tau = \langle x, p, 1_{\{x\}} \rangle$, is given by

$$1_{\{x_i\}}(v) = \begin{cases} 1 & \text{if} \quad J_i(v_i) > \max\{J_j(v_j), 0\} \\ 0 & \text{else} \end{cases}$$

where

$$J_i(v_i) = \frac{1}{2}(3v_i - 2v_T - \bar{v}_i) \tag{10}$$

and sets $x_i = 1/2 + \varepsilon$ if $1_{\{x_i\}} = 1$, $\forall i \in \{D, F\}$.

Proof: Follows from Lemma 2 and is omitted.

Thus, according to Proposition 1, the bidder which has the truly highest valuation does not always win control in the optimal mechanism. This is because bidder i wins the takeover game only if $J_i(v_i)$ is greater, not if its valuation v_i is greater. Hence, it is quite possible that $J_D(v_D) > J_F(v_F)$ while $v_D < v_F$, since the former condition only requires that $v_F - v_D < (\bar{v}_F - \bar{v}_D)/3$. The optimal takeover mechanism thus *discriminates* between the domestic and foreign bidders.

Note that the optimal takeover mechanism does not allocate *all* the shares to the winner. This is because the bidder's gains are increasing in the expected shareholdings, if it wins. Since this is a zero-sum game, target shareholders' gains are decreasing in the shareholdings of the winner. Consequently, the optimal mechanism for the target stockholders gives the bare minimum number of shares required to win control, i.e. a simple majority of shares. The optimal takeover mechanism is also not *ex post* efficient. The target stockholders may keep the control, even if a bidder's valuation exceeds the status quo value v_T, because of the condition that $J_i > 0$. In other words, the target sets a minimum reserve or floor price that a bid must exceed in order to be accepted.[3] Define the floor prices v_D^* and v_F^* as follows:

$$v_i^* = \frac{\bar{v}_i + 2v_T}{3} \quad \forall i \in \{D, F\}. \tag{11}$$

Clearly, the floor prices for the domestic and the foreign firms will be different since these firms' valuations are drawn from different distributions. The question of which bidding firm is discriminated against and which is favored depends on the relative values of these floor prices for the bidders. The following proposition shows that the optimal takeover mechanism favors the domestic firm at the expense of the foreign firm.

Proposition 2

$$v_D^* < v_F^*.$$

Proof. The claim follows equation (11) and the assumption that $\bar{v}_F > \bar{v}_D$.

This result can be understood as follows. Since the foreign firm knows that it values the target more than the domestic bidder (in the probabilistic sense), it may have an incentive to understate its bid. Setting the floor price higher for the foreign firm serves to induce it to bid higher. This increases the competition for the domestic bidder, forcing it to bid closer to its true value as well. Thus, by setting higher floor prices, the target stockholders can expect to receive higher bids from *both* the foreign bidder and the domestic bidder. On the other hand, higher floor prices lead the target stockholders to reject lower but perhaps acceptable bids from both the bidders, thus decreasing the probability that the firm will be taken over in the first place. The optimal floor price trades off the decreased probability of being taken over, because of the higher floor price, against the possibility of benefiting from a higher bid if the target firm is indeed taken over.

Since higher floor prices induce higher bids, a sample of target firms that have been taken over will, on average, exhibit higher gains for the target stockholders. From the above discussion, it follows that higher target gains are realized even if the winner is the domestic firm. Thus, the very presence of foreign bidder in the takeover contest serves to increase the target premiums from a takeover—but only if the share tendering strategies of the target stockholders conform to the optimal mechanism derived in Proposition 1. Given the relatively high participation level (23 percent) of foreign firms in the U.S. takeover market (Grimm, 1988), our results help explain the large premiums received by the target shareholders in the U.S. market.

Conclusion

This chapter has shown that modeling the problem of target shareholders facing takeover attempts by domestic and foreign bidders as a problem of designing an optimal takeover mechanism sheds light on the overall takeover activity in the domestic market. In particular, if the foreign bidders value the domestic target firms more (in a probabilistic sense), then target stockholders may discriminate between the foreign bidder and the domestic bidder by setting higher floor prices for the foreign bidder. This offers an international explanation for the relatively large premiums received by target shareholders in the United States.

The model given here can be extended in a number of directions. One is to incorporate more general distributions of bidders' valuations to determine the impact of distributional assumptions on the results. Another is to rigorously derive from first principles the source of the valuation differences between domestic and foreign bidders. A third extension may examine the optimal domestic regulatory policy for takeovers, given the high degree of participation by foreign bidders. Future work along these lines may go a long way to understanding the international implications for what has previously been regarded as a purely domestic takeover market.

Acknowledgement

We thank Rich Lyons for useful comments. The research support of SSHRC is gratefully acknowledged.

Notes

1. This assumption is made for notational simplicity. The analysis which follows can be extended to any finite number of bidders.
2. The interpretation here is that the valuations reflect the individual managerial skills of bidder i (or its management team, in the spirit of Jensen and Ruback (1983)) and not some value improving information that may be tradeable. The use of zero as a lower bound on value is purely for notational convenience.
3. Because the floor price is optimal *ex ante* but not *ex post*, the target stockholders need a *commitment* device (such as an agency contract) to turn down inadequate offers. For more on this problem, see Nagarajan (1995).

References

ADLER, M. and DUMAS, B. (1975) Optimal international acquisitions, *Journal of Finance*, 30, 1–19.

DASGUPTA, P., HAMMOND, P. and MASKIN, E. (1979) The implementation of social choice rules: some results on incentive compatibility, *Review of Economic Studies*, 46, 185–216.

DUMAS, B. (1989) Two-person dynamic equilibrium in the capital market, *Review of Financial Studies*, 2, 157–188.

ERRUNZA, V. and LOSQ, E. (1985) International asset pricing under mild segmentation: theory and tests, *Journal of Finance*, 40, 105–124.

ERRUNZA, V. and LOSQ, E. (1989) Capital flow controls, international asset pricing and investor's welfare: a multicountry framework, *Journal of Finance*, 44, 1025–1038.

ERRUNZA, V. and SENBET, L. (1981) The effects of international operations on the market value of the firm: theory and evidence, *Journal of Finance*, 36, 401–417.

ERRUNZA, V. and SENBET, L. (1984) International corporate diversification, market valuation, and size-adjusted evidence, *Journal of Finance*, 39, 727–743.

EUN, C. and JANAKIRAMANAN, J. (1986) A model of international asset pricing with a constraint on the foreign equity ownership, *Journal of Finance*, 41, 897–914.

HARRIS, M. and TOWNSEND, R. (1981) Resource allocation under asymmetric information, *Econometrica*, 49, 33–64.

HARRIS, R. and RAVENSCRAFT, D. (1989) The role of acquisitions in foreign direct investment: evidence from the U.S. stock market, Darden School Working Paper No. 89-27.

JARRELL, G. and POULSEN, A. (1989) The returns to acquiring firms in tender offers: evidence from three decades, *Financial Management*, 18, 12–19.

JENSEN, M. and RUBACK, R. (1983) The market for corporate control: The scientific evidence, *Journal of Financial Economics*, 11, 5–50.

MYERSON, R. (1981) Optimal auction design, *Mathematics of Operations Research*, 6, 58–73.

MYERSON R. and SATTERTHWAITE, M. (1983) Efficient mechanisms for bilateral trading, *Journal of Economic Theory*, 28, 265–282.

NAGARAJAN S. (1995) Delegated takeover resistance: The optimal auction design approach, *Research in Finance*, 12, 183–202.

SENBET, L. (1979) International capital market equilibrium and the multinational firm financing and investment policies, *Journal of Financial and Quantitative Analysis*, 14, 455–480.

SOLNIK, B. H. (1974) An equilibrium model of the international capital market, *Journal of Economic Theory*, 8, 500–524.

STULZ, R. (1981a) A model of international asset pricing, *Journal of Financial Economics*, 9, 383–406.

STULZ, R. (1981b) On the effects of barriers to international investment, *Journal of Finance*, 36, 923–934.

Appendix

Proof of Lemma 1

First, consider the only if statement. Rewriting the incentive compatibility condition, equation (5), yields

$$\Pi_i[v_i \,|\, \tau] \geq \hat{v}_i Y_i(\hat{v}_i) + Z_i(\hat{v}_i) + v_T[X_i(\hat{v}_i) - \alpha_i] - P_i(\hat{v}_i) + \bar{v}_i Y_i(\hat{v}_i) - v_i Y_i(\hat{v}_i)$$
$$= \Pi_i[\hat{v}_i \,|\, \tau] + (v_i - \hat{v}_i)Y_i(\hat{v}_i). \tag{A1}$$

Interchanging $\hat{v}_i$ and v_i yields

$$\Pi_i[\hat{v}_i \,|\, \tau] \geq \Pi_i[v_i \,|\, \tau] + (\hat{v}_i - v_i)Y_i(v_i). \tag{A2}$$

Combining equations (A1) and (A2) yields

$$(v_i - \hat{v}_i)Y_i(v_i) \geq \Pi_i[v_i \,|\, \tau] - \Pi_i[\hat{v}_i \,|\, \tau] \geq (v_i - \hat{v}_i)Y_i(\hat{v}_i). \tag{A3}$$

For $v_i \geq \hat{v}_i$, $Y_i(v_i) \geq Y_i(\hat{v}_i)$ and vice versa. Thus $Y_i(\,\cdot\,)$ is nondecreasing. Setting $\hat{v}_i \to v_i$ in equation (A3) yields

$$\Pi_i'[v_i \,|\, \tau] = Y_i[v_i] \quad \forall v_i \in [0, \bar{v}_i] \quad \text{a.e.}$$

and

$$\Pi_i[v_i \,|\, \tau] = \int_0^{v_i} Y_i[u_i]\, \mathrm{d}u_i + \Pi_i[0 \,|\, \tau].$$

Since $Y_i(\cdot)$ is nondecreasing, $\Pi_i[\cdot \mid \tau]$ is convex.

To prove the if statement, note that the convexity and the derivative condition imply equations (A2) and (A1), respectively, which are the incentive compatibility conditions.

Proof of Lemma 2

Substituting for $\alpha_T = 1 - \alpha_i - \alpha_j$, and $1_{\{x_T\}} = 1 - 1_{\{x_i\}} - 1_{\{x_j\}}$, where $i \neq j \in \{D, F\}$, into equation (9) and using equation (2) to simplify the expressions yields

$$\Pi_T[\tau] = \sum_{i \in N} \int_0^{\bar{v}_F} \int_0^{\bar{v}_D} v_i 1_{\{x_i\}}(v) \frac{1}{\bar{v}_D \bar{v}_F} \, dv_D \, dv_F$$

$$- \sum_{i \in \{D, F\}} \int_0^{\bar{v}_i} \Pi_i[v_i \mid \tau] \frac{1}{\bar{v}_i} \, dv_i - v_T.$$

Since τ is incentive compatible, by Lemma 1, $\Pi_i[v_i \mid \tau]$ can be expressed as equation (6). Substituting equation (6) into equation (A4) yields

(A4)

$$\Pi_T[\tau] = \sum_{i \in N} \int_0^{\bar{v}_F} \int_0^{\bar{v}_D} v_i 1_{\{x_i\}}(v) \frac{1}{\bar{v}_D \bar{v}_F} \, dv_D \, dv_F - \sum_{i \neq T} \int_0^{\bar{v}_i} \int_0^{\bar{v}_i} Y_i(u_i) \frac{1}{\bar{v}_i} \, du_i \, dv_i - v_T$$

$$= \sum_{i \in N} \int_0^{\bar{v}_F} \int_0^{\bar{v}_D} v_i 1_{\{x_i\}}(v) \frac{1}{\bar{v}_D \bar{v}_F} \, dv_D \, dv_F - \sum_{i \neq T} \int_0^{\bar{v}_i} \left[\frac{\bar{v}_i - u_i}{\bar{v}_i} \right] Y_i(u_i) \, du_i - v_T$$

(by changing the order of integration)

$$= \sum_{i \in N} \int_0^{\bar{v}_F} \int_0^{\bar{v}_D} v_i 1_{\{x_i\}}(v) \frac{1}{\bar{v}_D \bar{v}_F} \, dv_D \, dv_F$$

$$- \sum_{i \neq T} \int_0^{\bar{v}_i} \int_0^{\bar{v}_j} [\bar{v}_i - u_i] x_i(v) 1_{\{x_i\}}(v) \frac{1}{\bar{v}_j \bar{v}_i} \, dv_j \, dv_i - v_T$$

$$= \sum_{i \in \{D, F\}} \int_0^{\bar{v}_F} \int_0^{\bar{v}_D} \{(1 + x_i(v))v_i - v_T - \bar{v}_i x_i(v)\} \frac{1_{\{x_i\}}(v)}{\bar{v}_D \bar{v}_F} \, dv_D \, dv_F$$

after further simplification.

20

Foreign Bank Credit to U.S. Corporations: The Implications of Offshore Loans

ROBERT N. MCCAULEY AND RAMA SETH

International financial transactions have grown in recent years far faster than our ability to understand their significance for national economies. A case in point is the rise in bank loans from banks outside the United States to U.S. businesses. The rapid growth of such loans bears on issues ranging from the extent of the corporate debt buildup in the United States in the late 1980s, to the progress of securities markets in displacing intermediated corporate credit, to the loss of market share in U.S. commercial lending by U.S.-owned banks.

This chapter argues that the dramatic increase in offshore bank loans to U.S. businesses in the 1980s came about as foreign banks availed themselves of an opportunity to avoid the cost of the U.S. regulation, namely the reserve cost of banking loans in the United States. The slowdown in the growth of offshore loans after the Federal Reserve removed the relevant reserve requirements in 1990 is consistent with this explanation.

In addition, the chapter points to three implications of the rapid pile-up of offshore credit to U.S. businesses.

- The accumulation of debt by U.S. firms was even more rapid than was generally thought in the late 1980s, and the recent drop in bank lending far less striking.
- More of the corporate funding was supplied by banks, including foreign banks, and less by the securities markets than is generally thought. In other words, the usual reckoning of banks' loss of

corporate business to the securities markets in the 1980s overstates the case.

- Finally, the overwhelmingly foreign ownership of the banks responsible for the offshore lending means that the foreign bank share of the U.S. commercial lending market is higher than the frequently cited 30 percent figure that is based on loans booked in the United States. Instead, foreign banks have carved out a market share for themselves closer to 45 percent, putting commercial lending ahead of chemicals and auto-making in its command of the foreign share of the U.S. market.

The Build-up of Credit to U.S. Firms from Offshore

The Bank for International Settlements aggregates data on crossborder loans provided by 25 banking authorities from industrial countries and offshore banking centers.[1] These data show a very rapid rise in bank loans to U.S. borrowers other than banks: from about $50 billion in 1983 to $278 billion in 1991 (Fig. 20.1). Although publicly available information does not reveal where all the loans are booked, it is clear that the fastest growth has occurred in offshore

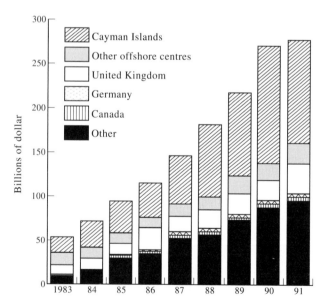

FIGURE 20.1 *Claims on U.S. Nonbanks by Banks in the BIS Reporting Area*
Sources: Bank for International Settlements, International Banking and Financial
Market Developments, Statistical Supplement to the Monthly Reports of the
Deutsche Bundesbank, Bank of Canada Review, Bank of England; national sources.

centers, particularly in the Cayman Islands, and 'other industrial countries', which include Japan.

Those borrowing in the United States from banks abroad include not only commercial and industrial firms, but also bank holding companies and their nonbank affiliates, securities firms, real estate companies, finance companies, and others. An estimate of the share of commercial and industrial loans in the offshore claims on U.S. nonbanks can be derived from the loans' share on the balance sheet of foreign banks' branches and agencies in the United States. This share is estimated to have remained steady at about 60 percent, at least since 1989.[2]

Estimated loans to commercial and industrial companies booked offshore rose from $37 billion in 1983 to $174 billion by the end of 1991 (solid line, Fig. 20.2). These sums are more than double the offshore loans captured in the Treasury International Capital (TIC) reporting system and reflected in the flow of funds data on aggregate corporate indebtedness published by the Board of Governors of the Federal Reserve System (dashed line, Fig. 20.2). Note that in one case the lender reports and in the other case the borrower reports.[3] The flow of funds data were capturing about 50 cents of every dollar of estimated offshore loans during 1984–1988, after which time they captured even less—only about 40 cents of every dollar by 1991.

In the mid-1980s, the Treasury's concern about the accuracy and completeness of the balance of payments data on U.S. corporate

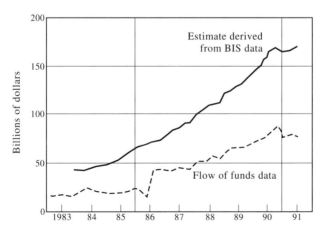

FIGURE 20.2 *U.S. Commercial and Industrial Loans Booked Offshore*
Sources: Board of governors of the federal reserve system flow of funds;
sources in Table 20.1

TABLE 20.1 Foreign Bank Share of the U.S. Commercial and Industrial Loan Market (Billions of Dollars Except as Noted)

	1983	1984	1985	1986	1987	1988	1989	1990	1991-I	1991-II	1991-III	1991-IV
Commercial and industrial loans to U.S. addressees	467	512	556	623	654	712	765	803	797	786	782	777
I. Loans by U.S.-owned banks	381	402	419	454	445	464	481	477	466	453	440	428
A. Onshore	364	382	401	439	431	446	460	454	443	430	417	407
B. Offshore	17	20	18	15	15	18	21	22	23	23	23	22
II. Loans by foreign-owned banks*	86	110	137	169	209	248	284	327	332	333	342	348
A. Onshore	66	78	92	109	130	153	168	179	185	186	191	196
B. Estimated offshore†	20	31	45	60	79	95	116	148	146	148	151	152
Memo: Foreign Share (percent)	18	21	25	27	32	35	37	41	42	42	44	45
A. Onshore	14	15	17	18	20	21	22	22	23	24	24	25
B. Offshore	4	6	8	10	12	13	15	18	18	19	19	20

Sources: Bank for International Settlements; Federal Financial Institutions Examination Council Reports of Condition Federal Reserve Form 2502; Federal Reserve Form 2951 Federal Reserve Bulletin, Statistical Table 4.3 Federal Reserve Bank of New York staff estimates.

Note: Banks in the United States include all banking institutions that file Reports of Condition with the Federal Financial Institutions Examinations Council.

*Includes branches agencies and subsidiaries with at least 10 percent foreign ownership.

†These figures are estimated in two steps. We calculate the commercial and industrial proportion of total claims on nonbanks of branches and agencies of foreign banks in the United States. Then assuming that the offshore proportion is the same, we apply this fraction 60 percent to the offshore claims on U.S. nonbanks of foreign banks. Also 1991-I Bahamian and 1991-I and 1991-II Cayman Islands figures for lending are carried over from end-1990.

TABLE 20.2 *U.S. Corporations' Motives for Using Foreign Banks (A Reason Index)*

	All foreign	Japanese	German	U.K.	Canadian	Swiss
Competitive loan pricing	15	27	1	0	0	-2
International service capabilities, domestic or offshore	11	-4	8	8	-3	9
Ability to propose innovative international banking alternatives	3	-3	-3	0	-3	6
Large lending capacity	-9	-14	-10	-14	-16	-13
Best at integrating merchant and commercial banking services	-9	-10	-14	-10	-10	-8
Reliable source of credit	-10	-17	-16	-12	-16	-9
Caliber of banking officers	-15	-28	-24	-17	-19	-17
Capital markets and corporate finance capabilities	-16	-20	-14	-24	-22	-5
Knowledge of innovative domestic banking alternatives	-18	-8	-6	-6	-6	-3
Historical relationship	-25	-39	-32	-36	-29	-39
Cash management	-46	-52	-58	-53	-41	-60

Source: Greenwich Associates *The Coming Shift in Bank Relationships* (Greenwich Connecticut, 1988), pp. 18–29.

Note: The index is the difference between the percentage of responses given for using foreign banks and that given for using domestic banks in 1988.

borrowing from abroad led it to put in place a new reporting form. In introducing the new form, the Treasury wrote:

"Information drawn from Treasury interviews with a number of major banks and nonbank firms has indicated that large amounts of offshore loans to U.S. nonbank residents are not being properly reported on the TIC forms. In large part, under-reporting of foreign loans may arise because the nonbank borrower is unsure where the loan is actually booked. This confusion is particularly likely in instances where a U.S. firm is granted a loan from a foreign source but all loan servicing transactions are handled by a bank or other intermediary in the United States."[4]

The result of the new reporting form was a jump in mid-1986 in the outstanding loans recorded by the Treasury (dashed line, Fig. 20.2). Nevertheless, the data reported to the Bank for International Settlements suggests to us that the U.S. data are still undercounting the offshore loans.

Foreign banks have made the bulk of the offshore loans to U.S. commercial and industrial firms. U.S. banks' branches held only $22 billion in such loans at the end of 1991, while foreign banks held an estimated $152 billion. Some of these loans are to U.S. affiliates of home country corporations. At least in the case of Japanese banks, however, such loans are not large enough to explain even their onshore loans.[5] We examine the reason for foreign banks' pre-dominance below. First, however, we place offshore lending by foreign banks in the context of their overall penetration of the U.S. commercial banking market.

Offshore Credit and Foreign Banks' Share of U.S. Commercial Lending

The conventional view of the foreign bank share of the U.S. commercial lending market only considers loans to businesses in the United States booked in the United States. Such loans totaled $196 billion at the end of 1991, when all commercial and industrial loans in the United States were estimated to total $603 billion. Subsidiaries accounted for $50 billion and branches and agencies accounted for $146 billion of the foreign banks' onshore lending.

Thus, the conventional view is that the foreign bank share had reached 33 percent in 1991, up from 15 percent in 1983. Sometimes loans to businesses in the United States booked at U.S. bank branches abroad are included in the definition of the market, but their modest size raises the conventional measure of the foreign bank share to only 31 percent in 1991.

The view taken here is that the U.S. commercial lending market is better conceived as borrowing by businesses located in the United

States: where a loan is booked is of secondary importance. To be sure, one reason for not considering commercial loans booked offshore by foreign banks is that we do not have a precise measure of them. The burden of our argument, however, is that a very accurate measure of a piece of the total is less useful than an approximate measure of the whole.

With this principle in mind, we calculate the foreign share of the U.S. commercial and industrial market to have grown from 18 percent in 1983 to nearly 45 percent in 1991 (Table 20.1, first memorandum line). Estimated offshore loans by foreign banks rose from 4 to 20 percent of the total market; this offshore growth represented almost half the growth in foreign banks' market share. Indeed, the increase in the offshore component of foreign loans was more rapid than that in the onshore component (lines IIA and IIB in Table 20.1). It is interesting that this pattern reversed itself between 1990 and 1991.

These estimates raise anew and with more force an old question: Why did foreign banks displace U.S. banks in their home market in the 1980s? In addition, the estimates raise a less familiar question: Why did foreign banks book such a high share of their new loans offshore in the late 1980s? We answer each question in turn.

Reasons for Foreign Banks' Gain in Market Share

Foreign banks appear to have drawn on two different kinds of advantages in bidding for U.S. corporate business in the 1980s. On the one hand, they could undercut the prevailing pricing and still satisfy the demands of their shareholders. On the other hand, they could offer international services and thereby persuade U.S. corporate treasurers to switch some business.

Price advantages. According to a recent study, continental and Japanese banks enjoyed substantially lower costs of equity than U.S. banks in the period 1984–1990.[6] In other words, investors in equities in Frankfurt, Tokyo, and Zurich put a higher price on a given, internationally comparable stream of bank earnings than U.S. investors. Such pricing in turn allowed continental and Japanese bank managers to target a smaller spread between the cost of funds and commercial lending rates than U.S., Canadian, or British bank managers could accept. U.S. banks' required spreads on commercial loans in the United States were on average more than 50 basis points, or one-half of a percent, wider than those of Japanese banks operating in the United States, 30 basis points wider than those of German and Swiss banks, and even 10 basis points wider than those of British and Canadian banks.[7] In the competitive world of commercial banking, these are telling differences.

Survey evidence supports the cost of capital interpretation of the penetration of foreign banks. Greenwich Associates conducted interviews with financial decision-makers at U.S. corporations of various sizes in 1988 and found that firms trimmed the ranks of their U.S. banks while increasing the ranks of their foreign banks between 1987 and 1988 (Fig. 20.3). Survey respondents cited, "competitive loan pricing" as their principal reason for favoring foreign—and, in particular, Japanese—banks (Table 20.2).

Nonprice advantages. The same surveys suggested that foreign banks benefited from their international presence in bidding for U.S. customers. U.S. corporate treasurers indicated that international service capabilities and knowledge of innovative international banking alternatives made foreign banks more attractive lenders than domestic banks (Table 20.2).

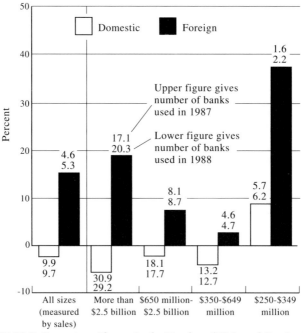

FIGURE 20.3 *Percentage Change in the Number of U.S. and Foreign Banks Used by the Average U.S. Company Between 1987 and 1988*
Source: Greenwich Associates, *The Coming Shift in Bank Relationships* (Greenwich, Connecticut, 1988)

Reasons for Foreign Banks' Offshore Bookings

We hypothesize that foreign banks arbitraged regulatory differences in booking U.S. commercial loans offshore. Under Federal Reserve Regulation D, which governs reserve requirements, a foreign bank branch or agency had to post a sterile 3 percent reserve when it sold a large 'Yankee' certificate of deposit in New York to fund a corporate loan (see box). In addition, once a foreign bank's U.S. offices had collectively run up net obligations to the bank's branches abroad, that bank had to post a sterile 3 percent reserve against additional Eurodollars borrowed abroad to fund U.S. assets, including corporate loans booked in the United States. However, a foreign branch or agency so bound by the Eurodollar reserve requirement could avoid it by booking a loan to a U.S. firm at a branch abroad.[8] If the foreign bank chose a jurisdiction with a reserve requirement lower than 3 percent, quite possibly one with no reserve requirement, it could be said to be engaged in *regulatory arbitrage*.

U.S. chartered banks could not play this game.[9] For them the Eurodollar reserve was assessed not only against net borrowings from affiliates abroad but also against loans to U.S. nonbanks booked at their foreign branches. The more inclusive reserve base was possible because U.S. chartered banks had to provide detailed information on their foreign branches and affiliates. As a result, a U.S. bank bound by the Eurodollar reserve requirement could not avoid it by booking a loan to a U.S. resident offshore.

Before we can confirm this interpretation of the rapid growth of foreign banks' offshore loans to U.S. firms, at least five conditions must be met.

1. Foreign banks must have been bound by the Eurodollar reserve requirement, or they would have no incentive to book offshore.
2. U.S. chartered and foreign banks must have differed in their booking behavior, since only the foreign banks had the opportunity to arbitrage regulations.
3. The jurisdictions in which the offshore loans were booked in fact must have offered regulatory advantages.
4. The configuration of onshore and offshore rates must have favored offshore booking by foreign banks.
5. Finally, the removal of the Eurodollar reserve requirement at the end of 1990 should have made booking loans offshore much less attractive.

We consider each condition in turn.

Were foreign banks bound by the Eurodollar reserve requirement? Data collected by the Federal Reserve indicate that many foreign branches

This box outlines the reserve requirements stipulated by Regulation D. Section 204.3 requires that "a depository institution, a U.S. branch or agency of a foreign bank, and an Edge or agreement corporation shall maintain reserves against its deposits and Eurocurrency liabilities."* Section 204.2 defines "Eurocurrency liabilities" as follows:

1. For a depository institution or an Edge or agreement corporation organized under the laws of the United States, the sum, if positive, of the following: (i) net balances due to its non-United States offices and its international banking facilities ('IBFs') from its United States offices . . . (ii) . . . assets acquired from its United States offices and held by its non-United States offices, by its IBF, or by non-United States offices of an affiliated Edge or agreement corporation; . . . (iii) *credit outstanding from its non-United States offices to United States residents* . . . (emphasis added).

2. For a United States branch or agency of a foreign bank, the sum, if positive, of the following: (i) net balances due to its foreign bank (including offices thereof located outside the United States) and its international banking facility after deducting an amount equal to 8 percent of the following: the United States branch's or agency's total assets . . ." (ii) assets (including participations) acquired from the United States branch or agency . . . and held by its foreign bank (including offices thereof located outside the United States), by its parent holding company, by its non-United States offices or an IBF of an affiliated Edge or agreement corporation, or by its IBFs.

Section 204.9 lists the reserve requirement ratios as follows:

Category	Reserve requirements
Net transactions accounts	
$0 to $40.5 million	3% of amount
Over $40.5 million	$1,215,000 plus 12% of amount over $40.5 million
Nonpersonal time deposits	
By original maturity	
(or notice period)	
Less than $1/_2$ year	3%
$1^1/_2$ years or more	0%
Eurocurrency liabilities	3%

On December 4, 1990, the Federal Reserve Board announced that reserve requirements would be reduced to zero on previously reservable nonpersonal time deposits and Eurocurrency liabilities on December 4, 1990.† The change was implemented in two steps. For depository institutions reporting weekly, the reserve ratios were reduced first to 1.5 percent in the reserve maintenance period that began December 13 and to zero in the following maintenance period that began December 27.

*Board of Governors of the Federal Reserve System, "Regulation D Reserve Requirements of Depository Institutions," 12 C.F.R. 204; as amended effective December 31, 1987.
†Federal Reserve Bank of New York, "Reserve Requirements," Circular No. 10406, December 4, 1990. See also amendment to Section 204.9 in Board of Governors of the Federal Reserve System, "Supplement to Regulation D."

in the United States indeed had clear incentives to book their loans offshore. By 1990, 123 out of 245 U.S. branches and agencies of foreign banks, representing over 50 percent of total assets of branches and agencies, had a positive net related Eurocurrency liability (Fig. 20.4); that is, they were bound by the Eurodollar reserve requirement. In addition, branches and agencies representing an additional 3.5 percent of total assets were nearly bound (that is, they were 1 percent of their assets or less away from having a reservable net due to position in relation to their foreign offices).

Bound in aggregate by the Eurodollar reserve requirement, U.S. branches and agencies of foreign banks were maintaining substantial sterile Eurodollar reserves, $485 million in October 1990, and could therefore fund a loan to a U.S. corporation more cheaply by booking it offshore. We consider below why some foreign banks were paying the Eurodollar reserve.

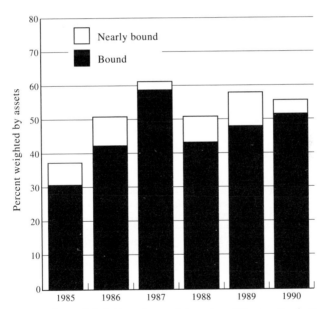

FIGURE 20.4 *Share of U.S. Branches and Agencies of Foreign Banks Bound by the Eurodollar Reserve Requirement*
Source: Federal reserve form 2951
Notes: Data are for second district banks only, for October of each year. Banks that had a positive net Eurodollar liability with related institutions are bound by the reserve requirement. Banks that had a small net 'due from' position with related institutions (less than 1 percent of their total assets) are classified as 'nearly bound'.

Did U.S. and foreign banks book differently? As described above, Regulation D called for different treatment of foreign branches and agencies, on the one hand, and U.S. chartered banks, on the other. This asymmetry in treatment was mirrored by the asymmetry in behavior: foreign banks' offshore loans to U.S. firms more than quintupled between 1984 and 1990, while U.S.-chartered banks' offshore loans showed little growth by comparison—5 percent during the same period.

The difference in regulation depended not on ultimate ownership but on the U.S. charter. Regulation D treated foreign bank subsidiaries like U.S.-owned banks rather than like foreign branches in the United States. The fact that foreign bank subsidiaries used their foreign branches no more than U.S.-owned banks (Table 20.3) therefore strengthens the regulatory interpretation.

Were foreign banks booking their U.S. loans in jurisdictions with lower regulatory burdens? Most of the offshore loans to U.S. nonbanks are booked in jurisdictions that impose no reserve requirements, such as offshore centers and the U.K. (Fig. 20.1). Jurisdictions that do impose relatively high reserve requirements, such as Germany, have not seen much growth in their loans to U.S. nonbanks.[10] We conjecture that the growth of loans from other industrial countries, including Japan, was concentrated in the Japan Offshore Market (JOM) in Tokyo. Since December 1, 1986, this market has permitted foreign loans to be funded with money not subject to reserve requirements.[11]

Clear evidence of regulatory arbitrage is seen in the use of shell branches in offshore centers such as the Cayman Islands

TABLE 20.3 *The Ratio of Commercial and Industrial Loans Booked Offshore to those Booked in the United States*
1990: Billions of dollars except as noted

	Loans booked	Loans booked	Ratio
Offshore Onshore (percent) Banking institutions not chartered in the United States	147	127	116
U.S.-owned banks	22	454	5
U.S. subsidiaries of foreign banks	1	52	2

Source: See Table 20.1.

Note: because reserve requirements were removed in 1991, 1990 data are provided for reference.

TABLE 20.4 *External Positions of Banks in the Cayman Islands in December 1990*

	Claims on	
	Banks	Nonbanks
Claims on residents of all countries (billions of dollars)	235	198
Claims on U.S. residents (billions of dollars)	106	134
As a share of total claims by all banks in the Cayman Islands (%)	45	68
As a share of total overseas claims on U.S. residents (%)	19	49
Share of banks not chartered in the United States (%)	77	85

Sources: National sources: Bank for International Settlements, International Banking and Financial Market Developments.

(Table 20.4).[12] More than two-thirds of all loans to nonbanks booked in the Cayman Islands were to U.S. addressees in 1990, and these loans amounted to nearly 50 percent of all offshore loans made to U.S. nonbanks.

As an aside, we note that foreign banks from different countries took varying advantage of the regulatory arbitrage possibilities (Fig. 20.5). Japanese banks, which had the biggest cost of capital advantage, engaged in regulatory arbitrage the least—perhaps, as suggested below, owing to the home country authorities' views. Japanese banks accounted for only 5 percent of nonbank loans made by all foreign banks in the Cayman Islands as opposed to 72 percent of the commercial and industrial loans made by all foreign branches and agencies in the United States. Continental banks, by contrast, appear to have exploited arbitrage opportunities.

The Japanese banks' small share of foreign bank assets in the Cayman Islands suggests that the Japanese share of the U.S. commercial banking market is overstated by foreign loans booked in the United States. For example, adding estimated commercial loans booked in the Cayman Islands to those booked in the United States reduces the Japanese share in foreign loans to U.S. corporations from 60 to 40 percent.[13]

To be sure, Japanese banks stood out in the 1980s for their increasing market share of U.S. commercial lending. However, contrary to the view that Japanese take every opportunity to gain advantage over their U.S. competitors, in this case the Japanese banks

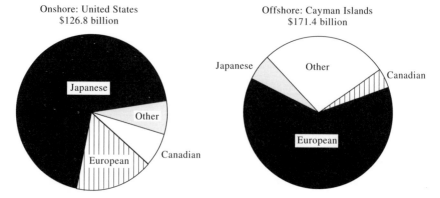

FIGURE 20.5 *Loans by Foreign Banks in the United States and Cayman Islands*
By nationality of bank, year-end 1990
Sources: Federal Financial Institutions Examinations Council,
reports of condition; national sources
Notes: Onshore loans are commercial and industrial loans by foreign bank
branches and agencies in the United States. Offshore loans are claims on all
nonbanks by foreign banks in the Cayman Islands

placed a modest third behind European and Canadian banks in exploiting shell branches.

Did the configuration of onshore and offshore rates favor offshore booking? At the beginning of the 1980s, U.S. wholesale certificate of deposit rates were substantially below the Eurodollar rate, that is, the London Interbank Offered Rate (LIBOR). In this circumstance, a foreign bank could fund a loan most cheaply in the U.S. money market, even if the foreign bank had to pay a Yankee premium (a premium paid by foreign banks to raise funds in the United States) of five basis points and to post the 3 percent reserve requirement.[14] Indeed, in the early 1980s, banks in the United States arbitraged the New York and London dollar markets by raising funds in the former and placing funds in the latter and thereby accumulated a net claim on their affiliates abroad.[15]

Through the 1980s, however, rates in the New York money market rose relative to those in the London dollar market (Fig. 20.6a, b). This change in relative rates was consistent with first the cessation of net bank outflows from the United States and then the reflux of net bank funds into the United States, both of which helped to finance the U.S. current account deficit. This reflux tended to make the Eurodollar reserve requirement bind.

Beginning in 1984 and regularly after 1985, a foreign bank choosing between (1) booking a U.S. corporate loan onshore and

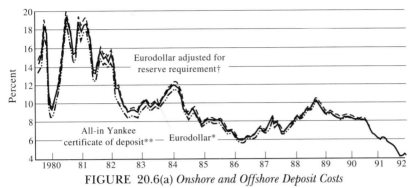

FIGURE 20.6(a) *Onshore and Offshore Deposit Costs*
Three-month interest rates
*London interbank offered rate (LIBOR) for the dollar
†LIBOR adjusted for 3 percent reserve requirement in effect until
December 1990
**U.S. certificate of deposit rate plus 5 basis point issuance costs and 5 basis
point premium. Rate is also adjusted for 3 percent reserve requirement in effect
until December 1990

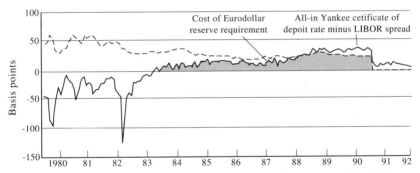

FIGURE 20.6(b) *Spread Between Cost of Reservable Deposits and LIBOR*
Sources: Federal Reserve Bank of New York; Board of Governors of the Federal
Reserve System

funding it with a reservable deposit, and (2) booking the loan offshore
and funding it with an unreservable Eurodollar deposit (see the
Appendix) faced a new incentive. Booking a loan to a U.S. company
offshore and funding it without holding any reserve became the
course that would minimize funding costs. (From 1984 the bold and
dashed lines on Fig. 20.6b are above the zero line, which represents
LIBOR.) In 1989–1990, it was cheaper to fund an onshore loan with
a reservable Eurodollar than with a Yankee certificate of deposit, but
it was still cheaper to book the loan offshore. (The dashed line in Fig.

20.6b cuts below the bold line, but both remain above the zero line.) The cost savings of booking a loan offshore varied with the relationship between onshore and offshore rates, but they reached about a quarter of one percent (Fig. 20.6b, shaded area).

In short, the opportunity to engage in regulatory arbitrage only became valuable to foreign banks in the United States as onshore rates rose relative to offshore rates. The more than doubling of the share of the U.S. commercial loans booked offshore by foreign banks in the years 1985–1990 (Table 20.1) is consistent with our reading of how the rate configuration created opportunities for regulatory arbitrage.

Has the removal of the Eurodollar reserve requirement made a difference? Once the Eurodollar reserve requirement was reduced to zero at the end of 1990, the growth of offshore loans slowed to a crawl after years of rapid growth. Loans booked at shell branches in the Cayman Islands actually fell for the first time in 1991 after growing steadily between 1983 and 1991 (Fig. 20.1).[16] In addition, responses to inquiries prompted by sizeable changes in U.S. claims of weekly reporting branches and agencies suggest that a fair amount of shell branch loans have been rebooked into the United States—at least $12 billion between February 1991 and May 1992.

Although the incentives to book offshore have clearly declined, it may be premature to consider them nonexistent. Some foreign banks fear that the reserve requirements lowered to zero in late 1990 might be raised again.[17] In addition, they fear the imposition of the Federal Deposit Insurance Corporation insurance premiums on their branches and agencies; bringing their loans onshore might increase some future burden. Finally, not only regulatory arbitrage but also tax arbitrage is a consideration in the booking of loans.

Why Didn't Foreign Banks Book All Their Loans Offshore?

As we have seen, loans booked at U.S. offices of foreign banks continued to expand in the late 1980s, and banks from different countries appear to have taken varying advantage of the opportunity to book loans offshore. These developments prompt us to ask why foreign banks as a group did not take fuller advantage and why some seem to have taken advantage more than others.

At the outset, recall that all foreign banks were not bound by the Eurodollar reserve requirement: only about half the foreign banks were (Fig. 20.4). In other words, about half the foreign banks could fund a loan at the margin with Eurodollars and not pay any reserves.[18]

Still, foreign banks and agencies did hold a Eurodollar reserve at the amount of $485 million as of October 15, 1990. At a 3 percent reserve ratio, this sum translates into over $16 billion of loans that might have been profitably rebooked offshore. Two rather tentative explanations maybe offered.

First some banks may have sought to avoid discussion with federal or state tax authorities over offshore loans. This consideration may apply particularly to Cayman Island shell branches managed in New York.

Second, some foreign banks bound by the Eurodollar reserve requirement may have been reluctant to book at Caribbean shell branches out of bankerly caution and the fear of official opprobrium. Over the years, the Federal Reserve has discouraged U.S. banks from using shell branches to relocate deposits and loans alike because of the implications for monetary control. Other authorities did not view shell branches with enthusiasm: the Japanese authorities were slow to authorize branches in the Cayman Islands, and perhaps as a consequence, Japanese banks used this option relatively little.[19] Italian banks may be under-represented in the Cayman Islands owing to official discouragement in the wake of the Banco Ambrosiano affair.[20]

How Large was the Cost Advantage From Regulatory Arbitrage in Relation to the Cost of Capital Advantage of Foreign Banks?

On balance the cost saving from regulatory arbitrage was smaller than foreign banks' cost of capital advantage. At most, foreign banks saved 26 basis points from funding at unreservable LIBOR rather than at reservable Yankee certificate of deposit rates. Over the period 1987–1990, the cost saving averaged no more than 15 basis points. Only for British and Canadian banks did the savings approach the size of their modest cost of capital advantage. For continental and especially Japanese banks, the passing advantage from regulatory arbitrage was quite small in relation to the measured cost of capital advantage. Certainly the large gains in market share in U.S. commercial lending were won by Japanese and continental banks, as one would expect if the cost of capital differences had dominated regulatory arbitrage.

Reassessing the Growth of Corporate Credit in the 1980s

Offshore bank loans to U.S. corporations grew at a rate faster than onshore loans until the U.S. reserve requirements on wholesale deposits were reduced to zero at the end of 1990.[21] Since the policy change, offshore loans have continued to grow faster than the aggregate of onshore loans, but at a rate lower than that of onshore loans extended by branches and agencies of foreign banks.

As argued above, the relatively fast growth of offshore loans in the late 1980s reflected reserve incentives that came into play only as offshore dollars cheapened in relation to onshore dollars and as banks in the United States tapped their foreign offices for funds. Behind these forces lay a U.S. current account deficit that placed dollar wealth in the hands of foreign investors who were more prepared than U.S. residents to hold Eurodollars.

Whatever its causes, rapidly growing and substantial unaccounted offshore credit to U.S. corporations has obscured the profile of U.S. corporate leveraging in the 1980s and the deceleration and decline in corporate borrowing since 1989. Again the flow of funds data (Fig. 20.7, broken line) serve as the point of reference for our restatement of bank credit (Fig. 20.7, solid line). The difference between credit growth as measured by the flow of funds data and credit growth according to our estimate widened fairly steadily after 1985 (Fig. 20.7). When we use a more comprehensive figure for offshore bank credit to U.S. corporations, the growth of corporate bank debt in the years of the merger and acquisitions boom of the 1980s emerges as even higher than conventional measures have suggested.

With a closer approximation of offshore loans, bank credit appears less squeezed after 1989. That is, the more inclusive measure of bank credit shows considerably less shrinkage in 1991—1 percent by our estimates, as opposed to 14 percent according to conventional measure-

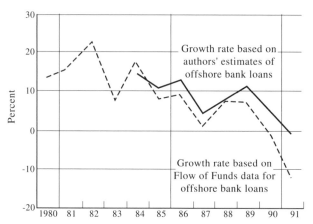

FIGURE 20.7 *Growth in Bank Debt of U.S. Nonfinancial Corporations*
Annual Growth Rate
Sources: Board of Governors of the Federal Reserve System, flow of funds; sources in Table 20.1

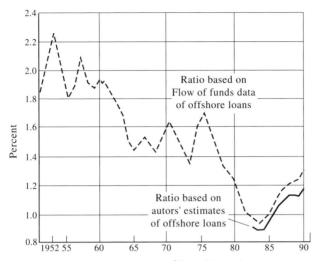

FIGURE 20.8 *Ratio of Securities to Loans*
Nonfinancial, nonfarm corporate business
Sources: Board of Governors of the Federal Reserve System, flow of funds:
sources in Table 20.1
Note: Ratio is the sum of outstanding bonds, commercial paper, and bankers'
acceptances divided by the sum of outstanding bank loans and finance company
loans

ment. By the same token, we estimate that bank credit also decelerated
less after 1987 that is generally believed. When offshore loans are taken
into account, foreign banks provided a greater offset to the contraction
of credit by U.S. chartered banks than has been appreciated.

Import of Offshore Lending to U.S. Firms for Securitization

The existence of a substantial sum of generally unrecognized bank
loans to U.S. corporations means that the rise in their reliance on
securities markets for borrowed funds in the 1980s has been
overstated. We compute the ratio of funding from the securities
markets—mostly corporate bonds, but also commercial paper and
bankers' acceptances—to funding from intermediated sources—
banks and finance companies. We calculate this ratio in two ways:
first, using the offshore loans as captured by the U.S. balance of
payments data in the flow of funds accounts (Fig. 20.8, dashed line);
second, using the offshore loans as we have computed them (Fig.
20.8, solid line). Our calculations suggest that the ratio of securities
borrowing to intermediated corporate credit rose less in the 1980s
than conventional measures have indicated.

Conclusions

In the latter half of the 1980s, U.S. reserve requirements interacted with money market interest rates to give foreign banks an incentive to book loans offshore. The rapid growth in this offshore component of foreign loans was in part missed by the U.S. reporting system, notwithstanding improvements in that system. This chapter argues that bank lending to U.S. corporations in the 1980s rose more rapidly, and securitization proceeded more gradually, than is usually thought. When the foreign loans booked offshore are estimated more comprehensively, foreign penetration of the U.S. market for commercial and industrial loans emerges as more extensive than generally recognized.

Notes

1. See Bank for International Settlements, Monetary and Economic Department, *Guide to the BIS Statistics on International Banking*, Bank for International Settlements, Basle (February 1988).
2. See notes to Table 20.1 for method of estimation. At least for one component of offshore loans to nonbanks, the 60 percent share is an underestimate. C I loans were 85 percent of loans to all U.S. nonbanks made by foreign branches of U.S.-owned banks in 1990.
3. Some of the problems with balance of payments data on nonbank flows are noted in "Final report of the working party on the measurement of international capital flows," International Monetary Fund, Washington, DC. February 3, 1992 (see footnote number 1 on p. 125).
4. Letter "To all nonbank business enterprises reporting on treasury international capital C-series forms" from Gary A. Lee, Manager, Treasury International Capital Reporting System, Office of Data Management, Department of Treasury, May 1, 1986.
5. See Rama Seth and Alicia Quijano, Japanese banks' customers in the United States, *Federal Reserve Bank of New York Quarterly Review*, 16, No. 1, Spring (1991).
6. Steven A. Zimmer and Robert N. McCauley, Bank cost of capital and international competition, *Federal Reserve Bank of New York Quarterly Review*, 15, 33–59, Winter (1991) .
7. Zimmer and McCauley, "Bank cost of capital," p. 49, Table 3. The title compares costs at branches.
8. No explicit guidelines against booking loans from offshore centers were given to foreign banks in particular. The Board of Governors of the Federal Reserve System, however, had discouraged U.S. banks from running U.S. business through their foreign branches. (See "Foreign branches—deposits unconnected with foreign business," Section 3-698 in the Board's Interpretation of Regulation K, June 1981, pp. 3.302–3.303.)
9. U.S. banks' foreign offices could, however, lend to multinationals' foreign offices free of reserves, and those offices in turn could rebook the funds to

their U.S. home offices. In this case, the regulatory arbitrage would show up in the balance of payments data as an intercompany loan, reducing U.S. direct foreign investment abroad (U.S.-based multinationals) or increasing direct foreign investment into the United States (foreign-based multinationals). For examples of the latter associated with acquisitions by British companies, see Robert N. McCauley and Dan P. Eldridge, The British invasion: explaining the strength of U.K. acquisitions of U.S. firms in the late 1980s, in *International Capital Flows, Exchange Rate Determination and Persistent Current Account Imbalances*, pp. 323, 324, Bank for International Settlements, June (1990).

10. Reserve requirements on domestic liabilities range as high as 12 percent in some cases (sight liabilities of more than DM100 million). Under an extended compensation regulation, however, foreign currency liabilities to nonresidents in an amount equal to corresponding book claims in foreign currency with maturities less than four years are exempt from reserve requirements.

11. The JOM in Japan is modeled after the IBFs in the United States. In addition to the reserve requirement exemption, such facilities are also exempt from deposit insurance, from withholding/stamp taxes, and from some income taxes, and there is no ceiling on deposit rates.

12. The distribution of assets across banks in the Cayman Islands further attests to the advantage enjoyed by foreign banks in booking loans offshore: 85 percent of these loans were booked by non-U.S. banks. U.S.-chartered banks might have realized tax advantages from booking loans in the Caymans, but they could not avoid the reserve requirements.

13. This calculation assumes that the Japanese share in loans to U.S. corporations made by all foreign banks in the Cayman Islands is the same as their share in all nonbank loans made by these foreign banks.

14. See for example Marsha Stigum's *The Money Market*, p. 539, Dow Jones–Irwin (1983). For a treatment of the foreign premium in the U.S. commercial paper market, see Robert N. McCauley and Lauren Hargraves, U.S. and Eurocommercial paper: Converging money markets?, *Federal Reserve Bank of New York Quarterly Review*, 12, 24–35, Autumn (1987).

15. See Lawrence L. Kreicher, The Eurodollar arbitrage, *Federal Reserve Bank of New York Quarterly Review*, 7, pp. 10–22, Summer (1982).

16. Most of the rebooking that did occur was on the liability side. Some foreign banks that had *not been bound* by the Eurodollar reserve requirement had found it cheaper to fund U.S. loans with unreservable Eurodollars as long as Yankee certificates of deposit were reservable. But once large nonpersonal time deposits, including Yankee certificates of deposit, were no longer reservable, these banks compared Eurodollar rates directly with the rates on Yankee certificates of deposit and found the latter attractive. If these banks were large, well-rated foreign banks with little paper outstanding in the U.S. market, money market mutual funds may not have cost them much of a premium over the best U.S. banks' rates. See Monetary policy report to the Congress, *Federal Reserve Bulletin*, 77, 701, September (1991).

17. Regulation D sets a range of reserve ratios on Eurocurrency liabilities and transaction and nontransaction accounts. In 1991 the Federal Reserve Board

determined that these ratios would be reduced to zero for Eurocurrency liabilities and all nontransaction accounts, but it did not *eliminate* reserve requirements. An act of law is not required to reinstate these requirements.

18. For instance, the foreign bank branches in the first half of 1991 were replacing unreservable Eurodollar funding with newly unreservable domestic liabilities (see note 8). These branches sold such a large volume of Yankee certificates of deposit that growth in M3 was distorted during this period.

19. Bank of Tokyo was the first to have a branch in the Cayman Islands. Nippon Long Term Credit Bank followed in 1982, Sumitomo Trust in 1983 and Sumitomo Bank in 1984. Subsequently, two banks started operations in 1986, one in 1987, five in 1988, and two in 1989.

20. A freeze was imposed on subsidiaries of Italian Banks in countries where the supervisory structure was inadequate and where the Bank of Italy did not have access to aggregate information. This freeze was lifted only in 1986 for reasons of international competitiveness. Although there was no explicit freeze on branches and agencies, shell branches in offshore centers of Italian banks were largely authorized after 1986.

21. Thus, before the reserve change, offshore lending never reached a mature phase of balanced growth in comparison to onshore lending. See Robert Z. Aliber, The integration of the offshore and domestic banking system, *Journal of Monetary Economics*, 6, 520 (1980).

Appendix: Loan Booking by a Foreign Branch—Onshore or Offshore?

This Appendix shows how the configuration of New York and London dollar money market rates interacted with the Eurodollar reserve requirement to provide an incentive for offshore booking. Rates characteristic of 1984 and 1989 will be examined under the assumption, first, that the Eurodollar reserve did not bind and then that it did. We begin with the configuration of rates in 1984

$$CD^{U.S.}_{1984} = 10.3 \text{ percent}$$

$$E\$_{1984} = 10.8 \text{ percent}$$

$$\left.\begin{array}{l} RR^{CD} \\ RR^{E\$} \end{array}\right\} = 3 \text{ percent},$$

where CD^{US}_{1984} is the secondary market yield of New York three-month certificates of deposit of prime U.S. banks, $E\$_{1984}$ is the Eurodollar offered rate payable by major internationally active banks for three-month deposits in London, and RR^{CD} and $RR^{E\$}$ are, respectively, the required reserves against large nonpersonal time deposits and required reserves against net Eurodollar liabilities (see "Revision of Regulation D," *Federal Reserve Bulletin*, 66, September, 1980, pp. 758–773). We estimate that foreign banks had to offer a premium on their certificates of deposit of 5 basis points; this so-called Yankee premium was consistent with the extra yield offered by foreign commercial paper issuers and reflected the same home-name preference on the part of managers of money market mutual funds, managers of trust accounts, and others (see Robert N. McCauley and Lauren A. Hargraves, Eurocommercial paper and U.S. commercial paper: converging money markets, *Federal Reserve Bank of New York Quarterly Review*, 12, 24–35, Autumn, 1987). In addition, we assume that issuing costs amount to another 5 basis points.

The foreign bank maximizes profit for a given yield on a loan by booking it where it can be funded most cheaply. The foreign branch faces an incentive to book a loan to a U.S. resident offshore if:

$$\begin{array}{ll} \text{cost of offshore} & < \text{cost of onshore} \\ \text{booking and} & \quad \text{booking.} \\ \text{funding} & \end{array}$$

This inequality will hold if

$$\begin{array}{l} \text{Cost of} \\ \text{offshore} \\ \text{booking} \quad < \text{minimum of} \\ \text{and} \\ \text{funding} \end{array} \left\{ \begin{array}{lll} \text{cost of} & & \text{cost of} \\ \text{onshore} & & \text{onshore} \\ \text{booking} & \text{or} & \text{booking} \\ \text{and onshore} & & \text{and offshore} \\ \text{funding} & & \text{funding} \end{array} \right\}$$

or if

$$E\$_{1984} < \min\left\{ \frac{(CD^{US}_{1984} + 0.05 + 0.05)}{1 - RR^{cd}}, \frac{10.8}{(1-0)} \right\}.$$

If the branch was not bound by the Eurodollar reserve requirement in 1984, the booking choice became:

$$10.8 \overset{?}{<} \min\left\{ \frac{(10.3 + 0.05 + 0.05)}{1 - 0.03}, \frac{10.8}{(1-0)} \right\},$$

or

$$10.8 \overset{?}{<} \min\{10.7, 10.8\}.$$

Since the inequality did not hold, the unbound branch faced no incentive for offshore booking. Onshore booking and funding minimized cost.

If the branch was bound by the Eurodollar reserve requirement, offshore funding of the loan booked onshore became more expensive

$$10.8 \overset{?}{<} \min\left\{\frac{(10.3+0.05+0.05)}{1-0.03}, \frac{10.8}{(1-0.03)}\right\},$$

or

$$\overset{?}{<} \min\{10.7, 11.1\}.$$

Since onshore booking and funding remained the least costly choice, the foreign branch faced no incentive for offshore booking. The New York market remains the cheapest source for dollars whatever the reserve position of the foreign branch. The net claim position of U.S. banks against their foreign branches is consistent with this observation.

Now revisit the problem in 1989

$$CD^{U.S.}_{1989} = 9.0 \text{ percent}$$

$$E\$_{1989} = 9.1 \text{ percent},$$

and RR^{CD} and $RR^{E\$}$ are unchanged. The unbound branch checked

$$9.1 \overset{?}{<} \min\left\{\frac{(9.0+0.05+0.05)}{1-0.03}, \frac{9.1}{(1-0)}\right\},$$

$$9.1 \overset{?}{<} \min\{9.4, 9.1\}$$

and concluded again that the strict inequity did not hold. The unbound branch was indifferent between onshore or offshore booking but found it cheaper to fund offshore. Thus, the unbound branch tended to become a bound branch.

The bound branch checked

$$9.1 \overset{?}{<} \min\left\{\frac{(9.0+0.05+0.05)}{1-0.03}, \frac{9.1}{(1-0.03)}\right\}$$

$$9.1 \overset{?}{<} \min\{9.4, 9.4\}.$$

Since the strict inequity held, the bound branch faced an incentive to book offshore. Convergent onshore and offshore rates interacted with the Eurodollar reserve requirement to induce offshore booking. Note that, according to the last two calculations, foreign branches not bound by the Eurodollar reserve requirement faced the greatest cost incentive not to sell Yankee certificates of deposit. And it was precisely these banks that increased their Yankee certificates of deposits outstanding when reserve requirements on such deposits were removed. (The banks switching from offshore to onshore liabilities affected M3 so noticeably that their behavior merited special attention in Chairman Greenspan's Humphrey-Hawkins testimony in mid-1991. Monetary policy report to the congress, *Federal Reserve Bulletin*, 77, September, 1991.)

Although no foreign branch would have had reason in 1989 to sell a Yankee certificate of deposit, certificates were in fact sold. The puzzle of foreign branch behavior is somewhat like the question why foreign banks did not book all their loans offshore. Recognizing the cost and time required to gain acceptance in domestic U.S. portfolios, banks may not have been quick to withdraw in response to a particular rate configuration that might prove temporary. In addition, the possibility of liquidity problems in the London deposit market that would not affect the New York dollar market would discourage extensive reliance on either market, given reasonable rate differentials. (See *Recent Changes in Liquidity Management Practices at Commercial Banks and Securities Firms*, New York Federal Reserve Bank of New York, 1990.)

21

Sovereign and Corporate Borrowing and Sustainable Growth: Strategies Model for the Design of Payments

EDGAR ORTIZ AND ENRIQUE ARJONA

Foreign Borrowing and Sustainable Growth

Development financing and international lending to support corporate activity and government plans in the developing countries (DCs) has become increasingly tied to international institutions and markets. Following World War II, public borrowing from foreign lenders became a permanent source to support public expenditures. Indeed, in the developing countries, foreign debt became the main mechanism to close their gaps in their balance of payments, in their savings and investments processes, and in their government revenues and expenditures. Results have been mixed, conditioned by the nature and magnitude of international business cycles, as well as by the levels of indebtedness and the degree of debt financing acquired through the international financial markets. During boom periods, credits for development have been relatively easy to acquire and developing countries have experienced greater economic growth. During recessive periods, credits have been tight and debt obligations have been exorbitant and often negative flows have taken place, leading to a 'definancing of development', and economic stagnation for many countries.

The intensity of the crisis ensued during recessionary periods has been also determined both at the domestic and international levels by the amounts of indebtedness, the participation of financial markets in development financing, and the level of exposure of financial intermediaries to sovereign debts. Higher levels of indebtedness increased the sensitivity of a nation to domestic and international booms and crashes. Similarly, the greater the levels of external funds obtained from private sources at international markets, the greater the sensitivity of a debtor country to international economic shocks, and the greater the sensitivity of the international economy to debt payments problems from borrowing countries.

These contrasting changes between debt and international financing induced growth and economic collapse clearly suggest that external debt, acquired by governments or enterprises from developing nations, has important trade-offs that must be considered to formulate a strategy consistent with short and long run economic growth and equilibria. Undue restrictions on foreign borrowing would forego its potential benefits. On the other hand, excessive indebtedness leads invariably to undesirable setbacks, as past experiences show. Hence, the issue is simply instrumenting sustainable debt levels. This mainly depends on whether or not domestic policies are consistent with economic growth goals set, considering internal conditions and adjustments needed to face external shocks. Thus, high external borrowing is uncalled for if the generation of funds for payments is limited and/or if adjustments needed—creation of surpluses of domestic savings over investments—to meet external obligations during downturns of the international economy would lead to sharp falls in domestic investment, thus failing to sustain desired levels of growth. In short, growth cannot be sustained with unsustainable foreign debt levels.[1]

The case of private financial lending institutions is similar. Long run growth in profits is inconsistent with overexposure to any kind of lending. Massive credits to a reduced number of risky clients can lead to high profits during periods of economic boom and stability. However, failures from clients, during economic stagnation and crisis, leads to sharp losses, decapitalization, falls in stock prices of the lending institutions, and even liquidity and bankruptcy problems.[2] Moreover, overexposure to sovereign debt or borrowing from corporations from developing countries is more complex and riskier than large scale lending to private clients from developed countries. Risks, highly related to domestic and international systemic factors, are not only more difficult to grasp and assess, but also more difficult to incorporate in credit allocation conditions. In addition, failures in sovereign borrowing transmit forcefully at the international level, and are more difficult to recuperate, for they involve complex negotiations, entailing even interests outside the contracting parties, i.e. governments from borrowing and lending nations and international financial institutions. Lending institutions therefore need to reconcile their long run growth strategies with their long run lending practices. A sustainable growth in profits is only feasible with a sustainable portfolio of credits, a portfolio which is diversified and generates a sustainable flow of revenues consistent with the interests of shareholders and all other stakeholders of the lending institutions. [3]

In this respect, to promote sustainable development levels for developing nations and sustainable profits growth for investment and banking institutions is imperative to reconcile their interests. Countries must set their economic growth levels not only considering their domestic conditions and needs, but also basing their goals on sustainable debt levels whose payments flows also take into account the needs and limitations of lending institutions. Similarly, investing and banking institutions must lend considering fully the potential of borrowing nations or their borrowing corporations, and setting up payments schedules consistent with their growth path. The key thus lies in reconciling economic development goals and debt capacity payment flows from sovereign borrowers or corporate borrowers from developing nations with long run profits goals and stability of investors and financial intermediaries. Since corporations from the developing countries are becoming important international borrowers, these principles should be extended to include their strategic growth needs and cash flow generation available for payments.

External Debt and Credit Failures

Economic development depends on both real and financial variables. Equilibrium conditions and steady-state growth of an economy are, therefore, determined by the functional relationships between these variables. Hence, disequilibria in the financial markets leads to overall economic disequilibria and vice versa. Moreover, disequilibria in the real sectors cannot be sustained with artificial credit creation and excessive money supply. However, public policy in the last few decades, prior to the 1990s, resorted excessively to these practices as a means to spur on economic activity, in both developed and developing nations as shown by their recurrent fiscal deficits. In the case of the developing nations this problem was compounded by the fact that foreign debt became a permanent mechanism to increase monetary resources and patch up insufficiencies in their real sectors.[4]

Before World War II, governments used public debt only as a limited and sporadic mechanism to finance some special development projects, mainly in infrastructure. Foreign debt was used even more sparingly. Moreover, banks issued bonds to governments and subsequently sold them to individual investors. They adjusted their portfolio holdings according to their preferences in risk, returns, and liquidity needs. Thus, if a borrowing government failed to meet its obligations, or stopped payments due to political reasons, security holders were the main party affected. During recessionary periods, such as the world-wide depression of the 1930s, banks were affected by defaults declared by foreign governments, but the burden of international credit failures was borne by individual investors, and many of them suffered devastating losses. Efforts to minimize losses basically confronted the individual investors and the failing government. Banks suffered losses mainly because of damages to their reputation.[5]

After World War II this situation changed radically. As a result of the Great Crash of 1929, investors preferences toward foreign bonds remained low. Particularly, developing nations found no alternatives to finance some of their infrastructure projects along the prevailing lines of the previous period. However, the emergence of a new international monetary system led to the creation of several bilateral and multilateral financial institutions whose role was to provide development financing. Following the reconstruction of Europe and Japan their loans were concentrated in the developing countries. Originally, their actions were positive and remained within manageable bounds. Several reasons account for this early success. First, although credits were tied up, for instance, to purchases of certain inputs exported by developed countries, funds were directly related to specific development projects. Moreover, consistent with conventional credit analysis, careful cost-benefit analysis was carried out. Projects selected, whether there existed competing alternatives or not, were those which would most benefit the borrowing nation and at the same time would generate foreign revenues, directly or indirectly, to insure payments. Second, these loans were preferential, so that interest rates remained low and were granted on a long-term basis. Third, foreign debt and debt servicing remained low in relation to Gross Domestic Product, exports, and other leading economic indicators of the borrowing nations. Thus, no credit failures really occurred. When payments problems emerged, these were rather due to balance of payments disequilibria, which in turn were due to the inability of those nations to transform their economy.

In fact, growth paths chosen by the less developed economies showed some inadequacies.[6] Among them must be cited the fact that industrialization relied heavily on import substitution. In its first phase, this was entirely inward oriented and limited to consumption goods. By the end of the 1960s and the beginning of the 1970s substitution of capital goods was attempted and some regional integration schemes were made. Exports were promoted, but the thrust of industrialization remained import substitution for domestic markets. The importance of foreign markets and their opportunities were neglected. Only a few countries, particularly in East Asia, follow-ed an export-led industrialization and development strategy, which has proved to be a real success to the extent that other countries are trying to follow that model now. Thus, although import substitution led to important changes in the developing nations, particularly in the case of the Latin American countries, it also led to severe socio-economic disequilibria. Moreover, industrialization was promoted neglecting the development of the agricultural sector and without technological and scientific support. Hence, previous disequilibria in international trade payments, which import substitution aimed to overcome, soon reappeared due to heavy imports of intermediate and capital goods. Imports of consumption goods also increased due to increases in income and limited increases in productivity in domestic production. Moreover, wages in the agricultural sector remained low and employment rather decreased in relative terms due to applications of agricultural machinery. All this also led to massive migrations to the urban centers, increasing demands for social services. The state responded by increasing economic inter-vention and swelling its bureaucratic apparatus.

Clear symptoms of disequilibria were present and recurrent adjustments were needed. Thus, governments from the developing nations began using foreign debt as an additional mechanism to offset their balance of payments and fiscal budgets disequilibria, and to overcome limited capital formation in the domestic markets. This practice remained within reasonable bonds until the early 1970s both because international financial institutions lent carefully and because borrowing countries acquired debt within manageable levels, albeit adjustments were often needed. However, adjustments were limited to the short run and were taken within the long-term import substitution development model. This scheme was possible to follow as long as international trade conditions remained favorable and the financial system remained stable.

The fall of the international monetary system, stagflation in the developed nations, and petrodollars changed this picture completely. Developed nations began experiencing severe disequilibria from the mid-1960s.[7] Concretely, the United States lost ground in productivity and at the international markets, while an opposite trend took place among the European nations, especially Germany, and in Japan. Additionally, the dollar weakened due to massive outflows related to trade imbalances, military expenditures abroad, and repressive financial regulations that led to the emergence of Eurodollars and the European capital markets.[8] These events weakened the international monetary system and its institutions. The main benchmark of this process was the end of the gold exchange standard in August 1971. Then, as a result of high balance of payments deficits, domestic economic problems and lack of confidence in the dollar, President Nixon suspended convertibility of the dollar into gold. Currencies began to adjust freely. The Smithsonian Agreement later that year attempted to re-establish order and confidence in the international monetary system. However, a period of uncertain financial instability followed, fixed exchange rates were substituted by managed floating rates and flexible interest rates were adopted in the international money and capital markets.[9] In addition, international financial institutions had limited resources for developing financing. To meet their needs, developing nations began to borrow from private sources at international capital markets. At first, foreign debt from these sources remained relatively low and manageable.

However, a sharp overturn occurred with the 1973–1974 oil crisis. International financial institutions were unable to lend enough funds to the developing nations to absorb such shock. Thus, these nations began borrowing large sums from private sources. Syndicated roll-over credits from commercial and investment banking institutions became the main vehicle for international lending. Moreover, international lending increased sharply, induced by huge petrodollar deposits made by oil exporting countries at private financial institutions from the developed nations. Although these countries engaged themselves in significant development projects, their limited capacity to absorb capital led them to superfluous consumption expenditures and to make large deposits at private financial institutions from the developed world. This led to excess liquidity in these institutions. Moreover, the opportunities to direct credits to the developed nations were limited, for investments opportunities there remained low due to their persistent stagflation as well as a result of oil crisis shocks.

This induced an explosive growth of foreign loans to the developing nations. They needed funds to face their sharp disequilibria brought on both by their structural development problems and the oil crisis shocks. In addition, many governments were committed to improve welfare and responded with populist policies. Indeed, foreign debt became a mechanism to achieve equilibria, forfeiting needed internal changes, particularly in tax reforms and the development of domestic capital markets. To avoid social pressures from both underprivileged and privileged groups, reforms were postponed and foreign debt became a mechanism to 'scape into the future'.[10] Additionally, private bankers were eager to lend to these nations.[11] Often their credit was not tied up to specific development projects and their capacity to generate foreign revenues. Often these loans were granted based on 'country risk analysis' alone, leaving aside detailed project analysis.[12]

This situation was of course unsustainable. Developing nations simply borrowed beyond their capacity to pay.[13] What triggered its end was the high increases in interest rates and restricted terms in credits at the international capital markets, which took place by the end of the 1970s and in the early 1980s. Careful risk analysis had not been made earlier. The sustenance of foreign debt obligations under international expected downturns in world economic activity had not been assessed. Thus, high amortization and interest payments pressed the developing nations beyond their capacity to pay and a severe crisis ensued among highly indebted countries.

Total foreign debt from the developing countries neared a trillion dollars in the early 1980s. In terms of world production this was really a modest amount. However, the nature of credit failures put in jeopardy the entire international financial system and world economic growth. Five important facts must be pointed out regarding this situation to draw lessons for the emerging patterns of inter-national lending and borrowing.

First, the debt crisis of the developing countries took place in the context of a generalized crisis of the entire world economy. The developed countries themselves had faced for several years severe economic problems and competition among them for world markets and investments had been sharp.

Second, holders of foreign debt from the developing countries were private financial institutions from the developed nations, mainly their leading commercial banks. Thus, credit failures from the developing nations weakened not only their credit portfolios but led to financial instability in the developed countries. Low returns and low liquidity in these institutions affected not only stockholders from these institutions, but also households and the governments from the lending nations, for they have traditionally backed the activities of their financial intermediaries through multiple insurance programs, which ultimately are supported by tax payers.

Third, most loans from the private financial institutions were made without tying them to specific projects. Funds were usually granted to the borrowing government, their development banks, or their leading public enterprises on the basis of country risk analysis alone. Those funds went to a general fund which was used by governments and public enterprises to support their activities. Moreover, even loans made to private enterprises proceeded on these basis, based on the guaranty given by the government from the borrowing nation. Hence a recuperation of funds lent could not be made through the sale of nonfinancial assets belonging to a borrowing government, a public enterprise, or even a private corporation.

Fourth, the burden of adjustment was mainly borne by the debtor nations. In spite of overexposure, lending diversification practices and state protection schemes enabled banks to cushion economic shocks. For the borrowing countries, on the other hand, foreign debt had become a key variable, but adjusting policies proved insufficient and costly in social terms. This situation led to the application of bail-out solutions which overextended the time and impacts of the debt problem to both lenders and borrowers.

Fifth, no alternatives had been made to overcome the problems of the international financial system. To a great extent, this has continued to operate only on a *de facto* basis. This is another reason why sound overall solutions to the debt problem were taken tardily.

Currently, the world economy is undergoing radical changes in industrial and technological development, which is inducing differential changes in productivity among nations, changes in world trade patterns, and high competition for world markets. This has led to an internationalization of production and a globalization of real and financial markets. Economic blocks have also been established, partly as a response to the shortcomings of international institutions, like GATT which has failed to reconcile the interest of its members in its Uruguay Round of negotiations, and partly as a result of a search of governments for complementariness with neighboring nations and main trade partners to attain greater productivity and a more competitive position in the world markets.

Simultaneously, the market has become the global mechanism for economic activity. Market economies, developed and developing, have enforced the role of markets by decreasing economic inter-vention of the state, privatizing state corporations, and implementing deregulating and liberalizing schemes in order to strengthen local markets and open them up to foreign trade and investments. State led economies have also turned to the market as the mechanism to promote their economic activity. Particularly, Eastern European countries and the countries which constituted the former Soviet Union are undergoing a rapid, albeit painful, transition towards market oriented economies.

Economic and financial globalization have changed profoundly the characteristics and operating mechanisms of international financial markets and institutions. These have become more complex and more competitive. They have also become the vasomotor of international competition in the real markets. Similarly, financial globalization has been accompanied by more volatile and interdependent markets. In turn, international financing to the developing countries is also taking new forms. Public borrowing continues to be important, but its role in development is clearer. It aims to strengthen local infrastructure and market conditions. However, significant flows are now being channeled to private corporations through innovative operations and securitization which interact local 'emergent' and international capital markets.[14] As a result the most advanced developing economies, and thanks to previous successful debt negotiations, are recovering their economic development paths, which seems will be extensive to other developing nations once their past debt problems are settled and the world economy recovers.

Nevertheless, although perspectives are positive, the possibility of another debt crisis in the future cannot ignored. The Mexican case shown in Table 21.1 underlines the complexity of the situation. At the

TABLE 21.1 *Mexican Foreign Obligations* (in Billion Dollars)*

Sector/type	Amount	Percent total	Percent GDP
Public	$ 79.0	53.56	29.04
Swaps Banco de Mex/IMF	6.0	4.07	2.21
Corporate	16.9	11.45	6.21
Banking	22.0	14.91	8.08
Total foreign debt	$123.9	84.00	45.54
Mexican treasury bills			
Held by foreigners	21.3	14.40	7.83
Other government titles			
Held by foreigners	2.3	3.59	1.95
	$23.6	16.00	9.79
Extended foreign debt	$147.5	100.00	54.22
ADRs & stock investments			
Held by foreigners	$54.5		20.03
Total foreign debt + quasi-debt	$202.0		74.25

*December 1993.
Source: Information from the World Bank, International Monetary Fund, Secretaria de Hacienda y Credito Publico, and Bolsa Mexicana de Valores. See note 14.

height of the debt crisis, in 1987 public debt reached a peak of 110.901 billion dollars, which amounted to 79 percent of Gross Domestic Product (GDP). Successful debt renegotiations which ended in 1990 and repurchases have led to a significant decrease of public debt. As shown in Table 21.1, public debt has decreased to $79 billion dollars.[15] However, international borrowing from private corporations and private banks at international capital markets has increased significantly. Outstanding disbursed debt to these sectors totals now $38.9 billion dollars, 14.29 percent in relation to GDP. Total public and private debt nears $150 billion dollars, 54.22 percent in relation to GDP. This situation gets more complicated once foreign holdings of public domestic debt, corporate stocks and American Depository Receipts (ADRs) held by foreigners are considered. Strictly, these holdings do not constitute debt in the traditional sense. Debt securities from the Mexican government are denominated and payable in pesos. However, free currency convertibility and freedom to repatriate capital makes these securities very akin to foreign debt. Holdings of stocks purchased in the Mexican Stock Market approach this situation. Furthermore, some domestic debt instruments, like *Tesobonos*, are tied to the value of the dollar. If local money and capital markets weaken, foreign investors might desire to take their money out. Finally, ADRs constitute quasi-debt since they imply a commitment to pay dividends.[16]

In summary, Table 21.1 shows that external borrowing is increasing and assuming new characteristics:[17] increased private borrowing, significant participation of local and international securities markets to mobilize resources to the governments and corporations from the developing countries;[18] and innovative forms of securitization. It is worth noting that capital markets in most developing countries are still thin and imperfect and greater integration with the international financial markets have made them highly sensitive to international changes in the real and financial markets. Similarly, crisis could reoccur in the developed countries and in international trade and finance. These facts could lead to a recurrence of an international payments crisis. On the other hand, credit analysis, particularly country risk analysis, has become more sophisticated, which should help to prevent undesirable events. Nevertheless, learning from past experiences, international lending and borrowing needs to be strengthened along some important lines.

First, the international financial system and its international developing institutions need to be reformed. A return to fixed exchange rates is out of order, but mechanisms to induce greater stability in the foreign exchange system are needed. Resources of the international development institutions should be increased so that their role in development financing follows current trends of economic globalization, market oriented activity, and association of countries in economic blocks. International monetary authorities should also promote and play a leading role in the adjustment processes of the industrialized countries, particularly those showing deficit in their external and public accounts.

Second, financing channeled to governments and corporations from developing countries must be planned to prevent and take into account downturns in international business cycles. Short run credits should be minimized to real liquidity needs to support trade and investment activities. Long-term credits should be promoted to truly support infrastructure and human capital development and long run market development promoted by governments; and strategic investments in technology and product development and sales—local and exports—by private corporations. Possible downturns in the international business cycles should be taken into account by incorporating in the payments schedule the capacity of the borrower to pay and the long run needs the lender. This would allow them to prevent crises, and share the costs of adjustment, if needed, for their mutual long run benefit. To complement these measures, countries should formulate and strengthen long run planning, corporations should practice strategic planning, and intermediaries should lend following stricter country risk and project risk analysis.

Third, state credit insurance should be redesigned to prevent indiscriminate credit granting and overexposure of lending institutions. Industrialized countries should take the lead in these changes since their institutions and international portfolio investors take the largest share in international lending. However, international agreements should be promoted, similar to those currently emerging for investment and commercial banking regarding capitalization ratios.

Finally, emerging securities markets should be strengthened. Deregulation and greater disclosure of corporate activity should be emphasized. Summing up, governments, corporations and international financial intermediaries need to incorporate the notion of sustainable growth and sustainable debt in development financing—sovereign borrowing—and international lending to corporations from the developing countries. An alternative to attain it is to incorporate the interests of borrowers and lenders in the external debt processes.

The Interests of Borrowers and Lenders

In many respects, borrowers and lenders have opposite interests, particularly when credit failures occur. However, it is possible to find a common ground from which a solution beneficial to both parties can be negotiated. In the case of foreign debt financing the main actors currently are: from the lending side, (1) international development financing institutions; (2) private international financial intermediaries, particularly commercial banks and investment banks; (3) institutional investors; and from the borrowing side, (4) sovereign borrowers; and (5) corporate and bank borrowers from the developing nations.

The common ground for international financial institutions and sovereign borrowers is clear and in affinity with the ideas set forth here: promote a sustainable development using sustainable levels of indebtedness and the formulation of appropriate domestic policies. In the past, discrepancies have occurred. Two important reasons lay behind those differences: Policy principles followed different orientations; and the lack of a thorough international monetary reform. Because their markets and institutions were in formation, governments from the developing nations intervened directly in economic activity. In addition they tended to over-regulate market activity, responding mainly to short run needs and tendencies, which resulted in unstable policy making and fiscal indiscipline. International monetary and development institutions, on the other hand, have felt responsible for international stability and growth along market oriented mechanisms. For that reason they have promoted, and enforced through adjustment programs, fiscal discipline and adjustment of local variables—exchange rates and wages prices—to international market trends. On the other hand, the lack of reforms in the international financial system made the developing economies more sensitive to changes in the international business cycles in investments, trade, and finance.

The rise of the market as the engine for economic activity puts developing countries and international monetary and development authorities in affinity. Thus, these two actors can encourage sustainable levels of development financing consistent with sustained growth by working closer in long-run development and financing plans. Payment schedules should be worked out taking into account the real capacity to pay, smoothing payments according to revenues from growth goals set in joint agreements. The capacity to pay of a nation can be determined assessing expected growth patterns and examining carefully expected inflows from exports of goods and services, net foreign direct investments flows, and net portfolio investment flows. These analyses should focus on the viability of specific projects. The support of development institutions to smooth debt payments should be extended to debt contracted with private financial institutions. These measures should be supported by promoting in the DCs consistency in policy making, and stability and fiscal discipline. International monetary and development institutions should promote the long awaited reform of the international financial system.

In relation to market sourcing for development, the needs and interest of sovereign borrowers are clear cut. They seek additional funds to complement local savings in order to induce greater rates of growth to overcome underdevelopment. In addition, they need credits which will not restrain their economic growth due to payments schedules which fail to appraise the nature of their investment flows and impacts of unfavorable business trends on them. That is, countries need payment schedules that allow them to grow and pay simultaneously; they need credits whose payments take into account their real capacity to pay and their economic potential.

Private financial intermediaries, particularly banks, on the other hand seek to maintain sound liquidity and capital adequacy and high and stable returns to meet the needs of their shareholders and other stakeholders. Bank liquidity, in addition to a means to meet demands for credits and payments on short-term liabilities, is a protection against risks due to losses resulting from the sale or liquidation of assets in adverse markets. Thus, underperforming and nonperforming foreign loans attempt against the ability of bankers to meet credit demands. The higher the ratio of bad foreign debts to deposits is, the more restrictive credit policies will have to be, in detriment of the local and international economies. Moreover, valuation of bank's stocks in the capital markets decline due to the psychological impact of bad debts and actions taken to shield their impact, such as increasing reserves for bad losses which occurred often during the 1980s debt crisis among U.S. banks. To overcome this problem foreign debt holdings must become credit worthy assets. This in turn means that continuous unplanned rescheduling of debt payments is inefficient. Credit agreements should contemplate regularization of amortization and interest payments.

Capital adequacy is a protection against insolvency. Thus, bankers must insure capital adequacy not only to comply with regulations, but above all to avoid bankruptcy and insure smooth operations in benefit of their stockholders. That is, bankers must insure from their credit operations returns consistent with the degree of risks undertaken so that enough profits are generated to shield shocks of economic instabilities, pay fair dividends to their stockholders and also insure increased valuation of their stocks in the capital markets. Weak foreign debt holdings have naturally attempted against all these needs, because such portfolios have decreased sharply in value, and returns obtained have been unsteady and subject to continuous negotiations. Easy ways out of this problem, albeit costly, are to wipe out foreign debt holdings through the acknowledgement of bad debts, recovering part of the investment by selling those assets in the markets, and the creation of reserves for bad debts. These alternatives have been taken by many banks in the past in an attempt to leave behind this problem and concentrate management of their operations on a new, 'more solid ground'. It was believed that although their stocks will be valued down at first at the capital markets, in the medium term favorable results will be obtained as the financial position of the banking institution becomes stronger without the 'noise' of bad foreign debt holdings. This position was somewhat justifiable, but rather myopic. It did not consider that a solution to the foreign debt problem was feasible. It considered the borrowing countries unable to meet their obligations and/or unwilling to negotiate their debt in terms consistent with the lenders interests. It also assumed that their own authorities and world financial and economic and political institutions could not give whatever supplementary support was necessary to strengthen agreements reached between lenders and debtors.

Although individual investors are acquiring securities issued by developing countries governments and firms, the bulk of investments not held by financial intermediaries themselves is in the hands of institutional investors, mainly mutual funds and pension funds from industrialized countries. Their interests are obvious. They need to meet their costs and the liquidity needs and required rates of return of their members. They also need guarantees with respect to solvency. Since the volume of resources managed by these institutions is large, the potential to mobilize them to governments or firms from developing countries is high. Borrowers, however, must be aware that they must offer risk premiums above returns offered in the developed nations to take care of local systematic risk and firm's intrinsic risk, when relevant. In this respect, the sustenance of debt obligations, and instruments to be held by foreigners in general, to be released privately or in the international securities markets should be well planned, so that the minimum of adjustment mechanisms and negotiations are needed to solve unexpected problems. In addition, governments from the developed countries and the international financial institutions should set up funds to smoothen the payments from sovereign borrowers and corporations from the developing countries, so that the revenues from institutional investors are stabilized and meet their required rates of return.

The interests of borrowing banking institutions and corporations from developing countries have similarities to the interests of lending banking institutions from the developed nations and sovereign borrowers. As private institutions, they seek high and stable returns to meet the demands from their shareholders and all stakeholders. Local banks must also maintain capital adequacy requirements. They resort to foreign borrowing to boost their lending capacity and increase returns. Nonfinancial corporations seek sufficient financing to support their growth and investment opportunities. Finally, as borrowers, both local banks and corporations need financing contracts that take into consideration both the patterns of cash inflows due to the intrinsic recuperation of investments made, i.e. their capacity to pay,[19] as well as the changes in flows due to unexpected changes in the markets, but that would not alter the sustenance of debt in the long run.

In sum, to reconcile debtor and lender interests what is needed is to schedule payments in such a way that they are made without unduly pressuring sovereign borrowers and their corporations and at the same time insuring a fair return to the institutional investors and international lending institutions.

A Model to Schedule Sustainable Debt Servicing According to Payments Capacity and Return Requirements

Taking into account the above considerations, to reconcile debtor and lender interests is necessary to schedule debt servicing according to the expected revenues from borrowers and required rates of return from lenders, stressing the strength of foreign exchange revenues and the convertibility and strength of the local currency. The capacity to fulfill international obligations might vary through time due to the maturing characteristics of projects, while payments required might also vary, due to amortization or changes in international financial conditions. From the lenders point of view is necessary to insure that those payments yield a fair return. In addition, to avoid instability of payments, the schedule of payments could be made smooth by supplementary support given by financial authorities from the lending nation and by the international financial institutions.

In analytical terms, what is needed is to prove whether or not expected payments yield the desired rate of return. In practical terms, this also means determining whether or not the expected payments are viable with the required rate of return. A model to solve this problem follows.[20]

Let

D = foreign debt contracted

F_i = present value of debt servicing (interest and amortization) per period; $i = 1, \ldots, n$

$$K = \frac{D}{\sum_{i=1}^{n} F_i}$$

and

R_i = required rate of return per period, $i = 1 \ldots n$
T_i = unknown interest rate to be earned per period so that the
     present value of the flow equals KF_i and all debt is paid; $i = 1 \ldots n$
C_i = capacity to pay per period; $i = 1 \ldots n$.

Then

$$C_1 = F_1(1 + R_1) = KF_1(1 + T_1)$$
$$C_2 = F_2(1 + R_1)(1 + R_2) = KF_2(1 + T_1)(1 + T_2)$$

.
.
.

$$C_n = F_n(1 + R_1) \ldots (1 + R_n) = KF_n(1 + T_1)(1 + T_n).$$

Hence

$$T_1 = \frac{1 + R}{K} - 1$$

$$T_2 = \frac{(1 + R_1)(1 + R_2)}{K(1 + T_1)} - 1 = \frac{(1 + R_1)(1 + R_2)}{\dfrac{K(1 + R_1)}{K}} - 1 = R_2$$

.
.
.

$$T_n = \frac{(1 + R_1)(1 + R_2) \ldots (1 + R_n)}{K(1 + T_1)(1 + T_2) \ldots (1 + T_{n-1})} - 1$$

$$= \frac{(1 + R_1)(1 + R_2) \ldots (1 + R_n)}{\dfrac{K(1 + R_1)(1 + R_2) \ldots (1 + R_{n-1})}{K}} - 1$$

$$= R_n.$$

That is, required rates of return to be earned and applied per period
are simply:

$$\frac{1 + R_1}{K} - 1, R_2, R_3, \ldots, R_n.$$

Hence, debt is sustainable if flows of payments, scheduled according to debt capacity (are positive and) meet the lenders expected rate of return

$$\frac{1+R_1}{K} - 1 > 0$$

$$\begin{aligned}
&\leftrightarrow 1 + R_1 - K > 0 \\
&\leftrightarrow R_1 - K > -1 \\
&\leftrightarrow K - R_1 < 1 \\
&\leftrightarrow K < R_1 + 1.
\end{aligned}$$

Therefore, the length of the first payment period must be such that the percentage and deficit in the flow of payments be less than or equal to expected $R + 1$ in that period. This means that the length of such a period can be negotiated. Further, payments can be smoothed up with the support of local and international authorities. That is, through programs in affinity with the existing Brady Plan, when expected payments are low, the U.S. government could give some fiscal incentives to the banks, diminishing taxes in revenues obtained from debt payments. Analogous types of incentives could be created to promote smooth revenues among institutional investors. Similarly, the international financial institutions can grant the lending institutions or the borrowers special credits for the amount needed to cover the payments developed according to the analytical conditions defined above. Table 21.2 depicts a situation like this. Assuming that a nation contracts foreign debt for 100 billion dollars to be paid in even payments for ten years at 10 percent,[21] the annuity necessary to

TABLE 21.2   *Smoothed Payments Schedule (000s Omitted)*

Year	Interest	Payments	Capacity	Smoothing
1	0.10	16,273,374	16,273,374	
2	0.10	16,273,374	16,273,374	
3	0.10	16,273,374	16,273,374	
4	0.10	16,273,374	16,273,374	
5	0.11	17,739,786	15,739,786	2,000,000
6	0.11	17,739,786	16,739,786	1,000,000
7	0.12	21,004,535	17,004,535	4,000,000
8	0.11	16,927,626	16,927,626	
9	0.10	11,695,451	15,695,451	(4,000,000)
10	0.10	11,695,451	16,444,154	(4,748,704)
11	0.10	4,991,176		

Figures within parentheses indicate repayment to the international financial institution.

liquidate the loan is $16,273,394,000. Let us assume that under normal circumstances this nation will be able to meet such obligations. However, if interest rates change and the price of the indebted nation exportable goods fall, payments will increase, but the nation's capacity to pay most likely will diminish. Column 2 shows the varying interest rates; column 3 shows the required new payments to liquidate the outstanding debt; and column 4 shows the debtor's changing capacity to pay. Since the lender interest rates of return cannot be covered, a renegotiation must take place, at most at the end of the 10-year period to extend payments for more years to meet the lenders required rate of return. For simplicity, in this case, given the debtor's capacity to pay, outstanding debt is marginal and can be covered in one more period, as shown in year 11. The last column shows the alternative balancing scheme through the intervention of an international financial institution, i.e. The World Bank. That is, during the years that the indebted nation falls short of required payments, this institution assists the indebted nation with the amount necessary to meet the payment. However, in the years that the indebted nation's capacity to pay is higher than the required payments, those surpluses are used to pay back the international lending institution. In this simple example, excess funds are sufficient to liquidate the additional debt with the international financial institution. The advantage of this approach is that payments to the private institution are smoothed up. In the case of the indebted nation, not only are pressures eased, but also further contracting of debts to meet outstanding obligations is avoided. These actions should promote international financial stability. In the case that the length of the payment period is already established, T must be determined again. However, the algorithm can be generalized so that a viable solution is established, thus benefiting debtors and lenders.

Indeed, from the preceding viability analysis it can be observed that a conciliation of debtor and lender interests is not feasible if $K > R_1 + 1$. Then, to maximize payment flows is necessary to determine a constant K_1 in lieu of K so that

$$K_1 = \min\left[\frac{D}{\sum\limits_{i=1}^{n} F_i}, R_1 + 1\right].$$

This transforms debt for another payment period and the adjusting factor of the flows becomes

$$\frac{D - K_1 F_1}{\sum_{j=2}^{n} K_1 F_j}.$$

This means that the following T_1 must be adjusted in a similar way, using a corresponding factor K_1. Generalizing this approach, the interest rate earned and applied in each period must be

$$\frac{1 + R_1}{K_i} - 1 \text{ with } K_i = \min\left[\frac{D - \sum_{j=1}^{i-1} K_1 \ldots K_j F_j}{\sum_{j=1}^{n} K_1 \ldots K_{i-1} F_j}, R_i + 1\right].$$

Therefore, the first element of the minimizing function is a ratio of initial debt minus all the preceding payment flows, each of them multiplied by adjustment constants and the sum of the remaining payment flows. It must be pointed out that once of one the constants K_1 are equal to one, from that period on the remaining T_1 correspond to the desired rate of return.

Finally, to make this model practical, only one final remark is in order. If the overall contracting period is short, flows must very high to make a solution feasible. Thus, if the debtor nation or corporation has a limited capacity of payment either the bank will be unable to recover its investment, or else the debtor will be highly pressured by debt payments and its own development will be hindered. Thus, based on the capacity to pay, the most important variable to determine is the length of the overall period to make the payments. The longer the period the lower the payments will be and hence easier to fulfill with those commitments. Similarly, the lender will insure its overall required rate of return. However, since during some periods the required rate of return can remain below its requirements, some support from its local authorities or from the international financial authorities might be necessary, as explained before. Since payments are made based on the capacity of the debtor to pay, such revenues must be estimated. The expected flows to the bank can be easily computed and can then be programmed whatever supplementary help is needed to insure that the lending institutions maintain their annual required rate of return, and hence maintain their liquidity and capital structure according to their stockholders interest.

If support is needed to make this sort of scheme feasible, international financial institutions could transfer funds to the private lenders based on the schedule of payments negotiated. These funds could be charged to a special account with the borrowing nation or corporation. That is, a new form of foreign debt can be issued. Clearing it would be a function of the borrower's capacity to pay. That is, as long as payment flows remain below the annual required rate of return from the bankers, the international financial institutions would smooth payments, charging them to an account of the debtor. When payment flows exceed the required rate of return, the borrowing nation would simply pay the lending institution the required rate of return and excess funds would be channeled to the international financial institutions to cancel its debt due to this scheme of smoothing up payment flows.

Conclusion

International lending currently presents a more complex set of factors than in the past. Funds for development financing and corporate activity are now channeled by a complex interaction of developed and emerging financial markets and institutions. These emerging patterns are the result of increased globalization of real and financial markets; the rise of the market and private corporations and institutions as the engines for economic activity; diminished intervention of the state in economic activity coupled with its stronger participation in overhead creation and the promotion of market activity through long run planning and adequate regulation; and the continued development of new technologies, increased competition for domestic and international markets, and the creation of economic blocks among nations as a response to meet the challenges of the emerging economic order.

Although several countries still suffer the effects of the debt crisis of the 1980s and adjustment and modernization process are still undergoing for most developing countries, economic development perspectives point towards positive results in the future. Innovative forms of intermediation and securitization are channeling international savings to public and private investments in the developing countries. However, the possibility of a crisis in international lending practices in the future cannot be ignored. Markets from the developing economies have become more integrated with world real and financial markets, but due to their thinness and inefficiencies still being present, their financial markets have particularly become more sensitive to changes in the international business cycles in investments, trade, and finance. [22]

To prevent future payments crisis originating in the developing countries, it is imperative to promote steady-state growth with sustainable levels of debt. To achieve this purpose it is necessary to promote a reform of the international financial system, promote consistent policy making and fiscal and monetary discipline among the developing countries, and promote long run lending and borrowing based on well thought-out development programs. In these new schemes of development financing, reconciling the interests of borrowers and lenders can play a key role. Payments should be scheduled taking into account the capacity of public and private borrowers to meet their international obligations and the liquidity, capitalization, and rates of return required by international portfolio investors and international private lending institutions. Since the interests for sustainable growth and sustainable debt levels are common to sovereign borrowers, private corporations from the developing countries, and international monetary and development institutions, the latter can play an important role in the design of development programs, development financing needs, and especially in creating mechanisms to smooth the payments from borrowers to meet the stake of lenders. The analysis and model offered in this chapter offer an alternative for its application.

Acknowledgement

Research support from Programa de Apoyo a Proyectos de Investigacion e Innovacion Tecnologica (PAPIIT) from Universidad Nacional Autonoma de Mexico is acknowledged.

Notes

1. The issue of sustainable debt levels and sustainable economic growth is assuming great relevance in the aftermath of the debt crisis of the 1980s. For important studies on the subject and related problems see van Wijnbergen *et al.* (1992); Vaggi (1992); and Bottome *et al.* (1992).
2. For a recent study on these problems, see Madrid (1992). Official international financial institutions such as the World Bank, the Interamerican Development Bank, and other development banks are not exempt of severe failures due to lax lending practices. No serious problems of this nature have arisen during the last five decades. However, development banks have experienced severe problems at the domestic level due to delinquent accounts and loan defaults. Concerning banking institutions (other international lenders are also identified in this work), the analyses and model presented in this chapter stress private commercial banks, but they also apply to the case of national development banks. They can also be applied to the case of multilateral official lending institutions. We assume that these institutions will not present major problems and that their liquidity and capital adequacy problems can be solved by additional agreements among member countries.
3. The principle of sustainable growth and sustainable debt levels has long been

applied to corporate and bank management. For an early analysis on bank management see Ortiz and Cramer (1983). For thorough discussions on sustainable corporate growth see Higgins (1977), Harrington and Wilson (1989).

4. The origins, causes, and implications of the debt crisis and stabilization and adjustment processes that followed it have been extensively studied. Detailed analyses on the issues summarized here can be found in Jorge and Salazar-Carrillo (1992); Felix (1990); and Sachs and Collins (1989, 1990).

5. See Madrid (1992).

6. For detailed views concerning the limitations of development strategies in developing countries see Chennery et al. (1974); Hewitt et al, (1992); Isbister (1993); Meier (1984); Nafziger (1984), Sheahan (1987); and Smith (1993).

7. For a good summary of the patterns of world economic development and changes in economic leadership see Maddison (1982).

8. Concerning the development of the Euromarkets, see Champion and Trauman (1982); Scott (1976); Seyffert (1972); Vazquez Seijas (1989); and Smith (1992).

9. Williamson (1983) and Serulle and Boin (1984).

10. This well-thought-out conceptualization has been put forth by Paniagua (1985).

11. Wellons (1986). Forceful views about the role of private banks in the debt problems and for the existence of limited solutions about it can be seen in Badford and Kucinski (1988) and Sampson (1981).

12. It must be recognized that country risk analysis involved complex evaluations and that sound analytical models were used. On this subject, see Hefferman (1986) and Solberg (1988).

13. See Malindretos and Kasibhatla (1992).

14. In relation to globalization issues about the capital markets, see Ghosh and Ortiz (1994) and Aggarwal and Schrim (1995).

15. Table 21.1 has been developed from information released by The World Bank, International Monetary Fund, and Secretaria de Hacienda y Credito Publico. See Acelerado Endeudamiento Privado, *El Financiero*, lunes 18 de octubre de 1993, 1, 4–5; Rendimientos Nacionales dos Veces Superior al de Estados Unidos, *El Financiero*, lunes 11 de Octubre de 1993, 3A and 11A; and Bolsa Mexicana de Valores, Indicadores Bursatiles, Diciembre 1993.

16. It is worth noting that not only economic but also political factors could lead to a crisis in payments in the developing countries. This is true even for countries traditionally knows as stable. For instance, Mexico has experienced a recessive economy since 1992, which has been accompanied by some political instability. An unexpected Indian uprise in the State of Chiapas in January 1994, and the assassination of Luis D. Colosio, candidate of the official ruling party on March 23, 1994, led to a massive outflight of capital estimated at 11 billion dollars. A crisis was avoided thanks to a short-term loan from the U.S. government amounting six billion dollars, enforced by President Clinton as part of the North American Free Trade Agreement.

17. These are macrotendencies. Each country shows a specific structure within these tendencies. Table 21.1 shows that properly of Mexico.

18. In Table 21.1, 77.5 percent of Mexico's total foreign obligations can be tied to international investments made at the local and international securities markets. This does not include recent placements of bonds made by the government and state enterprise (e.g. PEMEX, Nafin, Banco Nacional de Comercio Exterior, etc.) at the international markets. Conservatively, total obligations acquired through the securities markets borders 80.0 percent.

19. The capacity to pay for private borrowers is determined by the cash flows they can generate from investments made. Sound capital budgeting and adequate credit analysis can identify expected patterns of cash flows. At the international level some macroeconomic tendencies and policies should be incorporated in the analysis to assess their impact on cash flows. For instance, if a firm borrows to carry out domestic projects, high inflows will guarantee payments to the international lender only if national monetary and exchange rate policies are sound and there are no restrictions to currency convertibility. Preferably, international lending to private corporations from the developing countries should be associated with export projects.

20. An algorithm based on this model, available as a software package, has been developed by Enrique Arjona and tested in lending practices of a development bank in Mexico.

21. The example can also be applied to the case when the borrower is a private corporation and the lender a foreign bank. It can also be applied for the ease of domestic borrowing and lending.

22. Some recent studies dealing with financial liberalization and its impacts on the Asian and Latin American countries can be found in Faruki (1994).

References

AGGARWAL, R. and SCHRIM, D. C. (eds.) (1995) *Global Portfolio Diversification. Risk Management, Market Microstructure and Implementation Issues*, Academic Press, San Diego.

BADFORD, S. and KUCINSKI, B. (1988) *The Debt Squads. The U.S. Banks and Latin America*, Zed Books, London, NJ.

BOTTOME, R. *et al.* (1992) *In the Shadow of the Debt. Emerging Issues in Latin America*, The Twentieth Century Fund, New York.

CHAMPION, P. F. and TRAUMAN, J. (1982) *Mechanism de Change et Marche des Eurodollars*, Economica, Paris.

CHENNERY, H. *et al.* (1974) *Redistribution with Growth: An Approach to Policy*, Oxford University Press, Oxford.

FARUKI, S. (ed.) (1994) *Financial Sector Reforms, Economic Growth, and Stability. Experiences in Selected Asian and Latin American Countries*, The World Bank, Washington, DC.

FELIX, D. (ed.) (1990) *Debt and Transfiguration? Prospects for Latin America's Economic Revival*, M. E. Sharpe, Armonk, NY.

GHOSH, D. K. and ORTIZ, E. (eds.) (1994) *The Changing Environment of International Financial Markets. Issues and Analysis*, St. Martin's Press, New York.

HARRINGTON, D. R. and WILSON, B. D. (1989) *Corporate Financial Analysis*, Business Publications, Plano, TX.

HEFFERMAN, S. A. (1986) *Sovereign Risk Analysis*, Unwin Hyman, London.

HEWITT, T., JOHNSON, H. and WIELD, D. (1992) *Industrialization and Development*, Oxford University Press, New York.

HIGGINS, R. C. (1977) How much growth can a firm afford? *Financial Management*, Fall, 7–16.

ISBISTER, J. (1993) *Promises not Kept. The Betrayal of Social Change in the Third World*, Kumarian Press, West Hartfort, CT.

JORGE, A. and SALAZAR-CARRILLO, J. (eds.) (1992) *The Latin American Debt*, St. Martin's Press, New York.

MADDISON, A. (1982) *Phases of Capitalistic Development*, Oxford University Press, New York.

MADRID, R. L. (1992) *Over-exposed. U.S. Banks Confront the Third World Debt Crisis*, Westview, Boulder, CO.

MALINDRETOS, J. and KASIBHATLA, K. M. (1992) Sustainable levels of foreign debt: model and empirical examination of the Brazilian experience. Mimeo, New Jersey Institute of Technology.

MEIER, G. M. (1984) *Leading Issues in Economic Development*, Oxford University Press, Oxford.

NAFZIGER, E. W. (1984) *The Economics of Developing Countries*, Wadworth, Belmont, CA.

ORTIZ, E. and CRAMER, R. (1983) Inflation and bank capital adequacy: the Mexican and U.S. experiences. In ORTIZ, E. (ed.), *Current Economic and Financial Issues of the North American and Caribbean Countries*, NAEFA, Mexico, DF.

PANIAGUA RUIZ, R. (1985) *Prologomenos para una Teoria de los Limites Financieros del Estado: Problemas de la Deuda y Crisis Financiera*. UAM-Iztapalapa, Mexico, DF.

SACHS, J. D. and COLLINS, S. M. (eds.) (1989/1990) *Developing Country Debt and Economic Performance* (three volumes), University of Chicago Press, Chicago.

SAMPSON, A. (1981) *The Money Lenders*. Hodder and Stoughton, London.

SCOTT, B. (1976) The new euromarkets. A theoretical and practical study of financing in the eurobond, eurocurrency and related financial markets. Research Paper, Institute of International Relations, University of Dijon.

SERULLE, J. and BOIN, J. (1984) *Fondo Monetario Internacional: Deuda Externa Y Crisis Mundial*, IEPALA, Madrid.

SEYFFERT, L. R. (1972) *Analisis del Mercado de Eurodolares: Origen. Desarrollo y Consecuencias*, CEMLA, Mexico, DF.

SHEAHAN, J. (1987) *Patterns of Development in Latin America*, Princeton University Press, Princeton.

SOLBERG, R. L. (1988) *Sovereign Rescheduling: Risk and Portfolio Management*, Unwin Hyman, London.

SMITH, A. D. (1992) *International Financial Markets: The Performance of Britain and its Rivals*, Cambridge University Press, New York.

SMITH, S. C. (1993) *Case Studies in Economic Development*, Longman, New York.

VAGGI, G. (ed.) (1992) *From the Debt Crisis to Sustainable Development*, Macmillan, London.

VAN WIJNBERGEN, S., ANAND, R. CHHIBBER, A. and ROCHA, R. (1992) *External Debt, Fiscal Policy, and Sustainable Growth in Turkey*, The Johns Hopkins University Press/The World Bank, Baltimore.

VAZQUEZ SEIJAS, A. (1989) *Mercados Internacionales de Capital*. UAM-Azcapozalco, Mexico, DF.

WELLONS, P. A. (1986) Multinational institutions in the debt crisis. National interests and long term consequences. In CLAUDON, M. P. (ed.), *World Debt and Crisis. International Lending on Trial*, Ballinger, Cambridge, MA.

WILLIAMSON, J. (1983) *The Exchange Rate System*, Institute for International Economics, Washington, DC.

Author index

Subject index